Practical Intrusion Analysis

Practical Intrusion Analysis

PREVENTION AND DETECTION
FOR THE TWENTY-FIRST CENTURY

Ryan Trost

✦✦ Addison-Wesley

Upper Saddle River, NJ · Boston · Indianapolis · San Francisco
New York · Toronto · Montreal · London · Munich · Paris · Madrid
Capetown · Sydney · Tokyo · Singapore · Mexico City

The publisher offers excellent discounts on this book when ordered in quantity for bulk purchases or special sales, which may include electronic versions and/or custom covers and content particular to your business, training goals, marketing focus, and branding interests. For more information, please contact:

> U.S. Corporate and Government Sales
> (800) 382-3419
> corpsales@pearsontechgroup.com

For sales outside the United States please contact:

> International Sales
> international@pearson.com

Visit us on the Web: informit.com/aw

Library of Congress Cataloging-in-Publication Data:

Trost, Ryan.

  Practical intrusion analysis : prevention and detection for the twenty-first century / Ryan Trost.

    p. cm.

  Includes index.

  ISBN-13: 978-0-321-59180-7 (pbk. : alk. paper)

  ISBN-10: 0-321-59180-1

  1. Computer networks--Security measures. 2. Computer networks--Monitoring. 3. Computer security. 4. Computers--Access control. I. Title.

  TK5105.59.T76 2009

  005.8--dc22

                                                                2009019158

ISBN-13: 978-0-321-59180-7
ISBN-10: 0-321-59180-1

Text printed in the United States on recycled paper at R.R. Donnelley in Crawfordsville, Indiana.

First printing July 2009

Editor-in-Chief
Karen Gettman

Acquisitions Editor
Jessica Goldstein

Senior Development Editor
Chris Zahn

Managing Editor
Kristy Hart

Project Editor
Jovana San Nicolas-Shirley

Copy Editor
Sheri Cain

Indexer
Erika Millen

Proofreader
Debbie Williams

Publishing Coordinator
Romny French

Cover Designer
Chuti Prasertsith

Compositor
Jake McFarland

To my loving wife, Kasey, who is pregnant with our first beautiful child.

To my supportive families: To my parents, sister, and brother, who have supported me, motivated me and somehow sustained my endless IT ramblings. And to my wife's family, the Arbacas clan, who have only had to endure my InfoSec rambling for a couple years and still invite me to dinner. I very much appreciate all the help and support!

Contents

Preface

This book was developed to help fill multiple gaps in practical intrusion detection within a single cover-to-cover publication. Traditionally, intrusion detection books concentrate on narrow subject matter that focuses on vendor-specific information, like Snort or Cisco MARS, Intrusion Detection System (IDS) installation, and sensor placement or signature writing. This book incorporates the essential core knowledge to understand the IDS, but it also expands the subject matter to other relevant areas of intrusion interest, such as NetFlow, wireless IDS/Intrusion Prevention System (IPS), physical security, and geospatial intrusion detection. Don't get me wrong…the previously mentioned books are the foundation of my security knowledge, but as the industry matures to include various facets of incursion, its books should incorporate those facets into a single publication so security aficionados don't have to fracture their attention across so many titles.

WHO SHOULD READ THIS BOOK

This book's audience is any and all security practitioners; whether you're an entry-level security analyst, a chief security officer, or even a prospective college student researching a career in network security. Every chapter might not provide a silver-bullet solution that protects your company from every well-versed attacker. But, as you peel back the onion layers, you will find a combination of included security defenses that help ensure your company's security posture and out-endure even the most motivated attacker(s).

HOW TO READ THIS BOOK

Although, at first glance, the chapters might seem independent, a structure guides you from the first few chapters that provide a fundamental foundation, including Chapter 1 "Network Overview," and Chapter 2, "Infrastructure Monitoring," to more advanced chapters. Chapter 3 "Intrusion Detection Systems" starts to outline the blank canvas with cornerstone concepts and techniques. Chapter 4 "Lifecycle of a Vulnerability" is the perfect transition from beginner to more advanced topics of new intrusion detection strategies consisting of wireless IDS/IPS, network behavioral analysis (NBA), converging of physical and logical security, and geospatial intrusion detection. Several traditional chapters explore new approaches, including ones that cover IDSs, vulnerability signature dissection, and Web Application Firewalls (WAF).

I was lucky enough to have several knowledgeable friends that, with some begging and pleading, agreed to include their extensive security insight, experience, and opinions. I avoid duplicating materials presented in other books because I want to fill the gaps of current security initiatives and/or explore the arena of new concepts and strategies.

How This Book Is Organized

This book follows a compartmentalized organization because each chapter focuses on specific intrusion techniques. The beginning of this book introduces basic networking terminology, and it transitions into providing an overview of intrusion detection, which caters to the InfoSec newbies and finally dives into more sophisticated and advanced intrusion defenses. Here is a brief description of each chapter:

- Chapter 1, "Network Overview," focuses on basic network structure and briefly explains the anatomy of TCP/IP and OSI. Most IT-related books must include some introductory chapter to either define the foundation of the technology or refresh readers that might not deal with it in their daily lives; this book is no different. It is not meant to be an in-depth analysis, but it eases you into the more sophisticated work to come.
- Chapter 2, "Infrastructure Monitoring," explores some common network security practices, including vulnerability assessments, packet sniffing, IDS, file integrity checking, password auditing, wireless toolkits, exploitation toolkits, and network reconnaissance tools. Network security heavily relies on the tools used to "see" the traffic. However, as the chapter title indicates, a majority of this chapter concentrates on mainstream monitoring capabilities and the never-ending battle between using a tap or SPAN for monitoring purposes.
- Chapter 3, "Intrusion Detection Systems," provides you with insight into the IDS industry by introducing fundamental concepts and then progressively jumping into more complex topics, including evasion techniques, signature dissection, and a look into the Snort and BRO IDSs, while simultaneously providing as little duplication of previous material as possible. Most IDS books written in the past focus solely on Snort, snort.conf (Snort's configuration file), and the signature syntax. However, few publications truly clarify the distinction between writing a signature looking for an exploit versus writing a signature identifying a system's vulnerability. Finally, the chapter ends with an assessment of two open source systems, Snort and Bro, which take different approaches to intrusion detection.

- Chapter 4, "Lifecycle of a Vulnerability," steps you through the natural evolution of a vulnerability, from discovering the vulnerability, to capturing the packet stream, to analyzing the malicious content within the packet, and writing an efficient Snort signature to alert on it. It does all this, while simultaneously exposing you to a small subset of necessary tools to help you in your quest. The examples escalate in complexity and are specifically chosen to reflect relatively recent events, because they were all released within the past few months. For newcomers, the analysis of a packet might appear overwhelming and tedious, but if you segment it and step through the packet capture packet-by-packet, the process starts to fall into place. For the already skilled signature writers, the advanced examples, which use flowbits, PCRE, and newly shared object rules, shed some light on the thought process and technique that the Sourcefire VRT team uses.
- Chapter 5, "Proactive Intrusion Prevention and Response via Attack Graphs," examines proactive methods of attack risk reduction and response through attack graphs. Administrators and security analysts are overwhelmed by constant outside threats, complexity of security measures, and network growth. Today's status quo for network defense is often reduced to mere triage and post-mortem remediation. The attack graphs map potential paths of vulnerability through a network, showing exactly how attackers might penetrate a network. Attack graph analysis identifies critical vulnerabilities and provides strategies for protecting critical network assets. But, because of operational realities, vulnerability paths often remain visible. In such cases, attack graphs provide an ideal methodology for planning appropriate attack responses. This includes optimal placement of intrusion detection sensors, correlating intrusion alarms, accounting for missed detections, prioritizing alarms, and predicting the next possible attack steps.
- Chapter 6, "Network Flows and Anomaly Detection," explores the topic of network flow data: its collection for network security analysis and, specifically, an emerging field called Network Behavior Analysis (NBA). First, this chapter explores flow technology and analyzes the different flow formats: their characteristics, respective datasets, and key fields. It discusses how network flow deployments affect device performance and statistical sampling and then introduces possible data flow collection strategies. IDS and packet sniffing software are microanalytical tools that examine packet contents, data flow is a macroanalytical mechanism that characterizes large volumes of traffic in real time. Although traditional IDS/IPS technologies are still an environment staple, they are blind to specific attacks, whereas NBA fills those gaps and perfectly complements them because it excels at immediately detecting polymorphic worms, zero-day exploits, and botnet denial of service (DoS) attacks.
- Chapter 7, "Web Application Firewalls," exposes you to the terms, theories, advantages, and disadvantages of the Web Application Firewall (WAF), which is quickly

becoming a solution of choice for companies who operate mission-critical Web sites. With the explosion of the Internet, an entire new family of attack vectors has been created that redefine the traditional concept of a threat. Whether it is the database server, Web server or even the visitors of the targeted site, these threats are often embedded in seemingly innocent traffic that many IDSs do not have the power or capability to detect.

- Chapter 8, "Wireless IDS/IPS," details how wireless deployments have a whole new set of problems than traditional IDSs address. For the most part, intrusion detection focuses on the data passing from point A to point B. However, this is a limited view of data transmission, because it fails to consider the physical properties of the transmission process. Thanks to wireless networking, data no longer has to exist as electronic pulses on a wire, but can now live as radio waves in the air. Unfortunately, this means traditional IDS solutions are no longer qualified to fully protect this information, if only because they cannot interpret RF energy. In this chapter, you gain an understanding of the issues related to wireless security, the shortcomings of the network-based IDS, and the options available to those who want to keep a close eye on their wireless traffic.

- Chapter 9, "Physical Intrusion Detection for IT," gets IT security staffs thinking about how intrusion detection efforts can be bolstered by converging with the physical security team. This chapter includes an overview of physical security technologies to help IT security personnel understand the perspective of the physical security team and familiarize themselves with the physical security technology terrain. A few example scenarios illustrate the possibilities of what converged detection can offer.

- Chapter 10, "Geospatial Intrusion Detection," proves how the source IP address is one of the most overlooked and powerful components of an intrusion detection log. IDSs/IPSs are becoming more advanced, and geocoding source IP addresses is adding another layer of defensive intelligence. The ultimate goal of geospatial intrusion detection is to maximize situational awareness and threat visualization techniques among security analysts. Most attackers use multiple zombie machines to launch professional attacks, but even a zombie's network reconnaissance leaves geographic fingerprints that are easily picked up by pattern recognition algorithms from the Geographic Information Systems (GIS) industry.

- Chapter 11, "Visual Data Communications": Visualization of security data has become an increasingly discussed topic. As data retention policies increasingly capture the compliance spotlight, it is forcing companies to retain audit logs for extended time periods and, in some cases indefinitely. NetFlow is a perfect example of how beneficial visualizing data can be. As it samples the network traffic, an analyst can immediately identify suspicious patterns. Countless possible datapoints can be tracked and visualized within a company's network. The driving focus is to put into words that visualizing security alerts are left to interpretation because what helps me defend my network might not help you preserve yours. This chapter provides a broad view of the different visualization possibilities.

- Chapter 12, "Return on Investment: Business Justification," involves the nontechnical anomaly as it focuses on management decisions regarding intrusion detection security. This chapter conveys valuable insight on the compliance landscape, a breakdown on ROI strategies, and introduces cyber liability insurance. This chapter conveys valuable insight for both today's, and tomorrow's, security directors. Regardless of what your security tier, you're always training for the next escalation of privileges.
- Appendix, "Bro Installation Guide," provides some basic instructions and guidance to help security analysts/engineers install Bro. In comparison to the other popular open source IDS, Snort, the supporting documentation for Bro is significantly lacking. Although this doesn't drastically narrow the margin, it hopefully answers some initial questions.

Acknowledgments

I attribute my security success and drive to family, colleagues, and hard work. My fascination with network security all started with conversations with my little brother, Adam, who at the time was pursuing his computer science degree at the University of Virginia, all while I was finishing up my business management degree at York College of Pennsylvania. As I spoke of economics and statistics, he introduced me to programming, networking, and cryptography, and he awakened my calling with IT and network security. Immediately after completing my undergrad, the thirst for a more in-depth technical education level quickly became reality as I completed my master's degree in computer science from George Washington University. In addition to my brother, I want to thank my parents and sister for their support and always motivating me. Who said a little bit of sibling rivalry isn't healthy? Publications = Ryan +1.

Throughout my career, I have been privileged to work with some of the most intelligent and driven security professionals in the industry. I have been fortunate to work in atmospheres where managers welcome new ideas and coworkers share knowledge. I thank everyone at DeYoung & Associates for taking me under their wing (especially Marilyn) and introducing me to spaghetti code and computers. My next career move found me in the middle of a federal government project surrounded by an engineering and operations team, and the rules and regulations that all government-funded projects must comply with. I want to thank Margaret, Maryanne, Deb, Malek, Trung, Morales, Mohler, Farred, Dunia, Harwell, Assad, Roesch, Karabelas, Roney, Tom, Salim, Christina, Lisa, Mike, Dave, Dae, Jim, Stephanie, Quyen, Josh, and Tim.

My current residence at Comprehensive Health Services has been the most enriching, because it has the level of dedication and teamwork among the staff for which every CEO hopes. The company's highly dynamic environment proves challenging, motivating work, and truth be told, even my worst day is better than most people's best day. I thank the senior executives for the opportunity and I especially thank the IT team, including Chris, Todd, Dave, Peter, Foote, Wesam, Brian, Kasia®, Melissa, Christy, Ben, Chet, Jerry, PJ, Dan, Trish, Nadim, Mark, Christina, Bill, and the rest of the gang. I will continue to try and keep up if you continue to motivate and amaze me.

All security experts have an "inner circle" of security friends to whom they turn when they just are not 100 percent sure of a technology, a configuration setting, or even a suspicious event log. To Rob Kerns, Luis Sepulveda, Orlando Ferreiras, Nate Miller, and

Trevor Hawthorn at Stratum Security, Richard Bejtlich, and of course, the technical contributors: Thanks for all the great advice and guidance.

I am especially grateful to several industry professionals that expanded my vision and brought their subject matter expertise to several chapters—I cannot express how grateful I am. Andy Wilson, a senior systems engineer at Lancope, for all his help and insight on the NBA chapter. Jake Babbins, who on short notice, helped me refine the intrusion detection chapter, specifically Bro. Barbara Bennett and Marcy Wilder from Hogan & Hartson took time from their hectic schedule to educate me on HIPAA and the new presidential stimulus package. Stephanie Shelton ensured that my GIS interpretations weren't too far off the mark. Gary Connor at Quova opened his door and gave me a first-hand look at Quova's strategies and methodology for translating IP addresses to geographic coordinates…absolutely amazing! John McLaughlin helped me navigate through the cyber liability insurance obstacle course. I also want to express an ENORMOUS amount of gratitude to Ron O'Meara for assisting me with the organization and structure of several chapters, but specifically the Visualization chapter. To all: Your dedication, experience, and suggestions were intuitive and a saving grace.

I also greatly appreciate the invaluable feedback from the technical review committee for their expertise, time and effort, Jan Monsch, Raffael Marty, and Tom Jacobs, whose insight absolutely strengthened this book. I also thank the Pearson folks, who have been integral in the publication of this book: Jessica Goldstein and Romny French guided me through the publication process, and Chris Zahn provided integral writing feedback and somehow saw through my infamous sentence structure! And last but not least, Jovana San Nicolas-Shirley, Sheri Cain, and the rest of the Indianapolis crew for their final review and layout assistance. THANKS!

Most importantly, I thank my pregnant wife Kasey. (It's our first child!) She supports my every move, no matter how far over the stars I shoot. *And she was understanding when I VLANed her and her celebrity gossip Web surfing off my lab network.* Love always and forever!

About the Author

Ryan Trost is the Director of Security and Data Privacy Officer at Comprehensive Health Services where he oversees all the organization's security and privacy decisions. He teaches several Information Technology courses, including Ethical Hacking, Intrusion Detection, and Data Visualization at Northern Virginia Community College. This enables him to continue exploring his technical interests among the endless managerial meetings. In his spare time, Ryan works to cross-pollinate network security, GIS, and data visualization. He is considered a leading expert in geospatial intrusion detection techniques and has spoken at several conferences on the topic, most notably DEFCON 16. Ryan participated as a RedTeamer in the first annual Collegiate Cyber Defense Competition (CCDC) and now fields a team of students in the annual event. Ryan has been a senior security consultant for several government agencies before transitioning over to the private sector. In 2005, Ryan received his masters of science degree in computer science from George Washington University where he developed his first geospatial intrusion detection tool.

About the Contributing Authors

Seth Fogie is the CEO of Airscanner USA, where he oversees the research and development of security products for mobile platforms. Seth has coauthored several books, such as *XSS Attacks, Aggressive Network Self Defense, Security Warrior*, and even contributed to *PSP Hacks*. Seth also writes articles for various online resources, including Pearson Education's InformIT.com, where he is acting cohost for its security section. In addition, and as time permits, Seth provides training on wireless, Web application security, and mobile device security. He speaks at IT and security-related conferences and seminars, such as BlackHat, Defcon, and RSA.

Jeff Forristal, a.k.a. Rain Forest Puppy and creator of libwhisker, is a senior security professional with more than a decade of security-specific experience. He currently works for Zscaler, and he previously worked at HP, SPI Dynamics, and Neohapsis in senior positions related to security consulting and security research. Jeff has written multiple articles and cover stories for *Network Computing* and *Secure Enterprise* magazines on various topics, such as physical security, source code static analysis products, and network vulnerability scanners.

Dr. Steven Noel is the associate director and senior research scientist at the Center for Secure Information Systems at George Mason University. His research interests include cyber attack modeling, intrusion detection data mining, and visualization for information security. He received his Ph.D. in computer science from the University of Louisiana at Lafayette in 2000. His dissertation work was in information visualization and data mining for Web content analysis. He also earned an M.S. in computer science from the University of Louisiana at Lafayette (1998) and a B.S. in Electro-Optics from the University of Houston–Clear Lake (1989). From 1990 to 1998, Dr. Noel was a research scientist at the Naval Surface Warfare Center in Dahlgren, Virginia, where he worked in image/video compression, wavelets, neural networks, genetic algorithms, and radar signal processing. He has published numerous conference papers, journal articles, and technical reports.

Dr. Sushil Jajodia is a university professor, BDM International Professor of Information Technology, and the director of the Center for Secure Information Systems at the George Mason University, Fairfax, Virginia. He joined GMU after serving as the director of the Database and Expert Systems Program at the National Science Foundation. Before that, he was the head of the Database and Distributed Systems Section at the Naval Research Laboratory, Washington. He received the 1996 Kristian Beckman award from IFIP TC 11 for his contributions to the discipline of information security, the 2000 Outstanding Research Faculty Award from George Mason's Volgenau School of Information Technology and Engineering, and the 2008 ACM SIGSAC Outstanding Contributions Award for his research and teaching contributions to the information security field and his service to the ACM SIGSAC and the computing community. Dr. Jajodia is the founding editor-in-chief of *Journal of Computer Security* and on the editorial boards of *IET Information Security, International Journal of Cooperative Information Systems, International Journal of Information and Computer Security*, and *International Journal of Information Security and Privacy*.

Alex Kirk's earliest memories revolve around computers, including learning to type on his parents' TRS-80 Model III at the age of 4. Following a high school journalism career that included a stint as editor-in-chief of a paper ranked ninth in the country by the National Scholastic Press Association, Alex worked briefly as a freelancer for *The Sacramento Bee* before attending George Washington University as a journalism major. The fiscal lure of the dot-com boom led him to switch his career focus in 2000, when he took a job as a Web master contracting to the U.S. Department of Agriculture. After completing a degree in computer information systems at Strayer University and surviving a pair of post-bubble layoffs, Alex joined the Sourcefire Vulnerability Research Team in early 2004, and has since become an expert in all things Snort. Alex continues to write in his spare time, including an article published in the August 2001 issue of *SysAdmin* magazine on CheckPoint firewalls and work as a public relations officer for The Mars Society, a nonprofit space advocacy group. Since joining the Sourcefire team, Alex has become one of the world's leading experts on intrusion detection using Snort.

Network 1 Overview

Knowledge of the structure of Internet Protocol (IP) packets is a fundamental part of understanding the Internet and how information moves from one point to another. The benefits of such knowledge extend to virtually all networking disciplines, not the least of which is intrusion detection. Rules-based intrusion-detection mechanisms, for example, can flag packets as suspicious if their structure mimics that of a known malicious string. While this is happening, another rule might cause an action in response to a packet that has no conceivable reason to exist, as when both the SYN and RST flags are set. There are many ways to probe and attack from within a packet, and the problem only gets worse as a network gets larger. The shotgun approach of enabling all possible Intrusion Detection Systems (IDS) rules is sure to fail in most environments, particularly when busy, high-speed circuits threaten to overtax IDS deployments that must decode every packet on the wire. In IP networks, bit-level expertise cannot be overvalued when you are designing solutions or choosing the most appropriate defense technologies.

The topic of this chapter—the structure and functions of TCP/IP—is uniquely appropriate in any discussion of intrusion-detection techniques. This chapter begins with a clarification of key terms and concepts, and then it discusses the genesis of current reference models that were introduced in the early 1980s. Following that is a detailed examination of TCP/IP, and the final section describes modern networking.

KEY TERMS AND CONCEPTS

It is important to clarify certain key terms that this chapter uses. Readers who know the standards that are under review by more than one name will see them here as TCP/IP and the OSI Model, which represent *Transmission Control Protocol over Internet Protocol* and *Open Systems Interconnection*, respectively. Because all the popular terms are essentially correct, it is best to declare this common ground before the details are discussed.

When reading technical information or preparing for a network-analysis effort, it helps to have certain issues and concepts in mind. These items serve that purpose regarding TCP/IP and the OSI Model:

- All implementations are not created equal. Conforming to standards made by developers and manufacturers is practically voluntary.
- In nearly all real-world cases, the OSI Model nomenclature is used in documents and discussions, regardless of the technology.
- Although it can be made to work, communication between TCP/IP and the OSI Model systems can have undesirable effects, at least in the form of more difficult implementation.

BRIEF HISTORY OF THE INTERNET

The goal that was realized by the creation of this protocol mix, which is often called a "protocol stack," is a means for open communication between disparate computers. The driving forces behind the Internet was the United States Department of Defense (DoD), specifically the Defense Advanced Research Projects Agency (DARPA), and two international organizations: the International Organization for Standardization (ISO) and the International Telecommunications Union (ITU).

DARPA began work on its network, ARPANET, in 1968, which went into full production in 1970. At the time, the protocol in use was the ARPANET Network Control Program (NCP) host-to-host protocol, and the first five nodes added belonged to Bolt, Beranek, and Newman (BBN); Stanford University; UCLA; UC Santa Barbara; and the University of Utah.

The number of nodes on ARPANET grew considerably over the next few years, which lead to various problems that were largely viewed as symptoms of technical limitations. In July 1980, the Office of the Secretary of Defense directed that a set of DoD standard protocols be used on all defense networks. The protocols have the following official designations:

- RFC 791, Internet Protocol
- RFC 793, Transmission Control Protocol

These are the most current RFC numbers and descriptions; the authoritative organization of the day was the Internet Configuration Control Board (ICCB), who designated the original releases as RFC 760, DoD Standard Internet Protocol and RFC 761, DoD Standard Transmission Control Protocol.

In the mid to late 1970s, the ITU and ISO were working independently to develop an open set of standards for network architectures. This presented significant challenges that DARPA did not encounter, which, by comparison, operated in a controlled environment. The ISO and ITU architects faced the daunting task of convincing equipment manufacturers to agree with each and every standard.

ISO and ITU established a positive vendor relationship with Honeywell Information Systems, which worked with the international teams. In 1984, the ITU and ISO teams merged their respective standards work into a single document, and much of the final product came from Honeywell engineers. The standards document was released under the umbrella name Open Systems Interconnection, which is now referred to as the OSI Reference Model (or simply the OSI Model). The cooperating international organizations designate the specification as follows:

- ITU-T, X-Series Recommendation X.200
- ISO 7498, Open Systems Interconnection, Basic Reference Model

The ARPANET transition to TCP/IP happened between October 1981 and October 1983. During this time, the protocols were intensely researched and scrutinized by their developers. The official release came on January 1, 1983, and the Internet was born. The headstart that was gained by the development period and 1983 release date is said to be the reason that TCP/IP is now the global standard for Internet communications. Now that you have an abridged knowledge of the history of the Internet it's time to explore the OSI Model and TCP/IP.

LAYERED PROTOCOLS

Internet hosts communicate by using a special software mechanism called *layers* (or *layered protocols*). The OSI Model has seven layers, and TCP/IP has four.

NOTE

The depiction of layers might depend on which reference document is chosen as the authoritative model. Although most Internet Engineering Task Force (IETF) documents reference TCP/IP as having the four layers shown in Figure 1-1, RFC 1983, "Internet User's Glossary," lists the number of layers at five. Commercial documents also reflect this difference, but Cisco Systems, the current and long-standing leader in network technologies, teaches in *CCENT/CCNA ICND1 Official Exam Certification Guide* (Odom 2007) that TCP/IP has four layers.

Figure 1-1 makes it easy to understand why the world is comfortable with TCP/IP as the Internet standard protocol suite, but it still uses the OSI Model terms in documents and discussions. The end result is the same with both versions, but TCP/IP has an edge over the OSI Model in terms of simplicity. The Internet Society can divide TCP/IP into two areas of responsibility in support of developers and users: The lower three layers (link, Internet, and transport) are the communication layers, which focus on networking requirements, and the application layer covers host software. On the other hand, the OSI Model gives the technical community a clear set of terms for communication between humans. A minor point is the fact that many readers interpret Figure 1-1 to be based on "incorrect" names. For example, the link layer is also known as the access layer and media access layer.

As previously mentioned, OSI Model nomenclature is used in nearly all discussions and documents, even though TCP/IP is the Internet standard. Figure 1-1 shows that TCP/IP is at Layer 2 if the counting starts at the bottom and moves up; however, because it is functionally the same as the OSI Model network layer, referring to it as a Layer 3 protocol causes no problems.

Industry technical parlance involves specific names for data units in the context of the TCP/IP and OSI Model layers. For the data link layer, the term is frames, the network layer term is packets, and the transport layer term is segments. In the broader context of the Internet, a unit of data is called a *datagram* (or an IP datagram). This is a case of TCP/IP terminology being applied to the OSI Model layers, but it is technically accurate. Architects of the OSI Model devised a more elegant way to describe data chunks. OSI Model documents use the term Protocol Data Unit (PDU) for all units of data and, as a differentiator between layers, it simply uses the layer number as a prefix to PDU. As such, a TCP/IP Ethernet frame is an OSI Model Layer 2 PDU. Note that the word *datagram* is sometimes used interchangeably with *PDU* or *packet* in RFCs and commercial documents. Table 1-1 lists the TCP/IP and OSI Model layers and functions.

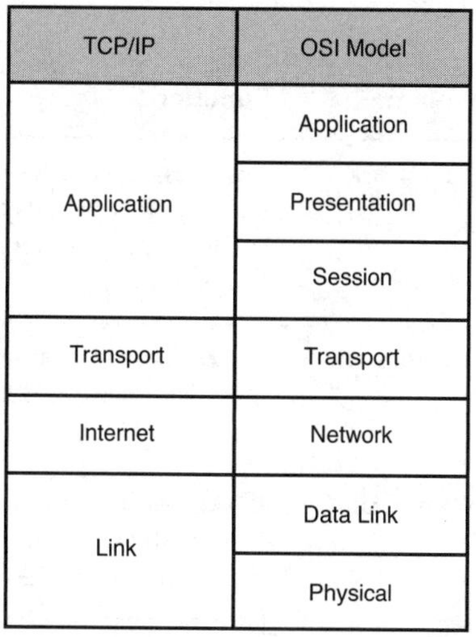

TCP/IP	OSI Model
	Application
Application	Presentation
	Session
Transport	Transport
Internet	Network
Link	Data Link
	Physical

Figure 1-1 TCP/IP and OSI Model comparison

Table 1-1 OSI Model Layers

TCP/IP Layer	OSI Layer	Name	Function
4 (commonly referred to as Layer 7)	7	Application	Facilitates communication services to user and network support applications. For example, the Simple Mail Transfer Protocol (SMTP) is a user application, and the Simple Network Management Protocol (SNMP) is a network-support application.
	6	Presentation	Performs code conversion when data is represented by different codes, such as Extended Binary Coded Decimal Interchange Code (EBCDIC) and the American Standard Code for Information Interchange (ASCII).
	5	Session	Starts, controls, and ends communications sessions; manages full-duplex and half-duplex conversation flows.
3 (commonly referred to as Layer 4)	4	Transport	Connection-oriented; responsible for congestion control and error recovery; assembles long data streams into smaller segments at the sending host and reassembles at the receiving host (segmentation); reorders segments that are received out of order (resequencing).

Table 1-1   OSI Model Layers

TCP/IP Layer	OSI Layer	Name	Function
2 (commonly referred to as Layer 3)	3	Network	Provides logical addressing and end-to-end delivery of packets. IP is routed at this layer by routing protocols, such as Open Shortest Path First (OSPF) or Routing Information Protocol (RIP).
1 (commonly referred to as Layer 2 with references to Layer 1)	2	Data Link	Places data into frames for transmission over a single link. Examples are Ethernet and Fiber Distributed Data Interface (FDDI).
	1	Physical	Interface to the physical network infrastructure. Handles bit-level encoding and manages electrical characteristics of the circuit.

Consider an analogy of what is required for a personal computer in Redmond, Washington, to converse with a mainframe computer in Armonk, New York:

1. The first, and most obvious, requirement is that both computers must be physically connected to a network that, in turn, has physical connectivity between the locations.

2. The computers need to be told that they can talk and decipher the communication that comes their way as being real or garbage (errors).

3. At least one of the computers in the conversation must know the address of the other computer and the wherewithal to initiate the data communication.

4. The data traffic might be heavy, so both computers need to know how to go with the flow and have their data arrive in one piece at the other end.

5. The participants must have the sense not to talk at the same time. They must know when to shut up!

6. Knowing that they are foreign to each other, an interpreter must be available.

7. The personal computer and mainframe can exchange information.

Disregarding that this analogy is fiction, the conversation became easier because traffic cops along the route did not spend time meeting all the same requirements. All they needed was physical connectivity, a common language for communication, and a list of recipient addresses that they could share.

The casual analogy of two computers that need to talk as people do describes a seven-layer communication model. Reality departs from such an analogy, mostly because of these details:

- **Same-layer interaction**. The layered networking model has a peer-to-peer interaction between equal layers on different computers.

- **Adjacent-layer interaction**. Layered networking involves an interaction between adjacent layers on the same computer.

The same-layer interaction is how each layer communicates its intended action to its peer on the receiving end of a connection. Adjacent-layer interaction involves attaching a PDU to a protocol header as it moves through the layers, which is a process called *encapsulation*. As its name implies, a header is at the front of the transmitted data and is the first thing that the receiving host interprets. It contains source and destination addresses, and it can include error checking or other fields. Figure 1-2 and Figure 1-3 show *same-layer* and *adjacent-layer* communications.

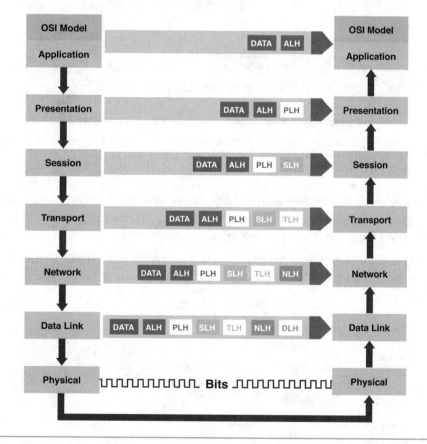

Figure 1-2   OSI Model same-layer and adjacent-layer interactions

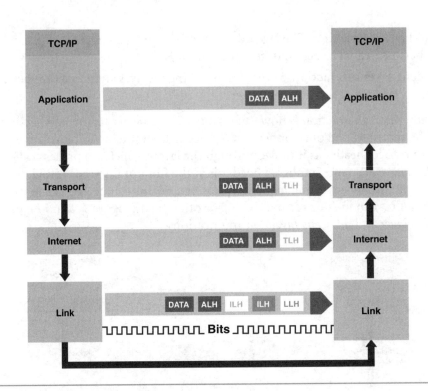

Figure 1-3   TCP/IP same-layer and adjacent-layer interactions

An example using TCP/IP hosts shows how layered protocols enable communication. Assume that a host application program needs to send data to another host that is several hops away. Figure 1-4 illustrates the following steps:

1. The application program at the originating host passes its data, the destination address, and other parameters required to the transport layer as arguments in a system call.

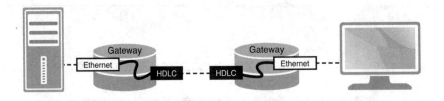

Figure 1-4   Data transmission

2. The transport layer encapsulates the data by attaching it to a header that it has created and then passes it to the Internet layer.

3. The Internet layer encapsulates the data inside an IP header and passes it to the link layer.

4. The link layer (in this example, Ethernet) encapsulates the data as a frame inside an Ethernet header and trailer for transmission by the physical media.

5. Data is encoded as bits on the physical medium. This is called *electrical encoding*.

6. The Ethernet frame arrives at the interface of a router that is on the same segment. The router also has a connection to the wide area network (WAN). This router functions as a gateway.[1]

7. The IP packet is extracted and routed to the next hop in the path. At this point, the entire operation is internal to the router, which effectively switches the packet from its Ethernet interface to a WAN interface; in this example, it is a serial interface. This is path switching, not switched Ethernet.

8. The serial interface is configured to use high-level data link control (HDLC) as the WAN protocol, so the packet is encapsulated inside an HDLC frame, and then forwarded over the WAN to the next hop in the path. HDLC is a Layer 2 protocol in OSI terminology.

9. At each hop, the IP packet is extracted, switched to an outbound interface, and encapsulated as required for transmission to the next hop.

10. Routing along the way to the final destination is facilitated by routing protocol operations in each hop. Path selection is based on IP address tables (routing tables) and routing algorithms, such as Open Shortest Path First (OSPF) and Interior Gateway Routing Protocol (IGRP). Large networks that are logically divided into "domains" also use special routing protocols for interdomain path selection, such as Border Gateway Protocol (BGP).

11. At the destination router, the IP packet is extracted and switched to an outbound Ethernet interface; the destination host is on this segment.

12. The packet is encapsulated inside an Ethernet header and trailer.

13. The Ethernet frame is encoded in electrical bits, transmitted over the physical medium, and delivered to the interface of the destination host.

---

[1] The word gateway references functionality, not a special type of device. In TCP/IP terms, gateway and router describe devices at hops in the routed path. The OSI Model equivalent is intermediate system (IS).

14. The Internet layer extracts the IP packet from the Ethernet frame and passes it to the transport layer.

15. The transport layer ensures that all segments are in order and delivers the data to the host application program.

TCP/IP PROTOCOL SUITE

Specifications in RFC 1122, "Requirements for Internet Hosts—Communication Layers," state that Internet hosts must implement at least one protocol from each layer of the TCP/IP protocol suite. In light of the fact that the link, Internet, and transport layer protocols must be operational for an implementation to work, it might appear as though the IETF is "requiring the obvious." Additional details clarify the requirement by distinguishing two categories of application layer protocols: *user protocols* that provide services to users, and *support protocols* that enable common system functions. RFC authors explain that the most common examples of each are as follows:

- **Application layer user protocols**. Telnet, File Transfer Protocol (FTP), and Simple Mail Transfer Protocol (SMTP).

- **Application layer support protocols**. Simple Network Management Protocol (SNMP), BOOTP, Reverse Address Resolution Protocol (RARP), and Domain Name System (DNS).

Tables 1-2 through 1-5 offer brief definitions of these protocols and others that are widely used today. To be consistent with typical industry language, OSI Model terms describe the layers at which each protocol operates.

Although developers have latitude for implementing the TCP/IP protocol suite, there are some stringent requirements to consider. A good example is the *robustness principle*, which stresses that software is written in such a way that it deals with every conceivable error condition. The principle also involves performance in a network-friendly manner and drives the point home with specific verbiage, such as "be liberal in what you accept and conservative in what you send."

To clarify, for applications that do not require reliable transport services, UDP is available. This is called a UDP/IP application, and it is distinct from TCP/IP.

The nuts and bolts of protocol operations exist as fields within the bit-level structure of each data unit, whether it is a frame, segment, or packet. According to the layered protocol discussion so far, those particular units, or chunks, of data will at some point exist within the same logical structure. The concept was described at a high level in the layered communications example earlier in this chapter (specifically at Step 4). At that point, application data and an application layer header—if required, an attribute that is unique to the application—were encapsulated inside an Ethernet header and trailer along with transport and Internet layer headers. The role of a TCP/IP protocol header is to convey information to the other layers and to its peer of the same protocol at the other end of the path. (This is the adjacent-layer and same-layer interactions, respectively.) Figure 1-5 shows application data encapsulated as an Ethernet frame, an IP packet, and a TCP segment.

Table 1-2 Application Layer Protocols

Application Layer Protocol	Description
Domain Name System (DNS)	A data query service that is used primarily to translate human-readable system names into IP addresses. The query parameter is an Internet host name that is associated with the address. It is called the Domain Name System instead of Host Name System because its services are of a global nature. For example, a Web site's host name can be as simple as ABCD; the fully qualified domain name (FQDN) would be ABCD.com, assuming that it is operated by a commercial entity. Country domain names, such as .us or .uk, are based on ISO specification 3166.
File Transfer Protocol (FTP)	Enables users to transfer files to and from other hosts. Typically, FTP is used to transfer large files that are not e-mail friendly, such as images, hefty database files, or in my case, wedding photos from the wedding photographer.
Hyper Text Transfer Protocol (HTTP)	Used on the Internet to transfer hypertext markup language (HTML) files. Since its creation, an increasing number of applications have been built for transferring information in Web pages with HTTP as the foundation.
Simple Mail Transfer Protocol (SMTP)	Transfers electronic mail. SMTP is completely transparent to users. Behind the scenes, SMTP connects to remote machines and transfers mail messages much like FTP transfers files.
Simple Network Management Protocol (SNMP)	The Internet standard protocol for device management. It reads data from device Management Information Base (MIB) tables, which can create performance and health reports. SNMP also sets parameters in remote devices, and it supports real-time event and alert generation. Software in the managed device is called an SNMP agent, while software at the operator's end of the network is called a network management system.

Table 1-2   Application Layer Protocols

Application Layer Protocol	Description
Kerberos	A widely supported security protocol for centralized authentication management. Kerberos uses a special application, called an authentication server, to validate passwords and encryption schemes.
Network File System (NFS)	A network file-sharing protocol developed by Sun Microsystems. It allows computers to access and use files on other systems over the network as if they were on a local disk. This is accomplished by a distributed file system scheme. It is the de facto Internet standard for remote file management.
Telnet	The Internet standard protocol for remote terminal connection services. Although it is intended for a hands-on user, many shops employ automation scripts that periodically open Telnet sessions to perform a particular function. This is negative from both security and performance perspectives because it transfers results over the network in unencrypted packets and generates much overhead traffic. Telnet is being replaced by Secure Shell (SSH), which provides encrypted and secure remote terminal access.
Server Message Block (SMB)	A network file-sharing protocol developed by Microsoft. It allows computers to access and use files on other systems over the network as if they were on a local disk.
Trivial File Transfer Protocol (TFTP)	A simplified version of FTP. It lacks security and uses UDP for transport services (as opposed to TCP). TFTP has fewer capabilities than FTP and is used frequently in an automated fashion without generating an undue amount of network overhead traffic.

Table 1-3   Session Layer Protocols

Session Layer Protocol	Description
Remote Procedure Call (RPC) Session layer	Implements the client-server model of distributed computing. Its main function is to remotely request the execution of a particular process.

Table 1-4 Transport Layer Protocols

Transport Layer Protocol	Description
Secure Shell (SSH)	Used for secure remote login capabilities over an otherwise unsecured network. It is slowly replacing Telnet as the preferred method of remotely accessing devices. SSH has three components: Secure Shell Transport Layer Protocol (SSH-TRANS), which provides server authentication and integrity; User Authentication Protocol (SSH-USERAUTH), which runs over the transport layer and authenticates the client side user to the server; and the Connection Protocol (SSH-CONNECT), which runs over SSH-USERAUTH and multiplexes the encrypted tunnel into logical channels.
Transmission Control Protocol (TCP)	The Internet standard transport layer protocol. It is connection oriented, which is why it is classified as a reliable transport protocol, and stream oriented. It is responsible for congestion control, error recovery, and segment assembly and sequencing, which is how it reorders data streams that arrive out of order.
User Datagram Protocol (UDP)	The Internet standard for connectionless transport layer services. The word user indicates its role to support management functions, unlike TCP, which is part of how payload data is transmitted successfully over the Internet. SNMP uses the UDP protocol because its nature is such that maintaining a connection is unnecessary. Other applications might use UDP for performance reasons because it has none of the limitations imposed by having to maintain a connection. UDP offers better response times than TCP, but it has no error-recovery functions, which are left to higher layer protocols designed for use with UDP services.

Table 1-5 Internet Layer Protocols

Internet Layer Protocol	Description
Internet Control Message Protocol (ICMP)	An extension to IP that facilitates the generation of error messages and test packets, and it manages informational messages. It has been a part of the TCP/IP protocol suite from the beginning, and it is an important part of making IP work. It is so important, in fact, that RFC 1122, "Requirements for Internet Hosts—Communication Layers," states a requirement that "the Internet layer of host software MUST implement both IP and ICMP."
Internet Protocol (IP)	The packet-switching protocol for TCP/IP; it uses logical addressing.

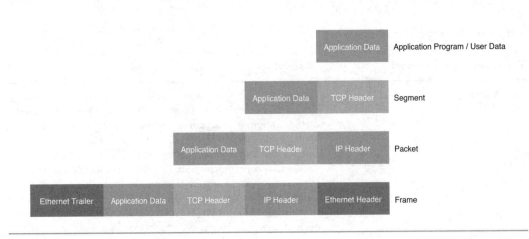

Figure 1-5   Datagram encapsulation

A common vehicle for malicious network activity is an altered header field. Attackers capture all (or part) of a message so that it can be used for illegal purposes. The first line of defense is to know which headers are subject to legitimate change and which headers need to be fixed at a specific value, either because of protocol requirements or local security policies. The following list includes high-level categories for expected header behavior. Detailed IP header information is displayed later in this chapter:

- **Inferred**. Values that can be inferred from other values. An example is packet length.
- **Static**. Values in these fields are expected to be constant throughout the packet stream's life; they must be communicated at least once. The IP version number is an example.
- **Static-Def**. Static fields whose values define a packet stream. IP source and destination addresses are in this classification.
- **Static-Known**. Static fields that are expected to have well-known values and do not need to be communicated, such as an IP version 4 (IPv4) header length field.
- **Changing**. These fields are expected to vary randomly within a limited value set or range; the TTL field is an example.

INTERNET PROTOCOL

IP is a primary protocol of the OSI Model and, as its name suggests, an integral part of TCP/IP. Although the word Internet appears in its name, IP is not restricted to use on the global Internet, where it is implemented on all participating hosts. So, what's in a name?

Readers interested in Internet history may enjoy visiting one of several Web sites that the Internet Society sponsors. The society rests at the top of a loosely formed organization of engineers, researchers, operators, and visionaries from the academic community. The IETF is connected to that hierarchy and, through its working groups, keeps the Internet running and is involved in its continued evolution. The URL for the IETF site is www. ietf.org/.

Because it is connectionless and uses logical addressing, IP is easily ported to networks that are isolated from the Internet. It is an excellent choice for managers of enterprise networks who need efficient, machine-to-machine communications today, but must prepare for Internet connectivity tomorrow. As a practical matter, when compared with non-IP networks, an existing IP infrastructure is cheaper to migrate to the Internet or to an extranet[2] connection with another organization. NetWare environments, where IPX is a competing protocol, face bigger challenges as the need for growth becomes a reality.

A key concept about IP is that it is a routed protocol, not a routing protocol. An IP packet knows where it is going in the network because it holds addressing information that is unique to its destination. Furthermore, it can only be destined for an IP host, which is termed as such because it contains an IP address. To reach that destination, the packet depends on a routing protocol to direct its path by creating routing tables in infrastructure devices (hence the term router). The dependency of *routed* protocols on *routing* protocols is only a small sample, albeit an important one, of a larger set of interactions between software entities that keep the electronic world connected.

IP serves two basic purposes: addressing and fragmentation. The protocol is rigidly structured, and the logical part of its addressing capabilities does not imply a logical or virtual circuit. Fragmentation and reassembly is used for traversing networks[3] where transmission units are smaller than at the packet's source.

Engineers who have supported Ethernet segments might have a better grasp of what connectionless means, at least in the context of TCP/IP. They learned quickly enough that, however voluminous the trouble calls were from first-level support personnel, collisions were generally a good thing. As a shared medium, Ethernet reported collisions when multiple hosts transmitted simultaneously, mainly so some would back off and wait in line to retransmit. Too many collisions were symptomatic of error conditions, but more often than not, there was no cause for alarm. Just as "management events" might have been a better term than "collisions," connectionless is a better term than "unreliable" when discussing IP. One of the reasons that IP is a robust, efficient protocol

---

[2] Extranet describes limited network connectivity, perhaps a single link, between autonomous companies or agencies.

[3] Remember that the Internet is a network of networks.

is that it leaves time-consuming tasks, such as looking up addresses in routing tables, to resident modules in devices along its path. By design, it is not involved in connection establishment and has no flow-control mechanism. When reliable delivery is necessary, the connection-oriented, higher layer protocol, TCP, produces that service.

The closest thing to flow control in IP—and it is not close at all—is the TTL field in its header. The upper bound of the TTL value is set at the sending side, and it is decremented by one at each point along the route. If the value reaches zero before the packet reaches its destination, the packet is destroyed, which prevents an infinite routing loop. IP packets do not have a checksum function for the data contents of their payload; that's only for header information.

IP provides for a maximum packet size of 65,535 octets, which is much larger than most networks can handle, hence the need for fragmentation. When the first fragment arrives at its destination, the receiving host's Internet layer starts a reassembly timer; if all fragments are not received by the time a predetermined value is reached, the received fragments are discarded. When fragments are received on time, the receiving host uses the identification field in the IP header to ensure that fragments are inserted back into the correct packet.

This fragmentation method is called *Internet fragmentation*, and it is documented in the specification for the IP protocol. An *intranet* fragmentation method is in existence that might be implemented by software developers, but it is outside of RFC specifications. It is a LAN-only method that is transparent to the Internet module in host software.

Attackers can use altered fragments to allow incoming connections on outgoing-only ports. In 2001, this was exemplified by the Tiny Fragment Attack and the Overlapping Fragment Attack, both of which are explained in RFC 3138, "Protection Against a Variant of the Tiny Fragment Attack." Do not confuse reassembling fragmented packets with situations where packets unexpectedly arrive out of order. Out-of-order packet arrival is symptomatic of one or more situations that are far more serious than a route through a small packet network. Some of the more worrisome causes for out-of-order packet arrival are

- Packets have been captured, tampered with, and then played back for intrusion or reconnaissance purposes. An example is a man-in-the-middle (MITM) attack (also called a replay attack).
- Asymmetric routing[4] is occurring, which, under certain conditions, causes out-of-order packet arrival. For example, when the return path has changed because of a

---

[4] Asymmetric routing is when a packet takes a different path on the inbound side of a link than it took on the outbound side.

circuit failure and the new path has higher propagation delays, an increase in the overall round trip time (RTT) is experienced. This particular condition is known to cause out-of-order packet arrivals.

- Certain router load-sharing configurations, where the outbound packet stream splits across multiple interfaces, can cause out-of-order packet arrival at the destination.

The IPv4 header is specified in RFC 791, "Internet Protocol," as being six 32-bit words in length when all optional fields are populated and with a minimum value of five words. It has no hardware dependencies and must be compatible with previous versions of IP. The requirement in RFC 791 for compatibility with earlier versions was important at the time because there had been six prior versions in production on ARPANET. This becomes relevant again as IP version 6 (IPv6) becomes a reality on the Internet. Figure 1-6 shows the IPv4 header layout.

0 1 2 3	4 5 6 7	8 9 10 11 12 13	14 15	16 17 18 19 20 21 22 23 24 25 26 27 28 29 30 31
Version (4 bits)	IHL (4 bits)	DSCP (6 bits)	ECN (2 bits)	Total Length (16 bits)
Identification (16 bits)			Flags (3 bits)	Fragment Offset (13 bits)
Time to Live (8 bits)		Protocol (8 bits)		Header Checksum (16 bits)
Source Address (32 bits)				
Destination Address (32 bits)				
Options (variable bit length)				Padding (variable bit length)

Figure 1-6 IPv4 header layout

A more detailed explanation of an IP packet structure is expounded in the following list. The field name is followed by its length and description:

- **Version Number** (4 bits). Contains the IP version of the packet, which is how gateways along network paths know how to interpret data in the packet. If the version number is incorrect, the packet is silently discarded, which simply means that no error message is sent.

- **Internet Header Length (IHL)** (4 bits). Reflects the total length of the IP header built by the sending host. The unit of measure is defined in RFC 791, "Internet Protocol," as 32-bit words. The minimum value is five.

- **Differentiated Services** (6 bits). Populated by the Type of Service parameter in the original specification, which has been updated by RFC 2474, "Definition of the

Differentiated Services Field (DS Field) in the IPv4 and IPv6 Headers." A further update, RFC 3168, "The Addition of Explicit Congestion Notification (ECN) to IP," added Explicit Congestion Notification (ECN), which is the next entry in this list. Differentiated services enable service discrimination by mapping the Differentiated Services Codepoint (DSCP) to a value that changes the treatment of packets by routers in its path. This essentially changes the per hop behavior (PHB).

- **Explicit Congestion Notification (ECN)** (2 bits). The bits are used together to indicate any of the following status conditions:

  00. Not ECN-Capable Transport (Not-ECT)

  01. ECN-Capable Transport (ECT 1)

  10. ECN-Capable Transport (ECT 0). This is the same as ECT 1; implementations may use either.

  11. Congestion Experienced (CE)

  Equipment manufacturers slowly adopted ECN, but it is now available in most IP devices as a configuration option. Its main benefit is that routers can actually send notifications of congestion instead of simply dropping packets.

- **Total Length** (16 bits).[5] Indicates the total length of the datagram, including the header and data; the unit of measure is octets. The length of the data field can be computed by subtracting the Internet header length from this value. A recommendation is given in RFC 791, "Internet Protocol," that hosts only send datagrams larger than 576 octets if there is assurance that the receiving end can accept large datagrams. The maximum Internet header length is 60 octets, although the most typical size is 20, which leaves ample room for a considerable amount of data. The liability of sending larger datagrams is that fragmentation can occur.

- **Identification** (16 bits). Holds an identifying value that is assigned by the sending host. This number is required when reassembling fragmented messages, which ensures that the fragments of one message are not intermixed with other messages.

- **Flags** (3 bits). Control flags used by the fragmentation process include the following:

  Bit position 0 is reserved and must be zero.

  Bit position 1 indicates either may fragment (0) or don't fragment (1).

  Bit position 2 indicates last fragment (0) or more fragments (1).

---

[5] In keeping with the rest of the list, this is the number of bit positions taken by the Total Length field. It should not be confused with the associated description.

- **Fragment Offset** (13 bits). Indicates where this fragment belongs in the datagram; it is measured in units of 8 octets. This enables IP to reassemble fragmented packets in the proper order.

- **Time to Live (TTL)** (8 bits). Also called the hop limit. Generally automatically set by the sender and is decremented by 1 at each hop during its journey to the destination node. If the value reaches zero before the datagram reaches its destination, the datagram, which is probably undeliverable anyway, is discarded. The purpose of the TTL field is to avoid the risk of eternal packets overwhelming the Internet.

- **Protocol** (8 bits). Identifies the next level protocol in the data portion of the Internet datagram as specified by the Internet Assigned Numbers Authority (IANA) in coordination with the IETF. A list used to be maintained in an RFC, but that was replaced by an online database at http://iana.org. Some examples include the following.

Decimal	Keyword	Protocol	Reference
0	HOPOPT	IPv6 Hop-by-Hop Option	RFC 1883
1	ICMP	Internet Control Message	RFC 792
2	IGMP	Internet Group Management	RFC 1112
3	GGP	Gateway-to-Gateway	RFC 823
4	IP	IP in IP (encapsulation)	RFC 2003
5	ST	Stream	RFC 1190 and RFC 1819
6	TCP	Transmission Control	RFC 793
7	CBT	CBT	Tony Ballardie
8	EGP	Exterior Gateway Protocol	RFC888 and David Mills

- **Header Checksum** (16 bits). Checksum for the header only. Because of changing header fields, such as the TTL value, the header checksum is recalculated and verified every time the Internet header is processed. The checksum algorithm takes the one's complement, which negates negative numbers by inverting each bit in the number of the 16-bit sum of all 16-bit words. This is a fast, efficient algorithm, but it misses some unusual corruption circumstances, such as the loss of an entire 16-bit word that contains only 0s. However, because the data checksums used by both TCP and UDP cover the entire packet, these types of errors usually can be caught as the frame is assembled for the network transport.

- **Source IP Address** (32 bits). The IP addresses of the sending host.
- **Destination IP Address** (32 bits). The IP addresses of the receiving host.
- **Options** (variable length). A mandatory implementation for all IP hosts and gateways; transmission of the field is optional. There are two possible use cases:

Case 1. One octet as option-type.

Case 2. One octet as option-type; one octet as option-length; and a variable amount of option-data octets.

The option-type octet has three fields that convey information:

- One bit for the copied flag (0 = not copied; 1 = copied).
- Two bits for the option class (0 = control; 1 = future use; 2 = debugging and measurement; 3 = future use).
- Five bits for the option number.

There are seven *control class* (0) options and one *debugging and measurement* (2) option, as shown in Table 1-6.

Table 1-6   Options

Class	Number	Length	Description
0	0	—	End of option list. Occupies one octet and has no length octet.
0	1	—	No operation. Occupies one octet and has no length octet.
0	2	11	Security. Carries security, compartmentation,* user group, and handling restriction codes.
0	3	Variable	Loose source routing. Routes datagrams based on information supplied by the source host. Allowed to use any route or number of intermediate gateways.
0	9	Variable	Strict source routing. Allows no deviations from the specified route. If the route cannot be followed, the datagram is dropped. Strict routing is frequently used for testing routes, but rarely for transmission of user datagrams. This is because of the increased chances of the datagram being dropped.
0	7	Variable	Record route. Used to trace the datagram route.
0	8	4	Stream ID. Carries the stream identifier.
2	4	Variable	Internet timestamp.

*Defined by the *Merriam-Webster Online Dictionary* as "division into separate sections or units."

- **Padding** (variable bits). Padding of zero values to ensure that the header ends on a 32-bit boundary.

ADDRESSING

Moving datagrams through the Internet or through an enterprise network requires the use of three important protocol components: name, address, and route. A name describes the target host; an address identifies where the target is located, usually its physical or logical location in a network; and a route shows how to get there.

In many ways, network addresses are analogous to the addresses that the postal service uses to deliver mail. Both have standard addressing conventions that everyone must use; the source and destination is included, although the postal service is flexible in that regard; there are times when the payload they are associated with is lost along the way. Where networks are concerned, *topology*, which shows computers and the links between them, is the deciding factor for choosing the correct addressing convention. Topologies are formed over one or more of the following network types:

- **Local area network (LAN)**. A link that operates mainly at the physical and data link layers. Examples of technologies are Ethernet, token ring, and FDDI.
- **Wide area network (WAN)**. Can include multiple, connected point-to-point links (hops); switched virtual circuits (SVCs), where the communication link is shared by multiple hosts that switch on data transmission and then release the circuit for use by others; permanent virtual circuits (PVCs), where multiple hosts are each assigned and permanently use one logical slice of the same communications link; Integrated Services Digital Network (ISDN), which is a telecommunications technology that carries voice, data, and video; and other physical media types. WAN operates at all TCP/IP and OSI Model layers or a subset thereof. Example technologies are HDLC, synchronous data link control (SDLC), Frame Relay, Asynchronous Transfer Mode (ATM), Frame Relay-to-ATM service interworking; and the Internet.
- **Metropolitan area network (MAN)**. Extends LAN capabilities to a geographic area that is the size of an average U.S. city. Operates mainly at the physical and data link layers, but with more instances of network layer operations than on most LANs. Examples are Ethernet, token ring, FDDI, and switched multimegabit data service (SMDS). Builders of MANs frequently take advantage of dark fiber, which are fiber-optic transmission facilities that are not in operation and were once installed for future use.

- **Mobile ad-hoc network (MANET).** Leverages wireless, satellite, and radio communications to create a network that is literally mobile. Many law enforcement and military applications have this type of network.

Addresses are either physical, which means that they are hard-coded in the equipment, or logical. Because they are not hard-coded, logical addresses can be changed through a software-configuration process. IP uses logical addressing.

Unlike logical addresses, physical addresses cannot be seen beyond the boundary of the connected link. Routing does not occur at this layer because it forwards frames based on Layer 2 header information. One way to view the concept is to compare troubleshooting scenarios for each technology. Analyzing traffic on a Layer 3 link means that there might be multiple hops involved and that the end-to-end path could enter and exit multiple devices; a diagram of each hop, or point, would be labeled *point A* to *point B* to *point C*, and so forth, depending on the number of hops; the same work on a Layer 2 link is limited to *point A* to *point B*.

In OSI Model terminology, the physical address is called the Media Access Control (MAC) address. It is a *data link layer* function, not a *physical layer* function as the name might imply. The data link layer is subdivided into a logical link control (LLC) sublayer and the *MAC sublayer*. LLC and MAC addresses are administered under the authority of the IEEE.

The length of the physical address varies according to the networking system, but Ethernet and several others use 48 bits. For communication to occur, two addresses are required: one each for the sending and receiving devices. The IEEE assigns a 24-bit organization unique identifier (OUI) so that organizations can assign the remaining 24 bits to suit their unique needs. Two of the 24 bits assigned as an OUI are control bits. The IEEE Ethernet and allied standards use another address for link service access points (LSAPs), which provide services to Layer 3 protocols.

IP ADDRESSES

TCP/IP within the IPv4 format uses a 32-bit address to identify a machine on a network and the network to which it is attached. IP addresses identify a machine's connection to the network, not the machine itself. The IP address is the set of numbers that many people see on their workstations, such as 127.40.8.72, which uniquely identifies the device. When such a device is connected to the Internet, as opposed to a closed enterprise, it is at the bottom of a global hierarchy for address assignments. End users "rent" an IP address from their Internet Service Provider (ISP), who receives address assignments from a global network of authoritative registries, whose protocol-related operations are coordinated by IANA. Registry organizations can be a Local Internet Registry (LIR), Regional Internet Registry (RIR), or National Internet Registry (NIR). The list of current registries and their areas of coverage is as follows:

- **AfriNIC**. Africa region.
- **APNIC**. Asia/Pacific region.
- **ARIN**. North America region.
- **LACNIC**. Latin America and certain Caribbean islands.
- **RIPE NCC**. Europe, Middle East, and Central Asia.

Of the, two available IP protocol versions—IPv4 and IPv6—IPv4 is by far the most widely used today. It was originally organized into classes:

- **Class A** (0.0.0.0 to 127.255.255.255) for general use. *Class A* addresses are for large networks; they use 8 bits for the network ID and 24 bits for the host ID.
- **Class B** (128.0.0.0 to 191.255.255.255) for general use. *Class B* addresses are for intermediate networks; they use 16-bit host addresses and 16-bit network addresses.
- **Class C** (192.0.0.0 to 223.255.255.255) for general use. *Class C* addresses have only 8 bits for the host address, limiting the number of devices to 256. There are 24 bits for the network address.
- **Class D** (224.0.0.0 to 239.255.255.255) multicast. *Class D* is for multicast purposes only; the manner of operation is that each multicast address represents a particular group of hosts. IANA assigns permanent addresses and allocates transient addresses through the network of registries.
- **Class E** (240.0.0.0 to 255.255.255.255) reserved. *Class E* addresses have historically been reserved for use by the IETF for experimental purposes, but IANA is currently in the process of changing the designation to *private use*. At the time of writing, it is unclear what *private use* means in this context, but it is likely that this is a stopgap measure to avoid running out of addresses while the world waits for IPv6.

Certain blocks of addresses within the available spaces are reserved for private Internets. For example, the Class C range (192.168.0.0 to 192.168.255.255) is available and is what many ISP customers see on their computers in their home network.

Classes A, B, and C are most germane to this discussion, particularly as a foundation for understanding Classless Inter-Domain Routing (CIDR), which is discussed at the end of this section. Readers can see that the classful addressing scheme that has served the Internet so well in past decades is virtually slipping away without notice. It is now officially considered as having a "historic" status.

The term *classful addressing* comes from the fact that a specific number of bits assign an address to a class, and there are different combinations of possible networks and hosts according to each one. The design accommodates the unique networking requirements of organizations by offering options that match their own distributed computing environment. For example, a national sales force with small operations in 1,000 cities needs a lot of network addresses, but few host addresses. That is how it connects teams of only five or six employees to the rest of the company. Centralized business operations, on the other hand, require the opposite—a lot of host addresses and few network addresses. Table 1-7 summarizes classful network addresses for general-purpose classes.

Table I-7   Classful Network Addressing

Class	Total Network ID Bits	Class ID Bits	Network ID Octets	Possible Networks		Total Host ID Bits	Possible Hosts
A	*8	0	0nnn	$8 - 1 = 7$	$2^7 - 2 = 126$	*24	$2^{24} - 2 = 16,277,214$
B	*16	10	10nn.nnnn	$16 - 2 = 14$	$2^{14} = 16,384$	*16	$2^{16} - 2 = 65,534$
C	*24	110	110n.nnnn. nnnn	$24 - 3 = 21$	$2^{21} = 2,097,152$	*8	$2^8 - 2 = 254$

Host IDs with all 0s and all 1s cannot be assigned, which reduces the number of possible hosts by two.

Class A network ID numbers 0 and 127 are reserved, so 2 bits are subtracted in calculations.

Because even centralized operations, where most of the company's workforce is in the same city, might need a campus network, classful addressing can subdivide a single network into several smaller ones, called *subnetworks*. Subnetting is accomplished by using subnet masks to change the meaning of an IP address. The subnet mask defines the network and host bits in an associated address and is one way to tell, at a glance, which class is in use. Table 1-8 shows the default masks in both dotted-decimal form and their full binary equivalents. It is customary to use a single zero in the dotted-decimal form to represent eight zeros in an octet.

A visual inspection of the masks shown here, along with the *total network ID bits* in Table 1-7, reveals that bit positions populated by ones align with the network ID. The reverse of that is true and is shown in the number of possible hosts. What is not implicit in the visual part of the scheme is the fact that changes to a subnet mask can increase/decrease the number of hosts, but not the possible number of networks.

Table 1-8   Subnet Mask translation

Subnet Mask	Dotted-Decimal Form	Binary Equivalent
Class A Subnet Mask	255.0.0.0	11111111.00000000.00000000.00000000
Class B Subnet Mask	255.255.0.0	11111111.11111111.00000000.00000000
Class C Subnet Mask	255.255.255.0	11111111.11111111.11111111.00000000

The following example uses a Class B subnet mask, where

- n = a decimal position in the network octet
- x = a decimal position in the host octet

	Dotted Decimal	Binary
Default Class B network mask:	255.255.0.0	1111111.11111111.00000000.00000000
Network and host octets:	nnn.nnn.x.x	

Modifications to the mask affect the address as follows:

Modified Class B network mask:	255.255.224.0	11111111.11111111.11100000.00000000
Network, subnet, and host octets:	nnn.nnn.x.x	11111111.11111111.00000000.00000000

The network and host octets do not change because this is still a Class B address according to the old classful addressing system. The change must be represented differently:

```
Address with default Class B mask:    <network-number>, <host-number>
Address with new subnet mask:         <network-number>, <subnet-number>, <host-number>
```

This form of notation is used in, among other documents, RFC 1812,[6] "Requirements for IP Version 4 Routers," where the rules are laid out for the use of this historical scheme in a CIDR environment. CIDR addressing uses the length/prefix notation for addresses where the prefix represented the number of bits in a subnet mask, but now, it is part of the official convention for addressing. A CIDR address is described as

IP address = <network-prefix>, <host-number>

In router configurations = n.n.0.0/16

---

[6] The term used in RFC 1812 for this addressing scheme is "classical." The word "classful" came after the RFC was authored.

This CIDR naming convention looks exactly like what the legacy Class B mask would be if it were written as such, but it is not a Class B address. Subnetting allows users to get more out of their assigned address space *within their own network*. Devices with Internet connectivity need to use only those addresses that are in the range and assigned by their local registry.

The lengths of each section of the IP address were carefully chosen to provide maximum flexibility in assigning both network and local addresses. The total length is fixed at 32 bits and is divided into four octets according to the notation used to type the address on a keyboard or write it on paper. To put that description in context, here is a basic example of how an IP address translates from four octets—as people see them—to the 1s and 0s that machines can read. This example uses a common internal IP address.

An IP address written as four octets looks like this:

```
192.168.1.101
```

Figure 1-7 shows a way to convert this IP address without a calculator or conversion chart.

192								168								1								101							
128	64	32	16	8	4	2	1	128	64	32	16	8	4	2	1	128	64	32	16	8	4	2	1	128	64	32	16	8	4	2	1
1	1	0	0	0	0	0	0	1	0	1	0	1	0	0	0	0	0	0	0	0	0	0	1	0	1	1	0	0	1	0	1

Figure I-7   Quick conversion of an IP address from octets to bits

To use this shortcut by hand, write the address' decimal version on paper and leave room in between each for the values underneath. Because each decimal value represents an octet, 8-bit positions are populated in the next line, as Figure 1-7 shows. The last step is to add whichever numbers from the 8-bit positions equal the decimal value; fill in 1s underneath those values and 0s underneath those that were not used. The result is a 32-bit binary representation of the IP address.

From the IP address, a network can determine if the data will be sent out through a gateway. If the network address is the same as the current address (routing to a local network device, called a direct host), the gateway is avoided, but all other network addresses are routed to a gateway to leave the local network (indirect host). The gateway receiving the data to transmit to another network must then determine the routing from the data's IP address and an internal table that provides routing information.

If an address is set to all 1s, it applies to all addresses on the network, so an IP address of 32 1s is considered a broadcast message to all networks and all devices. It is possible to broadcast to all machines in a network by altering the local or host address to all 1s so that the address 147.10.255.255 for a Class B network is received by all devices. Coding the address as all 0s refers only to the originating device. The all-zero format is used when the network IP address is not known, but other devices on the network can still interpret the local address. By convention, no local device is given a physical address of 0. It is possible for a device to have more than one IP address if it is connected to more than one network, as is the case with gateways. This is sometimes referred to as being multihomed.

The address 127.0.0.1 is reserved as the loopback address of a device. It is used for test purposes and cannot be assigned as a host ID, but here is a way to configure additional loopback addresses on a router for network-management purposes. Consider a router that has eight interfaces, all of which have a unique IP address. Remote network management systems (NMS) need a target address to reach the router in order to query its MIB. The address used is fundamentally just an open door for the NMS to collect MIB tables regarding the entire router, not just the interface associated with the address. If the circuit is down for the interface that happens to have the target address, data collection is interrupted. Most router vendors offer the capability to configure a virtual interface, using any valid IP address, as a loopback interface for network-management purposes. The main benefit is that it is available as long as the router is operational.

IPv6

IP version 6 (IPv6) was designed to address the issues inherent to IPv4. The major improvement with IPv6 is the capability to handle much larger address spaces, which eliminates any threat of running out of IP addresses. In addition to scalability, IPv6 offers improved security, ease of configuration, and network management. It has been tested on a worldwide, isolated network called 6BONE, which included participants in more than 30 countries.

The major changes brought about by IPv6 are as follows:

- **Greater address space**. The address space in IPv6 is 128 bits long, compared to IPv4's 32 bits.
- **Stateless addressing**. IPv6 networks can automatically route messages using the ICMPv6 discovery messages that send a broadcast to other routers with details of its network.
- **Link local address**. Automatically configured in the host; valid only in the local physical link.
- **Large packet support**. Enables packets up to 4GB instead of IPv4's limit of 64KB.

- Streamlined header that moves nonessential and optional fields to extension headers for increased efficiency in processing at intermediate nodes.

IPv6 addresses are usually written as eight groups of four hexadecimal digits separated by colons. So, if an IPv4 address is 205.154.89.200, an IPv6 address looks like 192a:0d8e:743b:92f2:a083:cf3e:6fe4:8237.

According to specifications in RFC 4292, "IPv6 Addressing Architecture," long strings of 0s can be compressed using the special syntax : :, as long as it appears only once in an address. The double-colon syntax can also be used for leading or trailing 0s.

Figure 1-8 shows what the IPv6 header looks like.

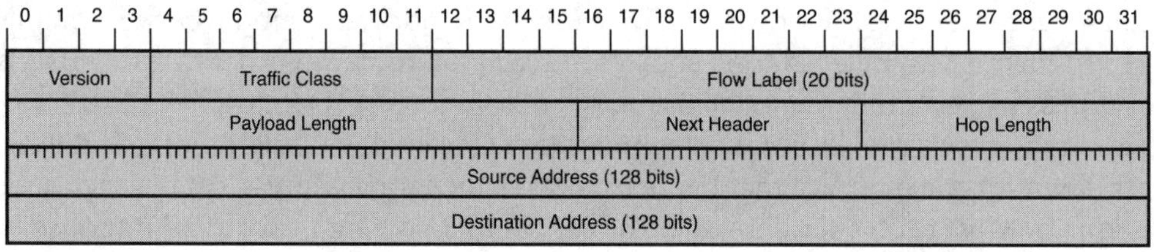

Figure 1-8   IPv6 header

The header itself is 320 bits long (40 octets) and contains the following:

- **Version.** 4-bit IP version
- **Traffic class.** A packet priority value
- **Flow label.** Used for quality of service (QoS) management (currently unused)
- **Payload length.** Number of bytes in the payload
- **Next header.** Next encapsulated protocol (compatible with IPv4 values)
- **Hop length.** TTL value from IPv4
- **Source address.** 128-bit IPv6 address
- **Destination address.** 128-bit IPv6 address

IPv6 was developed in the early 1990s. It was supposed to roll out in the late 1990s, but this never happened because of the differences in IPv4 and IPv6 and the cost of simultaneously supporting both protocols. IPv6 has been added as a viable protocol for the Internet only in the last two years, with full support along the backbone for IPv6 now in place. Although plans to phase out IPv4 in favor of IPv6 are touted, the sheer number of legacy devices that cannot support IPv6 means that a complete switchover is unlikely to happen for many years. Conversion efforts might be hastened by the U.S. Office of Management and Budget (OMB), which mandated that federal agencies convert to IPv6 by June 30, 2008. The 26 agencies in the mandate all made the deadline in some manner.

SUMMARY

Since its official birth in 1983, the Internet has grown beyond its fashionable description as the information superhighway to a communication mechanism that is a necessity, not just a convenience. Government and commercial entities depend on its services when it is necessary to communicate with people not part of their own isolated and secure networks. The Internet is so critical to global concerns that virtually every developed country in the world now has a hand in its continued evolution. The layered set of protocols that make it work enable innovation in many forms, and technical contributions are never in short supply.

Commercial and government enterprises, those networks that are isolated from public network connectivity, mirror the Internet in many ways. Layer 2 switching technologies on the LAN connect to Layer 3 routers in a way that enables personal computers, servers, printers, and various video and voice devices to connect on a global scale.

In the midst of such extensive global communication, a constant struggle against illegal activities exists. Network security professionals must participate in every aspect of network innovation, either as inventors or as students of technology.

Infrastructure Monitoring 2

The term *infrastructure monitoring* represents many different tasks and processes, depending on the context and the role of the person using the term. Infrastructure monitoring typically involves traffic analysis of data flowing through a network; it might also involve creating inventories of all devices connected to the network and their associated operating status (particularly their security posture).

A more specific application of infrastructure monitoring relates to security issues, both from a preventative and a corrective action viewpoint. With preventative network monitoring and analysis, the network is surveyed for potential security issues, and the solutions are hopefully implemented before an attacker exploits the security hole. Corrective network analysis is employed in reaction to an identified security incident. (Post mortem is a common phrase used in this scenario.)

Although network analysis is a somewhat nebulous term, you can examine it more specifically in terms of network security. This chapter begins with an overview of network-analysis tools, and it spends some time discussing packet sniffing. Next, it reviews the various methods to access packets on a network: network taps and switch SPANs. This chapter ends with the concept of defense-in-depth and how you can apply it to infrastructure monitoring.

NETWORK-ANALYSIS TOOLS

A wide range of network-analysis tools are available for use; some tools are relatively new and some have existed for decades. This section quickly looks at the various tools and their purposes, and a later section then examines packet sniffers.

Network complexity has steadily increased over the last two decades. Simple local area networks (LANs) started with ring or hub/spoke topologies using devices such as concentrators and hubs. Bridges interconnected two different networking technologies (for example, Token Ring and Ethernet). Eventually, Ethernet emerged as the preferred LAN technology, and hub devices eventually evolved into network switches. Now, you must handle multiple LANs connected via wide area networks (WANs); provide redundant connections to the Internet; and manage the availability and configuration of communication backbones, remote-access servers, and all the failover communication equipment. Increasing awareness of security issues brought about firewalls, and support for several protocols (such as IPX and NetBIOS/NetBEUI) and TCP/IP added protocol-conversion issues into the mix. When wireless technologies began appearing, they required a new approach to security that lacked convenient physical boundaries, and it was necessary to restructure network design and architecture to accommodate these new network-connection points.

Today, the demands of high-speed Internet access, road-warrior virtual private network (VPN) remote connections to internal networks, and data-capable personal peripherals (such as PDAs, smartphones, and Blackberry devices) add more complexity to a typical network environment. The rise of e-commerce and 24/7 accessibility expectations requires redundancy in firewalls, multiple network connections, and server farms equipped with failover capabilities to preserve connectivity with minimum downtime. As networks evolve, the demands on network administrators and security groups also change, because a continual reassessment of preventative and reactive measures is needed to keep everything secure.

When networks were evolving and new network technologies were emerging, many network-analysis tools materialized to help administrators and security analysts. These useful network-analysis tools emerged over time (find a more extensive list at http://sectools.org):

- **Vulnerability assessment (VA) scanners.** Typically software suites that assess/audit the security of a computer system or network; the goal is to identify any potential or actual security problems. The scanners typically search for misconfigurations, known vulnerabilities, and missing security patches/updates. The most popular freely available scanning tools include Nessus, Nikto, Microsoft Baseline Analyzer (MSBA), Nipper, and router audit tool (RAT). Commercial scanners include Cenzic

Hailstorm, HP WebInspect, Qualys, GFI Languard, IBM (formerly ISS) Internet Scanner, eEye Retina, and countless others.

- **Packet sniffers (also called packet analyzers or protocol analyzers).** Captures network traffic (such as packets) that traverses the network. Bare minimum packet sniffers take the received network data and save it to a file or display a terse representation of the data. More comprehensive packet sniffers dissect the packets and the data within them, which gives detailed representations of the protocol being used and the associated context of the data. These software packages are usually graphical by design and include various statistic or graph representations of network/traffic activity. The most popular freely available packet sniffers are Wireshark (formerly Ethereal), TCPDump (WinDump is the Windows equivalent), and Ettercap. Commercial applications often include more comprehensive analysis capabilities. (OmniPeek, PacketTrap, and Clearsight are notable examples.) The section, "Packet Sniffing," looks at packet sniffers in more detail.

- **Intrusion Detection Systems (IDS).** Monitors network traffic and identifies suspicious patterns that might indicate a network or system attack. Large organizations often heavily rely on both IDSs and firewalls to provide detection and defense against the myriad types of attacks that occur on a continuous basis on the Internet. Two popular open source IDS software packages are Snort and Bro. Commercial IDS software vendors include, Sourcefire, IBM (ISS), NetClarity, nCircle, GFI, Lancope, NetWitness, NFR, Q1 Labs, and TriGeo. IDSs are a core concept of this book, and they are discussed at length in later chapters.

- **File integrity checker.** Generates and monitors checksums on directories and files to ensure that nothing has been modified by unauthorized personnel. A checksum is calculated by applying a mathematical algorithm, such as secure hash algorithm (SHA) or message digest 5 (MD5), to the contents of a file or directory. The checksum is theoretically random and unique to the exact contents of that file or directory; any change to the content—no matter how miniscule—results in an entirely different checksum value. Thus, a file integrity checker can detect when a file is modified because the checksum of the current file won't match the previously stored checksum of the same file. Tripwire, RANCID, and AIDE are popular file integrity toolkits. Related to file integrity checkers are file hash database/whitelist tools. A file hash database/whitelist is essentially a precomputed list of checksums for common files often found on many systems (such as all the DLL and EXE files shipped with Windows). File hash databases/whitelists tend to be popular in forensic processes because they approximately provide the same type of functionality as the file integrity checkers without having to explicitly create the initial checksum list of the files ahead of time.

- **Password auditing.** Can equally serve both good and bad users. Password-auditing tools use various password-cracking techniques to recover a user's password, including dictionary attacks, brute force attacks, and hybrid attacks (where possible passwords are transformed by replacing certain characters with popular replacements, like "i" is replaced with the number "1"). In corporate network environments that must audit password policies to ensure compliance with an industry regulation (such as HIPAA, PCI, SOX, and GBLA), password-auditing software evaluates user passwords against the password format requirements. In other words, administrators can leverage password crackers to find users who have weak passwords and ask them to strengthen their passwords. Popular password-auditing applications are John the Ripper, Cain and Abel, Proactive Password Auditor (PPA), Brutus, RainbowCrack, and my favorite, Atstake/L0pht's LC5, which Symantec acquired years ago and is now discontinued. Many password-auditing software packages now use rainbow tables to expedite auditing. *Rainbow tables* are essentially specialized lists of precomputed hashes and their equivalent passwords. Rainbow tables take advantage of the "time versus space" tradeoff common to computer applications. (For example, you can usually save computing time if you have ample space available to store precomputed results.) In terms of rainbow tables, a single table can easily consume 64GB (or more) of disk space. The Internet offers a handful of application-specific password-cracking applications that allow a user (theoretically, a document owner or system administrator) to crack forgotten passwords for specific file types, such as .zip, .doc, .xls, .ppt, .tar, .txt, and .pdf. ElcomSoft is a popular vendor of such tools.

- **Wireless security toolkits.** Although wireless networks are still not fully accepted in particularly conservative organizational network environments, wireless networking technology has hit ubiquitous status (especially in the U.S. consumer market). Wireless networks provide many benefits, such as lower network-connectivity costs (because installing network cables through walls and ceilings is expensive or even prohibited in historic buildings) and higher mobility/freedom (because users can carry their laptops and still access their network). However, with this new technology comes the need to secure and audit it. Therefore, an entire selection of tools emerged that married traditional network-utility functions (such as packet sniffing and IDS) with the particulars of wireless networks. Examples of wireless security applications include Kismet, AirSnort, NetStumbler, Omnipeek, and AirCrack.

- **Vulnerability exploitation tools.** A notable concern to system administrators and security analysts. These toolkits are point-and-click attack tools that automate the complex process of constructing working exploits and running those exploits against target systems. These tools serve both good and bad purposes. They are typically extremely simple, automated, and powerfully effective. The old-school belief that certain vulnerabilities can be "too complex for most attackers to exploit, thus they pose less threat" is outdated because these toolkits allow novice attackers to easily exploit complex vulnerabilities.

Vulnerability exploitation tools overlap somewhat with VA scanners in terms of operation (for example, they test systems by trying to break into them), but the overall intent of each is different because VA scanners look to provide thorough identification and coverage of all security problems, while vulnerability exploit tools focus on breaking into the system via only one or two particular vulnerabilities. System administrators and security analysts often use vulnerability exploitation tools on development environments to confirm the results of a vulnerability assessment report. Vulnerability exploitation tools can help verify VA tool findings and weed out the false positives. In a more nefarious setting, YouTube tutorials provide potentially lethal step-by-step guidelines on how to use exploitation tools to target victims.

As with everything in the security industry, the exploitation toolkits come in both open source and commercial versions. The most notable is the open source toolkit Metasploit, which personally has provided hours of entertainment. On the commercial side, both CORE Impact and Immunity CANVAS have earned the security industry's respect. Somewhat related to the singular exploitation toolkits are specialized exploitation tool collections. BackTrack is an extremely powerful and comprehensive exploitation toolkit that is freely available; it comes in the form of a bootable CD/DVD that launches a ready-to-go Linux system with many preinstalled attack tools at a user's disposal.

- **Network reconnaissance toolkits.** Are all about gathering a system's or network's information. These tools widely vary in their purpose and the type of information they collect. Network reconnaissance tools include Hping2, nmap (and amap), DSniff, ping, Sam Spade, traceroute, SuperScan, Fport, NBTScan, Firewalk, XProbe2, SolarWinds, ngrep, and ntop. Davix and BackTrack are powerful collections of toolkits that can extend into the network reconnaissance category.

These tools were voted the most favorite by many IT professionals in the periodic security tools survey (hosted by sectools.org). But of all the known network-security issues, a majority of troubleshooting is based on sheer packet analysis, so this subject is worth looking at in detail.

PACKET SNIFFING

Just because a network is functioning correctly doesn't mean it is secure. Networks are configured by system administrators or network architects who might not know much about security. Even if they do, they can still make an honest mistake and misconfigure a device, which results in it being unsecure. The previously mentioned tools, such as VA scanners, help find many misconfigurations, but they are far from perfect. Therefore, it helps to monitor what is happening in a network to see if there are any attempts to attack a known or unknown security problem. This concept is similar to familiar physical security setups, such as a locked door to prevent unauthorized entry and a security camera to record that door. In a perfect world, the door is 100 percent effective at keeping unauthorized people out and letting authorized people in, so the need for the camera is redundant. However, a door is not exactly a perfect security control, because it can be left unlocked, propped open, or forcibly opened. There is also significant value in knowing if an unauthorized person is trying to forcibly open the door, regardless of whether he succeeds. Thus, the security camera provides extra protection and notification that complements the security control provided by the door. On a network, a packet sniffer is the equivalent to a security camera.

A packet sniffer (also known as a packet analyzer, protocol analyzer, or networkanalyzer) monitors network traffic by watching the packets as they pass the sniffer. Originally intended to troubleshoot and optimize networks, packet sniffers are easily used for less honest work, particularly eavesdropping. The threat of eavesdropping via a packet sniffer is one of the significant reasons for the shift to use encrypted protocols, such as secure sockets layer (SSL) and Secure Shell (SSH). Without encryption, someone using a packet sniffer can see all the transmitted plaintext information, which can include Telnet system login credentials, e-commerce data, and database records.

The simplest packet sniffers capture all the data that passes through the sniffer's location, which is typically a specific machine. This is actually a shortcoming of sniffers: They can only see the traffic that immediately passes them. If you want to sniff a particular traffic stream, you must position a sniffer so that desired traffic stream is delivered to the sniffer. More sophisticated packet sniffers and sniffing functionality can be installed/enabled on gateways, switches, and routers; thus, it can monitor an entire network, not to mention any traffic passing in/out of the network to the Internet or a remote LAN. (The section, "Accessing Packets on the Network," discusses some of these options.) Another approach is to deploy remote sniffing agents to collect traffic at remote locations and transport it to a central location for analysis and review. Some vendors have started to include packet sniffers into their products to aid system administrators in troubleshooting network issues. (For example, Citrix Access Gateway [CAG] includes a packet sniffer with it.)

Grabbing raw traffic data off the network is the fundamental operation of a packet sniffer; however, this raw blob of bits and bytes is difficult for a human to directly interpret. That is why most sniffers analyze the data content to varying degrees and break it apart according to the proper protocol. This gives the human reviewer more context for

PROMISCUOUS AND RFMONITOR MODES

The phrase *promiscuous mode* is often heard when talking about packet sniffers. Ethernet hardware technologies conceptually use a shared medium, such as wire, to transmit different data between different hosts. The data is encapsulated in frames, and these frames use MAC addresses to indicate to which network interface card (NIC) the frame should be transmitted. Because many frames might exist on the shared wire that are not destined to a particular NIC at any given time, that NIC often ignores/drops those frames at a hardware level; the host never knows that those frames existed. Only frames that are specifically destined to that NIC's Media Access Control (MAC) address or frames that go to a MAC broadcast address (meant for everyone) get passed from the NIC to the host for further processing. Thus, the NIC performs a certain degree of hardware filtering for frames not destined to it. Under these conditions, a sniffer running on that host can only see traffic for that host/NIC or broadcast traffic.

Promiscuous mode refers to an operating mode in the NIC where you can turn off hardware filtering. The NIC just passes all frames seen on the wire to the host, including frames that were never destined for this NIC. This mode is particularly advantageous for sniffing because it allows the sniffer to see all the frames on the wire, not just the frames for that one host. Promiscuous mode is typically achieved by using a command utility that informs the NIC to enable/disable it.

RFMonitor mode is conceptually similar to promiscuous mode, but it is specific to wireless network hardware. RFMonitor mode on a wireless NIC allows the wireless NIC to relay all wireless frames that are being transmitted to any system, not just the wireless frames destined only to that wireless NIC.

the data. One such analysis involves looking at Internet Protocol (IP) packet headers. By analyzing the headers, the packet sniffer can build a picture of the network composition, including the number of machines on the network, their IP addresses, where they are likely situated in the network topology, and the types of traffic they generate. By analyzing the content of the packets, packet sniffers can see all the data passing between these machines. This separates the large jumble of network traffic into individual conversations between specific systems. At that point, a basic review of those conversations can be done to see if a particular set of conversation partners seems strange. (For example, system X starts a conversation with system Y, but system X has no operational reason to talk to system Y...so something is fishy.)

As helpful as packet sniffers are to system administrators, they equally help attackers. Treat the notion of an unauthorized packet sniffer running on your network as a significant concern. Unfortunately, an unauthorized packet sniffer is typically difficult to detect because the eavesdropping operation of the sniffer is entirely passive and doesn't necessarily cause any noticeable effects, especially ones that are remotely detectable via the network itself. There are a few commonly discussed tactics for discovering unauthorized sniffers, and they all have varying degrees of effectiveness:

- Remotely log in to every system on the network and look at the network adapter properties to see if they are in promiscuous mode, which possibly indicates sniffing. However, many legitimate applications use promiscuous mode.

- Remotely log in to every system on the network and scan the file system for known packet sniffer software packages/components that are installed.

- Rely on any installed host-based antivirus scanner to find installed sniffer software packages. Many antivirus scanners can detect packet sniffer software as a "potentially unwanted program/application" (although these detections might not be enabled by default).

- Monitor reverse Domain Name System (DNS) lookups to catch systems that perform an excessive number of lookups for a wide range of local IP addresses. This behavior is typical of either a network scanner or sniffer that is trying to figure out the host names for all the IP addresses that the scanner/sniffer sees.

- Witness an unexplained slowdown/latency increase on a system/device performing routing or bridging functionality. The increased latency might be caused by the additional processing needed to sniff and process every packet.

- Look for hosts sending responses to traffic that was not destined for that host. Because sniffers cause the host to receive all packets, the host's IP stack might erroneously respond to someone else's packets.

Although it is difficult to efficiently detect unauthorized sniffers, the general threat of sniffers can be significantly reduced by using network switches. Ethernet switches effectively remove the concept of a shared wire in the Ethernet topology and only place frames on the wire (more specifically, the wire connected to a particular switch port) to which the destination NIC is connected. For example, if four hosts are connected to an Ethernet network (hosts A, B, C, and D) in a legacy Ethernet topology using a hub, all traffic from D to A is also seen by B and C. Figure 2-1 illustrates this example. Security implications aside, this actually creates unnecessary congestion on the wires connecting to B and C and delays the capability to send traffic to B and C until traffic from D is done using the wire. When a switch is used, the switch receives the frames from host D on switch port D, sees that the frames are destined for host A, and only transmits those frames on switch port A. Those frames are never transmitted on switch ports B and C, so those hosts never see those frames. This actually enhances performance, because B and C can simultaneously transmit or receive frames on their associated connected network cables, and do not have to worry about collisions or contention caused by host D's traffic. The side effect of this operational change is that traffic to host A is no longer sent to other hosts, which renders the threat of sniffing (by either hosts B or C) moot.

Packet sniffing functionality is a core capability embedded in intrusion detection sensors because all IDS/IPS devices *must* be able to read data streams off the wire. Therefore, the IDS/IPS needs to be positioned so that it can see as much network traffic as possible.

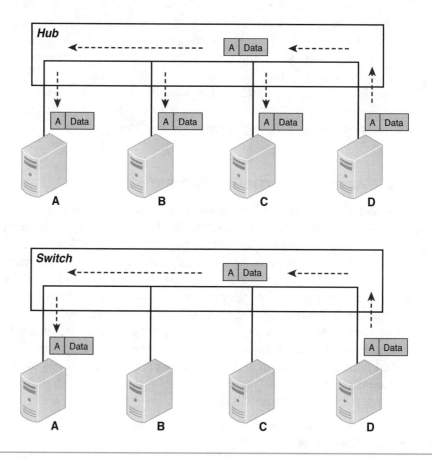

Figure 2-1 Host D sending a frame destined to host A through an Ethernet hub (top) versus an Ethernet switch (bottom)

FIGHTING FIRE WITH FIRE...ERR, SNIFFER WITH SNIFFER

Address Resolution Protocol (ARP) spoofing (also known as ARP poisoning) is a particular type of low-level network attack that involves sending fake ARP messages to redirect arbitrary traffic to an attacker's system. Generally, systems find each other on an Ethernet network by sending a broadcasted ARP message to everyone that essentially says, "What is the Ethernet MAC address of the system that has IP address x.x.x.x?" The destination system with the corresponding IP address sends an ARP response that indicates the correct MAC address, and then the sending system transmits Ethernet traffic directly to the destination system using the correct MAC address. An attacker abuses this process by sending ARP responses that essentially say someone else's IP address is located at the attacker's MAC address. ARP spoofing tools often use a built-in packet sniffing capability to help execute this type of attack in order to monitor the existing ARP traffic on the network.

One effective method to detect ARP spoofing is to use another specialized sniffer, such as Arpwatch, that tracks and correlates all IP addresses and MAC addresses on a network. If the MAC address for a given IP ever changes, Arpwatch immediately sends an administrative alert message to indicate that something is fishy.

ACCESSING PACKETS ON THE NETWORK

A core security goal of corporate environments is to ensure that packets passing on a network are examined for threats or other liabilities. IDSs or packet sniffers can perform such packet analysis, but copying the packets off the network and delivering them to the analysis system is not a trivial process. As previously mentioned, network switches actually work to partition traffic among switch ports and, thus, prevent widespread sniffing, so connecting a sniffer to a normal switch's port is not an effective way to access network traffic. An alternative approach is needed to gain access to the packets.

Two common techniques have emerged to accomplish aggregate network sniffing: Switched Port Analyzers (SPANs) and network taps (sometimes thought to be an acronym for Test Access Point). Both SPANs and taps create passive access to network traffic, so they are useful IDS/IPS or packet sniffers. However, they work in different ways and have a different set of benefits and limitations.

SPANs (PORT MIRRORING)

Some managed network switches provide a port mirroring functionality, which sends a copy of particular network packets to a second destination port. The previous example (refer to Figure 2-1) mentioned how hosts B and C will not receive the traffic frames being transmitted from host A to host D. With port mirroring, a switch can be explicitly told to copy (mirror) all traffic on port D to port C; this results in host C seeing all the same traffic that host D sees. In this example, you attach a sniffer on port C of the switch and still see all the traffic passing through port D, which is something a normal switch does not allow. Cisco Systems named this feature Switched Port Analyzer (SPAN), but the term has been adopted, generalized, and applied outside the realm of Cisco equipment. Port mirroring is completely internal within the switch and usually enables several source and destination ports to be configured.

Port mirroring is enabled by standard switch-configuration means, and, by default, it is most often disabled. Usually, any of the switch's ports can be configured as a SPAN source port. In Figure 2-2, all input and output traffic traversing ports A, B, C, and D is copied as output to port E. Some switches also allow multiple ports to be configured as SPAN destination ports. Ultimately, the SPAN/port mirroring capabilities are dependent on the hardware and software capabilities of the switch in question.

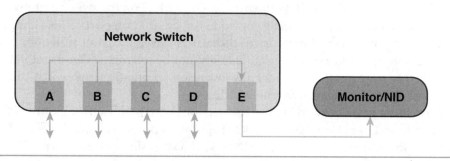

Figure 2-2   All input and output traffic from ports A–D is copied to port E.

Deployment

Assuming that the target network switch supports port mirroring/SPAN, network port mirroring can be deployed without modifying any network infrastructure. This is because it does not require any network-connection interruption or rewiring. A simple switch reconfiguration is all that is necessary, and within a moment's notice, copies of network traffic are sent to a SPAN destination port. Switches that do not support port mirroring/SPANs need to be replaced with ones that do, and that can cause some interruption.

Some switches support Remote SPAN (RSPAN), which encapsulates copied traffic into a specified virtual LAN (VLAN) and then forwards the traffic to another remote switch. The remote receiving switch is configured to copy this VLAN-encapsulated SPAN traffic out to a port. The end result is that multiple switches can use RSPAN to copy traffic and send it to a remote core switch where the packet sniffer is waiting; the packet sniffer doesn't have to be physically connected to the switch running the SPAN/RSPAN. This provides greater flexibility in using SPAN.

Advantages

The primary advantage of port mirroring is that no additional hardware investment is required if existing switches support port mirroring/SPAN. This also implies that no additional point of failure needs to be added to the network topology. Furthermore, enabling or changing port mirroring configurations are done via switch configuration with virtually no interruption to traffic. Port mirroring also tends to be scalable, because the switch can mirror many source ports to a single destination port (and attached sniffer).

Disadvantages

Port mirroring can consume additional CPU and memory resources on the switch, which affects the switch's overall performance. Depending on the switch architecture, mirrored traffic can either be directly copied to the destination port or it might need to be processed by the CPU and memory of the switch. Given the latter situation, if the switch runs low on resources, some traffic might not be mirrored. This is not necessarily exclusive to just port mirroring; under any low resource situation, the switch could fail to properly partition and forward normal traffic.

Heavily saturated switches handling connections with high traffic amounts (such as those often found in network cores/backbones) might not be suitable hosts for SPAN, because the full-duplex links hosted by the switch can easily produce mirrored traffic that exceeds the destination port's maximum capacity. It is important to ensure that the combined bandwidth of all source ports being mirrored does not exceed the bandwidth of the destination port(s); otherwise, traffic might be dropped. For example, take an eight port gigabit switch that has an additional 10 gigabits per second (Gbps) port. Ethernet traffic is full-duplex, which means that the Ethernet connection can both simultaneously transmit and receive the entire bandwidth capacity; thus, a single giga-bit port could, theoretically, transmit the maximum 1Gbps of data while also simulta-neously receiving 1Gbps of data. A SPAN configured to monitor both incoming and outgoing data on a single gigabit port could actually result in 2Gbps (1Gbps outgoing plus 1Gbps incoming) of total traffic to be copied. If this 2Gbps of data is destined to be mirrored to another gigabit port, a significant problem occurs: The maximum out-put of the single gigabit port is only 1Gpbs. The SPAN destination port does not have enough bandwidth to handle the maximum potential traffic passing through another gigabit port to be mirrored. To keep up, the switch must drop some traffic. In such a situation, the solution is to either mirror only one direction (incoming or outgoing) of the source port to a destination port of the same speed, mirror the source port traffic to multiple destination ports, or mirror the source port traffic to a higher bandwidth destination port. In our example, the switch is also equipped with a 10Gb port, which is sufficient to theoretically handle up to five full-duplex gigabit port mirrors. If you are confident that all the source ports will never simultaneously use their full capacity, you can take the gamble of adding more source ports to the SPAN configuration, even though the total theoretical maximum might exceed the destination port. In other words, you can add all eight gigabit ports of the example switch into a SPAN that is mirrored to the 10Gb port. The theoretical maximum mirrored traffic for eight gigabit ports is 16Gbps, which is far more than the single 10Gb port can handle. But as long as the aggregate traffic across all eight gigabit ports stays below 10Gbps at any point in time, everything is all right.

NETWORK TAPS

Network taps are specialized hardware devices that physically connect multiple network connections while also regenerating traffic seen on those connections onto additional connections. Network taps contain three ports at a minimum: two ports act as a bridge/passthrough and one port is an additional monitor port. The bidirectional traffic passing through the passthrough ports are copied to the monitor port(s) as output, which creates a self-contained port mirroring situation for a single passthrough network connection. Figure 2-3 shows the basic tap operation.

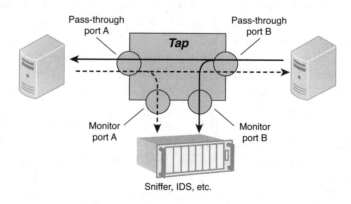

Figure 2-3   Basic network tap operation

Every tap model varies slightly on its features, so it is recommended that you understand these technical features as they relate to your environment. When talking about taps, a lot of terms are used, such as passive, regenerating, and aggregating. However, not all vendors use these terms consistently (and they tend to be marketing-driven) so avoid them for the time being and focus on the actual functionality, regardless of what vendors call it.

Some network taps require power, others do not. In particular, fiber taps often do not require power because they use nonelectronic optical components to literally just split the incoming fiber laser beam into two halves and then forward the two halves to the respective output ports. Wire-based taps (that tap a RJ-45 unshielded twisted pair [UTP] connection) need a power source to power the tap electronics responsible for performing the logical data copy operations and generating the electronic transmission signals on the monitor ports (and possibly the passthrough ports, depending on how the tap was designed). It's also important to read the tap vendor's fine print regarding what happens when a powered tap loses power: Does it fail open or closed? Does it continue to bridge the passthrough traffic if there is no power, or does it essentially sever the passthrough network connection? This is a critical question to answer when evaluating a powered tap. Fortunately, the current generation of taps has mostly eliminated this problem, because it is no longer practical to sell a tap that will inhibit the passthrough connection upon power loss. Also, many taps now ship with dual power-supply capability for redundancy.

Taps can intermix multiple connection mediums in the tap process, which makes it a bit like a media converter. For example, the tap might target a fiber gigabit link, but provide UTP (wire) gigabit monitor ports. This can be particularly useful and convenient if your monitoring systems (sniffers and IDSs) have readily available UTP network connections but no fiber network connections. The lower tap in Figure 2-4 shows a fiber tap that offers two UTP monitor ports.

The number of monitor ports on a tap can also vary. This chapter previously discussed the bandwidth issues of mirroring the full-duplex traffic of one port to another monitor port with a SPAN; the maximum full-duplex capacity of one port (transmit and receive) is double the maximum transmit capacity of a monitor port of the same speed, which potentially causes packet loss. This is also an issue for taps. Simple taps actually provide two monitor ports: one for each direction of passthrough traffic. For example, the tap might be monitoring traffic between hosts A and B. One monitor port receives passthrough traffic going from A to B, and the other monitor port receives all passthrough traffic going from B to A. No packet loss occurs because neither directional passthrough transmission bandwidth capacity exceeds the transmission capacity of the monitor port. The downside of this configuration is that now *two* monitor ports need to

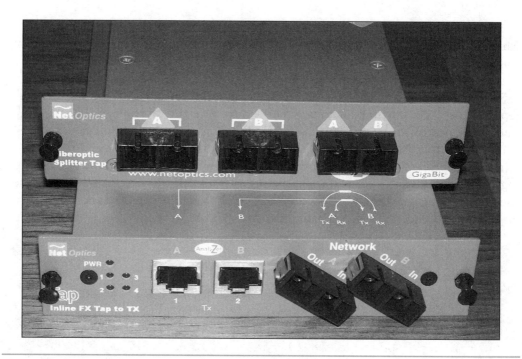

Figure 2-4   Two NetOptics network taps

be monitored to get a view of incoming and outgoing traffic. A directly attached sniffer/IDS/ needs to have two network interfaces and watch both of them. Trying to use a normal packet-analysis application can be slightly frustrating if the application isn't capable of sniffing multiple interfaces at once, because any traffic analysis from only one interface only provides half the picture. You can potentially leverage any link bonding or channel bonding capabilities of your operating system (OS) to logically combine traffic from both network interfaces into one larger virtual interface, which can then be easily monitored.

Higher end taps provide traffic-aggregation capabilities within the tap itself, such that the tap only contains one high-speed monitor port that usually handles multiple lower speed passthrough ports. This is similar to the previous SPAN example, where five 1Gbps ports can have their full-duplex traffic mirrored to a single 10Gbps monitor port. More common, however, is to use another device, called a tap aggregator (also known as a link aggregator), which essentially combines multiple incoming low-speed data connections onto one single outgoing high-speed data connection. This way, you can take the output from multiple tap monitor ports (or SPAN destination ports) and combine it into one high-speed data connection to your monitoring system (sniffer, IDS, and so on).

Some new-breed taps offer a lot of native processing capability within the tap itself, which is a departure from the historical "just copy the traffic" function of taps. These are sometimes referred to as *hybrid taps*. These taps can actually be accessed for remote management and report functional errors via Simple Network Management Protocol (SNMP) alerts. They can also provide a basic amount of traffic statistics collection and reporting. Another tap function growing in popularity is the capability to filter traffic. Rather than mirroring all the passthrough traffic to the monitor port, the tap can be configured with a list of filters of what traffic to include/exclude for monitoring. Filtering/preprocessing the traffic at the tap allows less traffic to be sent to the monitoring system(s). This keeps them from becoming overloaded and potentially allowing the use of a less expensive monitoring technology (such as 1Gbps-capable systems, which are far less expensive than 10Gbps-capable systems).

802.1AE: DEATH TO TAPS

The IEEE 802.1ae standard (also known as the IEEE MAC Security Standard [MACsec]) provides point-to-point security features on an Ethernet LAN. These features include Ethernet frame encryption, integrity checking, and frame origin authentication. In other words, 802.1ae provides a Layer 1 and 2 capability to know what device created a frame, whether the frame was tampered with during transmission, and encryption to keep the frame's contents safe from unauthorized eavesdropping during transmission. Think of it like a type of VPN, but the endpoints of the secured tunnel are only the immediate devices on the same Ethernet network. If a host has to go through multiple hops before it reaches the final destination, each link between the hops is configured independently for 802.1ae. The 802.1af standard documents the key agreement protocol used by 802.1ae.

How does this impact network monitoring? 802.1ae is meant to prevent unauthorized tapping. The Ethernet frames can now be encrypted between the transmitting device and the receiving device. Any taps (authorized or unauthorized) put within the path of those two devices can't understand the traffic if 802.1ae is enabled. Thus, if you want to tap a link with 802.1ae enabled on it, you either need to disable 802.1ae or tap elsewhere.

Deployment

Network taps are deployed inline between two devices. The actual network connection between the two devices must actually be severed to connect it to the tap. Therefore, installing a tap temporarily disrupts network connectivity. It is recommended that you include taps in your network architecture design and deploy them as you initially build your network.

Because taps only provide access to traffic passing through them, place them on a network connection that carries all the target network traffic. You can achieve higher visibility by placing taps on common backbone or gateway connections. Complex network environments that feature many redundant and load-balanced connections can prove problematic for tapping, because traffic essentially can flow through multiple routes to get between two points. Figure 2-5 shows an example. The goal is to monitor all traffic to and from the Internet. This can be done by placing taps on connections A, B, D, and F for thorough coverage, but that requires four taps (and, most likely, a tap aggregator). A better solution is to place taps on connections C and E, which still see all the same traffic but only require two taps. It is impossible to monitor all the desired traffic using only one tap.

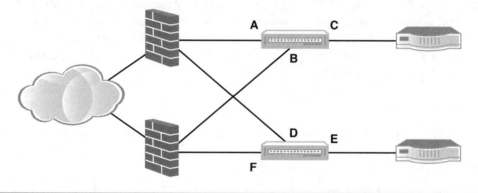

Figure 2-5 Network tap location choices in a redundant/complex network setup

NOTE

If you are extremely concerned about tap failures, placing taps on links A, B, D, and F might actually be a justifiable solution because a single tap failure on any of those links still allows traffic to be routed around the problematic tap.

Advantages

Once deployed, a network tap allows for easy monitoring of a point-to-point link. Monitoring devices can be connected and disconnected from a network without interrupting the link or causing any stress on the network infrastructure (particularly the switch, as can happen with SPANs). For the most part, taps are immune to resource constraints caused by high amounts of traffic; a tap won't bog down and cause issues because it is spending too much time processing critical traffic loads. They can continuously operate at full line rate with no ill effects. More advanced functionality of the newer hybrid taps (basic traffic statistics gathering, monitor output filtering, and so on) can also prove advantageous to monitoring efforts.

Disadvantages

At the end of the day, network taps introduce a new possible point of failure within a network. Tap vendors go to great lengths to ensure taps continue to pass traffic in the event of a failure, but the general possibility of failure affecting network traffic still must be considered. Also, taps can be tricky to deploy on existing links that already carry traffic; the link must be interrupted while the tap is installed. Powered taps require additional reliable power sources at the point of tapping, and all taps require the physical space to place them (such as a space on an equipment rack).

The number of tap monitor ports that need to be monitored can get out of hand as you deploy additional taps. A tap aggregator essentially becomes required after two or three taps, unless you want to use a monitoring system that has six or more network interfaces. The tap aggregator, again, introduces yet another point of failure, although fortunately, a failure in the tap aggregator only affects the monitoring traffic and not the network passthrough traffic.

TO TAP OR TO SPAN

Whether to use SPANs or network taps is somewhat of a debate among network engineers and security analysts. As previously discussed, both have various advantages and disadvantages. Keep these questions in mind:

- Do your existing deployed switches support SPAN? If so, you're already set. If not, it might be more cost effective to use a few taps instead of upgrading your switches to models that are SPAN-capable.

- Are your switches heavily utilized? If so, you might not want to use SPAN because it will further impact your already constrained switch performance. Taps do not cause additional burdens to your switches.

- How many connections do you need to monitor? SPANs tend to be more manageable when dealing with monitoring a large number of connections; SPANs are also easier if large numbers of those connections terminate on the same switch. Managing a sizable fleet of deployed taps takes extra infrastructure, such as tap aggregators, to realistically wield effectively.

- What is the overall bandwidth utilization of the monitored connections? SPANs can cause more performance burden on the switch when monitoring heavily saturated connections; additionally, switches need a higher speed port with enough bandwidth to cover the aggregate bandwidth of all SPANned ports. Taps operate fine on a fully saturated link.

- Can the existing link to be monitored be temporarily interrupted? If not, you won't be able to deploy a tap on it. SPANs (assuming the existing switch supports them) can be turned on and off without affecting the traffic on the link.

- Do you need to monitor only certain traffic on a heavily saturated link? If yes, a filtering tap is a good choice. A filtering tap handles high levels of traffic without problems while filtering it, and the tap provides only your target traffic on the monitor port.

- Are you paranoid about adding additional points of failure to your network? Although the latest generation of taps is generally designed to be resilient to passthrough connection failures, taps still represent a possible point of failure. SPANs, on the other hand, occur on the already existing switches and do not add any new failure points.

- Do you need oversight and change control regarding which links are being monitored? SPANs are controlled by normal switch configurations; those configurations can be centrally managed and automated through normal network device configuration-management platforms. Taps involve manually keeping track of where the physical taps are deployed and require a lot of human effort to oversee.

- Will you need to frequently change what links are monitored? Physically splicing taps into links and then later reconnecting the link after the tap is removed can prove cumbersome if it's done often. SPANs can be enabled, disabled, and reconfigured as often as desired without the overhead of recabling the link for every change.

- Does your monitoring system only have one network connection for monitoring input? If so, use a tap aggregator, regardless of whether the actual packet monitoring is done by SPAN or tap.

- Are you using jumbo frames or other abnormal packet/MTU sizes on your network? SPANs should be fine, but carefully read the specifications for taps and tap aggregators, as support widely varies.

- Are you using 802.1ae (link encryption) on your links? If so, taps do not help unless you disable link encryption. SPANs are not affected by 802.1ae.

Overall, there is no absolute answer on whether a SPAN or network tap is most appropriate. The decision must always be evaluated within the context of what you are trying to monitor and how each possible solution (SPAN or tap) impacts the surrounding network environment.

DEFENSE-IN-DEPTH

Defense-in-depth (or depth-in-defense) is a broad buzzword that is often repeated by many security practitioners. The true context is the practice of implementing multiple security controls within your network's boundaries, even if these controls overlap or are considered redundant. This is already common practice in many organizations that simultaneously use firewalls, IDS/IPS, antivirus, antispam, and server security products. If an attacker can manage to evade the firewall, hopefully, the IDS/IPS identifies it and alerts you about the attacker's presence. A piece of malware situated as an e-mail attachment might be missed by the mail server's antispam filter but the antivirus software on a user's desktop might catch it.

Some entities take the defense-in-depth strategy further and explicitly deploy different vendors for the same security control. The strategy isn't particularly unique to computer security; it's widely accepted by many experts (particularly those in biology-related fields) that a heterogeneous ecosystem is more resilient to afflictions than a homogenous one. Think about it: If you deploy 40 firewalls from vendor X, and that firewall is found to contain a critical flaw that allows an attacker to walk right past it...well, the security control value of your 40 firewalls has been reduced to zero. Imagine if you had instead deployed 20 firewalls from vendor X and 20 firewalls from vendor Y. Now, the security value of vendor X's firewalls has been negated, but vendor Y's firewalls still continue to provide security control. This strategy is fairly effective, but is not used often in the real world because of additional financial complexities, additional device management overhead, and overall sophistication added to the network. It is more common to find this strategy used for Internet Service Providers (ISPs) than for security controls. (For example, many companies make ISP connectivity deals with different providers. If, for some reason, one ISP's service fails, the company relies on the other ISP to maintain connectivity.)

NOTE

Anticipation of ISP service interruptions is sometimes referred to as the backhoe theory, aptly named after the amount of documented network-service failures caused by construction crews using digging equipment (backhoes). The digging erroneously severed buried fiber-optic network backbone cables and caused connectivity outages.

What does this have to do with infrastructure monitoring? This theory applies to IDS/IPS technology, too. Some companies want to maximize their IDS/IPS effectiveness and, therefore, deploy monitoring sensors from multiple vendors. This approach provides the company with a better chance of detecting an attacker that is capable of evading one of the vendors. The sensors do not need to monitor the same traffic; instead, they can be scattered on different network segments to provider larger overall coverage. Thus, an attacker who can "fly under the radar" of the first IDS sensor might, within a hop or two, be caught by the other IDS sensor.

When you start intermixing multiple monitoring products, you quickly realize the need to correlate what one product sees against what the other product sees. This is where network security management (NSM) and security information management (SIM)/security information and event management (SIEM) systems lend a hand. The products receive information from multiple monitoring products and correlate it into a unified, holistic picture. They take care of the messy details of figuring out whether you are experiencing two different attacks or the same attack from two different vantage points.

SUMMARY

Effective infrastructure monitoring capabilities are a prerequisite to most tasks tackled by a security analyst. Using network-analysis tools such as the ones mentioned in this chapter help you not only build a picture of your network and its behavior, but also detect unwelcome attackers who want to examine your network traffic or use network resources for nefarious purposes. Detecting and containing security incidents are a necessary part of every network administrator's job, and keeping an accurate and updated picture of the network's security posture is crucial. Proper analysis of your network environment, determining the most appropriate and efficient packet-capturing method, and maintaining a defense-in-depth strategic view of your network's monitoring and security controls provides a significantly better chance of successfully securing your network.

Intrusion Detection Systems

For readers not already familiar with the basic concepts of an Intrusion Detection/ PreventionSystem (IDS/IPS), the following brief overview enables you to wisely use the rest of this chapter. Numerous publications revolve around Snort how-to books, IDS configurations, and sensor placement, and although some overlap of material is inevitable, this chapter attempts to refrain from reinventing the wheel and regurgitating that same literature. Instead, this chapter provides potentially new insight into common evasion techniques, detection strategies (signature versus anomaly), and deeply digs into signature analysis. This chapter finishes up with a side-by-side, apple-to-orange comparison of Snort and Bro—both are considered as the two most commonly used freeware IDSs available, even though they take separate approaches. However, the frequency of use is hugely in favor of Snort—it boasts 3 million public downloads. At the smaller end of the spectrum, Bro is an IDS that has only a handful of site deployments around the world, but it has an extremely knowledgeable following. If you have already run an IDS/IPS, you are a network security analyst with a couple years of experience or you at least know what these sorts of systems are all about, so feel free to skip to Chapter 4, "Lifecycle of a Vulnerability."

NOTE

Bro has significantly less documentation online and in print; therefore, the Appendix, "Bro Installation Guide," provides a crash course for installing and deploying it.

IDS GROUNDWORK

In a nutshell, IDSs detect attacks against a given set of computer assets from a single desktop PC to a major corporate enterprise network. IPSs are essentially the same thing (often, IPS solutions are simply an IDS configured differently) with the key difference being that, whenever they detect an attack in progress, an IPS blocks the activity detected as malicious. In both cases, attacks are detected by looking for a predetermined set of criteria that is not present during normal daily use. IDS solutions maintain their flexibility against ongoing security threats by having a framework that enables these criteria to be updated over time without modifying the core underlying software package. This is similar to the way that an antivirus product downloads new definitions to detect new threats without touching the scanning engine.

At their highest level, IDSs break into two primary categories: host-based and network-based. As their names imply, these categories are delineated based on the IDS' location, with host-based IDS solutions being installed directly on the hosts they are designed to protect, and network-based IDSs running as independent systems at critical network junctures (typically points of ingress/egress, such as immediately behind a firewall). Because the relative merits of the two system types have been exhaustively discussed elsewhere, this book does not revive that debate; it simply focuses on network IDSs.

Historically, IDSs were labeled either signature based or anomaly based, both of which are detailed later in this chapter. However, the natural evolution of this defensive strategy has transitioned to several other niche IDSs: behavioral IDS and statistical IDS. Behavioral deployments generate a baseline of known network traffic from data flows and alert when deviations occur. It is specifically addressed in Chapter 6, "Network Flows and Anomaly Detection." Statistical deployments are a specialized case and use the IP and port level header information to correlate malicious intentions. Chapter 10, "Geospatial Intrusion Detection," addresses a particular methodology of statistical IDS.

Among network IDS systems, the distinction between IDS and IPS is one of the more crucial ones, even if many existing products can be run in either mode by simply tweaking configuration options. As recently as four years ago, the debate still raged among the network security community about whether an IPS should ever be deployed on a production network, because of its potential to cause major disruptions to end users. Any time that legitimate activity is incorrectly flagged as malicious (commonly referred to as false positives), it is blocked. Unfortunately, that activity is effectively shut down until a network administrator identifies the problem and updates the IPS' configuration. In some environments, this process can take days or weeks. Conversely, many people in the industry—particularly security-sensitive end users, such as defense contractors and law enforcement—felt that detecting an attack after the damage was done had little value, and that it was worth dealing with occasional service interruptions to ensure that no malicious traffic made its way into the networks. Although that debate has been resolved in favor of giving individual security engineers/architects the choice of which methodology to use, the question of whether to block suspicious network traffic or simply flag it for analysis is one that network security analysts still face today.

FROM THE WIRE UP

First, a bit of housekeeping: For the remainder of this chapter, IDS generically refers to any system that scans network traffic for malicious activity, whether it is an IPS or IDS. If a particular point applies only to one system, that specific system is acknowledged.

Before getting into how an IDS analyzes network traffic, it is worth taking some time to discuss IDS evasions that exist at the network and transport layers of the OSI Model and how IDS deals with those evasions to ensure that it sees all the traffic destined for the network it protects. Not only is this the first bit of work an IDS must do after it acquires each packet off of the wire, but it is fundamentally one of the most important pieces of the IDS puzzle, because low-level evasions can make even the best-researched detection methodologies worthless by preventing the higher levels of the IDS from seeing what they need to see.

This chapter discusses four different IDS evasion techniques and what can be done to overcome them: denial of service (DoS), IP fragmentation, TCP stream manipulation, and the use of target-based reassembly.

DoS ATTACKS

One of the oldest attacks on the Internet is DoS attacks—and its close cousin, distributed denial of service (DDoS) attacks, which is when traffic comes from a large number of hosts distributed across the Internet instead of one or more hosts on a single network—are the simplest to understand and implement, yet they are some of the most difficult attacks to effectively prevent. Chapter 6 extensively discusses DoS attacks, but this section discusses them in the context of IDSs.

The concept of these attacks is straightforward: By flooding a given device, whether it is an IDS, a Web server, or some other resource with enough traffic, an attacker can exceed its ability to process inbound requests in a timely fashion. This causes the device to slow dramatically, or in some cases, become completely unavailable. Flood DoS attacks are the most common type of DoS attacks, because they require the fewest resources to conduct. The attacks seek to saturate a given system with hundreds, thousands, millions, or billions of connections, depending on the environment's bandwidth, or with an abnormally large amount of data flowing across a normal number of connections. Depending on the capacity of the attacked host, a flood DoS attack can be conducted by a single person using a single attacking system. For example, an attacker with a powerful server connected to an OC-3 line can easily take out a home-based system with more moderate hardware, connected to the Internet via a digital subscriber line (DSL) line or a cable modem.

Flood DDoS attacks are often nearly as easy to conduct, despite the inherent requirement that an attacker use multiple systems to carry out his plans. Software designed to break into desktop PCs—be they home or corporate systems—and then turn the infected hosts into a botnet capable of launching DDoS attacks is easy for any motivated individual to find. Legitimate computer-security penetration-testing framework projects, such as Metasploit, can be used with malicious intent to create DDoS networks. Even those with virtually no network-security or programming knowledge can launch a DDoS attack simply by persuading enough people to visit a given Web site, which is commonly known as the slashdot effect, after the propensity of the tech news Web site Slashdot.org to accidentally make Web servers unavailable after its millions of readers attempted to read an article posted on a third-party Web site.

Unfortunately, an IDS can do little to protect itself from a flood DoS or DDoS attack, because there is generally no way for an IDS to distinguish this type of traffic from a legitimate spike in network activity, especially because, sometimes, legitimate traffic can actually constitute a DDoS. IDS administrators concerned about these attacks need to look at more generic anti-DDoS technologies, including load-balancing perimeter segments, anti-DoS cleansing appliances, or implement a network-behavior analysis tool.

More sophisticated attackers, however, can perform a DDoS with a considerably smaller amount of actual traffic moving across the network. By understanding an IDS in depth, an attacker can pinpoint the types of network traffic that cause the IDS to work particularly hard and shape his attack accordingly. An excellent, if not exactly plausible, example comes from the TurboSnort.com Web site, which came online in mid 2005 as a way for people to check the speed of their Snort rules. The site allowed users to submit any rule whatsoever; their submissions were run against a collection of packet captures with speed metrics being gathered along the way.

To prove a point about both the vulnerability of such a service and the potential for a poorly written Snort rule to slow down an IDS to the point where it's unusable, Brian Caswell, a well-respected IDS aficionado and author, submitted the following rule for analysis:

```
alert tcp any any -> any any (pcre:"/.+\n.+/";)
```

If you do not know why this rule is problematic, you will by the end of Chapter 4, which discusses Snort rule performance. In short, by running a recursive regular expression against every single packet analyzed by the IDS, he was able to keep the remote system busy for nearly a day, when it typically returned results under an hour. Although no IDS analyst in their right mind would run such a rule on a production network, the essential point remains: If an attacker knows about a particularly resource-intensive piece of detection that an IDS is doing, and can shape his traffic to trigger that detection, he can cause the remote system to burn resources so quickly that it becomes unusable, with a minimal amount of traffic actually sent across the network.

IP FRAGMENTATION

Another type of IDS evasion comes from a perfectly legitimate IP feature: packet fragmentation, which was originally implemented to allow packets to be routed through systems that have a smaller maximum transmission unit (MTU) size than the originating host. Packets fragmented at the IP layer contain an offset, which specifies where in relation to the beginning of the original packet the given fragment must be placed when performing reassembly; for example, an IP packet of 1,500 bytes that was broken into three fragments of equal size might have offsets of 0, 500, and 1000. With this information, the receiving host can reassemble the fragments into the original piece of data, regardless of the order in which the fragments arrive.

Where the matter becomes complex, and thus a target for IDS evasion, is the way that operating systems (OSs) reassemble overlapping fragments. For example, if the same 1500 byte packet was broken into fragments with offsets of 0, 1000, and 1200, with respective fragment sizes of 1000, 400, and 300 bytes, an overlap occurs, with bytes 1200 through 1400 present in both the second and third IP fragments. Figure 3-1 visualizes this packet fragmentation.

In such a scenario, the authors of the receiving OS are forced to make a choice as to which fragment the data should be pulled from—should they use the one that arrived first, the one that arrived last, or use some completely different criteria set to determine from which fragment to pull the data?

Because different OSs have different methods of reassembling overlapping fragments, it is possible that an IDS protecting a heterogeneous environment might not reassemble the fragments in the same way as each different OS it is protecting. This allows an attacker to evade the IDS by choosing the appropriate IP fragmentation scheme because IP packets can, of course, be manually fragmented. Thomas Ptacek and Timothy Newsham first outlined this method in their landmark 1998 whitepaper distributed by

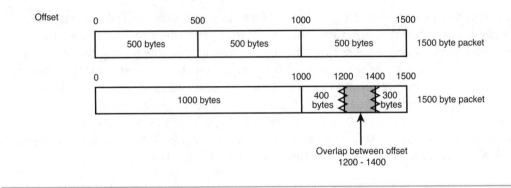

Figure 3-1   Packet fragmentation example

Secure Networks, Inc., "Insertion, Evasion, and Denial of Service: Eluding Network Intrusion Detection." Umesh Shankar and Vern Paxson expanded on this method in their May 2003 academic whitepaper, "Active Mapping: Resisting NIDS Evasion Without Altering Traffic," in the Proceedings of IEEE Symposium on Security and Privacy.

TCP STREAM ISSUES

A more complex set of problems arises from the nature of Transmission Control Protocol (TCP), which by design often carries application-layer payloads in multiple packets. The first, and most obvious, problem is the real possibility that attack data does not all exist inside a single packet, but is split across two or more packets. Such a scenario is particularly common when dealing with client-side exploits, such as a malformed piece of HTML that crashes certain browsers; although the maximum size of a TCP payload running on a standard Ethernet network with an MTU of 1500 bytes is 1446 bytes, the average Web page sent to a browser is often considerably larger, up to hundreds to a few thousand bytes. Thus, if two pieces of data were necessary to exploit a given vulnerability in, say, Internet Explorer, and one piece was present in the page's header and another in the body, the two pieces of data can easily come across the wire in separate packets. Without some sort of mechanism to combine multiple packets sent in a given TCP stream, it can be a trivial task to evade an IDS.

Even when an IDS implements some form of TCP stream reassembly, the potential for attacks to span multiple packets exists. Because an IDS must, by definition, store the contents of all packets that it wants to reassemble in memory until it is ready to put them back together and send them through its detection engine, all IDS software must have some sort of policy regarding what they do with large streams of data. More specifically, there must be a standardized way for the IDS to say, in essence, "Okay, there's too much data here for me to keep spooling it up. I'm sending everything I have now through the detection engine. Then, start spooling up fresh data on this connection." Skilled attackers with knowledge of the IDS that they are trying to evade can take advantage of this policy to time the data they send through specifically so that it splits across multiple flushes of the data stream buffer. Of course, the same effect can also be achieved purely by chance even when an unskilled attacker or automated worm sends large chunks of traffic, so this scenario must be taken into account by anyone attempting to detect an attack that could be present in a large TCP stream.

Similar to the situation with IP fragmentation, it is also possible to legitimately have two TCP packets that contain the same data slice. This often occurs in the real world when a connection between a pair of hosts is unreliable; if the receiving host does not acknowledge receipt of a given packet within a certain amount of time, the sending host retransmits that packet in order for the receiving host to piece back together the entire data stream being sent. Much more complex scenarios exist. For example, if the receiving host acknowledges receipt of a packet, but that acknowledgment does not make its way back to the sending host, the sender retransmits the packet, thinking that the data never reached the receiving host. In some cases where the original packet never reached the receiving host before the sending host retransmitted the data, the original packet arrives after the retransmission (either before or after the retransmitted packet). Like IP fragmentation, different OSs have different policies for handling these conflicts, and a skilled attacker can evade the IDS by exploiting the differences between the way that the target OS and the IDS protecting it reassemble a TCP stream.

Finally, idiosyncrasies in the way that OSs deal with the close of a TCP session can cause the IDS to see application-layer traffic differently than the receiving host. A TCP connection can be closed, either through a graceful exchange of FIN and ACK packets or by a RST packet, which need not be ACKed, but is sometimes anyway by poorly written TCP stack implementations. For example, if a host sends a FIN packet to close a connection, and receives a final piece of TCP stream data before the remote host acknowledges the FIN, a determination must be made as to whether to accept the last piece of data. If the receiving host chooses to honor the data, but the IDS discards it as invalid, the IDS misses any attack that was present in the final piece of data.

TARGET-BASED REASSEMBLY

Given all these potential ways to evade an IDS, a good system must ensure that it not only implements anti-DoS technology, IP fragment reassembly, and TCP stream reassembly and management, it must do so in a way that is consistent with all the OSs it defends. This ensures that the IDS sees the same traffic as the end hosts.

This concept, known as *target-based reassembly*, is something of a Holy Grail among today's IDS systems, because no existing IDS automatically does target-based reassembly. Perhaps the closest any system comes is Snort, which via its frag3 and stream5 preprocessors, enables users to specify which reassembly policy needs to be used for which segments of the network (or even individual IP addresses). Anyone interested in how target-based reassembly works must read the Ptacek/Newsham and Shankar/Paxon whitepapers previously mentioned and "Target-Based Fragmentation Reassembly" (Judy Novak 2003) and "Target-Based TCP Stream Reassembly" (Judy Novak & Steve Sturges 2007), both of which are available on the Snort.org Web site.

Two Detection Philosophies: Signature and Anomaly Based

All IDS software performs at least some types of traffic normalization previously discussed to ensure that it has a reliable and valid picture of network traffic. However, some IDSs can be split into two major groups:

- A *signature-based IDS* works by scanning through packets, looking for a particular set of well-defined characteristics that, when seen together, typically constitute an attack in progress. As a result of this architecture, a signature-based IDS is only as good as its signatures; it cannot possibly detect attacks for which it has no signatures. A poorly written signature can either cause an enormous number of false positives or allow legitimate attacks to go undetected (commonly referred to as "false negative").

- An *anomaly-based IDS* approaches the problem from a different angle: It monitors the characteristics of the network traffic it sees and searches for changes from some predefined normal set of characteristics. For example, if a dedicated Web server suddenly begins initiating a large number of outbound Simple Mail Transfer Protocol (SMTP) connections, an anomaly-based IDS raises an alert, likely indicating that a spam relay had been installed on the Web server. Here, the key factor in the quality of the system is its capability to determine what is normal versus what is abnormal; without some sort of baseline to compare traffic to, an anomaly-based IDS is likely to generate too many or too few alerts.

The remainder of this chapter examines these two approaches to IDS through the lens of a pair of real-world products: Snort is the example tool using signature detection, and Bro performs anomaly detection. Snort is a pure signature-detection IDS, whereas Bro can be categorized as a network-application framework because it has the capability to allow the security analyst to perform anomaly detection, signature detection, and behavioral detection in various capacities. However, this chapter focuses more on the anomaly-detection capabilities.

Snort: Signature-Based IDS

At its heart, Snort—like any other signature-driven IDS—spends most of its time searching for particular malicious traffic patterns inside of packets. A well-written signature has search criteria that are narrow enough that the analysis process does not overwhelm the IDS, but broad enough that all potential variants of the traffic being sought can be found. To demonstrate how a signature works, a few simple Snort rules are provided that would alert on real-world traffic. (These are not based on any real exploits, because several of them are covered in Chapter 4.) Snort newbies can find a plethora of online documentation and how-to books about Snort, and therefore, these details are omitted here.

For the first scenario, suppose that you run a Web site that has some pages that you do not want Chinese search engines to access because of, say, ITAR restrictions.

Note

ITAR stands for International Traffic in Arms Regulations. It is a set of self-preservation U.S. government regulations that dictates import and export laws pertaining to defense and military related technologies, such as cryptographic algorithms.

As you peruse your Web server's logs, you see that, despite your best efforts, in robots.txt, the spider from Baidu.com—China's top search engine—continues to access those pages. Looking at the packet data for these requests, you see HTTP payloads similar to the following:

```
GET /site/secrets/coolpage.html HTTP/1.1\r\n
Host: www.yoursite.com\r\n
Connection: close\r\n
User-Agent: Baiduspider+(http://www.baidu.com/search/spider.htm)\r\n
Accept-Language: zh-cn,zh-tw\r\n
Accept-Encoding: gzip\r\n
Accept: */*\r\n
\r\n
```

The Snort rule to block access from the Baidu spider to this page is as follows:

```
drop tcp $EXTERNAL_NET any -> $HOME_NET $HTTP_PORTS (msg:"Block Baidu Spider
From coolpage.htm"; flow:established,to_server;
uricontent:"/site/secrets/coolpage.html"; nocase; content:"User-Agent¦3A¦";
nocase; content:"Baiduspider"; nocase; distance:0;
pcre:"/^User-Agent\x3A[^\r\n]+Baiduspider/smi"; classtype:misc-activity;)
```

Several important pieces of this signature tell Snort what packets to look at, where to look inside of those packets, and for what exactly it is looking. These pieces break down into two logical groups: header-specific, which is concerned with the IP and TCP layers; and payload-specific, which is concerned with the remainder of the packet.

The header-specific options begin with the `tcp $EXTERNAL_NET any -> $HOME_NET $HTTP_PORTS` piece of the rule. This first tells Snort that it should only look for TCP packets as opposed to UDP, ICMP, and so on. Next, the rule uses a group of predefined Snort variables to tell the IDS to only examine packets that come from an external IP address (one outside the zone being defended) to an internal IP address (one inside the zone being defended), bound for TCP port 80 (or any other port that houses Web traffic on the defended network). With this simple first signature piece, the IDS can discard irrelevant traffic it sees as it processes this particular signature.

The other piece of the header-specific section of the signature is `flow:established, to_server;`. Because every TCP packet has an associated state, specifying that state enables the IDS to further trim the number of packets it needs to inspect. Here, the rule first states that the packet it is looking for must be part of an open, established TCP stream. More importantly, in terms of discarding irrelevant packets, the rule states that the packet must be headed to the machine considered to be the server per the established TCP stream (meaning the system that *received* the initial SYN packet at the start of the three-way handshake). This distinction is particularly relevant when dealing with situations, such as peer-to-peer traffic, in which a single machine can be both a server and a client. By relying on the TCP-based definition, a rule written for such a situation can still specify that it only applies to packets headed in a particular direction, thus eliminating the need to examine in detail potentially half or more of the packets passing to the IDS.

The payload-specific section of the signature begins with the `uricontent` piece, which tells Snort to search only through the HTTP Uniform Resource Identifier (URI) portion of the TCP/IP payload—the packet portion that is typically visible within a Web browser's location bar—for the string `/site/secrets/coolpage.html`. The following word `nocase` simply means to make the search case insensitive, which is necessary, because IIS Web servers return a page properly no matter how the request for it is capitalized. (Apache Web servers are case sensitive.)

The following two content pieces of the signature both search through the entire TCP/IP payload for the specified strings. If—and only if—the string `User-Agent:` is found (note that `|3A|` is simply the hexadecimal encoding for ":", which is required because colons are special characters in Snort rules), Snort looks through the payload for `Baiduspider`. Because this string is followed by the option `distance:0;`, Snort only searches from the end of the string `User-Agent:` to the end of the packet. This speeds the process and simultaneously helps eliminate false positives, because the string Baiduspider is only relevant if it follows User-Agent:.

The final, and perhaps most relevant, piece of detection is the pcre option. For readers not familiar with this option, PCRE stands for Perl-Compatible Regular Expressions, whose job is to do complex string matching. Given PCRE's complexity, covering it in any sort of depth is outside this book's scope; instead, this section explains what any expressions given in this chapter and the next are supposed to do, without going into detail about how they do so.

In this case, the expression ensures that the string User-Agent: begins at the start of a line and allows for one or more characters that are not new lines before the string Baiduspider. The rationale behind the first requirement is simple, but it goes to the heart of how signature-based IDSs work: Because Snort has no concept of the state of the HTTP conversation, and thus no idea whether it is looking at form data being sent to a server, HTTP headers, or even HTML being returned from the server, it is the signature writer's job to help Snort self-locate or determine whether the data it sees is in the right part of an HTTP conversation to be relevant. Because all HTTP headers begin at the start of a new line, requiring that the string be found there makes it 99 percent (or more) likely that the string that has been matched is actually an HTTP header and not, say, the contents of a blog entry being posted to a remote server.

The second requirement enforced by the PCRE has a more subtle rationale, but it is again central to how a signature-based IDS works. Although the single string User-Agent: Baiduspider works well for the packet previously shown, detection immediately ceases working if any change is made to the string in question (for example, if a future version of the crawler sent User-Agent: *GoldenBaiduspider* instead). By allowing one or more non-newline characters between the first and the second string, the signature remains flexible in the event of eventual change or even intentional attempts to evade detection and will still trigger an alert.

NOTE

The /smi attributes at the end of the PCRE statement in the signature are PCRE-compatible modifiers and can be found at www.snort.org/docs/snort_htmanuals/htmanual_2832/node274.html.

Of course, self-location is even more important when a signature-based IDS looks for attempts to exploit software vulnerabilities. For example, say that you are defending a network where many people use ChatOL, a (fictional) open source chat client that talks to the AOL Instant Messenger (AIM) community via the OSCAR protocol (that AOL released in March 2008). A security researcher just discovered that ChatOL contains a buffer overflow, where messages greater than 1024 bytes cause memory corruption on the machine using ChatOL, and possibly allow an attacker to gain control over the machine. The Snort rule to detect this attack is

```
alert tcp $EXTERNAL_NET 5190 -> $HOME_NET any (msg:"ChatOL oversized message
buffer overflow attempt"; flow:established,to_client; content:"¦2A¦";
depth:1; byte_test:2,>,1024,3,relative; classtype:attempted-user;)
```

After setting your header-specific options based on the fact that inbound AIM messages are coming from port 5190 to a client inside of your protected network, you get to the meat of this signature: the payload-specific portion. From reading the OSCAR specification (http://dev.aol.com/aim/oscar/), you know that all messages using that protocol begin with a single hexadecimal byte, 0x2A. To confirm that the data you are looking at is actually OSCAR traffic and not some other protocol using this port (a situation that happens too frequently on ports above 1024), the signature must first find this byte at the start of the packet. Thus, it uses the Snort keyword depth, which modifies the previous content clause by specifying the number of packets into the payload to search. Because the byte in question must be at the very beginning, set a depth of 1, which allows only Snort to examine the first byte of the payload.

If this check succeeds, you have determined that you are most likely at the start of an inbound OSCAR/AIM message and can proceed to check for the malicious condition: a message size greater than 1024 bytes. Because the OSCAR protocol declares message length in the fourth and fifth byte of the packet encoded as an unsigned hexadecimal 16-bit integer, the byte_test option examines those specific bytes and generates an alert if they are larger than the specified size.

NOTE

The byte_test option can test a byte field against a specific value, both binary values, or by converting byte strings to its binary equivalent. The Snort Manual, section 3.5.10, "byte_test," and section 3.11.5, "Testing Numerical Values," provide a more in-depth explanation of byte_test.

Why is this such a good example of the importance of self-location? Suppose for a moment that Snort had no feature to constrain the area in which to search for a given string or byte; instead, Snort always searched through the entire packet payload to look for the strings specified in the signature. In the first example, the chances of finding both

User-Agent: and Baiduspider strings in the same packet in any order besides the one you want is relatively low. More importantly, a human can quickly look at the packet that was blocked by the IDS because Snort, like any other IDS, logs any packets that match a signature to determine whether the two terms appear in the right places, and, if necessary, update the signature to no longer alert on the false positive case. In the second example, however, the likelihood of finding 0x2A, which is an ASCII "*", somewhere else in the packet is extremely high; if Snort processes the byte_test after finding one of these other 0x2As, it is also likely that it would find a pair of bytes that, when interpreted as a size (instead of, say, the body of the chat message), exceeded 1024 bytes. Thus, the potential for false positives is huge and more problematic, because the chances of the analyst looking at the logged packet understanding a binary protocol like OSCAR are substantially lower than the chances of that same analyst understanding the basics of HTTP.

Of course, the more flexible the language of a signature-driven IDS, the more likely it is able to detect malicious traffic with a high degree of precision. For example, the introduction of PCRE into early versions of Snort was a major breakthrough in signature writing, because it allowed analysts to use a more feature-rich Regular Expression (REGEX) style of signature writing. However, because of the flexibility of the Bro framework, it uses the UNIX style of FLEX REGEXs. This is because the REGEX is used by more than just the signature engine of Bro, and is, in fact, tied into the scripting language internal to Bro. The byte_test operator in Snort is of little use without the option to examine bytes represented in little-endian order, as is the case with all Microsoft file formats. Snort's relatively new shared object signatures, which are written in C (making use of an Application Programming Interface [API] that allows for the use of any standard Snort keyword within the C code), provide signature writers with essentially limitless flexibility.

Equally important in terms of a signature-based IDS' capability to do its job well is its use of high-level protocol decoding, implemented in Snort by preprocessors. By performing certain bits of inspection and/or normalization on all pieces of data within a certain known protocol family, an IDS can provide signature writers with additional tools to inspect traffic that let them do their job in a more precise, reliable, and high-performance way. The most widely used preprocessor in Snort is http_inspect, which operates on all HTTP traffic running over ports specified by the system administrator; thus, it examines the concept of protocol decoding in a signature-based IDS.

One of the biggest benefits of protocol decoding is the IDS' capability to break a protocol into its component pieces, which allows for the creation of signatures that examine only the protocol stream's relevant parts. As previously shown, http_inspect provides the uricontent Snort keyword, which limits inspection to an HTTP URI; in addition, an updated version of the preprocessor released in Snort 2.8.3 provided keywords, such as http_cookie, which restricts searches to cookie data being sent back to a remote server. By searching only within the appropriate protocol structure, a signature can work more rapidly because it has a smaller buffer to search through. An analyst can have a higher degree of confidence that she has found the condition necessary to trigger a given vulnerability.

Another important benefit of protocol decoding is normalization of different common encodings used within the protocol. The classic example is URL encoding, in which a character is represented by taking the associated hexadecimal character from the ASCII set and preceding it with a percent sign (for example, %20 for a space, or %41 for A). Originally developed to allow reserved characters to be present in a URL without causing problems, URL encoding is a dream come true for an attacker attempting to evade an IDS, because it allows for a massive number of different ways to express the same set of data in a URL. Without a way to normalize URL-encoded characters back into standard ASCII, a signature writer has no choice but to write a signature (or group of signatures) that look for every possible combination of encoded and nonencoded characters or simply have a single signature that was extremely prone to false negatives. Clearly, protocol normalization is an extremely important piece of the puzzle for an effective signature-based IDS.

The other main benefit of protocol decoding is that it enables the IDS to generate alerts whenever it detects badly formed protocol structures or finds common conditions that are technically legal per the protocol specification, but often result in the exploitation of poorly written software. For example, http_inspect can be set to alert you whether characters prohibited by the HTTP RFC are present in a URL or to alert whether an HTTP header exceeds a certain specified size. This sort of detection helps find software that might be poorly configured or otherwise cause problems on a network for detecting suspicious activity, such as an attacker probing for network vulnerabilities, and, in some cases, detecting exploits that abuse not-yet-public software vulnerabilities.

The main drawback to the protocol-decoding model in a signature-based IDS is the simple fact that additional features must be added to the IDS to do the protocol decoding, which—depending on the IDS' complexity—can be a long and complex process. Worse, a talented network security analyst might not be proficient in C or whatever programming language the IDS is written in to develop new protocol-decoding software for his IDS, or he might be completely unable to do so if he is running a closed-source system. It is even possible that newly written protocol-decoding routines might contain software vulnerabilities themselves, thus exposing the IDS to attack!

TWO SIGNATURE WRITING TECHNIQUES

Given all the capabilities of a signature-based IDS, one major question rem̲____ ̲ ̲ ̲ ̲or̲ any-one developing signatures: *How exactly do I go about picking the criteria for my signature?* Although this answer clearly differs for every signature that an analyst writes, there are two major schools of thought in developing IDS signatures. Both approaches strongly influence the way that the criteria for a given rule are chosen, sometimes to the point that the signature essentially writes itself, because there is only one real option for writing a given signature while still adhering to the principles of the school of thought to which the writer adheres.

Unique Pattern Mentality

The first of these two schools is what this book calls the Unique Pattern school. As its name implies, analysts who adhere to this school of thought are primarily concerned with finding some string or other piece of data, such as packet size, that is unique for a given exploit or other piece of malicious traffic. Signatures written in this fashion typically search for one or more strings of 10 or more bytes and do not commonly make use of advanced features, such as `byte_test` and PCRE.

This school of signature writing has a pair of important positive aspects associated with it. First and foremost, writing signatures this way makes for rapid and easy signature development. An analyst does not need to know anything about how a vulnerable piece of software actually operates—much less how a given exploit abuses that software to gain control over it—in order to create a functional signature. All that is necessary for signature development are samples of normal network traffic being sent to the vulnerable piece of software, which are then compared to samples of malicious traffic sent to the same piece of software. By examining the two side-by-side and searching for differences, an analyst can quickly narrow down the data that is available for writing a signature. With a little common sense, and hopefully at least a vague understanding of the vulnerable software, that data can be whittled down to what is present each time in an exploit, and a signature can be written that looks specifically for that data. An analyst with good command of his tool set and some practice developing signatures via this method can often create a functional signature in about 15 minutes once he has the network traffic he needs.

The other main benefit of the Unique Pattern school of signature writing is that, by sticking primarily to simple string matches and other IDS basics, signatures written in this fashion tend to be especially high performance. Some of the great minds of computer science have refined the science of string matching over the last several decades, giving the creators of IDSs several excellent string-matching engines that they can simply integrate into their products. Perhaps more importantly, it is virtually impossible to foul up the process of string matching; simply select the strings your signature will look for and put them in. By contrast, from personal experience, it is too easy to write a recursive regular expression that chews up CPU like a starving person suddenly entering an all-you-can-eat buffet.

The main negative issue associated with this school of signature writing is its relative inaccuracy. Although it is possible to create a signature that works reliably 100 percent of the time in this manner, it's not likely; the reality of the situation is that such signatures are far more likely to be prone to false positives, or worse yet, false negatives (where an exploit sneaks by the IDS undetected).

The most common cause of false negatives among strictly pattern-based signatures is the use of shellcode as part of the string chosen to create the signature. For readers unfamiliar with shellcode, it is the piece of software that bridges the gap between simply crashing a vulnerable service and taking control of the system running the vulnerable service/application. It is comprised of a sequence of processor-level instructions that cause the targeted system to spawn a shell, download and execute a particular file, or perform some other operation that an attacker chooses. Because shellcode travels across the network as byte code, it looks nothing like human-readable protocols, such as HTTP or SMTP, and it often contains sequences of bytes that are nowhere to be found (even in binary protocols). The fundamental problem with writing a signature based on shell-code, however, is that an attacker can easily alter his shellcode to evade the signature while still achieving the desired goal of taking control of the remote system.

To demonstrate just how problematic this issue is, look at some shellcode generated by the Metasploit project's Web shellcode generation interface—arguably the best shell-code-generation tool available today, and certainly one of the most widely respected—at http://www.metasploit.com/shellcode/. Going with the Windows Execute Command option, you generate some classic proof-of-concept shellcode, which causes calc.exe to run on the remote system, and then use the Structured Exception Handler (SEH) method to return control to the OS:

```
/* win32_exec - EXITFUNC=seh CMD=calc.exe Size=164
Encoder=PexFnstenvSub http://metasploit.com */
unsigned char scode[] =
"\x29\xc9\x83\xe9\xdd\xd9\xee\xd9\x74\x24\xf4\x5b\x81\x73\x13\x91"
"\xc9\x2d\x3c\x83\xeb\xfc\xe2\xf4\x6d\x21\x69\x3c\x91\xc9\xa6\x79"
"\xad\x42\x51\x39\xe9\xc8\xc2\xb7\xde\xd1\xa6\x63\xb1\xc8\xc6\x75"
"\x1a\xfd\xa6\x3d\x7f\xf8\xed\xa5\x3d\x4d\xed\x48\x96\x08\xe7\x31"
"\x90\x0b\xc6\xc8\xaa\x9d\x09\x38\xe4\x2c\xa6\x63\xb5\xc8\xc6\x5a"
"\x1a\xc5\x66\xb7\xce\xd5\x2c\xd7\x1a\xd5\xa6\x3d\x7a\x40\x71\x18"
"\x95\x0a\x1c\xfc\xf5\x42\x6d\x0c\x14\x09\x55\x30\x1a\x89\x21\xb7"
"\xe1\xd5\x80\xb7\xf9\xc1\xc6\x35\x1a\x49\x9d\x3c\x91\xc9\xa6\x54"
"\xad\x96\x1c\xca\xf1\x9f\xa4\xc4\x12\x09\x56\x6c\xf9\x39\xa7\x38"
```

```
"\xce\xa1\xb5\xc2\x1b\xc7\x7a\xc3\x76\xaa\x4c\x50\xf2\xe7\x48\x44"
"\xf4\xc9\x2d\x3c";
```

As expected, from the previous data, an analyst can choose from a wealth of unique strings from which to create a signature. Unfortunately, an intelligent attacker also has a wealth of options to choose from when he attempts to evade a signature based on the previous bit of shellcode. For example, calc.exe runs successfully regardless of what command-line arguments are passed to it, because it simply ignores options that it doesn't understand. Thus, if you return to the Metasploit shellcode-generation page and change the command you want to run from calc.exe to calc.exe -evasion, you get different shellcode, which serves the exact same purpose:

```
/* win32_exec -  EXITFUNC=seh CMD=calc.exe -evasion Size=172
Encoder=PexFnstenvSub http://metasploit.com */
unsigned char scode[] =
"\x33\xc9\x83\xe9\xdb\xd9\xee\xd9\x74\x24\xf4\x5b\x81\x73\x13\xf0"
"\xa0\xe7\x25\x83\xeb\xfc\xe2\xf4\x0c\x48\xa3\x25\xf0\xa0\x6c\x60"
"\xcc\x2b\x9b\x20\x88\xa1\x08\xae\xbf\xb8\x6c\x7a\xd0\xa1\x0c\x6c"
"\x7b\x94\x6c\x24\x1e\x91\x27\xbc\x5c\x24\x27\x51\xf7\x61\x2d\x28"
"\xf1\x62\x0c\xd1\xcb\xf4\xc3\x21\x85\x45\x6c\x7a\xd4\xa1\x0c\x43"
"\x7b\xac\xac\xae\xaf\xbc\xe6\xce\x7b\xbc\x6c\x24\x1b\x29\xbb\x01"
"\xf4\x63\xd6\xe5\x94\x2b\xa7\x15\x75\x60\x9f\x29\x7b\xe0\xeb\xae"
"\x80\xbc\x4a\xae\x98\xa8\x0c\x2c\x7b\x20\x57\x25\xf0\xa0\x6c\x4d"
"\xcc\xff\xd6\xd3\x90\xf6\x6e\xdd\x73\x60\x9c\x75\x98\x50\x6d\x21"
"\xaf\xc8\x7f\xdb\x7a\xae\xb0\xda\x17\xc3\x86\x49\x93\x8e\x82\x5d"
"\x95\x80\xca\x40\x86\xc1\x94\x4c\x9f\xce\xe7\x25";
```

Know-the-Vulnerability Mentality

Exactly this sort of problem led to the existence of the second school of thought among IDS signature writers, which this books calls the Know-the-Vulnerability school. Analysts who adhere to this school of thought begin the signature-creation process by determining the nature of the vulnerability that affects the software in question—either by reading public information, such as vendor advisories or the code of public exploits, or by performing their own original research—and from there figuring out precisely what criteria must be present for the vulnerability to be triggered. A classic example is a case where a vendor announces that its File Transfer Protocol (FTP) server is prone to a buffer overflow when processing a given command, such as PWD. An analyst of the Know-the-Vulnerability school immediately downloads and installs a vulnerable copy of the FTP server and begins sending it PWD commands with successively larger arguments until he crashed the server. Based on this work, the analyst is certain that any exploit that attempted to use this vulnerability would require that a PWD command with at least the discovered length be sent to an FTP server—no matter what sort of shellcode an attacker might use.

The positive aspect of this school of signature development is obvious: By determining the minimum criteria necessary for an exploit to occur and searching for those criteria, an analyst can create a signature that is 100 percent reliable. This assumes, of course, that the IDS has supplied a reliable picture of the application-layer data being sent across the network. Of course, not all such signatures are 100 percent reliable. If an alternate way of encoding data at the application layer is used that the analyst does not anticipate or the IDS cannot properly handle, such as a command string being sent in Unicode or a JavaScript exploit being obfuscated by concatenating multiple strings to make up the name of the vulnerable command, false negative cases still exist. More commonly, if an analyst misunderstands the nature of a vulnerability or misses one or more of the criteria for exploitation, any signature he writes is fundamentally flawed and prone to either false positives or negatives. Even so, the possibility of attaining 100 percent signature reliability—or even 80 or 90 percent reliability—is such a dramatic improvement over the Unique String school of signature writing that many professional IDS analysts choose to follow the Know-the-Vulnerability school of thought at all times.

The most frequently encountered drawback of this school of signature development is, of course, the relative complexity involved. In the previous scenario of a publicly available FTP server being prone to a buffer overflow, all but the most novice analysts can easily go through the process of determining the nature of the vulnerability. However, it is often an analyst's job to work with more complex vulnerabilities, with considerably fewer details about the way that they work. A classic example is the monthly security patches that Microsoft releases, which typically contain no details about the nature of the vulnerability and require an analyst to either reverse-engineer the patches to determine what has changed in the vulnerable software (and thus what was previously vulnerable to attack) or simply start throwing malformed data at the vulnerable application until he can reliably cause a crash. The process of determining the nature of the vulnerability can take hours, days, or even weeks in these sorts of scenarios—time that an analyst often does not have when he is tasked with defending a vulnerable network from imminent attack.

The other drawback inherent in the Know-the-Vulnerability school of signature writing is that checking for the conditions necessary to exploit the vulnerable software can often be a complex task; thus, it can require rules that do not perform particularly well on a live network. An excellent example of this problem comes from the Microsoft Security Bulletin MS05-038, which includes CVE-2005-1988, "JPEG Image Rendering Memory Corruption Vulnerability." The nature of this problem occurred if two portions of the JPEG Huffman table laid out their indexes in different sequences (for example, 1, 2, 3, and 4 in the first index and 2, 1, 3, and 4 in the second). The Snort rule written to check for this condition includes a 244-character regular expression, which is not only difficult for even PCRE masters to read, but it takes a considerable amount of resources for Snort to evaluate.

A great example of the difference between writing a signature that detects an exploit and one that detects the underlying vulnerability can be seen by comparing those written by the Sourcefire Vulnerability Research Team and the Bleeding Edge Threats project for detection of the threat identified in the Microsoft Security Bulletin MS04-011. It is more commonly recognized as the vulnerability that led to the Sasser worm, which was one of the largest and most destructive computer viruses of all time.

NOTE

The Bleeding Edge ruleset was created by Matt Jonkman and was organized to allow Snort followers to submit 'homegrown' rules. The rules are usually released quicker than Sourcefire VRT release theirs but undergo significantly less testing and evaluation. A necessary evil at times, users implement these rules at their own discretion. The Bleeding Edge Threats project drastically lost support when Matt Jonkman transferred employers. The Bleeding Edge signatures have followed Matt to his new signature project, Emerging Threats (www.emergingthreats.net). Although Bleeding Edge is dead, the methodology of signature creation remains consistent at Emerging Threats. The next section demonstrates the lack of uniformity and standard within the public ruleset and although they play a significant role in IDS signature, they are considered "cowboy-ish" by certain conservative IDS engineers.

The vulnerability underlying the Sasser worm was in Microsoft's implementation of the Distributed Computing Environment/Remote Procedure Call (DCE/RPC) system, in particular in the Local Security Authority Subsystem Service (LSASS). The nature of DCE/RPC is similar to many other RPC systems in that a client wanting to perform a RPC must specify the subsystem to which it wants to address its commands. In DCE/RPC, this is done via a process known as a bind, which occurs through a sequence of one or more request/response packets sent between the client and the server. Once bound to the subsystem or service in question, the client optionally performs authentication and then issues commands for the service in a predetermined format. Sasser exploited a buffer overflow in a particular command sent to the LSASS service.

A small collection of signatures was published by the Bleeding Edge Threats group, including SIDs 2000032, 2000033, 2000040, 2000046, 2000047, 2001056, 2001057, and 2001548 (shown in Figure 3-2). SIDs 2000033, 2000040, and 2000046 do not specifically state, in the associated message string, that they are searching for particular variants of the Sasser worm or that side effects of its behavior are all based solely on long string matches, and all look for inbound attacks to come to TCP port 445. The SID 2001056 and 2001057 signatures look for W32/Sasser.worm.a and W32/Sasser.worm.b, which also use pure string matching but fail to retain the speed benefit associated with such simple

SID 2000032	alert tcp any any -> $HOME_NET 445 (msg: "BLEEDING-EDG EXPLOIT LSA exploit"; flow: to_server,established; content:"I31313131313131313131313131313131 3131313131313131313131313131313131313 13131313131313131313131313131313131 31313131313131313131313131313131I"; offset: 78; de classtype: misc-activity; reference:url,www.eeye.com/html/research/advisories/AD 0501.html; reference:url,www.upenn.edu/computing/virus/04/w32.sas worm.html; sid: 2000032; rev:6;)
SID 2000033	alert tcp any any -> any 445 (msg: "BLEEDING-EDGE EXPLO MS04011 Lsasrv.dll RPC exploit (WinXP)"; flow: to_server,established; content:"I95 14 40 00 03 00 00 0 00 01I"; content:"I78 85 13 00 AB5B A6 E9 31 31I"; clas activity; sid: 2000033; rev:5;)
SID 2000040	alert tcp any any -> any 5554 (msg: "BLEEDING-EDGE Sass Traffic"; content: "up.exe"; flow:to_server,established; classtype: misc-activity; sid: 2000040; rev: 2;)
SID 2000046	alert tcp any any -> any 445 (msg: "BLEEDING-EDGE EXPLO MS04011 Lsasrv.dll RPC exploit (Win2k)"; flow: to_server,established; content:"I00 00 00 00 9A A8 40 0 00 00 00 00 00I"; content:"I01 0000 00 00 00 00 00 9A 00 00 00I"; classtype: misc-activity; sid: 2000046; rev:5;
SID 2000047	alert tcp any any -> any 9996 (msg: "BLEEDING-EDGE Sass Transfer up.exe"; content: "I5F75702E657865I"; depth: 2 flow:established,to_server; classtype: misc-activity; sid: 20 rev: 2;)
SID 2001056	alert tcp $EXTERNAL_NET any -> $HOME_NET any (msg:"B EDGE W32/Sasser.worm.b [NAI])"; content:"I58 BC 0C FF5 31 BD EC 34 64 6E D6 E3 8D 65 04 68 58 62 79 DF D82 BA 13 74I"; reference:url,securityresponse.symantec.com/avcenter/ve ta/w32.sasser.worm.html; classtype:misc-activity; flow:established; sid:2001056; rev:2;)
SID 2001057	alert tcp $EXTERNAL_NET any -> $HOME_NET any (msg:"B EDGE W32/Sasser.worm.a [NAI])"; content:"IBC 3B 74 0B5 E8 46 A7 3D 09 85 B8 F8 CD 76 40 DE 7C 5B 5C D7 2AA 96 25 24I"; reference:url,securityresponse.symantec.com/avcenter/ve ta/w32.sasser.worm.html;classtype:misc- activity;flow:established;sid:2001057;rev:2;)

Figure 3-2   Signatures published by the Bleeding Edge Threats group

detection by searching on all IP addresses and TCP ports (for example, using any any -> any any in the header of the signature), and only requiring that a TCP session be established, instead of checking the directionality of the data being sent. The remaining three signatures, 2000032, 2000047, and 2001548, look for FTP traffic associated with some variants of Sasser. The signatures are generic almost to the point of completely uselessness but they have a miniscule silver lining. Useless in the sense that two signatures look for up.exe in the packet payload and the other looks for packets greater than 150 bytes that begin with the string PORT, the silver lining is the fact that they require the traffic to be headed to the TCP server of an established connection on TCP ports 5554 or 9996, which are not typically associated with FTP traffic.

By contrast, 224 signatures generate an alert on the vulnerability used by Sasser, and a large number of associated signatures that set necessary flowbits, which were not designed to generate alerts, were published by the Sourcefire VRT. Flowbits are detection plug-ins that use the flow preprocessor to track rule state across transport protocol sessions. This is most useful for TCP sessions, as it allows rules to generically track the state of an application protocol. Table 3-1 shows one of the contrasting Snort Sasser signatures. The large volume of signatures was primarily due to the fact that they accounted for every possible vector by which an exploit could arrive, including TCP ports 135, 139, 445, and from 1024–65535; UDP ports 135 and 138; little-endian byte order versus big-endian; and in both ASCII and Unicode. However, the primary value of these signatures was not so much in all the vectors that they covered; it was in what precisely they looked for before an alert was generated.

Table 3-1   Sourcefire sample Sasser signature

SID	Signature
SID 9419	`alert tcp $EXTERNAL_NET any -> $HOME_NET 445 (msg:"SPECIFIC-THREATS sasser attempt"; flow:established,to_server; flowbits:isset,dce.bind.lsass; content:"¦00¦"; depth:1; content:"¦FF¦SMB%"; within:5; distance:3; byte_test:1,&,128,6,relative; pcre:"/^.{27}/sR"; content:"&¦00¦"; within:2; distance:29; byte_jump:2,-6,relative,from_beginning,little; pcre:"/^.{4}/sR"; content:"¦05¦"; within:1; byte_test:1,&,16,3,relative; content:"¦00¦"; within:1; distance:1; content:"¦09 00¦"; within:2; distance:19; byte_test:4,>,256,0,little,relative; content:"¦EC 03 00 00¦"; within:4; metadata:policy balanced-ips drop, policy connectivity-ips drop, policy security-ips drop; reference:bugtraq,10108; reference:cve,2003-0533; reference:nessus,12205; reference:url,www.microsoft.com/technet/security/bulletin/MS04-011.mspx; classtype:trojan-activity; sid:9419; rev:4;)`

Thus, the simple fact that the Sourcefire VRT rules use `flowbits` to look for a successful bind to that service before performing any further detection serves as an important first step in focusing on only potentially malicious packets. This reduced the potential for false positives and the need to waste the IDS resources on known harmless packets, such as DCE/RPC calls to other nonvulnerable services. From there, the signatures walk their way through the structure of the DCE/RPC packets, checking for things such as the version of DCE/RPC being examined, the opnum (or function ID) being called, and so on. Only after the precise type of function that was actually vulnerable had been found did the signatures look for an overflow condition. Such precise parsing of the network traffic ensures not only a low to nonexistent rate for false positives, it ensures that low rate no matter what piece of software attempted to exploit the vulnerability. Thus, it ensures that the signatures caught all variants of Sasser, with no further work required by those looking to defend their networks.

BRO: AN ANOMALY-BASED IDS

Coming at the process of intrusion detection and prevention from a completely different standpoint are anomaly-driven IDSs. This chapter uses the Bro IDS, which is a product of Lawrence Berkeley National Laboratory (LBNL) at the University of California, Berkeley (found at www.bro-ids.org), as an example of an anomaly-based IDS. Bro IDS takes a different approach to examining network traffic than a traditional IDS platform, Figure 3-3 shows.

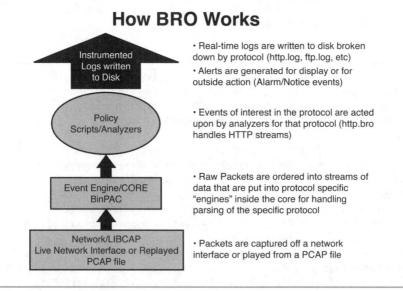

Figure 3-3   Internal workings of Bro

The Bro process captures traffic using LIBPCAP much like other network IDS platforms. Then, these packets are passed into the Bro core, which is where they are grouped by packets into streams of data for analysis. For example, all the packets related to a single HTTP client/server connection get grouped into one data stream. This stream then passes into a protocol decoder "engine" for handling HTTP traffic based on protocol verification checks and port checks, such as is the connection on 80/TCP, which is the standard for HTTP; or making sure that somewhere in the packet payload there is a string common to HTTP protocols to use for verification. After this determination is made, the data stream is passed, internal to the core, to the HTTP application decoder. Finally, the analyzers (or policy files) instrument what information is output from the core related to that specific protocol, This information can then perform actions, such as writing out the information to a log file, alerting an operator, or various other actions. For readers interested in learning more about Bro, an installation guide is included in the Appendix.

Using the policy scripts/analyzers, ASCII text logs, which relate to the applications, are generated (http.log for HTTP traffic, ftp.log for FTP traffic, and so on). These logs tell an operator that problematic events have occurred, such as potential attempts to exploit a vulnerable service, malformed but not necessarily malicious traffic, new services starting that should not be running, or users violating a corporate policy, for example, by using instant messaging (IM).

Bro has two different types of event handlers for information notification that might interest the operator/analyst. The notice function handles everything from errors to engine messages to notification of potentially bad information. By default, a notice is stored in the notice.log file and looks like the two following examples:

```
#
# This is an internal information statistic that can be filtered showing
# the number of events processed and what the packet statistics are
# passing the libpcap interface we are sniffing off of
1235768116.329282:ResourceStats:NOTICE_FILE::::::::::::mem=114MB
pkts_proc=166063 events_proc=208886 events_queued=208885 et=60.00
lag=0.001324sec util=22.3% pkts_rcv=0 pkts_drp=0 pkts_link=7991807:
#
#This is an example showing how alert information is first logged through
# the notice function
# This is showing that a "hot word" of "sex" was seen over an IRC connection
# as can be seen by the destination port of 6667/tcp.
1234554674.711527:IRC_HotWord:NOTICE_ALARM_ALWAYS::10.1.1.1:2566/tcp:19
2.168.5.5:6667/tcp:::::::IRC hot word in\: mec ch mec pour parler de
sexe::@1
```

By using some filtering options, these events can be limited or even stopped, depending on the operators' preferences. Then, using Bro's filtering options, you can choose to either just log specific notice events to the notice file or you can pass them to the second function, Alarm(). In the following example, a NOTICE event is triggered for every attempted TCP connection to a remote IP for port 6881/TCP. This is the default port for a BitTorrent Peer-to-Peer (P2P) client connection:

```
#
# This analyzer uses the IP connection (conn) information
# to determine when an IP has been attempting to connect
# to a bad port
#
# Can be invoked with a live network connection using
#  bro -I <interface> tcp <this_file_name>
#
# Cabe be invoked with a stored packet capture file
# bro -r <filename.pcap> tcp <this_file_name>

# Loading the basic Connection event handler/analyzer file
@load conn
# Loading the NOTICE event handler/analyzer
@load notice
# Loading local information such as local networks
@load site

module Addison;

# Constant values

# in this example it's the BitTorrent Default port
const BAD_PORT = 6881;
# Set the limit on the connections before doing something
const BAD_MIN_CONNECTIONS = 20;

# Add in our NOTICE event names
redef enum Notice += {
     BadPortConn,
};

# Setup our local network(s)
redef local_nets {
     192.168.1.0/24,
     192.168.2.0/24,
};

# Use a BRO stock event for attempted TCP connections
event connection_attempt(c: connection)
```

```
{
     # local variables for IP and port information
     local src_ip = c$id$orig_h;
     local src_port = get_port_number(c$id$orig_p); # converting port/protocol pair
into just port number
     local dst_ip = c$id$resp_h;
     local dst_port = get_port_number(c$id$resp_p); # converting port/protocol pair
into just port number

     # Check that the source IP is internal to your network and the destination IP is
external
     if ( (is_local_addr(src_ip) && (! is_local_addr(dst_ip) ) {
          # To reduce false positives Check that the Source port is emperical (>1024)
          # and then check for the bad port on the connection
          if ( (src_port > 1024) && (dst_port == BAD_PORT) ) {

               NOTICE([$note=BadPortConn, $conn=c,
                         $msg=fmt("Attempted BitTorrent
Connection: %s:%d %s:%d", src_ip, src_port, dst_ip, dst_port)]);
          }
     }
}
```

When run against either a live network SPAN/tap or a stored datastream file, the Bro analyzer creates an entry in the notice.log file for every attempted TCP outbound connection to destination port 6881. As Figure 3-4 shows, this process generates an excessive amount of network traffic, so one method is to filter those events before they get a chance to get written to the log file or perform some other action, such as sending them to another function.

If you tack on the following example of notice filtering to the analyzer just discussed, the entries won't log to the notice file any attempted connection from a specific IP:

```
# Use the NOTICE Filtering to ignore connection
# attempts to a specific IP on the bad port
refef notice_policy += {
     [$pred(n: notice_info) = {
          return n$note == Addison::BadPortConn && n$src == 192.168.1.5;
     },
     $result = NOTICE_IGNORE]
};
# Another example used to filter for a variable instead
# a specific IP
# add these 3 lines to analyzer to enable it to work
#
# const user_segment: set[subnet] &redef;
```

```
# redef user_segment += {
#       192.168.3.0/24,
#       192.168.2.0/24,
#       192.168.1.0/24,
# };
#
# refef notice_policy += {
#     [$pred(n: notice_info) = {
#             return n$note == Addison::BadPortConn && n$src in user_segment ;
#     },
#     $result = NOTICE_IGNORE]
#};
```

```
Host:bro_xx user$ ./src/bro -r ../trace-1.pcap policy/addison.bro | more
964954218.120391 BadPortConn Attempted BitTorrent Connection: 10.99.34.3:1777 85.75.45.2:6881
964954218.120391 BadPortConn Attempted BitTorrent Connection: 10.99.34.3:1778 85.75.45.3:6881
964954218.120391 BadPortConn Attempted BitTorrent Connection: 10.99.34.3:1779 85.75.45.4:6881
964954218.120391 BadPortConn Attempted BitTorrent Connection: 10.99.34.3:1780 85.75.45.5:6881
964954218.120391 BadPortConn Attempted BitTorrent Connection: 10.99.34.3:1781 85.75.45.6:6881
964954218.120391 BadPortConn Attempted BitTorrent Connection: 10.99.34.3:1782 85.75.45.7:6881
964954218.120391 BadPortConn Attempted BitTorrent Connection: 10.99.34.3:1783 85.75.45.8:6881
964954218.120391 BadPortConn Attempted BitTorrent Connection: 10.99.34.3:1784 85.75.45.9:6881
964954218.120391 BadPortConn Attempted BitTorrent Connection: 10.99.34.3:1785 85.75.45.10:6881
964954218.120391 BadPortConn Attempted BitTorrent Connection: 10.99.34.3:1786 85.75.45.11:6881
964954218.120391 BadPortConn Attempted BitTorrent Connection: 10.99.34.3:1787 85.75.45.12:6881
964954218.120391 BadPortConn Attempted BitTorrent Connection: 10.99.34.3:1788 85.75.45.13:6881
964954218.120391 BadPortConn Attempted BitTorrent Connection: 10.99.34.3:1789 85.75.45.14:6881
964954218.120391 BadPortConn Attempted BitTorrent Connection: 10.99.34.3:1790 85.75.45.15:6881
964954218.120391 BadPortConn Attempted BitTorrent Connection: 10.99.34.3:1791 85.75.45.16:6881
964954218.120391 BadPortConn Attempted BitTorrent Connection: 10.99.34.3:1792 85.75.45.17:6881
964954218.120391 BadPortConn Attempted BitTorrent Connection: 10.99.34.3:1793 85.75.45.18:6881
964954218.120391 BadPortConn Attempted BitTorrent Connection: 10.99.34.3:1794 85.75.45.19:6881
964954218.120391 BadPortConn Attempted BitTorrent Connection: 10.99.34.3:1795 85.75.45.20:6881
964954218.120391 BadPortConn Attempted BitTorrent Connection: 10.99.34.3:1796 85.75.45.21:6881
964954218.120391 BadPortConn Attempted BitTorrent Connection: 10.99.34.3:1797 85.75.45.22:6881
964954218.120391 BadPortConn Attempted BitTorrent Connection: 10.99.34.3:1798 85.75.45.23:6881
964954218.120391 BadPortConn Attempted BitTorrent Connection: 10.99.34.3:1799 85.75.45.24:6881
964954218.120391 BadPortConn Attempted BitTorrent Connection: 10.99.34.3:1800 85.75.45.25:6881
964954218.120391 BadPortConn Attempted BitTorrent Connection: 10.99.34.3:1802 85.75.45.2:6881
964954218.120391 BadPortConn Attempted BitTorrent Connection: 10.99.34.3:1803 85.75.45.3:6881
964954218.120391 BadPortConn Attempted BitTorrent Connection: 10.99.34.3:1804 85.75.45.4:6881
964954218.120391 BadPortConn Attempted BitTorrent Connection: 10.99.34.3:1805 85.75.45.5:6881
964954218.120391 BadPortConn Attempted BitTorrent Connection: 10.99.34.3:1806 85.75.45.6:6881
964954218.120391 BadPortConn Attempted BitTorrent Connection: 10.99.34.3:1807 85.75.45.7:6881
964954218.120391 BadPortConn Attempted BitTorrent Connection: 10.99.34.3:1808 85.75.45.8:6881
964954218.120391 BadPortConn Attempted BitTorrent Connection: 10.99.34.3:1809 85.75.45.9:6881
964954218.120391 BadPortConn Attempted BitTorrent Connection: 10.99.34.3:1810 85.75.45.10:6881
964954218.120391 BadPortConn Attempted BitTorrent Connection: 10.99.34.3:1811 85.75.45.11:6881
```

Figure 3-4   BitTorrent connections in notice.log file

This flexible filtering can enable a more granular and noiseless reporting that can be accomplished with most of today's network detection and prevention systems. Also, as this example illustrates, you can perform a series of actions for one or more of the NOTICE events within your analyzer.

If you have events that need to be bubbled up to an analyst/operator, use the `Alarm()` function to filter or report on specific criteria, such as the example hot word seen in the first example, when the string/word "sex" was seen in an Internet Relay Chat (IRC) connection. In that example, the `NOTICE` event has a filter and action set to force every instance that a hot word is used in a connection to generate an alarm for that content of data:

```
# Check for a list of Hot or bad words in the content of an IRC chat connection
If ( s == hot_words )
            NOTICE([$note=IRC_HotWord, $conn=c,
                $msg=fmt("IRC hot word in: %s", context)]);
    }
       # Then add it to the alarm list,
 refef notice_policy += {
      [$pred(n: notice_info) = {
            return n$note == IRC::IRC_HotWord;
      },
      $result = NOTICE_ALARM_ALWAYS]
};
```

This creates a formatted alarm in the alarm.log file and the notice.log file (shown in Figure 3-5). Searching the alarm file tells an analyst that an event triggered that might require his attention or can be redirected to a multitude of other devices/systems. As a side note, all alarm events are logged to the local syslog facility. This can be useful if your organization monitors or pulls all syslog logs to a central syslog-collection platform.

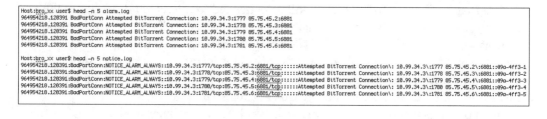

Figure 3-5   Formatted alarm included in the notice.log file

Finally, an alarm can be used in place of a `NOTICE` event if there is a trigger or indication that should always be looked at, such as a root account login observed over Telnet or an FTP file uploaded that should only be saved and passed around locally to your network. The following example is taken from the stock analyzer login.bro. If a plaintext protocol (Telnet or the UNIX R-services) allows a user to successfully authenticate without entering a password, skip NOTICE and directly report an ALARM showing the account and the connection information:

```
event login_success(c: connection, user: string, client_user: string,
                 password: string, line: string){
...... <cut for brevity>
    # else if ( password == "" )
          alarm fmt("%s %s <no password>", id_string(c$id), c$addl);
...... <cut for brevity>
```

As you can see, there is a bit of flexibility and control over how and what Bro reports to the analyst/operator. This can be taken to even more actions using some of the supported functionality of Bro and its scripting language. For example, several shipping scripts can take actions, including alerting the security analyst running Bro (NOTICE/ALARM), communicating with a router to tweak access control lists (ACLD developed internally at LBNL source code [ftp://ftp.ee.lbl.gov/acld.tar.gz]), or even directly terminating a TCP connection (using TCP RESETs to force both sides of a connection to stop communicating, which is not an inline block of the packet stream as with a commercial IPS vendor). As with most IDS platforms, Bro cannot only interpret live network data captured in real-time, it can also read back captured traffic as long as the traffic is in libpcap format. The power of searching through an entire connection at the application level opens the door for better and quicker detection of attacks, because they have moved into the application streams from the days of single packet identification of malcode.

In most organizations, one major deterrent to wider adoption of the Bro tool is the rich data that it provides and the high skill level needed to operate and configure the tool. Using a tool such as Bro means that your analyst must understand how common protocols, such as HTTP, SMTP, and DNS, work to efficiently evaluate and determine what is normal for that protocol and what is not. This is not to convey that Snort users are not highly knowledgeable but Snort is extremely supported and as such is significantly easier for security practitioners to quickly "wrap their arms around."

A main difference between an anomaly-driven IDS and a signature-based IDS is that anomaly-driven systems are not necessarily geared toward detecting known attacks; instead, they focus on finding behavior of any sort that is outside what is considered normal on a given network. For example, a sudden spike in traffic on a given host/port combination might indicate a compromised system, because why would a pair of hosts that normally do not communicate suddenly establish a large number of open connections to each other? A client system that has a large number of attempts to connect to an open port might indicate an unauthorized service being run on the machine. The possibilities for finding anomalous traffic are virtually limitless. They also can be something as nonthreatening as being able to identify hosts and software via banner information sent over the network, which violate standards or compliance. Two examples are running an older than approved version of software and using an unapproved browser.

The obvious benefit to this setup, as opposed to a signature-driven IDS, is that an anomaly-driven IDS can detect previously unknown attacks or classes of attacks, and it can see the lingering after-effects of a successful attack that it might have previously missed. Unfortunately, however, this benefit is inexorably linked with a drawback that must be managed well for the benefit to be useful. Generating alerts on all activity that appears suspicious, whether or not it is actually known to be so, can quickly overwhelm a security analyst with large amounts of irrelevant information. Although it's not unique to anomaly-driven IDSs—any analyst who has run a signature-driven IDS like Snort knows that a poorly tuned system can generate a huge volume of alerts—the problem is especially pronounced with an anomaly-driven IDS because of the number of potential situations on a network that fall outside the norm but are not actually a problem, such as new systems being connected, legitimate services being installed, and so on. However, if an analyst tunes his system in a way that it takes a large amount of anomalous activity to begin generating alerts, he might easily miss stealth attacks that generate little network traffic.

One key component of an anomaly-driven IDS is its capability to understand different network protocols. The key difference is that an IDS, like Bro, attempts to understand as much of any given protocol as possible to generate as many types of events as possible. This gives an analyst a larger number of data pieces to choose from when examining activity that occurs in the specified protocol. By contrast, many Snort preprocessors only understand small slices of the protocols they examine, and they are often geared toward presenting the analyst with a small amount of data to examine.

A side effect of understanding numerous protocols is that Bro can detect well-formed protocol activity on nonstandard ports. (For example, a Web server running on port 8000 or an SMTP server running on port 2500 and report the traffic as anomalous, depending on configuration or simply examine the data flowing on the nonstandard port as if it were completely normal traffic.) This allows Bro to detect rogue or unauthorized services running on a network by generating alerts about services running places where they should not. Additionally, it allows for the protection of legitimate assets that users might be running in nonstandard locations without the knowledge of the network security team (for example, a Web server that is running on a nonstandard port in a university environment that a signature-based IDS might miss because of its policy of only examining traffic bound for certain ports defined by the analysts running the system). The major drawback of this approach, however, is that scanning network traffic running on all ports dramatically increases the processing load on the IDS, which easily leads to an underpowered system dropping packets and missing potential attacks.

The other major difference between an anomaly-driven IDS and a signature-driven IDS is the process of installing and tuning the IDS. By definition, to determine what is anomalous on a given network, an analyst must have some concept of what constitutes normal behavior for that network. Although this can be a simple task for a small office or a home, defining "normal" becomes exponentially more difficult as network size increases. This is particularly true if the network is an open environment, such as a university campus. For a more locked-down environment, such as a major corporate network with enforceable practices and policies, it is easier to establish "normal" network behavior. In contrast, a signature-based IDS can be turned on and begin generating alerts, or it can be reconfigured to an IPS and begin blocking attacks almost immediately, even if some tuning must still be done to separate relevant alerts from irrelevant ones.

SIMILARITIES BETWEEN THE SYSTEMS

Despite the different angles that Snort and Bro take to the problem of network intrusion detection, they have numerous similarities, many of which represent the core functionality of any IDS tool. For example, as previously noted, both do some form of protocol parsing to give analysts the ability to more finely control what they want to search for when examining a given protocol.

Additionally, both systems are capable of doing each other's specialties. Bro includes a facility to perform signature-based detection and a tool called snort2bro that converts Snort signatures to Bro signatures. The snort2bro tool is part of the distribution as a legacy application, and it will likely be removed in a future release. However, the Emerging Threats community is working to keep the Bleeding Edge/Emerging Threat Snort rules converted to Bro signatures to enable the same detection signatures on a Bro platform (http://www.emergingthreats.net/index.php/component/content/article/1-latest/80-bro.html). Running the signatures requires some work because you have to load the signature engine and the specific signature set you want:

```
Prompt> bro -i <sniffing interface> -s <BRO_sig_file> <BRO analyzers to run>
Prompt>bro -i eth0 -s emerging-bro-all.sig tcp signatures alarm weird
```

This code starts Bro listening on interface eth0 (Linux interface name) with the TCP, signature, alarm, and weird analyzers loaded. Then, after the signature engine is loaded, the signatures in the file emerging-bro-all.sig are loaded into the signature engine to be used when checking packets that pass the system over TCP.

Similarly, Snort signatures can be written to search for anomalous traffic on a given network; however, this capability is limited by which "stream" based interpreter the signature system can understand when finding anomalous traffic. For example, the Snort

DNS handler only understands DNS A record requests and replies as opposed to the other DNS record types. To fill the gap, Snort leaves in terms of anomaly detection, and many of its users have turned to the commercial Real-time Network Awareness (RNA) program. RNA is a passive network-analysis tool that quietly listens to traffic on a given network, building a map of all hosts on that network along with the OSs they run, the services they make available, and so on, based on the characteristics of the traffic flowing across the network. Used in conjunction with an active vulnerability scanning tool, such as the open source solution Nessus, RNA can help network administrators determine what sorts of vulnerable software might be running on their networks, which helps them direct a patching program that ameliorates the vulnerabilities (even on its own, by building a profile of a normal network). RNA visualizes and displays events that combine attack profiles with known asset/host information. For example, if an IDS signature for MS Windows IIS Web server occurs against a known Linux Web server, the color and score of the visual event is set to a lower "threat" color than if the attack was used against an IIS server.

Both Snort and Bro also contain mechanisms to deal with multistage attacks. Snort's detection in this area is primarily stream-oriented: Through the use of its `flowbits` keyword, Snort can tag a given TCP stream or even, more recently, a UDP pseudo-stream (an active UDP conversation as having had part of the components necessary for a successful attack without actually generating an alert). In such a case, a second or third rule then becomes active on the stream in question, which generates an alert only if its criteria are found while the session is still active. This capability can also be used in reverse, telling certain rules not to scan further traffic in a session if a given piece of data has been found that prevents a particular exploit from ever being exploited. An excellent example of this capability in action comes from DCE/RPC attacks, which must first successfully bind to a service before sending a malicious payload.

Bro's signature-matching facility has functionality identical to Snort's `flowbits`, through its use of the `requires-signature` keyword, which directs a given signature not to match unless the specified other signature has matched. The following example is from the stock Bro distribution, and it uses the `requires-signature` keyword to report only vulnerable Web servers to the operator rather than all Web servers observed on the network:

```
#file ssl-worm.sig
# This signature searches for any TCP stream on port 80/tcp destined for a "local"
network range
# that has a packet content that contains the string "GET HTTP/1.1
<non_ASCII_characters>"
# for full BPF filtering options check out the tcpdump or wireshark sites
Signature sslworm-probe {
```

```
      Header ip[9:1] == 6
      Header ip[16:4] == local_nets
      Header tcp[2:2] == 80
      Payload /.*GET \/ HTTP\/1\.1\x0a\x0d\x0a/
      Event "Host may have been probed by Apache/SSL worm"
}


# this signature also uses a BRO function "sslworm_is_server_vulnerable" to check if
the web #server might be a vulnerable version using banner information observed in
network traffic
# from the server, such as "Apache/3.1 PHP/4.1"
Signature sslworm-vulnerable-probe {
      Requires-signature sslworm-probe
      Eval sslworm_is_server_vulnerable
      Event "Host may have been probed by Apache/SSL worm and is vulnerable"
}
```

Finally, both systems have mechanisms that enable them to generate active responses to an ongoing attack. Snort has several logging-related mechanisms; most notable are the `logto` keyword, which separates the packets matching a given alert into a special log file for easier monitoring by external programs; and its `tag` keyword, which logs packets for a specified interval after an alert is generated (for example, the next 60 seconds or the next 100 packets). Additionally, the `resp` keyword allows Snort to close sessions by sending TCP RST packets or ICMP unreachable messages, which causes most remote hosts to terminate the associated connection. In addition, numerous custom products, both open source and commercial, exist that watch Snort logs and perform actions based on what is seen in those logs, including e-mail or SMS notification, management of firewall rules, and so on.

Also, the Snort-inline project (http://snort-inline.sourceforge.net/) is a custom, open source project that enables Snort to examine and drop or pass traffic in real-time by placing a Snort device inline on a network. This functionality is now a compile time option for Snort, and it is documented on the snort/Sourcefire Web site. It was implemented into the Snort download version in the Snort 2.3.0 RC1.

Bro has a similar amount of flexibility in response to any given event, with the main difference being that instead of relying on third-party products that read its logs and act on what is found there, Bro has a built-in `system()` function, which allows its policy scripts to call any program on the OS running Bro, with any arguments it chooses to pass. The default Bro distribution includes some basic programs that are designed to be called by this feature, such as the `RST` program for terminating connections. As with any program where a direct call to `system()` can be made, however, users need to be cautious about how they use this feature, because improper usage might potentially result in serious problems for the system running Bro.

NOTE

A common newbie misconception is that issuing a client and server TCP RST kills the malicious connection. Actually, the TCP RST solution for an IDS/IPS vendor is basically a crap shoot, especially on large networks because it's highly unlikely that your "bullet after a bullet" actually gets to both sides of the connection to stop it. If you want to issue system commands to drop a connection, a more efficient technique is to use a timed ACL block on the routers to deny the connection for, say, 30 minutes. This defeats or slows down things like scanners or brute-force Web server/SSH/FTP server attacks.

SUMMARY

This chapter provided insight into the IDS industry by introducing fundamental concepts and progressively jumping into more complex topics, including evasion techniques, signature dissection, and a look at Snort and Bro IDSs. Most IDS books written in the past focus solely on Snort and snort.conf (Snort's open source configuration file) and even explain the signature syntax, but none of them truly clarify the distinction between writing a signature looking for an exploit versus writing a signature identifying a system's vulnerability. Finally, this chapter closed with an assessment of two open source systems: Snort and Bro. (A side-by-side comparison is slightly unjust because both systems do not use the same approach.) Snort and Bro are both extremely powerful, and the ideal deployment depends specifically on your environment and skill set. The next chapter deciphers a vulnerability's lifecycle from start to finish and shares the methodology and strategy to successfully create a solid signature.

Lifecycle of a Vulnerability

This chapter walks you through the process of providing Intrusion Detection System (IDS) coverage for a security vulnerability from start to finish, using practical examples and highlighting popular and useful open source tools. After the process is introduced, this chapter focuses on how to write Snort signatures for more complex vulnerabilities by using features such as flowbits, Perl-Compatible Regular Expressions (PCRE), and the relatively new shared object rules, which allow Snort to leverage all the power of the C programming language.

A VULNERABILITY IS BORN

The vast majority of new software vulnerabilities are announced on public forums, such as the SecurityFocus Bugtraq mailing list (www.securityfocus.com/archive/1); official government sites, such as US-CERT (www.us-cert.gov/) or NIST's CVE database (http://cve.mitre.org/); or directly on vendor Web sites or mailing lists, such as Microsoft's monthly security bulletin releases. These sites tend to cross-reference each other and typically sync vulnerability references and information within a matter of a day or two. Thus, for all but the newest vulnerability announcements, just about any major information source suffices.

In many cases, the details associated with a vulnerability release are vague; any IDS analyst who's been in the field for more than a few months is familiar with statements like, "Sending malformed packets cause the application to crash, which creates a denial of service condition." This lack of detail is usually the result of a conscious decision by the vendor to make one last stab at security through obscurity, essentially hoping that, by not releasing the exact mechanism of exploitation, it can save its users from having their software hijacked because no one takes the time to figure out how to use the newly announced security hole.

Although most users of a piece of affected software generally find this practice laudable, refusing to release technical details about a vulnerability usually only serves to annoy IDS analysts and challenge malicious adversaries. For the IDS analyst, the problem is obvious: Without details of how a successful exploit can be accomplished, it's impossible to determine what that exploit looks like coming across the network; thus, it is impossible to create an IDS signature to detect such behavior. For others, a newly announced vulnerability can be anything from a potential profit center (for example, for criminal crackers using it to further their nefarious goals) to a fascinating puzzle (see the excellent XKCD comic "Nerd Sniping" at http://xkcd.com/356/).

Given these pressures, a large number of vulnerabilities that are initially disclosed without details are soon followed by proof-of-concept code or an actual working exploit. (The difference between the two being that the latter actually injects shellcode into the vulnerable piece of software, which causes it to spawn a shell, open a TCP connection, or do something else that the cracker finds useful; the former simply crashes the application.) Generally speaking, the wider the installed base of the software, the more high-profile the vulnerability and the less complex the software, the more likely it is that a working exploit emerges soon after the initial announcement. For example, a buffer overflow in Microsoft Exchange almost certainly has a working exploit released within a day or less of the initial announcement; conversely, a format string bug in an obscure piece of proprietary software might never have one developed.

Luckily for IDS analysts, especially those without ties into the network security underground, several good publicly accessible Web sites publish working exploits, sometimes even before a vulnerability announcement is made. Sites such as Milw0rm, Packet Storm, and Metasploit serve as repositories for thousands of publicly available exploits, along with detailed information on how to break software, commonly used network security tools, and so on, all of which are extremely valuable to IDS analysts.

FLASHGET VULNERABILITY

Let's start out with a relatively simple buffer overflow exploit written in Perl, which is a language that about any Linux or BSD user has installed by default and that can be easily installed on Windows (www.milw0rm.com/exploits/6256). By selecting something that's easily readable for anyone who knows Perl and that takes no effort to get running, you can focus on the necessary tools to do the analysis and get into the details about the actual analysis later. Note that the console listings are straight copy and pastes from the machines used to actually run this exploit—you see exactly what I saw while I ran it.

The vulnerable software is FlashGet, which is a popular download manager for numerous protocols, such as HTTP, FTP, and BitTorrent. As originally disclosed on August 13, 2008, FlashGet is prone to a buffer overflow when parsing the FTP command PWD, and successful attacks can lead to remote code execution (for example, an attacker can run whatever it wants on the victim machine).

First, download the exploit to a machine that can have clients connect to it on TCP port 21, the standard FTP port, and verify that you can run it properly. (Note that if you simply use a tool like wget to fetch the file, it comes down as HTML that you need to clean up; it's simpler to copy and paste the exploit manually into a file.)

```
alex@gateway: ~$ sudo perl flashget-overflow.pl
usage: flashget-overflow.pl [1,2,3]
  1 -> Windows XP SP1
  2 -> Windows XP SP2
  3 -> Windows XP SP3
```

This result isn't too surprising. It tells you that you need to choose the operating system (OS) that you want to exploit. This often becomes a choice between different service packs of Windows XP, because each service pack includes different security mechanisms and each has important kernel functions that the shellcode uses for actually executing code in different memory locations. If you have a vulnerable copy of this software, try running the exploit first for the incorrect XP service pack and then the right one—you see that the first attack fails and the second works, popping up calc.exe on the compromised machine.

Because there isn't actually a vulnerable client on the receiving end of the exploit—as an IDS analyst, it's often more hassle than it's worth to set up the actual vulnerable software when recording an exploit—I arbitrarily choose to do SP2, because that's the most common version of XP. Running the command again with 2 as the argument, no prompt returned. The program simply sat and waited. To verify that it is actually listening properly, I used another window on the machine and ran netstat, which is a standard Linux/BSD command that displays open sockets:

```
alex@gateway: ~$ netstat -tna
Active Internet connections (including servers)
Proto Recv-Q Send-Q  Local Address     Foreign Address   (state)
tcp        0      0  *.21              *.*               LISTEN
tcp        0    320  68.55.r.s         71.163.x.y        ESTABLISHED
tcp        0      0  *.22              *.*               LISTEN
```

The first line of actual data confirms that there is something listening to port 21. Because I am not running an FTP server on this machine, it's clearly the exploit.

COLLECTING A SAMPLE PACKET CAPTURE

Now that you are ready to test the exploit, let's pause for a moment to ensure that you can actually record the traffic that it sends across the wire; after all, an exploit is useless to an IDS analyst if he can't see what it actually looks like on the network. Although some people can directly read exploit code in Perl, C, Python, or whatever other language it's written in, to determine precisely what the network traffic looks like, this is only useful for the most basic of exploits. Even a veteran IDS analyst can easily miss something if he attempts to rely solely on reading the exploit. Having an actual packet capture in hand prevents human error and helps immensely when it comes time to test the IDS' new detection capability.

Two primary options exist for capturing a copy of an exploit as it crosses the wire: tcpdump and Wireshark (which is the packet-analysis tool formerly known as Ethereal). Because Wireshark is primarily useful when you capture packets on a local system and have access to a graphical user interface [GUI]—and because it's trivial to figure out how to capture packets properly with that interface—I use tcpdump for this exploit, which is handy on any system where an IDS analyst has command-line access.

With both tools, the user capturing the packets needs to have either root access or has been granted permissions to set the interface he wants to capture on into promiscuous mode. Although this feature sounds like some kind of bad joke thought up by a lonely programmer, its name is actually reasonable when you consider what it means: Promiscuous mode sends all packets that a given interface sees up the network stack to the application listening on it, instead of only sending packets destined specifically for that interface. Although promiscuous mode is usually not particularly useful when an IDS analyst attempts to record a specific attack, it has distinct network-watching benefits in other situations and is required for packet-sniffing tools to properly function.

With that said, here's the command line I used to capture the exploit and the initial output from tcpdump letting me know that it was recording:

```
alex@home: ~/pcaps$ sudo tcpdump -n -i eth0 -s0 -w flashget.pcap host
68.55.225.129 and port 21

tcpdump: listening on eth0, link-type EN10MB (Ethernet), capture size 65535 bytes
```

Let's step through this piece by piece to ensure that you understand what you're looking at. The first option, -n, tells tcpdump not to do Domain Name System (DNS) lookups on the Internet Protocol (IP) addresses it outputs. You're free to leave this out if DNS helps you, but most of the time, an IDS analyst has no need for DNS when capturing a sample exploit. Also, any kind of issues with the DNS setup might slow tcpdump to the point that it drops packets while waiting for the DNS lookup to finish.

The second option, `-i eth0`, specifies the network interface to use for recording packets. On Linux systems, this often defaults to `eth0`, which is the standard name for the first network interface on the system. (Although on some machines, it might default to `lo0`, the loopback operator, which doesn't help when you're sending an exploit across the network.) If you've got multiple interfaces on the system, or you're running a BSD system (where network cards are named after the driver used to power them, such as `xl0` for 3Com, `nve0` for nVidia, and so on), it's worth specifying this explicitly. If nothing else, it's a habit worth getting into, in case you end up recording traffic on an unfamiliar system.

The third option, `-s0`, specifies the amount of data per packet that you want to capture, which the tcpdump manual calls the *snaplen*. A value of zero obviously doesn't mean that you want to record no data; instead, it specifies that tcpdump needs to capture the entire packet, regardless of its size. (OpenBSD users: `-s0` is invalid on that platform, so use an arbitrary large value, such as `-s2000`, to achieve the same effect.) It's particularly important to set this option, because if you don't, you end up with errors such as `[Packet size limited during capture]` in Wireshark or `IP Len field is 98 bytes bigger than captured length (ip.len: 180, cap.len: 82)` in Snort. These are signs that the data you want is simply not there.

The fourth option, `-w flashget.pcap`, is as simple as it gets: It specifies the file to which you want to write the packets, which generally has the extension .pcap (or, for people more accustomed to the old-school Windows eight/three notation, .cap). As obvious as this option might seem, it's worth highlighting because of the number of people who might simply redirect the output of tcpdump into a file, which produces an ASCII file with lines like this:

```
20:20:39.273666 IP 192.168.1.4 > 64.233.161.99: ICMP echo request, id
53591, seq 1, length 64

20:20:39.283251 IP 64.233.161.99 > 192.168.1.4: ICMP echo reply, id
53591, seq 1, length 64
```

A file like this is completely useless to a program like Wireshark or Snort, because it doesn't actually contain the packet's contents. By having tcpdump record directly to a file, however, a binary file is created with an exact copy of every single byte transmitted across the network. This enables analysis tools to dig as deeply as they need into the packet data.

The final piece in the sample command line, `host 68.55.225.129 and port 21`, isn't necessary and isn't something that's within the scope of this chapter. However, a brief example or two is illustrative. You are looking at a Berkeley Packet Filter (BPF) filter, which is a virtual interface directly into the structure of packets. BPF filters provide a straightforward syntax to specify what portion of a packet you're interested in examining and to filter packets out. Simple examples include host 192.168.1.1, port 25 or a combination of the two, such as host 10.1.1.10 and port 80. More complex options that allow for fine-grained control, such as selecting the type of Internet Control Message Protocol (ICMP) message, specific IP fragmentation flags, and so on, can be found in the tcpdump manual page.

Although an analyst can create a perfectly valid packet capture without using a BPF filter, using one makes it easier to identify the packets that actually contain an exploit or that you're interested in analyzing if capturing a sample of live traffic on an unknown entity. For example, capturing a simple visit to a site, such as www.google.com, without a BPF filter could easily collect ARP traffic, the DNS lookup for that address, and so on. If you're on a busy system that's doing a lot on the network, the capture might accidentally pick up things like a Secure Shell (SSH) session running in another window, an HTTP file transfer going on in the background, and so on. It's trivial to end up with tens to thousands of unwanted packets in your capture if you're not using a good BPF filter. This does nothing but frustrate you and any analysts with which you want to share the packet capture.

Now that that's out of the way, let's get to the interesting part: actually running the exploit. I used the simple built-in command-line FTP client on my Ubuntu Linux system to run the client side of things:

```
alex@home: ~$ ftp 68.55.225.129
Connected to 68.55.225.129.
220 Hello ;)
Name (68.55.225.129:alex):
331 pwd please
Password:
230 OK
Remote system type is CWD.
ftp> pwd
257 "AAAAAAAAAA...<lots of nonprintable characters>" is current
directory.
ftp>
```

Switching over to the window with tcpdump running, I hit Control-C to stop the capture and got the following output:

```
24 packets captured
24 packets received by filter
0 packets dropped by kernel
```

This output indicates that the capture succeeded. If, for some reason, the number of packets captured is larger than the number received by the filter, they might have been lost before they could be run through the filter and recorded, if applicable, or more importantly, if the kernel had dropped packets. This indicates that there are missing packets and the data is coming in faster than the system can process it. This means that either there's too much traffic on the wire or something else is hogging a huge amount of system resources. Dropping or missing packets occurs when the kernel-level buffer for the holding packets received by the network card (before they're processed by tcpdump or similar application) does not have the resources necessary to keep up.

Now that the exploit is recorded, it's time to open it in Wireshark. Certainly, you can use tcpdump's -r option to play it back or use Snort's equivalent option to dump the data. However, Wireshark includes several excellent analytical tools and features that make an IDS analyst's life easier, so unless there's a good reason not to do so, always use Wireshark when you examine your packet captures. Doing so on my system, Wireshark shows the results (see Figure 4-1).

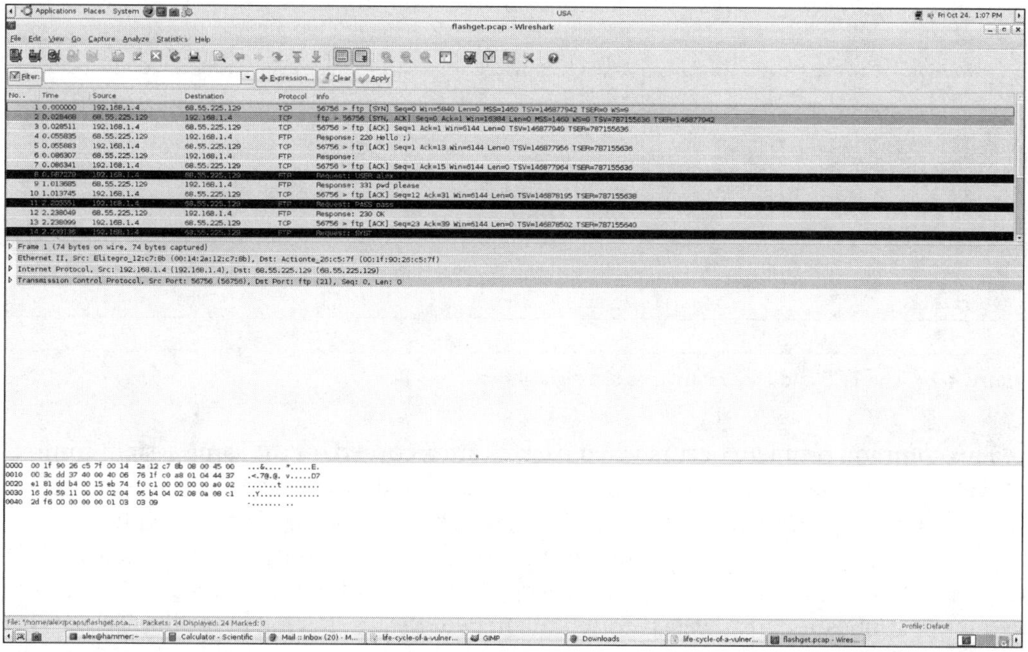

Figure 4-1   Wireshark results

One item that immediately sticks out is that several packets are highlighted in black with red letters. Looking at the first such packet more closely, you can see that Wireshark highlighted the TCP line in red. Expanding the drop-down menu reveals that the checksum line is also highlighted in red (see Figure 4-2). Reading it closely, you see the following error:

```
Checksum: 0xe796 [incorrect, should be 0x0635 (maybe caused by "TCP checksum offload"?)]
```

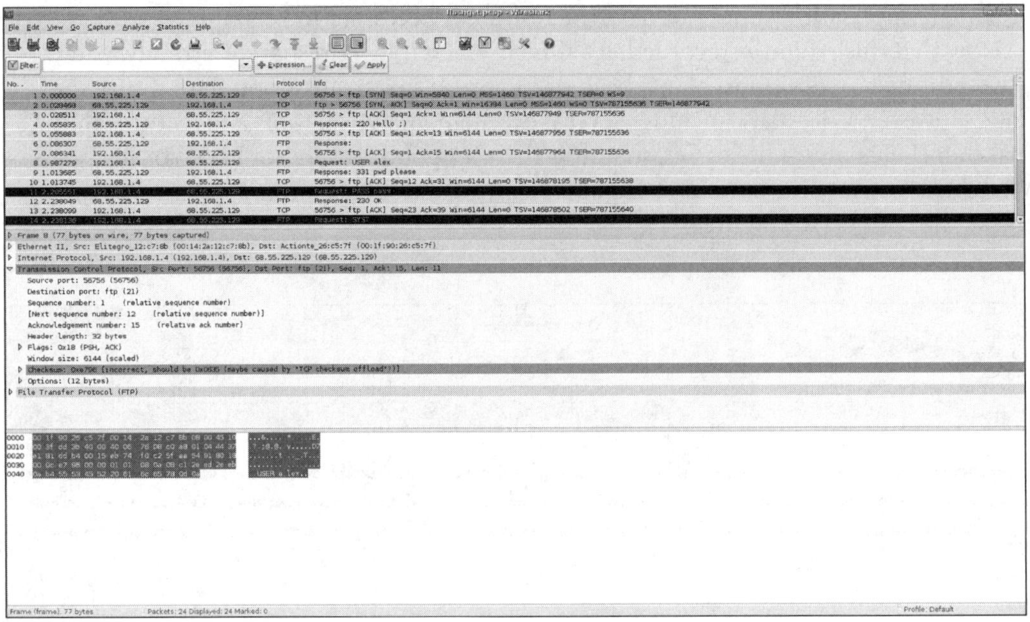

Figure 4-2   The TCP and checksum lines are highlighted.

This common problem occurs when packets are recorded on the same system from which they're being sent. Many Ethernet cards can calculate checksums for packets they're sending out directly on the card itself, which saves the CPU of the sending machine the overhead of calculating the checksum. As noted in the error message, this is known as *TCP checksum offloading*. When a packet destined for an external host is created by an application, it travels through the network stack, having items like TCP and IP headers added along the way. When TCP checksum offloading is enabled, the OS simply inserts a fake checksum into the header (whose data is essentially random for this chapter's purpose), knowing that the Ethernet card calculates the actual value and places it at the appropriate location in the packet before sending it to the network. Because the kernel-level packet buffer gets its copy of the packet before the real checksum is calculated, any capture tool reading out of this buffer gets the invalid checksums that the kernel generates.

Although this is a good system design and use of resources, it's frustrating for IDS analysts, because, by default, tools like Snort skip packets with bad checksums when they read them in. (This is logical, because a host receiving a packet with a bad checksum in the real world simply discards it.) The good news is that Brian Caswell wrote a free Perl script that fixes a packet's checksums (www.shmoo.com/~bmc/software/random/ fix-cksum.pl). (You need the free Perl modules Net::PCAP and NetPacket, which are available from CPAN, to run this tool.) Running it is as simple as

```
alex@home: ~/pcaps$ perl fix-cksum.pl flashget.pcap flashget.pcap.fixed
```

Now, the errors are gone in Wireshark, and you can get to the interesting part: actually analyzing the packets and creating a Snort rule based on the nature of the vulnerability.

PACKET ANALYSIS AND SIGNATURE-WRITING

By scrolling through the packets in flashget.pcap, it's obvious which packet contains the exploit (see Figure 4-3).

Note that Wireshark shows the command line as [truncated], which is not surprising, because it's 1332 bytes long, obviously much too long to display as a single line onscreen. Having an exploit packet generate errors in Wireshark is common, because the malicious packets are typically malformed to achieve their intended effect. In fact, Wireshark has been vulnerable over the years to numerous exploits that might be triggered by reading back a malicious packet capture. Of course, it's not worth discarding it as an analytical tool just because of these errors; it often correctly renders 99.99 percent of a packet capture. As an IDS analyst, keep in mind that an error in Wireshark doesn't mean you've done something wrong.

At this point, the question that must be answered is simple: What makes a malicious server response distinct from a legitimate one? Given that the vulnerability is a buffer overflow—in which data is copied into a fixed-size buffer in memory without ensuring that the data is actually the size of, or smaller than, the buffer—the answer is: The size of the response is going to be problematic.

This, of course, leads to a follow-up question: Just how big of a response should the Snort signature look for? The answer is deceptively simple: exactly the number of bytes necessary in order to overflow the vulnerable buffer in FlashGet. To get that number, an analyst has several options: relying on published information about the vulnerability to tell him the size of the buffer in question; directly testing the vulnerable software to determine how much data must be sent to cause a crash; and using a binary analysis

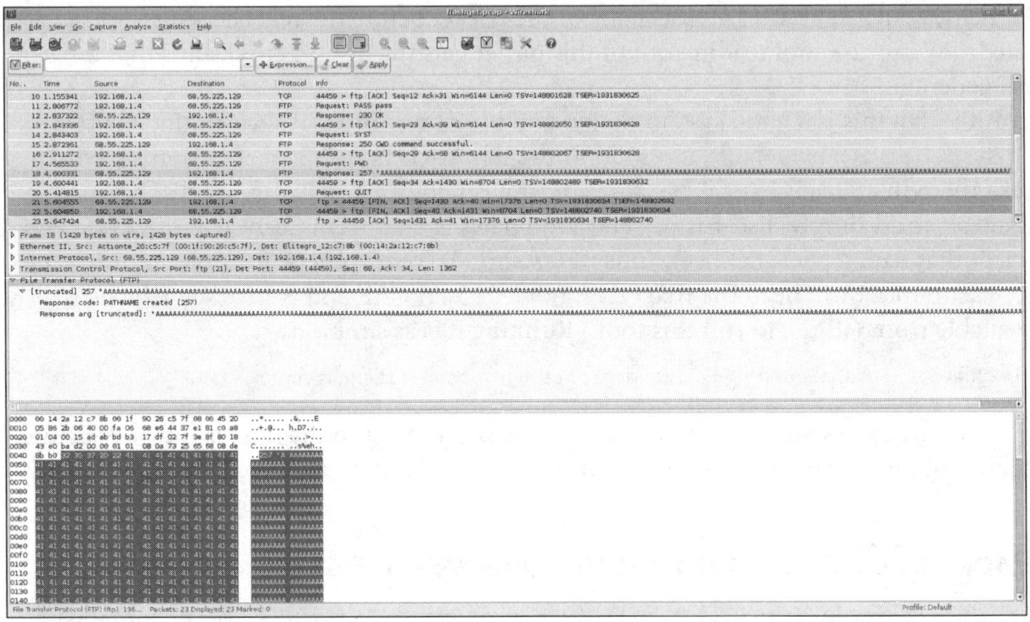

Figure 4-3   The packet containing the exploit

tool, like WinDBG or IDA Pro, to locate the vulnerable buffer in the program and determine its size by examining a disassembly of the program.

As an IDS analyst, chances are good that you're often going to be short on time, either
because you've got a ton of analysis to do or because you're dealing with a newly released
vulnerability that you must immediately create detection for. Given these constraints,
when writing a Snort signature, an intelligent strategy is to start with the easiest possible
methods and move on to more complex analysis later, if necessary. In this case, because a
public exploit exists, the first thing to do is to check for publicly available information
about the nature of the vulnerability. Because the Common Vulnerabilities and
Exposures (CVE) database usually has the most comprehensive list of links to known
information about any given vulnerability, it is a good place to start.

For this vulnerability, the URL to the appropriate CVE page is http://cve.mitre.org/
cgi-bin/cvename.cgi?name=CVE-2008-4321. Digging through the available links, you
quickly note that www.securityfocus.com/bid/30685/exploit has three distinct exploits
available for this vulnerability: two in Perl and one in Python. Because you want to
ensure that your signature detects all available exploits, go ahead and examine all three.

As it turns out, the last exploit available is a copy of the Milw0rm exploit. This makes things easier, because now there are only two more exploits to capture samples of in action.

After you run through the previous exercise to get samples of these exploits, it becomes immediately obvious that far fewer than the 1332 bytes worth of payload in the first exploit are actually necessary. In fact, the Python version of the exploit has only 356 bytes worth of payload. With no other information available in any of the public advisories regarding the size of the buffer required to perform the exploit, 356 is a reasonable size value to check for in the signature; it is a value that has been arrived at with a minimal amount of time spent examining the vulnerability.

Based on what the previous chapter covered (or your previous knowledge of Snort, of course) and what is known of the vulnerability and FTP, the basics of a signature should be fairly obvious. Malicious packets must be directed at TCP port 21 (used for FTP commands) and must come from a TCP server. All malicious packets contain the string 257, which is the response code sent along with a reply to a request for PWD, followed by at least 356 bytes that are not a newline (as a newline character terminates an FTP command). This makes for the following Snort signature:

```
alert tcp $EXTERNAL_NET 21 -> $HOME_NET any (msg:"FTP Flashget PWD response
buffer overflow attempt"; flow:established,to_client; content:"257"; nocase;
pcre:"/^257[^\n]{356,}/smi"; classtype:attempted-admin; reference:bugtraq,30685;
reference:cve,2008-4321;)
```

Before moving this signature to any sort of production system, however, you must first test it. The simplest way to do this is to put it into the local.rules file on a system where you've unpacked and compiled a current version of Snort. (Note that you don't need to have installed Snort anywhere; so long as all the paths in the snort.conf file are set appropriately, you can run any version of Snort out of any directory on a system, which is handy if you don't have administrative access on the machine on which you want to do the testing.) From there, manually call Snort with a command line similar to this:

```
alex@home: ~/downloads/snort-2.8.3$ src/snort -c etc/snort.conf -q -A
cmg -r ~/pcaps/flashget-python.pcap
```

Let's step through the arguments to ensure that you know exactly what's happening. First, note that the command is actually src/snort, and not just snort. This is because it's being executed out of the directory it was unpacked into, and you are specifying the direct path to the Snort binary compiled in there instead of letting the system search through its path to find a binary matching the name "snort." This enables multiple versions of Snort to be running on the same system, because you simply specify which Snort you want to run each time you call it. The next option, `-c etc/snort.conf`, specifies the configuration file that Snort should use. Again, it's key that this is manually specified, not just so you know exactly what file it's using, but because directly specifying it like this allows for different versions of Snort to nicely coexist.

The second and third options, `-q` and `-A cmg`, aren't strictly necessary for analysis, but they make dealing with Snort's output much easier. The `-q` flag tells Snort to be quiet (for example, to not bother outputting its initiation messages, protocol statistics, and so on), which is usually just unnecessary crud on your screen when your goal is verifying a signature. The `-A cmg` option tells Snort to output all alerts to standard output (such as your screen) so that you don't have to dig through an alert file to see if the signature you're testing just fired. Finally, the `-r` flag tells Snort that it should read an existing packet capture instead of pulling packets from the network.

With that done, the output from an initial run of Snort with the previous rule pasted in is as follows:

```
ERROR: etc/../rules/local.rules(1) => Each rule must contain a Rule-sid
Fatal Error, Quitting..
```

Although this might seem like a simple error to fix—adding `sid:99999;` to the end of the signature does the trick—it's worth pointing out, because it gives us a chance to briefly discuss Snort IDs (SIDs). Snort uses SIDs to keep track of rules, and they are included in Snort's output so users can tell what signature generated a given alert (and thus how legitimate it is and what service might have been exploited). What is less obvious is the debugging nightmare that can arise if you accidentally use an identical SID for two different rules. This is a mistake that most longtime IDS analysts who regularly use Snort have made. Because Snort silently overwrites the first rule with the second when it encounters an identical SID, it's possible to spend hours trying to figure out why a perfectly good signature isn't firing if you've made this mistake. Because no major public signature sets currently use the SID space between 10000 and 99999, SIDs in that range are easy to use for testing purposes.

After modifying the rule to include a SID, Snort's output is much happier:

```
10/24-14:23:26.067596  [**] [1:99999:0] FTP Flashget PWD response
buffer overflow attempt [**] [Classification: Attempted Administrator
Privilege Gain] [Priority: 1] {TCP} 68.55.225.129:21 ->
192.168.1.4:57564
```

```
10/24-14:23:26.067596 0:1F:90:26:C5:7F -> 0:14:2A:12:C7:8B type:0x800
len:0x1AD

68.55.225.129:21 -> 192.168.1.4:57564 TCP TTL:250 TOS:0x20 ID:47844
IpLen:20 DgmLen:415 DF

***AP*** Seq: 0xA9E10DAB  Ack: 0x553E2909  Win: 0x43E0  TcpLen: 32

TCP Options (3) => NOP NOP TS: 104617918 149029958

32 35 37 20 22 41 41 41 41 41 41 41 41 41 41 41   257 "AAAAAAAAAAA
41 41 41 41 41 41 41 41 41 41 41 41 41 41 41 41   AAAAAAAAAAAAAAAA
41 41 41 41 41 41 41 41 41 41 41 41 41 41 41 41   AAAAAAAAAAAAAAAA
41 41 41 41 41 41 41 41 41 41 41 41 41 41 41 41   AAAAAAAAAAAAAAAA
41 41 41 41 41 41 41 41 41 41 41 41 41 41 41 41   AAAAAAAAAAAAAAAA
41 41 41 41 41 41 41 41 41 41 41 41 41 41 41 41   AAAAAAAAAAAAAAAA
41 41 41 41 41 41 41 41 41 41 41 41 41 41 41 41   AAAAAAAAAAAAAAAA
41 41 41 41 41 41 41 41 41 41 41 41 41 41 41 41   AAAAAAAAAAAAAAAA
41 41 41 41 41 41 41 41 41 41 41 41 41 41 41 41   AAAAAAAAAAAAAAAA
41 41 41 41 41 41 41 41 41 41 41 41 41 41 41 41   AAAAAAAAAAAAAAAA
41 41 41 41 41 41 41 41 41 41 41 41 41 41 41 41   AAAAAAAAAAAAAAAA
41 41 41 41 41 41 41 41 41 41 41 41 41 41 41 41   AAAAAAAAAAAAAAAA
41 41 41 41 41 41 41 41 41 41 41 41 41 41 41 41   AAAAAAAAAAAAAAAA
41 41 41 41 41 41 41 41 41 41 41 41 41 41 41 41   AAAAAAAAAAAAAAAA
41 41 41 41 41 41 41 41 41 41 41 41 41 41 41 41   AAAAAAAAAAAAAAAA
41 41 41 41 41 41 41 41 41 41 41 41 41 41 41 41   AAAAAAAAAAAAAAAA
41 41 41 41 41 41 41 41 41 41 41 41 41 41 41 41   AAAAAAAAAAAAAAAA
41 41 41 41 41 41 41 41 41 41 41 41 41 41 41 41   AAAAAAAAAAAAAAAA
41 41 41 41 41 41 41 41 41 41 41 41 41 41 41 41   AAAAAAAAAAAAAAAA
41 2F 22 20 69 73 20 63 75 72 72 65 6E 74 20 64   A/" is current d
69 72 65 63 74 6F 72 79 2E 0D 0A                  irectory...
```

=+=

This alert contains a wealth of information, most of which can be safely ignored during the regular course of packet analysis. The most important piece is in the first line: [1:99999:0] tells you that SID 99999 generated the alert, meaning that Snort behaved as expected; the leading 1 specifies that the alert came from generator ID 1 (reserved for plain Snort rules, as opposed to 3 for shared object rules); and the trailing 0 tells you that the SID had no associated revision number. The other relevant piece is the payload, which is represented as hexadecimal digits on the left and ASCII characters on the right. It tells you that the alert was generated on the appropriate packet.

At this point, you have successfully written a Snort signature to detect this vulnerability. That said, the analysis process is only partially complete; there's still signature tuning to do, either immediately or in the future after the rule is deployed on a production system.

SIGNATURE TUNING

Signature tuning generally falls into two categories: detection tuning and performance tuning. Although the two categories are heavily intertwined—doing proper detection for some vulnerabilities can be highly performance-intensive and require IDS analysts to make best-guess tradeoffs between more accurate detection and better performance—it's worth discussing them separately so that the steps involved in each are fully outlined.

DETECTION TUNING

The process of detection tuning is better defined and more straightforward than performance tuning. Only two real pieces are involved in detection tuning: false negatives (when a signature fails to alert on a valid exploit) and false positives (when a signature alerts on valid and/or unrelated traffic).

Continuing with the example of FlashGet, assume that another exploit is released that has a payload of only 300 bytes long. Clearly, the previously signature written would have a false negative, because this new 300-byte exploit does not meet the minimum requirement of 356 bytes necessary to trigger an alert. A simple fix is to alter the rule to look for 300 or more bytes:

```
alert tcp $EXTERNAL_NET 21 -> $HOME_NET any (msg:"FTP Flashget PWD response
buffer overflow attempt"; flow:established,to_client; content:"257"; nocase;
pcre:"/^257[^\n]{300,}/smi"; classtype:attempted-admin; reference:bugtraq,30685;
reference:cve,2008-4321; sid:99999; rev:2;)
```

Faced with this new piece of information, many analysts might decide to drop the minimum size requirement even further—say, to 200 bytes—just to ensure that their systems were covered in case a newer, smaller exploit was released later. Unfortunately, this might lead to false positives when working on systems with multiple layers of nested directories, because a legitimate long path name might trigger an alert. If these types of false positives were rare—no more than one or two a day—were coming in IDS mode, and not fouling up the network in IPS mode, it is advisable to simply ignore them as they come in, because it's better to be safe than sorry. If they became common, however, it is worth revisiting the signature and at least applying some programming common sense to the number chosen for the overflow size: 256 is often a reasonable number, because it's a common buffer size that C programmers use and a size associated with a large number of buffer overflows.

PERFORMANCE TUNING

Performance tuning is a considerably less intuitive business. First of all, few people are familiar enough with the internals of Snort or any other IDS to know what tweaks impact performance. A more important consideration, however, is the fact that there is no hard-and-fast set of rules that can be applied to signature writing to speed performance across all environments. Although some things can be done that always improve performance, the nature of the network traffic that an IDS examines so heavily influences its performance that it's impossible to predict performance without detailed knowledge of the traffic. Thus, as you attempt to tune an IDS signature for performance reasons, keep in mind that testing it with someone else's network traffic has limited value, if there is any at all.

In the signature discussed so far, I have intentionally left room for performance so that I can introduce some of the most common performance optimizations with it. As discussed in the previous chapter, the signature already has numerous optimizations in it, simply by virtue of the fact that it's looking only for packets coming from TCP port 21 outside your network to some location inside your network and that it's constrained to established TCP sessions, and from there, only to packets being sent to the TCP client. Again, although these might seem like trivial optimizations, being specific about the nature of the involved TCP flow is one of the most important things you can do to improve a signature's performance.

In terms of the actual content of the packet(s) in question, one of the first things that you need to look for when attempting to speed up a rule is whether you can restrict the amount of data that the signature wades through to find what it's looking for. This is particularly true if the IDS searches for any fixed strings that are small, because, in essence, the smaller the fixed string, the more iterations the IDS must make through the packet to attempt to match the string. Because the signature you are looking to speed up has only one string that it must match in the packet, specified by content:"257"; nocase;, it is particularly slow. However, you know that, as an FTP response code, "257" must come at the beginning of the packet. By adding the option depth:3; after the nocase; option, you tell Snort to only search through the first three bytes of the packet for the string in question. This suddenly reduces the number of necessary string match operations from hundreds (or possibly even thousands) to one.

To illustrate this point, take a brief detour into a discussion of one of Snort's lesser known features: rule profiling (available as a configuration option and fully documented in the README.PerfProfiling file within the doc/ directory of Snort). By simply adding config profile_rules to your snort.conf, you get basic rule-performance data to print at the end of each run to Snort. For example, here is the output from running the original signature without the `depth` clause against the Milw0rm exploit for FlashGet:

```
Rule Profile Statistics (all rules)
===========================================================
SID   Chcks Matches Alerts Microsecs  Avg/Check  Avg/Match Avg/Nonmatch
===   ==== ======= ====== =====       =========  ========= ============
99999   2     2      1     563         281.8       0.5         0.0
```

The first and third columns (Num and GID, respectively) have been redacted to ease reading and properly display the the columns in print. They are just information on which signature the statistics are being reported. The second column in our print version, Checks, provides information about the number of signature-matching operations performed on the payload in question; each item, such as content and pcre, constitute a distinct check. (Often, the number of checks won't line up exactly to the number of rule operations and potentially matching packets, because Snort sometimes performs a given check more than once on a single packet. Also, issues such as reassembled packets out of a TCP stream often come into play.) The third column, Matches, is closely correlated: For each performed check, the operation can result in either a match (meaning that the check succeeded because the data being sought by the rule is present) or a nonmatch (failure). These two columns, in combination, provide a useful piece of information about a given signature. If the number of checks is considerably higher than the number of matches, some portion of the signature is being found in a large number of packets that are eventually determined to be uninteresting (because they don't contain all the criteria necessary for an exploit). Because this scenario causes Snort to do much unnecessary work, if at all possible, make the option that is matching frequently have more specific results in a faster signature; this cuts the number of packets that Snort evaluates as it looks for an exploit.

The four options grouped together (Microsecs, Avg/Check, Avg/Match, and Avg/Nonmatch) provide information about the amount of CPU time used while a given signature is processed, sliced into several different measures. (Note that CPU time can differ from wall-clock time if the system you're running the tests on is under heavy load and has many other processes competing for CPU time.) Although these options might seem like the most useful pieces of available information, a large number of factors limit their usefulness unless examined properly. For example, the number of microseconds spent evaluating a signature varies wildly between machines, because different CPU speeds result in considerably faster or slower signature processing. Additionally, other uncontrollable factors, such as hard drive caching of a packet capture, the load placed on the system by other processes, potential memory swapping, and so on, can equally dramatically impact the speed of signature evaluation, even on a single system.

Given this potential for unreliable output, an IDS analyst can do two things to pull useful information out of Snort's signature-profiling feature. First, running the same test a large number of times (preferably 10 or more) and pulling median values from that data set help eliminate some of the noise inherent in the generated statistics. The second is to look at a group of signatures all running simultaneously and look for those that require the longest amount of time to evaluate. Because a given group of signatures is being run simultaneously, their performance relative to each other—particularly if it holds true over repeated tests—is a reasonably valid measure of which signatures might need performance improvements.

With this in mind, the fact that the signature profiling output from ten runs each of the original rule and the updated rule (with the depth clause included) against the sample packet capture yielded a median value of 598 microseconds in the first case and 300 microseconds in the second case validates the fact that constraining the amount of packet data to search through sped up the signature. Although that conclusion should have been obvious, confirming it with Snort's signature-profiling feature highlights that feature in an easy-to-deal-with way. This is helpful if you ever choose to use it to debug more complex signature-performance issues.

Another optimization that can be added to the signature is an isdataat clause, which is integrated into the signature as follows:

```
alert tcp $EXTERNAL_NET 21 -> $HOME_NET any (msg:"FTP Flashget PWD response
buffer overflow attempt"; flow:established,to_client; content:"257"; nocase; depth:3;
isdataat:300,relative; pcre:"/^257[^\n]{300,}/smi"; classtype:attempted-admin;
reference:bugtraq,30685; reference:cve,2008-4321; sid:99999; rev:2;)
```

The concept behind the isdataat keyword is simple: It checks to ensure that the number of bytes specified is actually present in a given packet. By specifying the relative modifier, isdataat checks for the required number of bytes following the current location in the packet (for example, after all previous content operations are performed), instead of simply checking for packets of at least the required size. As it applies to the FlashGet vulnerability, the value of isdataat is obvious: If 300 bytes are required for a buffer overflow to occur, ensuring that there are at least that many bytes remaining in the packet after the string "257" enables Snort to rapidly skip packets that cannot possibly contain an exploit. The advantage of using isdataat becomes more obvious when you consider that it boils down to a simple piece of math on an existing packet structure, instead of the CPU-intensive process of calling into the PCRE library and performing a search that has to check each character as it moves along.

The final optimization that can be done on this signature is the most subtle. It is actually a feature of PCRE itself and not Snort specifically. By changing the expression from

```
/^257[^\n]{300,}/smi
```

to

```
/^257[^\n]{300}/smi
```

You can eliminate unnecessary work by the PCRE library on packets that contain more than 300 bytes of non-newline data following the string 257. By removing the comma from the repetition quantifier, you allow PCRE to end the process of matching as soon as it finds the 300 bytes necessary for an exploit to occur, instead of letting it continue to match until it runs out of data at the end of the packet, wasting CPU cycles as it goes.

ADVANCED EXAMPLES

Thus far, this chapter highlighted a simple vulnerability to keep the focus on the process of taking a known vulnerability and bringing it through the process of IDS analysis to create a Snort signature. Now that you understand at least the fundamentals of this process, let's get into some more advanced examples, highlighting additional useful tools and more advanced features of the Snort signature language. For ease of reading, this section focuses on a single vulnerability at a time and provides a brief header at the start of each analysis.

CitectSCADA ODBC Server Buffer Overflow: Metasploit

Given the increase in concern about the security of Supervisory Data Acquisition and Control (SCADA) systems, which monitor critical infrastructure, such as power grids or water distribution networks, this vulnerability is a natural choice, both for attackers interested in testing those systems and IDS analysts concerned with protecting them. The fact that the exploit comes in a handy Metasploit module provides us with a chance to go over that framework.

The initial disclosure of this vulnerability came via a Core Security Technologies advisory on June 11, 2008 (www.coresecurity.com/content/citect-scada-odbc-service-vulnerability). By reading the technical details of the advisory, it's immediately noted that the signature is listening on TCP port 20222 and that there is a 5-byte content match at the start of the packet. It's also clear that some sort of size check is happening. However, the initial advisory lacks critical details; without knowing the nature of the fixed 5-byte header, for example, you can't search for it. Without sample packet captures for this application, or the time and desire to reverse-engineer a vulnerable copy of the application, no signature could be created.

All that changed when the Metasploit module was released for this vulnerability on September 5, 2008. With a functioning exploit in hand, an IDS analyst looking to create a signature for this could suddenly determine what the fixed header string is, get an idea of how large the buffer must be for the overflow, and test detection against a packet capture of a valid attack.

After downloading the latest version of the Metasploit framework and extracting it to a handy directory, you can run any of its included exploits with ease (assuming that you already have a copy of the Ruby programming language installed on your system, because the current version of Metasploit is written in Ruby). The process of running this exploit is walked through here for readers unfamiliar with operating Metasploit by using the msfconsole version of the system (which is by far the simplest way to run Metasploit if you're just starting out or are unfamiliar with a given exploit). On load, you're greeted with a friendly piece of ASCII art, some summary information, and a UNIX-style prompt:

```
alex@home: ~/packages/framework-3.1$ ./msfconsole


      _____
     < metasploit >
      -----------
            \    ,__,
             \   (oo)____
                 (__)    )\
                    ||--|| *



            =[ msf v3.1-release
  + -- -- =[ 262 exploits - 117 payloads
  + -- -- =[ 17 encoders - 6 nops
            =[ 46 aux

msf >
```

Use the show exploits command to look for the name of the exploit you want to run. If the exploit you're looking to run is not included—which is often the case, particularly with a fresh exploit—it's trivial enough to add it to the system. For example, by October 31, 2008, the CitectSCADA module was still not included in the base distribution available on the web. All Metasploit modules include a comment near the top of the file that gives the path and name of the module file. This exploit was published to Milw0rm (www.milw0rm.com/exploits/6387), and the path is exploit/windows/misc/citect_scada_odbc. By creating the file modules/exploits/windows/misc/citect_scada_odbc.rb with the contents of what's on Milw0rm and reloading Metasploit, the module is loaded into the system. With the string windows/misc/citect_scada_odbc appearing as the name of the module, you can easily select it for execution:

```
msf > use windows/misc/citect_scada_odbc
msf exploit(citect_scada_odbc) >
```

The first time you run a Metasploit module, the first thing you'll want to do after selecting it is see what options you need to specify to run it:

```
msf exploit(citect_scada_odbc) > show options
```

```
Module options:
   Name    Current Setting   Required   Description
   --      --------------.   ----       -----.

   RHOST                     yes        The target address
   RPORT   20222             yes        The target port
```

Each option can be set by a simple statement, such as set RHOST 68.55.225.129 (for readers not familiar with Metasploit RHOST means remote host, whereas, LHOST means local host – RPORT and LPORT follow suit. Finally, before sending your exploit, you need to select a payload, which controls what the remote system does on a successful exploit. (In some cases, you also need to specify a target, which specifies the OS on which the vulnerable software is running.) Available options can be shown with show payloads (and show targets, if necessary) and is set with the same method as any of the other configuration options. From there, after you set up the remote system to listen properly and get a packet capture started with tcpdump, you simply type exploit and let Metasploit do its magic:

```
msf exploit(citect_scada_odbc) > exploit
[*] Started bind handler
[*] Trying target CiExceptionMailer.dll on XP Sp2 or SP3 5.42...
[*] Space: 329
[*] Using Windows XP Target
```

```
[*] Sent malicious ODBC packet..
```

With that done, pull up the packet capture and look at the payload. As expected, after reading the Core advisory, there are two packets with data from the client: one with 4 bytes, which you know to be the length of the following packet, and another with the actual exploit in it (see Figure 4-4). The aforementioned attack packet with the 4 bytes of data is the fourth packet in the packet capture.

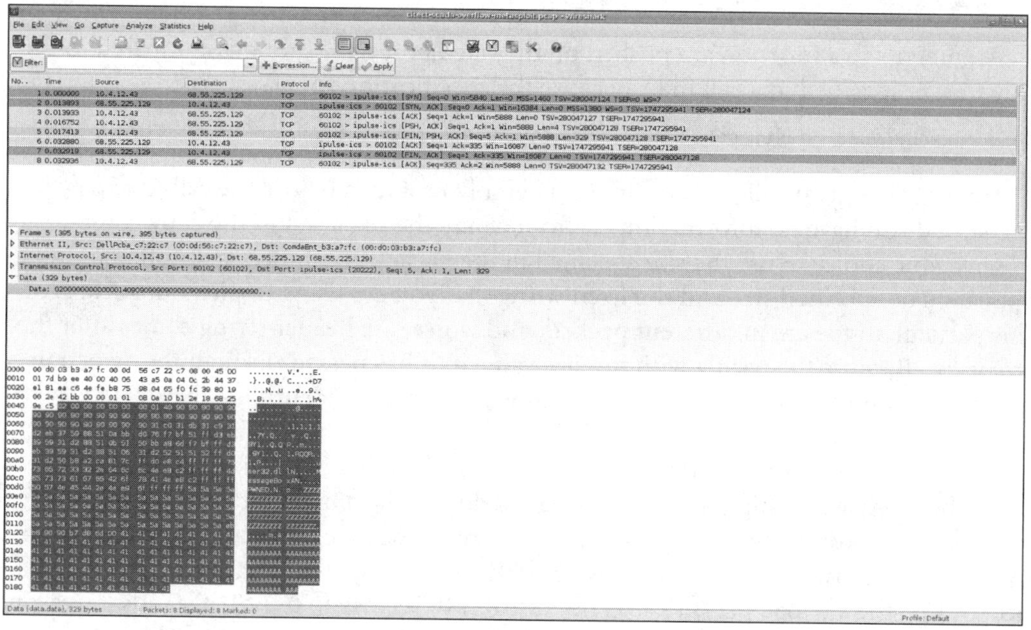

Figure 4-4 The CitectSCADA packet capture

The first question necessary to write a signature is easily answered: The fixed header is the sequence of hexadecimal bytes 02 00 00 00 00. You also have a decent idea of the sort of size you're looking for to cause an overflow; with 329 bytes of payload data, a reasonable default is probably 256 bytes or more. Because the size is declared in the data stream sent to the vulnerable system, check that size instead of relying on the size of the payload seen by Snort, because most software simply discards data that goes beyond the declared size and because, in some cases, software copies the amount of data specified in the packet even if it's not present on the wire, reading random bytes out of memory, and so on.

Had Core's advisory told you from where the size for the call to memcpy was coming, you might refine the signature to check for the appropriate behavior; unfortunately, the disassembly left out that argument:

```
.text:0051BC33 loc_51BC33:
.text:0051BC33 lea      ecx, [ebp+pDestBuffer]
.text:0051BC39 push     ecx      ; stack based buffer
.text:0051BC3A mov      edx, [ebp+arg_0]
.text:0051BC3D push     edx      ; class that contains packet
.text:0051BC3E call     sub_52125A ; memcpy
```

Arguments to a function are pushed on the stack in reverse order as compared to the way they're specified in a call in C. Because the specification for memcpy is

```
void *memcpy(void *dest, const void *src, size_t n);
```

You only have two calls to push in the assembly provided before the call to memcpy is made, and you have no information on from where the size used in the copy comes.

Given the choice to use the size specified in the packet, an immediate problem appears: The specified size and the fixed string that you are using to pick out packets of this particular type are in different packets, and worse, the header string comes after the size value. Because the packet with the size value in it has passed through the detection engine and out of Snort's memory by the time the header is identified, there's no way to check that value.

As it turns out, this roadblock is not permanent. Looking at the payload packet for clues about what else might be a triggering condition, the 4 bytes after the header string jump out as a possibility: 00 00 01 40. What makes these bytes special? Looking at the 4-byte size packet, the value contained is 00 00 01 49, which is the hexadecimal representation of 329, the payload packet's size. Because 0x140 is close to 0x149, it stands to reason that it might be another length value; subtracting the 5 bytes worth of fixed header, and the 4 bytes of potential size, you're left with 0x140 bytes of remaining payload. This information is confirmed by line 157 of the exploit:

```
wakeup = [0x0000000002].pack('Q')[0..4] + [mal.length].pack("N") + mal
```

With this new information in hand, writing a rule becomes trivial: Check for the header at the start of the packet and then check the size value contained in the next four packets for values above 256 bytes:

```
alert tcp $EXTERNAL_NET ANY -> $HOME_NET 20222 (msg:"MISC CitectSCADA buffer
overflow attempt"; flow:established,to_server; content:"¦02 00 00 00 00¦";
depth:5; byte_test:4,>,256,0,relative; reference:bugtraq,29634;
reference:cve,2008-2639; classtype:attempted-admin; sid:99999;)
```

After confirming that this generates an alert when run against the Metasploit packet capture, the signature is ready for production. There's no further specificity that can be added to it, there are no known false negatives or false positives, and no performance tricks can be employed to increase its speed.

FASTSTONE IMAGE VIEWER BITMAP PARSING

Along with several other popular Windows image viewers, the FastStone Image Viewer system was discovered to be vulnerable to integer overflow bugs when processing bitmap image headers in April 2007 (documented as Security Focus Bugtraq ID 23312). Although this might seem like an older vulnerability, a new script was released to exploit this problem on Milw0rm on October 5, 2008. Because this vulnerability exists in a client-side piece of software, and because many home users (or corporate desktop users) do not regularly update their software, it makes sense that it is still being exploited in the wild.

The Milw0rm script actually produces a malicious bitmap file. Because hosting a malicious image on a Web site is one of the simplest ways to exploit vulnerable users—there are a myriad of tricks for getting people to visit Web sites that an attacker con-trols—detecting a malicious file transfer over HTTP is likely to be one of the most effective means of mitigation an IDS can provide for a vulnerability like this. Thus, after generating the file based on the Milw0rm code, the first step in your research is to host the file on a Web server that you control and then download it, grabbing a packet cap-ture as you go. (Of course, remove the image after you have the packet capture.) Figure 4-5 shows the packet capture.

Looking at the actual bitmap data, it's not immediately obvious where the problem is. So, more research is necessary into the nature of the vulnerability. In the References tab of the Security Focus writeup, a link exists to a blog entry written by Ivan Fratric (http:// ifsec.blogspot.com/2007/04/several-windows-image-viewers.html), who discovered the vulnerability. In his section, "Experimental Results," you see that the files listed as wh3intof.bmp and wh4intof.bmp in his writeup caused FastStone Image Viewer to crash. Reading the descriptions of those files, the nature of the vulnerability becomes clear: If image width * image height * 3 is greater than the maximum size of a 32-bit integer (0xFFFFFFFF, or 4,294,967,295), an integer overflow occurs. More specifically, if a total value of, say, 0x100000001 (4,294,967,295) were arrived at by this calculation, a 32-bit system would actually store the result as 2, or the actual size minus the maximum size of an integer on that platform. Because memory is allocated to store the actual bitmap data based on that size calculation, causing this sort of an overflow might lead to the dynamically allocated memory buffer being overflowed, and thus causing a potential remote code execution.

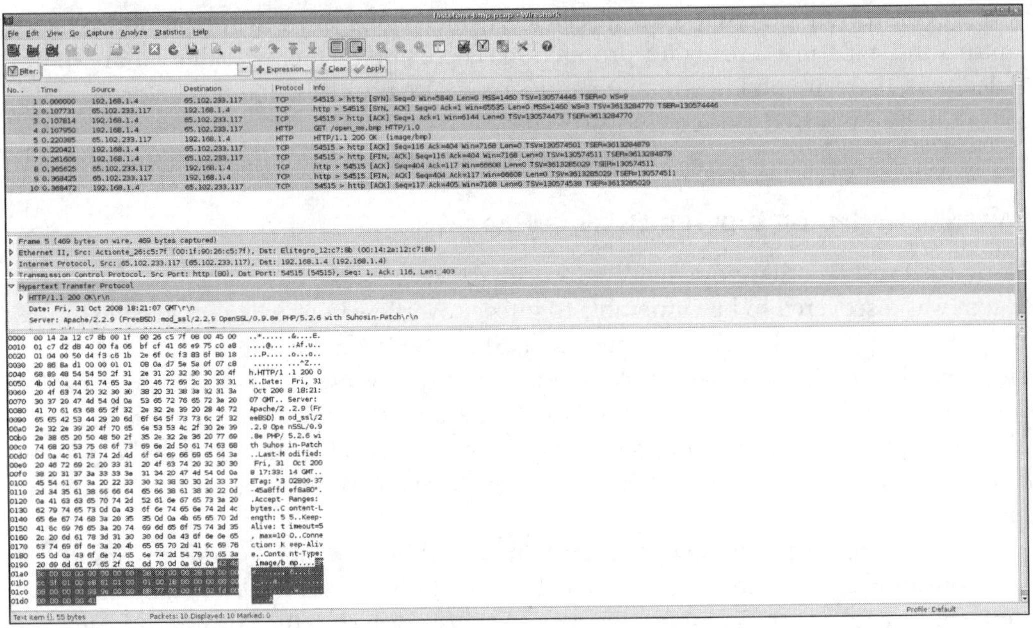

Figure 4-5   The FastStone Image Viewer packet capture

Because Wireshark doesn't parse out bitmap images for you, you are forced to go look up the bitmap specification to determine where in a bitmap file the width and the height are stored. The good news is that the Windows Bitmap Official Specification is now available online (www.fileformat.info/format/bmp/spec/e27073c25463436f8a64fa789c886d9c/view.htm). Some image or file formats do not have public documentation, and therefore require painstaking reverse-engineering to understand properly.

From the specification, the high-level layout of a bitmap file is as follows:

```
BITMAPFILEHEADER bmfh;
BITMAPINFOHEADER bmih;
RGBQUAD          aColors[];
BYTE             aBitmapBits[];
```

Because chances are good that something like image width and height are defined in a header, look to the definition of the bitmap file header and the bitmap info header:

```
typedef struct tagBITMAPFILEHEADER {    /* bmfh */
    UINT     bfType;
    DWORD    bfSize;
    UINT     bfReserved1;
```

```
    UINT      bfReserved2;
    DWORD     bfOffBits;
} BITMAPFILEHEADER;

typedef struct tagBITMAPINFOHEADER {      /* bmih */
    DWORD     biSize;
    LONG      biWidth;
    LONG      biHeight;
    WORD      biPlanes;
    WORD      biBitCount;
    DWORD     biCompression;
    DWORD     biSizeImage;
    LONG      biXPelsPerMeter;
    LONG      biYPelsPerMeter;
    DWORD     biClrUsed;
    DWORD     biClrImportant;
} BITMAPINFOHEADER;
```

These structures tell you everything you need to know to find the bitmap's width and height within a given file, because all the size specifications used for different structure members are fixed, and you know that they're the first two structures present in a bitmap file. Looking more closely at the definition of the bitmap file header, you see that the bfType item must always be set to BM, which makes for a handy string to use during detection.

Armed with that information, you are ready to write a signature. Unfortunately, a problem immediately arises: There's no feature built into the Snort rules language to do math, even simple arithmetic. Thus, the best possible detection that can be done is to look for unreasonably large values for the image width or the image height. By examining the Milw0rm exploit again, you see that those values are set to 0x15FCC (90,060) pixels and 0x161E8 (90,600) pixels, respectively. (Keep in mind that Microsoft typically records multibyte integers in little-endian order—with the least significant bytes first.) Because the total number is 0x5B30556A0 (24,478,308,000), it's obviously large enough to cause an integer overflow and so large that it's not particularly useful in terms of setting a minimum size for which you can look. Instead, some simple math helps provide a reasonable number: If you take 0xFFFFFFFF, divide it by 3, and take the square root of that number (because you want the smallest possible number that could appear as both the width and the height and still trigger an overflow), you end up with 0x93CD (37,837). Because no computer screen is anywhere close to being that large, you can safely set the size values that you're looking for to a number even smaller than that (say 35,000) without the likelihood of a large number of false positives.

With that conquered, the next problem is the small size of the fixed string you can search for in the signature: BM might easily appear in all sorts of HTTP traffic that have nothing to do with bitmaps. Even requiring that it appear at the start of a line (which you can do, because HTTP headers are delimited by a carriage-return new line sequence) does not help in terms of eliminating false positives. Knowing this, you need to examine the rest of the sample packet capture for anything useful (see Figure 4-6).

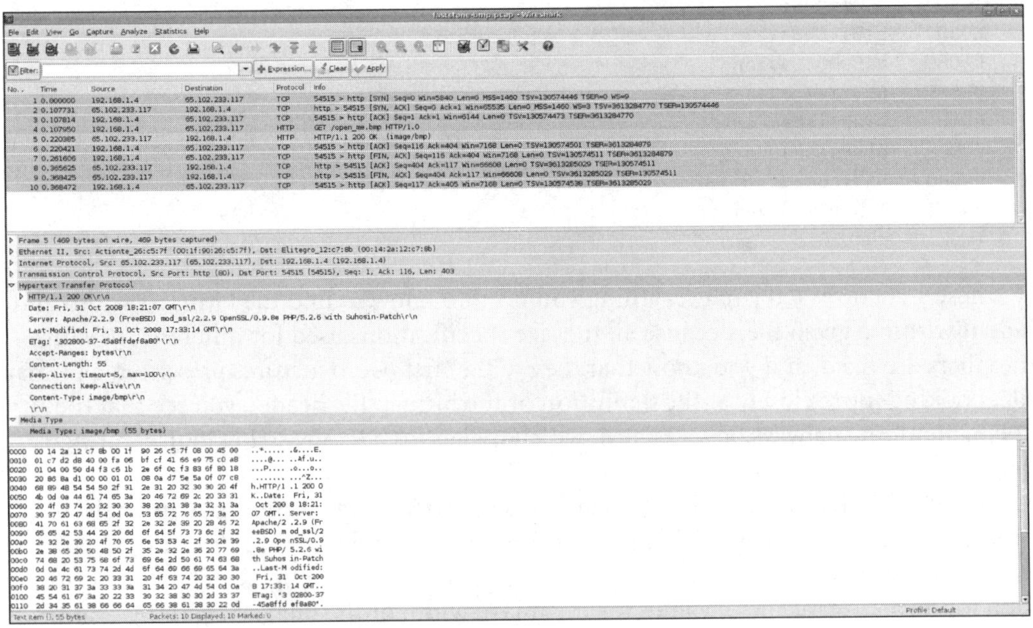

Figure 4-6   Remainder of the sample packet capture

The good news is that the HTTP headers actually provide a useful clue: the `Content-Type` header, which is set to image/bmp in the sample capture. Because all Web servers supply this header set to this value (even a malicious, custom-written server has incentive to do so, because such a header might trigger a helper application to view the malicious image), you can use it as a long content string for finding bitmap images. The resulting Snort signatures look like this:

```
alert tcp $EXTERNAL_NET $HTTP_PORTS -> $HOME_NET any (msg:"WEB-CLIENT FastStone
Image Viewer integer overflow attempt - oversized width"; flow:established,to_client;
content:"Content-Type¦3A¦"; nocase;
content:"image/bmp"; nocase; distance:0;
```

```
pcre:"/^Content-Type\x3A\s*image\x2Fbmp/smi"; content:"BM"; distance:0;
byte_test:4,>,35000,16,relative,little; reference:bugtraq,23312;
reference: cve,2007-1942; classtype:attempted-user; sid:99999;)
```

```
alert tcp $EXTERNAL_NET $HTTP_PORTS -> $HOME_NET any (msg:"WEB-CLIENT FastStone
Image Viewer integer overflow attempt - oversized height"; flow:established,to_client;
content:"Content-Type¦3A¦"; nocase; content:"image/bmp"; nocase; distance:0;
pcre:"/^Content-Type\x3A\s*image\x2Fbmp/smi"; content:"BM"; distance:0;
byte_test:4,>,35000,20,relative,little; reference:bugtraq,23312;
reference: cve,2007-1942; classtype:attempted-user; sid:99998;)
```

Both signatures fire on the Milw0rm packet capture as expected. However, these are not the final rules that need to go on a production system. Some Web servers send all the HTTP response headers in one packet and then begin data transmission in the next. This separates Content-Type: image/bmp from the actual bitmap data. Because Snort's stream-reassembly mechanism is not guaranteed to put these two packets into a single stream buffer and flush them through the detection engine, proper detection requires the use of the flowbits mechanism in Snort, which tags TCP streams so that a signature looking at a packet can tell if a necessary precondition has occurred in the stream. To do this, begin by setting a flowbit when the Content-Type header is seen:

```
alert tcp $EXTERNAL_NET $HTTP_PORTS -> $HOME_NET any (msg:"WEB-CLIENT bitmap
transfer"; flow:established,to_client; content:"Content-Type¦3A¦"; nocase;
content:"image/bmp"; nocase; distance:0;
pcre:"/^Content-Type\x3A\s*image\x2Fbmp/smi"; flowbits:set,http.bitmap;
flowbits:noalert; sid:99997;)
```

Here, the rule is virtually identical to the start of the previously written rules; the only difference, besides the message string, are the keywords flowbits:set,http.bitmap; flowbits:noalert;. The first of these creates a flowbit on the current TCP session named http.bitmap (essentially any arbitrary name, composed of letters, digits, and/or periods, is valid); the second tells Snort that even when the signature detects everything necessary to generate an alert, it should not actually log that alert (which is particularly useful in a case like this, because generating an alert for every single bitmap downloaded over HTTP on a given network generates a huge volume of alerts). With this done, you can now tweak the other two rules to look for that flowbit:

```
alert tcp $EXTERNAL_NET $HTTP_PORTS -> $HOME_NET any (msg:"WEB-CLIENT FastStone
Image Viewer multipacket integer overflow attempt - oversized width";
flow:established,to_client; flowbits:isset,http.bitmap; content:"BM"; distance:0;
byte_test:4,>,35000,16,relative,little; reference:bugtraq,23312;
reference: cve,2007-1942; classtype:attempted-user; sid:99999;)

alert tcp $EXTERNAL_NET $HTTP_PORTS -> $HOME_NET any (msg:"WEB-CLIENT FastStone
Image Viewer multipacket integer overflow attempt - oversized height";
flow:established,to_client; flowbits:isset,http.bitmap; content:"BM";
distance:0; byte_test:4,>,35000,20,relative,little; reference:bugtraq,23312;
reference: cve,2007-1942; classtype:attempted-user; sid:99998;)
```

Finally, because alerts are not reliably generated when a flowbit is set and then checked successfully on the same packet, you need to bring back the original two rules, only with different SIDs, and possibly an updated message string that reflects that the attack occurred in a single packet.

LIBSPF2 DNS TXT RECORD SIZE MISMATCH

The final vulnerability this chapter discusses is a DNS bug released by Dan Kaminski in October 2008, a buffer overflow in libspf when parsing DNS TXT records. (I'm specifically avoiding the DNS cache poisoning vulnerability he released earlier that year because that vulnerability has already been widely discussed.) Because DNS often contains multiple records and does not have clear string matches that allow Snort to find the start of each record, this vulnerability excellently showcases the power of Snort's new shared object rules, which are written in C and can do anything you can do in a C program.

As discussed in Dan's writeup (www.doxpara.com/?page_id=1256), the nature of this vulnerability is straightforward. One of the types of DNS resource records is TXT, which contains an ASCII text string. All DNS resource records have a 2-byte data length field immediately preceding the actual payload. Because TXT records are of type character-string, according to RFC 1035, they have a single-byte length field, followed by the actual string itself. The problem is that many DNS implementations do not perform a sanity check to ensure that the two values work together. In some cases, such as libspf, the 2-byte length field allocates a buffer in memory and the single-byte field is the size of the memcpy, which leads to a buffer overflow if that value is larger than the 2-byte value. For this signature, assume that any time the character-string length is not equal to the resource record length minus one (to account for the length byte), something suspicious is going on and you should generate an alert. Additionally, because Dan's example uses a TXT record in the answers section, concentrate your search there and skip the possibility that such a record might be present in an authority or additional resource record (for simplicity's sake, especially because you should have the knowledge necessary to check those other sections if you choose after reading the rest of this chapter).

After downloading Dan's tool and generating a sample packet (see Figure 4-7), which can easily be done by running `dig @ <ip of host running script> www.google.com TXT`, several things present themselves as obvious criteria for detecting this vulnerability.

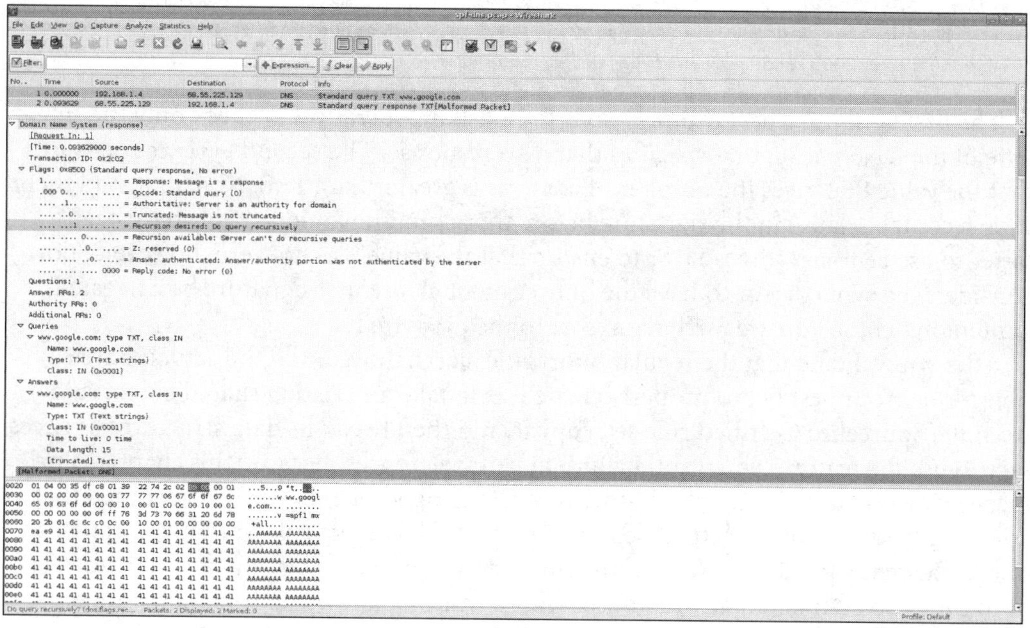

Figure 4-7 The Libspf2 packet capture

First, the packet must be inbound to your network from UDP port 53. Second, it must have the DNS response flag set, because you're looking for TXT records in answers, and answers are only present in DNS replies. Third, it must have more than zero answers listed in the header. Finally, at least one answer must contain a TXT record with a mismatched size.

Before venturing into the sometimes complex world of shared object rules, it's in your best interest to start with a standard Snort rule, add in as much detection as you can with the regular rules language, and ensure that the regular rule generates an alert on your sample packet capture. This helps you avoid dumb mistakes and frustration attempting to track down any problems in your build environment when the nature of the signature itself is the problem.

Here, check everything but the size mismatch portion in a regular Snort signature:

```
alert udp $EXTERNAL_NET 53 -> $HOME_NET any (msg:"DNS mismatched txt string
size"; byte_test:1,&,128,2; byte_test:2,>,0,6; reference:bugtraq,31881;
reference: cve,2008-2469; classtype:attempted-admin; sid:99999;)
```

The first `byte_test` performs a C-style bit masking operation to check only the single byte of the DNS packet that specifies that it's a response. The second `byte_test` ensures that the value that gives the number of answers is greater than zero. Note that, had there been a content clause in the signature before that point, it would actually have been faster to use `content:!"¦00 00¦";` to ensure that the value was not zero; however, Snort considers it a syntax error to have the only content clause in a signature be a negated content match, so you are forced to resort to the `byte_test`.

After you validate that the regular Snort rule alerts, move on to the actual shared object rule. Your best bet to properly create it is to take an existing shared object rule from the Sourcefire Certified rule set, copy it, and then tweak its data structures as necessary to use the features you want, including your references. Because this chapter is primarily concerned with the actual process of detecting vulnerabilities, it's assumed that you already know how to actually compile your shared object rule or that you can use one of the many good resources on the Internet to figure it out if you don't already know. It's also assumed that you have at least a working knowledge of C's fundamentals, because those are beyond this chapter's scope. Finally, note that the line numbers referenced correspond to those listed in the full source of this program (available at www.informit.com/store/product.aspx?isbn=0321591801).

After some initial standard setup that ensures that Snort actually gave the shared object rule a packet to work with, the first custom piece of this signature comes on line 139, where you check to ensure that at least 12 bytes of payload data are in the packet (the size of a DNS header) before doing anything else. This, along with all the other size checks performed throughout the rest of the rule, might seem pedantic; however, they're extremely critical, because if Snort, for some reason, passed in a malformed packet or, for some other reason, the shared object rule attempted to read data beyond the end of the packet, it is trivial to crash Snort (or even possibly cause exploitable memory corruption, if a skilled attacker had the source to a properly broken shared object rule).

The next two pieces of the rule call into the shared object API to run the `byte_tests`; if either test fails, you're not interested in the packet, so you return out of the rule without generating an alert. Continuing on, the rule sets the variable `cursor_raw` to point at 4 bytes from the start of the packet's payload, and then pulls out the number of queries and the number of answers declared to be in the DNS payload by using some simple C-bit shifting. Because this rule is not concerned with the other types of records that could be present, it simply skips those two numbers, sets the `end_of_payload` variable so that it can check itself before skipping anywhere within the DNS payload, and then moves on to the start of the payload.

Parsing the DNS queries is a fairly simple business. According to RFC 1035, each query is composed of a variable-length name, a 2-byte type, and a 2-byte class. Because the name portion of the query is terminated by a null byte, the easiest way to skip over each query is to loop, byte-by-byte, over the query until a null byte is encountered. (Each step along the way, check that you've not hit the end of the payload.) After this is done, the rule can skip over the next 5 bytes (the null byte itself and then the 4 bytes of data you're not interested in), and then proceed either to the next query if more are present or to the answer section of the payload.

Now you reached the interesting piece: the section where the vulnerability might be present. Looping over each of the answers noted as present in the packet, start by skipping over the name, because it's irrelevant to detection. For simplicity's sake, and based on all the DNS packets I've seen in my time as an IDS analyst, I've chosen to assume that the name is compressed using the mechanism outlined in section 4.1.4 of RFC 1035, and thus is always 2 bytes long. Next, check the 2-byte type field to ensure that it's 0x0010, which signifies a TXT record. Because the rule must skip the Time to Live (TTL) and class values of the record, from there, extract the record data size, irrespective of what type of record it is (because we'd need that value to skip over the actual data of non-TXT records). The rule simply sets a flag if the record is not of type TXT, so that it can easily be checked later. Finally, after the rule finds a TXT record, it compares the single-byte size value supplied in the packet to the data size in the previous 2 bytes and generates an alert if the values do not line up as expected.

SUMMARY

This chapter walked you through the natural evolution of a vulnerability, from discovering the vulnerability, capturing the packet stream, analyzing the malicious content within the packet, and writing an efficient Snort signature to provide an alert for it. Simultaneously, you were exposed to a small subset of necessary tools and Web sites to help you, including tcpdump, Wireshark, Metasploit, CVE, and milw0rm. The examples escalated in complexity and were specifically chosen because they were all identified within the past few months. (This shows you the unavoidable lag time for publishing a book.) For newcomers, packet analysis might appear overwhelming and tedious, but if you segment it and step through the packet capture packet by packet, the process falls into place. Unfortunately, the process can be tedious and frustrating, but be honest—that is the challenge and enjoyment of finally comprehending it. For already skilled signature writers, hopefully the advanced examples that used flowbits, PCRE, and newly shared object rules shed some light on the thought process and technique used by the Sourcefire VRT team.

Proactive Intrusion Prevention and Response via Attack Graphs

Network security is inherently difficult. Protocols are often insecure, software is frequently vulnerable, and educating end users is time-consuming. Security is labor-intensive, requires specialized knowledge, and is error prone because of the complexity and frequent changes in network configurations and security-related data. Network administrators and security analysts can easily become overwhelmed and reduced to simply reacting to security events. A more proactive stance is needed.

Furthermore, the correct priorities need to be set for concentrating efforts to secure a network. Administrators and analysts often have a vertical view of the particular component they are managing; horizontal views across/through the infrastructure are missing. This, in turn, shifts the emphasis to vulnerabilities at the interfaces. Security concerns in a network are also highly interdependent (for example, susceptibility to an attack depends on multiple vulnerabilities across the network). Attackers can combine such vulnerabilities to incrementally penetrate a network and compromise critical systems.

Generally, however, traditional security tools are point solutions that provide only a small part of the picture. They give few clues about how attackers might exploit combinations of vulnerabilities to advance a network attack. It remains a painful exercise to combine results from multiple tools and data sources to understand your true vulnerability against sophisticated multistep attacks. Even for experienced analysts, it can be difficult to recognize such risks, and it is especially challenging for large dynamically evolving networks.

Security is not a one-time single-point fix; it's a continuous process, as exemplified in the *protect-detect-react* lifecycle. To *protect* from attacks, you take steps to prevent them from succeeding. Still, you must understand that not all attacks can be averted in advance, and there must usually remain some residual vulnerability even after reasonable protective measures are applied.

Indeed, the more important question is not the vulnerability itself, but the magnitude of damage in case of an incident. You rely on the *detect* phase to identify actual attack instances. But, the detection process must be tied to residual vulnerabilities, especially ones that lie on paths to critical network resources. After attacks are detected, comprehensive capabilities are needed to *react* to them based on vulnerability paths. You can thus reduce the impact of attacks through advance planning and by knowing the paths of vulnerability through your networks, based on preemptive analysis of network vulnerability scan results. To create such a proactive stance, you must transform raw data about network vulnerabilities into attack roadmaps that help you prioritize and manage risks, maintain situational awareness, and plan for optimal countermeasures.

This chapter describes the latest advances in an innovative proactive approach to network security called *Topological Vulnerability Analysis (TVA).*[1,2] By analyzing vulnerability interdependencies, TVA builds a complete map that shows all possible paths of multistep penetration into a network, organized as a concise attack graph. The TVA attack graph then supports proactive network defenses across the entire protect-detect-react lifecycle. This includes identifying critical vulnerabilities, computing key security metrics, guiding the configuration of IDSs, correlating and prioritizing intrusion alarms, reducing false alarms, and planning optimal attack responses. You can also implement the TVA approach as a working tool, available commercially through limited distribution.

The remainder of this chapter is organized as follows:

- **Topological Vulnerability Analysis (TVA)**. Reviews the TVA approach and provides a visual example.
- **Attack modeling and simulation**. Describes the process of capturing network attack models in TVA to simulate multistep penetrating attacks.
- **Optimal network protection**. Discusses how to apply attack graphs for optimal network protection.
- **Intrusion detection and response**. Covers the application of attack graphs to intrusion detection and response.
- **Summary**. Summarizes our approach and suggests possible future advances.

TOPOLOGICAL VULNERABILITY ANALYSIS (TVA)

Because of vulnerability interdependencies across networks, a topological attack graph approach is needed, especially for proactive defense against insidious multistep attacks. The traditional approach that treats network data and events in isolation, without the context provided by attack graphs, is clearly insufficient. TVA combines vulnerabilities in ways that real attackers might, discovering all attack paths through a network, given the completeness of scan data used for your analysis. Mapping all paths through the network provides defense-in-depth, with multiple options for mitigating potential attacks, rather than relying on mere perimeter defenses.

This section overviews the TVA attack graph analysis and gives an example attack graph as an illustration. It then discusses the limitations of this modeling/simulation approach to attack graphs analysis.

OVERVIEW OF APPROACH

Figure 5-1 shows the overall flow of TVA. It begins by building an input attack model, based on the network configuration and potential attacker exploits. Network configuration data might include vulnerability scan reports, hosts inventory results, and firewall rules. Because you *model* network penetration versus actually exploiting vulnerabilities, you need to represent the fact that a given vulnerability can potentially be exploited. In fact, assume the worst case and model exploitation cause/effect, even if working exploit code is yet unreported for a given vulnerability. This model is explained in the section, "Attack Modeling and Simulation."

From this input attack model, TVA matches modeled exploits against vulnerabilities to predict multistep attacks through the network. From the resulting attack graph, it generates recommendations for optimal priority of hardening vulnerabilities, as described in the section, "Vulnerability Mitigation." The attack graph can also be explored through interactive visualization. (For more in-depth risk analysis, including what-if scenarios, see the section, "Attack Graph Visualization.") The TVA attack graph also supports computation of various metrics for measuring overall network security (see the section, "Security Metrics").

The attack graph guides optimal strategies for preventing attacks, such as patching critical vulnerabilities and hardening systems and services. However, because of realistic operational constraints, such as availability of patches or the need to offer mission-critical services, there usually remain some residual attack paths through a network. At this point, the residual attack graph provides the necessary context for dealing with

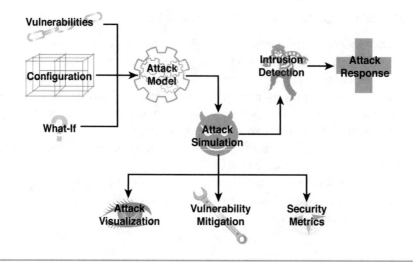

Figure 5-1   Visual representation of the Topological Vulnerability Analysis (TVA) overview

intrusion attempts. This includes guidance for the deployment and configuration of IDSs, correlation of intrusion alarms, and the prediction of next possible attack steps for an appropriate attack response.

For example, the attack graph can guide the placement of intrusion detection sensors to cover all attack paths, while minimizing sensors redundancy. As in all cases for TVA analysis, the attack graph must be kept current with respect to changes in network vulnerabilities. The attack graph then can filter false intrusion alarms, based on known paths of residual vulnerability. The graph also provides the context for correlating isolated alarms as part of a larger multistep attack penetration. It also shows the next possible vulnerabilities that an attacker might exploit, and whether they lie on attack paths to critical network resources. This in turn supports optimal planning and response against attacks, while minimizing the effects of false alarms and purposeful misdirection by an attacker.

ILLUSTRATIVE EXAMPLE

As a simple illustration of the attack graph approach, consider the small network in Figure 5-2. In this network, assume that the mail server and file server are only for internal use. However, outside access to the Web server is needed. Thus the firewall allows incoming Web connections to the Web server and blocks all other traffic from the outside. In this attack scenario, you want to know if an attacker on the outside can compromise the mail server through one or more attack steps.

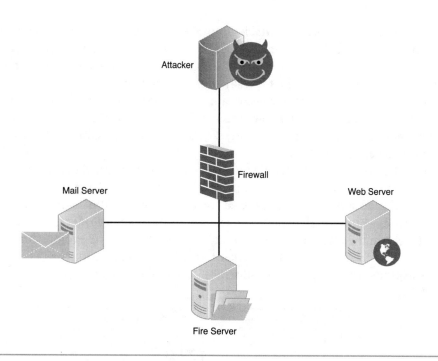

Figure 5-2 Small example network. The firewall allows Web traffic to the Web server, and blocks all other incoming traffic.

To model this scenario, you need to capture elements of the network configuration relevant to attack penetration. This includes the existence of vulnerable software (services) on hosts and the connectivity allowed to vulnerable services. You also need a set of potential attacker exploits that might work against the vulnerable services. In general, you rely on existing security tools to scan the network and build the input model.

For example, you can run a vulnerability scanning tool, such as Nessus,[3] against the hosts in the internal network to map their vulnerabilities and feed this into the TVA model. You then rely on your database of modeled exploits, which is prebuilt to cover exploitable vulnerabilities detected by Nessus. Assume the worst case, such as a vulnerability is exploitable (leads to an exploit) as long as it is reported as giving sufficient control over the victim machine. This is independent of any particular code or procedure that might actually carry out such exploitation.

To incorporate the connectivity-limiting effects of the firewall, scan the firewall. Also, scan behind the firewall to capture vulnerabilities that are available after an attacker reaches the internal network. Alternatively, you can process the firewall rules directly for building the network model.

Figure 5-3 shows the resulting attack graph for this scenario. There is a path from the outside to the inside mail server via a critical vulnerability exposed through the firewall. Figure 5-3(a) is a high-level view of the attack graph. It shows one vulnerability being exploited (implicitly, through the firewall) from the outside to the inside. In other words, the attack graph indicates that one vulnerability is exposed from the outside with the potential to be exploited, which allows the attacker to progress inside. This exploit, along with all others in this model, gives the attacker the ability to execute arbitrary code at an elevated privilege.

Figure 5-3(b) offers a more detailed view. It shows that an attacker can exploit a vulnerability on the Web server from the outside. Then, from the Web server, the attacker can attack the mail server. The box labeled "inside" represents the inside network, and implicitly, all machines on the inside can exploit one another's vulnerabilities. In Figure 5-3, the label 1 in the attack graph edge indicates that there is one exploit (implicitly, one exploitable vulnerability) from the attacker to the Web server. Inside the network, there are three exploits (three exploitable vulnerabilities on the Web server).

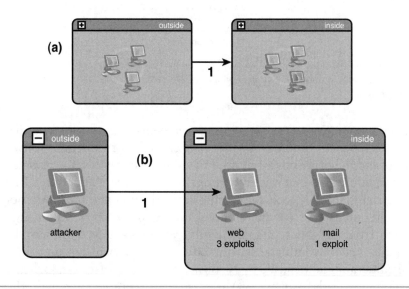

Figure 5-3   The critical vulnerability path from an outside attacker to the inside mail server from Figure 5-2

Of the three exploitable vulnerabilities on the Web server, only one is exploitable from the outside. TVA identifies this critical vulnerability. In other words, if the single vulnerable service from the attacker to the Web server is mitigated, the attacker has no other path to the mail server. Of course, other vulnerabilities can be mitigated, but the vulnerability from the attacker to the Web server is clearly a high priority.

This simple example shows how hosts on a network can be exploited through multiple steps, even when an attacker cannot directly access them. It is not directly possible to compromise the internal mail server from the outside because of the policy enforced by the firewall. But, TVA shows that the attack goal can be reached indirectly (in this case, through a sequence of two exploits). Furthermore, it shows that addressing a single critical vulnerability from among four within the internal network can prevent this attack scenario.

By constraining the attack graph to particular start and goal points, you focus the analysis on protecting a critical asset against an assumed threat source. For example, the file server does not appear in the attack graph because it does not play a part in this scenario. In other words, there are no attack paths from an attacker to the mail server that involve the file server. Also, Nessus and other vulnerability scanners generate many alerts that are merely informational and not relevant to network penetration. The TVA tool excludes such extraneous alerts from its database of modeled exploits.

In general, many different combinations of critical vulnerabilities might prevent an attack scenario. For enterprise networks, analyzing all attack paths and drawing appropriate conclusions requires extensive analysis.

LIMITATIONS

TVA is fundamentally a modeling/simulation approach. It relies on existing tools to gather network configuration and vulnerability information. It also needs to be prepopulated with a database of modeled exploits that can potentially be applied to a network. So, in this sense, the attack graph results are only as complete as the input model.

The benefits of a modeling/simulation approach include the capability to easily change the model for what-if analysis. But the modeling taxonomy needs to be carefully defined to reflect the realities of the network attack environment, while keeping model complexity manageable. That is, there is a tradeoff between model fidelity and model complexity that you must balance. Also, different analysis tasks might call for variations in model details. For example, the level of detail needed for information-operations support might differ from what is needed for patch management. The TVA tool is written to accept general models, in terms of exploit preconditions/postconditions. The only requirement is to create a database of the modeled exploits needed and to create network models that match exploit conditions.

ATTACK MODELING AND SIMULATION

TVA decomposes attack graph generation into two phases: capture of an input network attack model and using the model to simulate multistep network penetration. The attack model represents the network configuration and potential attacker exploits. In attack simulation, the input model is analyzed to form an attack graph of causally interdependent exploits, according to user-specified constraints.

NETWORK ATTACK MODELING

The network attack model includes aspects of the network *configuration* relevant to attack penetration and a set of potential attacker *exploits* that match attributes of the configuration. The TVA approach can apply to many different types of attack models, even noncyber models, as long as a common schema is employed across the model.

Figure 5-4 shows an example of one such schema for network models. This schema simply shows the hierarchical relationships among model elements (for example, a parent element "contains" its children). For clarity, the various attributes of the model elements are not shown, such as name attributes for machines and domains.

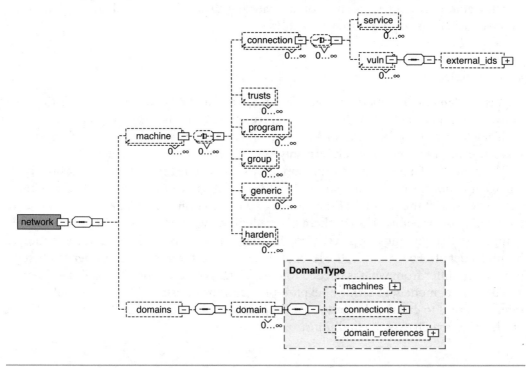

Figure 5-4 Example schema of network models

In this model schema, a network is comprised of machines and/or machines organized into protection domains. *Protection domains* capture the idea that the set of machines in a domain implicitly have unrestricted access to one another's vulnerable services. This abstraction is a scalable alternative to having a completely connected subgraph within the attack graph. The domain reference allows for domains within domains (subdomains).

A machine includes subelements and attributes relevant for modeling network attack penetration (exploits). This includes operating system (an attribute of machine, not shown) connections to vulnerable services on other machines, sets of machines that are trusted, application programs on a machine, groups to which the machine belongs (for example, Windows NT domains), and user-defined generic attributes. A harden element defines the hardening of a vulnerability. (For example, exploitation of a given vulnerability on a given machine is omitted from the attack graph.)

A connection describes how a machine connects to potentially vulnerable services across the network, to ports on other machines, or to its own ports. This mirrors the Transmission Control Protocol/Internet Protocol (TCP/IP) reference model, in which a layered connectivity structure represents the various network architectures and protocols.[4] A service connection indicates a running service on a destination machine, to which a source machine can connect.

Each connection is composed of a service or application type at the appropriate TCP/IP layer. For example, an HTTP connection specifies the Web server name/version at the Transport layer. Link-layer connectivity models exploit against the Address Resolution Protocol (ARP). This scopes attacks based on traffic sniffing, such as man-in-the-middle (MITM) attacks based on ARP poisoning. Application-layer connectivity models exploits rely on particular application configurations, trust relationships, or other high-level details.

To keep pace with emerging threats, you must continually monitor sources of reported vulnerabilities and add those to your database of modeled exploits. Attack graphs model an attacker exploit in terms of preconditions and postconditions and for generic attacker and victim machines, which are subsequently mapped to the target network. For convenience, map vulnerable network connections to known standard vulnerability identifiers, such as CVE[5] and Bugtraq.[6]

For populating models automatically, map outputs of network-scanning tools to the network schema, which in turn provide preconditions for attack graph exploits. Figure 5-5 shows example output data for Centennial Discovery,[7] which is a network-asset management tool. A Discovery agent deployed on a network host machine reports detailed host configuration data, such as product/manufacturer/version for each detected software component.

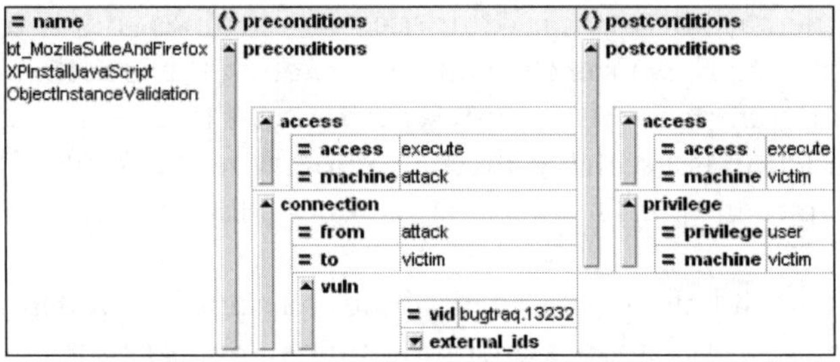

≡ name	() preconditions	() postconditions
bt_MozillaSuiteAndFirefox XPInstallJavaScript ObjectInstanceValidation	▲ preconditions	▲ postconditions

preconditions:
- ▲ access
  - ≡ access execute
  - ≡ machine attack
- ▲ connection
  - ≡ from attack
  - ≡ to victim
  - ▲ vuln
    - ≡ vid bugtraq.13232
    - ▼ external_ids

postconditions:
- ▲ access
  - ≡ access execute
  - ≡ machine victim
- ▲ privilege
  - ≡ privilege user
  - ≡ machine victim

Figure 5-5   Red Hat Fedora discovered by the network-asset management too

The discovered host software information is then mapped to preconditions for modeled exploits. Figure 5-6 shows the preconditions and postconditions for exploitation of a Bugtraq vulnerability, in terms of generic attacker/victim machines. The preconditions are that the attacker can execute code on the attacking machine, and a vulnerable connection exists from attacker to victim, identified as Bugtraq 13232.

≡ bugtraq.id	() service	
13232	▲ service	
	≡ product	fedora-release
	≡ manufacturer	Red Hat, Inc.
	≡ version	4

Figure 5-6   The preconditions and postconditions for the identified Red Hat Fedora machine

Symantec DeepSight,[8] a Web service direct feed of the Bugtraq database, gives the vulnerable software components for each reported vulnerability. Host configuration data gathered from an asset management tool, such as Discovery, generally differs from software descriptions in DeepSight. So discovered host software components need to be mapped to corresponding vulnerability records, as Figure 5-7 shows. This figure also shows a Discovery software description for Red Hat Fedora 4 mapped to Bugtraq vulnerability 13232. Symantec DeepSight has fields that correspond to product/manufacturer/service that help you with this mapping by matching against Discovery through regular expressions.

Figure 5-8 illustrates a resulting connection to vulnerable software (Bugtraq 13232) on the host machine. This connection is built into the attack model by mapping the discovered host software to a known vulnerability. Then, because a connection with Bugtraq 13232 is a precondition for a particular exploit, this exploit might be included in this network's attack graph.

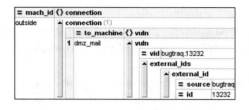

```
≡ mach_id () connection
outside        ▲ connection (1)
                     ≡ to_machine () vuln
                  1  dmz_mail      ▲ vuln
                                        ≡ vid  bugtraq.13232
                                        ▲ external_ids
                                              ▲ external_id
                                                    ≡ source  bugtraq
                                                    ≡ id      13232
```

Figure 5-7   Software-to-vulnerability mapping indicates that a version of Linux has a particular Bugtraq vulnerability

```
machine (1)
   ≡ mach_id () services
1  dmz_mail   ▲ services
                   ▲ service
                         ≡ product       fedora-release
                         ≡ manufacturer  Red Hat, Inc.
                         ≡ version       4
```

Figure 5-8   Network connection to vulnerable software specifies that a particular machine connects to another, with a given Bugtraq vulnerability on the destination machine

The Discovery asset management tool also defines protection domains, such as sets of machines with full connectivity to one another's vulnerable services (see Figure 5-9). Each protection domain is identified along with its member machines.

```
domain (3)
   ≡ domainid () machines
1  ClientLAN   ▲ machines
                    ▲ machine (2)
                          ≡ mach_id () services
                       1  client1     ▾ services
                       2  client2     ▾ services
2  DMZ         ▲ machines
                    ▲ machine (2)
                          ≡ mach_id () services
                       1  dmz_web     ▾ services
                       2  dmz_mail    ▾ services
3  ServerLAN   ▲ machines
                    ▲ machine (3)
                          ≡ mach_id () services
                       1  srvr_web    ▾ services
                       2  srvr_db     ▾ services
                       3  srvr_mail   ▾ services
```

Figure 5-9   Protection domains reported by the asset management tool

The purpose of modeling the network configuration is to support preconditions of modeled attacker exploits. As this chapter has shown, you can map software components to their reported vulnerabilities. Alternatively, you can run remote vulnerability scans with tools such as Nessus, Retina,[9] or FoundScan.[10] With this approach, the tool actively tests for the existence of host vulnerabilities. The scanner reports a detected vulnerability explicitly by using a standard vulnerability identifier instead of reporting a particular software component. The corresponding exploit precondition is written in terms of this vulnerability identifier.

An advantage of this approach is that you can capture the effects of connectivity-limiting devices, such as routers and firewalls. That is, you scan from different network vantage points, targeting hosts through firewalls. The idea is that the scanner assumes the role of an attacker who reaches a certain point in the network. Thus, you avoid creating any special firewall exceptions for the scanning machine, which is typically done for network vulnerability scans.

You then combine multiple scans from various network locations, building a complete map of connectivity to vulnerable services throughout the network. Alternatively, you can directly analyze firewall rules, adding the resulting vulnerable connections to the model. In this case, only local subnet scans are needed.

ATTACK SIMULATION

In attack simulation, modeled exploits are matched against the network configuration model, which forms an attack graph of causally interdependent exploits, according to user-specified simulation constraints. Because the model is prepopulated through network scans and vulnerability databases, all that remains is defining the attack scenario (for example, the starting point, the attack goal, and any what-if changes to the network configuration).

In other words, given an input model of network configuration and attacker exploits, the exploits are instantiated for specific attacker/victim machine pairs in the network. Preconditions for instantiated exploits are tested, and resulting postconditions are matched with preconditions of other exploits. Figure 5-10 shows an exploit that has been instantiated for particular machines in the network model. The attacker and victim machines are no longer generic; they are defined for actual machines in the network.

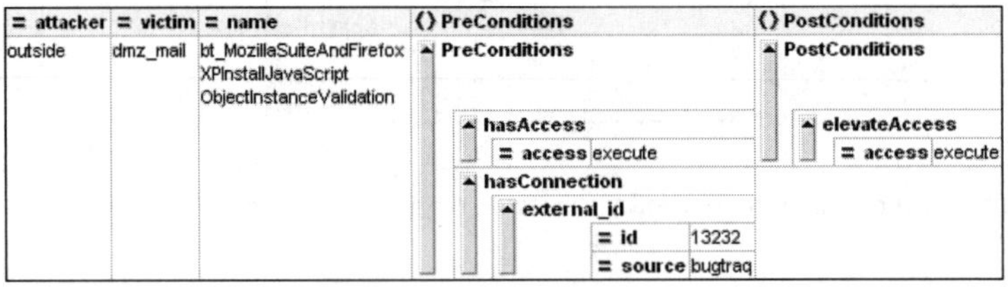

Figure 5-10   Exploit instantiated for particular network. Attacker and victim are actual network machines, and preconditions are satisfied from the network model.

An attack graph also needs to follow the structure of protection domains defined for the network. Within a protection domain, it is assumed that each machine has unrestricted connectivity to vulnerabilities on all other machines in the domain. This implies that the attack graph is completely connected with a domain.

Figure 5-11 shows example protection domains in attack graph data. Within each domain, the set of all member machines is specified, as well as exploits relevant to each domain. Two possible types of exploits exist: within-domain and across-domain. Within-domain exploits are only accessible to machines within the protection domain. Thus, it is sufficient to specify only the victim machine, because the attacking machines are implicit. Across-domain exploits are those that attack machines in other domains. Those exploits have both attacker and victim machines specified.

ProtectionDomain (2)									
= name	() Machine	() Exploit							
1 Internet	▲ Machine (1)	▲ Exploit (3)							
		= name	= attacker	= victim	= name	= withinPdom	() PreConditions	() PostConditions	
		1 outside	1 outside	dmz_mail	bt_MozillaSuiteAnd FirefoxXPInstallJav aScriptObjectInsta nceValidation	false	☑ PreConditions	☑ PostConditions	
			2 outside	dmz_mail	bt_MozillaSuiteAnd FirefoxDocumentO bjectModelNodesC odeExecution	false	☑ PreConditions	☑ PostConditions	
			3 outside	dmz_web	bt_MicrosoftWindo wsMediaPlayer_A SXBufferOverflow	false	☑ PreConditions	☑ PostConditions	
2 DMZ	▲ Machine (2)	▲ Exploit (5)							
		= name	= attacker	= victim	= name	= withinPdom	() PreConditions	() PostConditions	
		1 dmz_web	1 dmz_mail	srvr_mail	bt_MicrosoftWindo wsMediaPlayer_A SXBufferOverflow	false	☑ PreConditions	☑ PostConditions	
		2 dmz_mail	2 dmz_mail	srvr_mail	bt_WindowsMedia Player_ASXBuffer Overflow	false	☑ PreConditions	☑ PostConditions	
			3	dmz_mail	bt_MozillaSuiteAnd FirefoxDOMPropert yOverridesCodeEx ecution	true	☑ PreConditions	☑ PostConditions	
			4	dmz_mail	bt_MozillaSuiteFire foxAndThunderbir dMultiple	true	☑ PreConditions	☑ PostConditions	
			5	dmz_web	bt_MicrosoftIntern etExplorerURIDeco ding	true	☑ PreConditions	☑ PostConditions	

Figure 5-11   Protection domains in attack graph data

An attack graph can be completely unconstrained (for example, all possible attack paths regardless of assumed starting and ending points in the network). In such a scenario, the source of the threat is assumed unknown, and no particular critical network assets are identified as specific attack goals. Figure 5-12 shows an example of such an unconstrained attack graph.

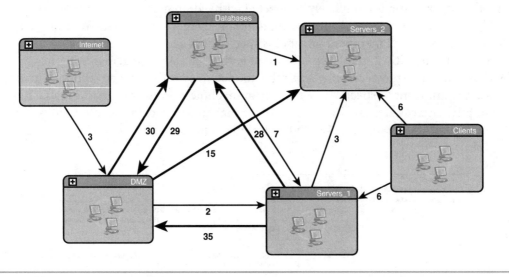

Figure 5-12   An unconstrained attack graph scenario

Another option is to constrain the attack graph to a given starting point (or points) for the attack. The idea is that the origin of the attack is assumed, and only paths that can be reached from the origin are included. Figure 5-13 shows an example attack graph in which the attack starting point (Internet) is specified.

Another option is to constrain the attack graph so that it ends at a given ending point (or points) serving as the attack goal. Here, the idea is that certain critical network assets are to be protected, and only attack paths that reach the critical assets are included. This option can be exercised alone, with an unconstrained starting point, or combined with a constrained starting point. Figure 5-14 shows an example of the latter, in which both the attack starting point (Internet) and attack ending point (Databases) are specified.

The motivation for constraining the attack graph is to reduce the scope of the graph to the expected attack scenarios, which eliminates unnecessary clutter. For example, in Figure 5-14, the outgoing edges from the Database protection domain are omitted. If the primary goal is to protect the databases, attacks *away* from there are less important, (because, for example, the databases have already been compromised). Similarly, any attacks *into* the starting point can be omitted, because the attacker already has control of it.

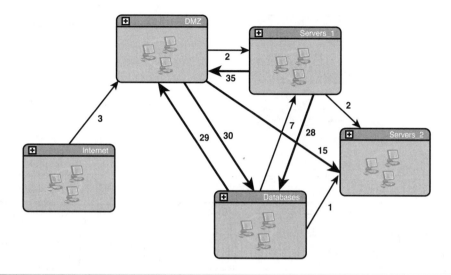

Figure 5-13 An attack graph with constrained starting point

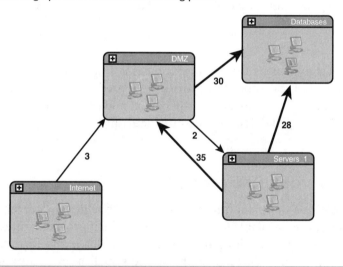

Figure 5-14 Attack graph with constrained starting and ending points

Particularly important attack paths to consider are the most direct ones, such as the shortest paths from attack start and/or attack goal (see Figure 5-15). Two scenarios are considered. In Figure 5-15(a), the graph shows direct (shortest) paths from a given starting point. In Figure 5-15(b), both the attack starting point and goal points are given. The graph shows all direct paths from the starting point to the goal point.

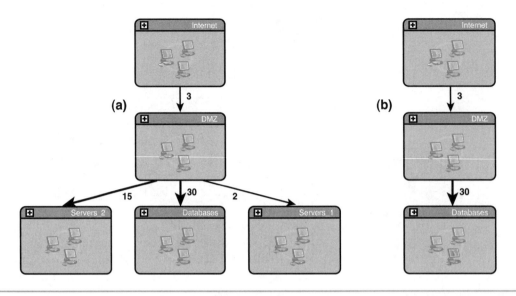

Figure 5-15   Attack graph constrained to direct attacks from (a) the given starting point and (b) the given starting and ending points

Again, the idea is to identify the most critical paths and vulnerabilities, for preattack network hardening and real-time alarm correlation, prediction, and response. Thus, given the assumed threat sources, attacker behavior, and critical network resources, you can tailor your analysis and defensive measures accordingly.

OPTIMAL NETWORK PROTECTION

Attack graphs provide a powerful framework for proactive network defenses. Various analytical techniques are available for attack graphs, which provide context for informed risk assessment. Attack graphs pinpoint critical vulnerabilities and form the basis for optimal network hardening. Through sophisticated visualization techniques, purely graph-based and geospatial, you can interactively explore attack graphs. This section's visualizations effectively manage graph complexity without getting overwhelmed with the details. These attack graphs also support numerous key metrics that concisely quantify the overall state of network security.

VULNERABILITY MITIGATION

Attack graphs reveal the true scope of threats by mapping sequences of attacker exploits that can penetrate a network. You can then use these attack graphs to recommend ways to address the threat. This kind of automated support is critical; manually finding such solutions is tedious and error prone, especially for larger networks.

One kind of recommendation is to harden the network at the attack source (the first layer of defense). This option, shown in Figure 5-16, prevents all further attack penetration beyond the source. Here, you use the same attack scenario (starting and ending points), as Figure 5-14 showed. However, the network configuration model is changed slightly, with a resulting change in the attack graph. In particular, the numbers of exploits between protection domains have changed.

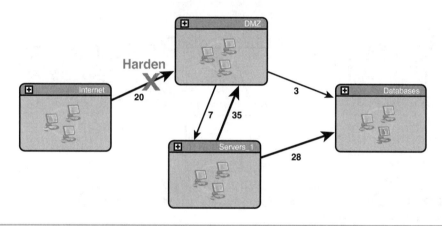

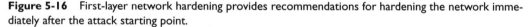

Figure 5-16 First-layer network hardening provides recommendations for hardening the network immediately after the attack starting point.

For first-layer defense for this network configuration, the recommendation is to block the 20 exploits from the Internet to DMZ. The idea is not to simply rely on preventing these 20 exploits for complete network protection. Instead, it is necessary to point out these critical first steps that give an attacker a foothold in the network. Understanding all known attack paths, not just the first layer, provides defense-in-depth. But, the first layer, which is critical, certainly must be highlighted.

Figure 5-17 shows a different kind of recommendation for network hardening, which is hardening the network at the attack goal at the last layer of defense. This option protects the attack goal (critical network resource) from all sources of attack, regardless of their origins. Here, as always, the assumption is that the compromise of the victim (DMZ) does not imply granting legitimate access to a subsequent victim (database server). If that is the case, such access is included as a potential attacker exploit.

The attack graph shown in Figure 5-17 is the same as Figure 5-16 (first-layer defense). For last-layer defense, the recommendation is to block the three exploits from DMZ to Databases plus the 28 exploits from Servers_1 to Databases, for a total of 31 exploits. As with first-layer defense, you do simply rely on preventing these last-layer exploits for complete defense-in-depth. Instead, the idea is to highlight these direct attacks against critical assets, which are reachable from anywhere an attacker might be.

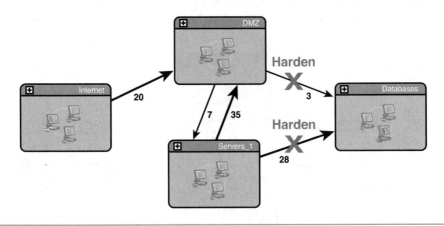

Figure 5-17   Last-layer network hardening provides recommendations for hardening the network immediately before the attack ending point.

Another kind of recommendation is to find the minimum number of blocked exploits that break the paths from attack start to attack goal. In other words, break the graph into two components that separate start from goal, which minimizes the total number of blocked exploits.[11]

Figure 5-18 shows this concept. For the minimum-cost defense, the recommendation is to block the three exploits from DMZ to Databases plus the seven exploits from DMZ to Servers_1, for a total of ten exploits. This is a savings of ten blocked exploits compared to first-layer hardening and a savings of 21 blocked exploits compared to last-layer hardening. As for first-layer and last-layer defenses, the idea is to highlight critical vulnerabilities that break the attacker's reach to the critical asset. After these are addressed, the residual attack graph can be analyzed for further defense-in-depth.

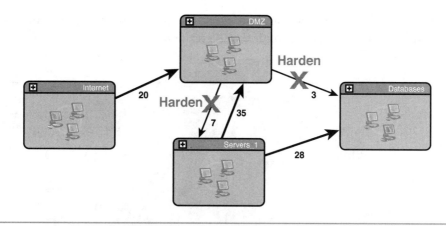

Figure 5-18 Minimum-cost network hardening provides recommendation for hardening the network involving the fewest number of vulnerabilities blocked.

ATTACK GRAPH VISUALIZATION

One of the challenges in this attack graph approach is managing attack graph complexity. In early forms, attack graph complexity is exponential[12,13,14,15] because paths are explicitly enumerated, which leads to combinatorial explosion. Under reasonable assumptions, attack graph analysis can be formulated as monotonic logic, which makes it unnecessary to explicitly enumerate states leading to polynomial (rather than exponential) complexity.[16,17,18] The protection domain abstraction further reduces complexity, to linear within each domain,[19] and complexity can be further reduced based on host configuration regularities.[20]

Thus, although it is computationally feasible to generate attack graphs for reasonably large networks, complex graphs can overwhelm an analyst. Instead of presenting attack graph data in its raw form, you present views that aid in the rapid understanding of overall attack patterns. Employing a clustered graph framework,[21] a clustered portion of the attack graph provides a summarized view while showing interactions with other clusters. Arbitrarily large and complex attack graphs can be handled in this way, through multiple levels of clustering.

Through sophisticated visualization,[22] graphs can be rolled up or drilled down as the graph is explored. Figure 5-19 shows a visualization interface for attack graph exploration and analysis. The main view of the graph shows all the possible paths through the network based on the user-defined attack scenario. In this view, the analyst can expand or collapse graph clusters (protection domains) as desired, rearrange graph elements, and select elements for further details. In Figure 5-19, two domains are expanded to show their specific hosts and the exploits between them.

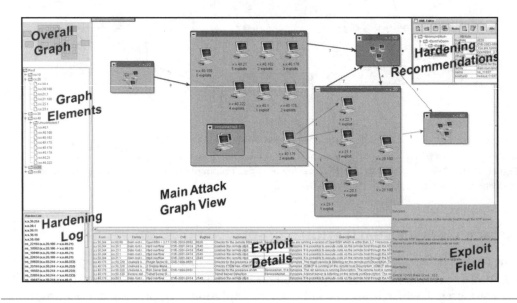

Figure 5-19   Attack graph visualization interface

When an edge (set of exploits) is selected in the main view, details for the corresponding exploits are provided. Each exploit record contains numerous relevant fields that describe the underlying vulnerability. A hierarchical (tree) directory of all attack graph elements is provided, linked to other views. A view of the entire graph is constantly maintained, providing the overall context as the main view is rescaled or panned. Automated recommendations for network hardening are provided, and the specific hardening actions taken are logged.

The visualization interface in Figure 5-19 provides an abstract, purely cyber-centric view of network attacks. But, in some situations, understanding the physical location of possible attacks might be important, such as assessing mission impact. Given the locality of network elements, you can embed the attack graph into a geospatial visualization. Figure 5-20 illustrates this. Here, elements of the attack graph are clustered around major network centers, and the graph edges show exploits between centers. Interactive visualization capabilities can support drilldown for further details at a desired level of resolution.

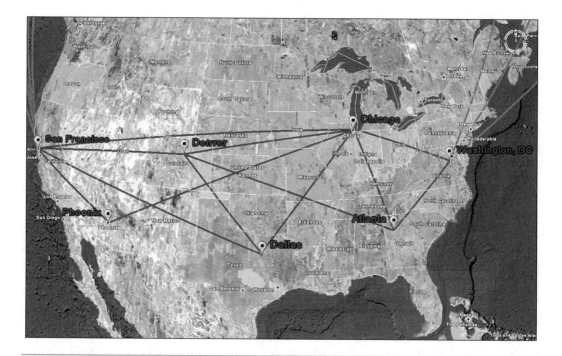

Figure 5-20   Geospatial attack graph user interface

SECURITY METRICS

You face sophisticated attackers who might combine multiple vulnerabilities to penetrate networks with a devastating impact. Assessment of attack risk must go well beyond simply counting the number of vulnerabilities or vulnerable hosts. Metrics, like percentage of patched systems, ignore interactions among network vulnerabilities; such metrics are limited, because vulnerabilities in isolation lack context.

Attack graphs show how network vulnerabilities can be combined to stage an attack, providing a framework for more precise and meaningful security metrics. Attack graph metrics can help quantify the risk associated with potential security breaches, guide decisions about responding to attacks, and accurately measure overall network security. Informed risk assessment requires such a quantitative approach. Desirable properties of metrics include being consistently measurable, inexpensive to collect, unambiguous, and having specific context.[23] Metrics based on attack graphs have all these properties.

Some early nonquantitative standardization efforts resulted in the System Security Engineering Capability Maturity Model (SSE-CMM).[24] The National Institute of Standards and Technology (NIST) publications outline processes for implementing security metrics[25] and establishing a security baseline.[26] The Common Vulnerability Scoring System (CVSS)[27] provides a way to score vulnerabilities based on standard measures. But, in all these cases, vulnerabilities are treated in isolation without considering their interdependencies on a target network.

In contrast, attack graph metrics are holistic measures that take into account patterns of vulnerability paths across the network. These can also be tailored for specific attack scenarios, including assumed threat origins and/or critical resources to protect. They provide consistent measures over time, so that an organization can continually monitor security posture through the course of network operation. They can also evaluate the relative security of planned network changes so that risks can be assessed and alternatives compared in advance of actual deployment.

One basic metric might be the overall size (vertices and edges) of the attack graph. For example, for a given attack scenario, the attack paths might constitute only a small subset of the total network vulnerabilities. This could be for a given attack starting point with the attack goal unconstrained, thus measuring the total forward reach of the attacker. Or it could be for a given attack goal with the attack start unconstrained, measuring the backward susceptibility of a critical asset. Alternatively, it could be computed for constrained start and constrained goal, measuring joint attack reachability/susceptibility.

Although the attack graph size provides a basic indicator, it does not fully quantify levels of effort for defending against attacks. For example, the number of exploits in the first-layer hardening recommendation quantifies the effort for blocking initial network penetration. Similarly, the number of exploits in the last-layer recommendation quantifies the effort for blocking final-step critical asset compromise. The minimum-effort recommendation quantifies the overall least effort required to block an attacker from a critical asset.

Another idea is to normalize metrics by the size of the network, which yields a measure that can be compared across networks of different sizes. You could also extend your attack graph models to deal with uncertainties. For example, given that each exploit has individual measures of likelihood, difficulty, and so on, you can propagate these through the attack graph, according to the logical implications of exploit interdependencies. This approach can derive an overall measure for the network, such as the likelihood of a catastrophic compromise. Such a measure might then be included in more general assessments of overall business risk. You can then rank risk-mitigation options in terms of maximizing security and minimizing business cost.

The kind of precise measurement provided by attack graphs can also help clarify security requirements and guard against potentially misleading "rule of thumb" assumptions.[28] For example, suppose a network has many vulnerable services, but those services are not exposed through firewalls. Then, another network has fewer vulnerable services, but they are all exposed through firewalls. Comparing attack graphs, from outside the firewalls, the first network is more secure.

Making network host configurations more diverse, presumably to make the attacker's job more difficult, might not necessarily improve security. For example, this might provide more paths leading to critical assets. By taking into account the diversity of configurations in the model, the attack graph metrics give precise measures for analyzing these situations.

INTRUSION DETECTION AND RESPONSE

Attack graph analysis identifies critical vulnerability paths and provides strategies for optimal protection of critical network assets. This enables you to make optimal decisions about hardening the network in advance of an attack. But, you must also recognize that because of operational constraints, such as availability of patches and the need for offering mission-critical services, residual vulnerability paths usually remain. But, the knowledge that TVA provides enables you to plan in advance and maintain a proactive security posture even in the face of attacks. For example, TVA attack graphs provide the necessary context for deployment and fine tuning of IDSs, for correlation and prioritization of intrusion alarms, and for attack response.

INTRUSION DETECTION GUIDANCE

Knowledge of vulnerability paths through your network helps you prepare your defenses and your responses. Attacks graphs can guide the optimal deployment and operation of IDSs, which are tailored to your network and its critical assets.

In deploying IDSs, you must decide where to place detection sensors within the network. Traditionally, intrusion detection sensors are placed at network perimeters, with the idea of detecting outside attacks. But, with this deployment, traffic in the internal network is not monitored. If an attacker avoids detection at the perimeter, subsequent attack traffic in the internal network is missed.

On the other hand, deploying sensors everywhere might be cost prohibitive and can overwhelm analysts with floods of alerts. You must strike a balance, where you cover known residual vulnerability paths using the fewest necessary sensors. TVA attack graphs provide this balance.

Consider the attack graph shown in Figure 5-21. Assume that this is the residual attack graph after network hardening measures are applied. So, now the goal is to map this attack graph to the network topology and embed intrusion detection sensors in the network to cover all the vulnerability paths (with the fewest sensors).

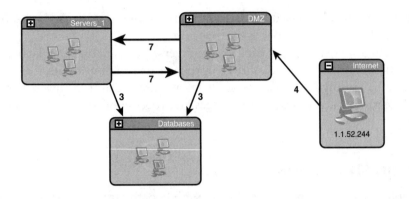
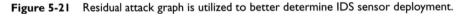

Figure 5-21 Residual attack graph is utilized to better determine IDS sensor deployment.

Figure 5-22 shows the network topology, overlaid by the attack paths from Figure 5-21. This simplified network diagram illustrates the problem of sensor placement for attack graph coverage. It omits firewalls, which limit connectivity as reflected by the attack graph. Also, the elements labeled router A, router B, and subnet *n* are abstract network devices capable of monitoring traffic through them (for example, via SPAN ports).

Analysis of the joint topology/attack representation in Figure 5-22 shows that detection sensors placed at router A and router B cover all vulnerability paths with the fewest sensors. An alternative is to place sensors at subnet 1, subnet 4, and subnet 8, which also covers all paths, but requires three (versus two) sensors.

In this network, deploying a sensor at the perimeter alone (router B) misses attack traffic from Servers_1 to Databases. In the opposite extreme, you might decide to deploy sensors at each of the four subnet *n* devices to catch all potential attack traffic. But, TVA shows that no critical vulnerability paths involve subnet 6, so deploying a sensor there is wasteful, including continually monitoring alerts generated from there. Again, sensors deployed at router A and router B are sufficient to cover all vulnerable paths.

For enterprise networks, performing this kind of analysis requires automation to maximize efficiency. The attack graphs bring together information from various sources over multiple network layers into a concise map. Although the sensor-placement problem itself is hard, a heuristic algorithm scales well and provides near-optimal solutions.[29] After sensors are deployed and generate intrusion alarms, you can further leverage attack graphs for alarm correlation and prioritization. This requires mapping alarms to their corresponding elements (exploits) in the residual attack graph. This in turn requires that you represent alarms in a common format, using alarm identifiers that match the identifiers used in the attack graph model.

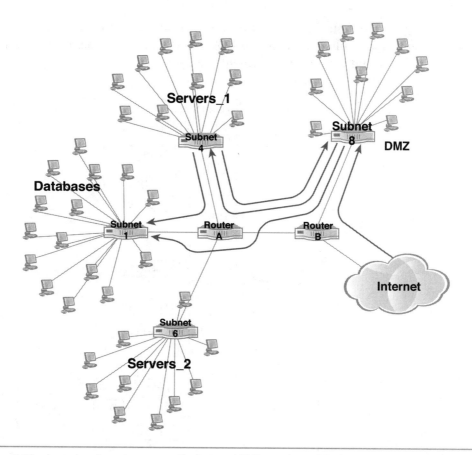

Figure 5-22 Intrusion detection sensor deployment. TVA attack graphs guide the placement of sensors to cover all vulnerability paths while minimizing the number of deployed sensors.

In this regard, specifications such as Intrusion Detection Message Exchange Format[30] (IDMEF) or the ArcSight[31] event log format define data formats for information sharing between IDSs and TVA. For example, one implementation option is the IDMEF plug-in[32] for Snort.[33] This plug-in allows Snort to output alerts in the IDMEF message format. Data exchanges in IDMEF are in XML with the format enforced through a formal schema.

Figure 5-23 shows the structure of an IDMEF alert. The IDMEF model represents alerts in an unambiguous fashion, while explicitly assuming that alert information is heterogeneous. Alerts from different tools might have varying amounts and types of information about an event, which the IDMEF data model accommodates. The critical data is source and target (attacker and victim) network addresses and an alarm identifier that can be mapped to a vulnerability in the TVA model. In IDMEF, these are supported by the *Source, Target,* and *Classification* elements, respectively.

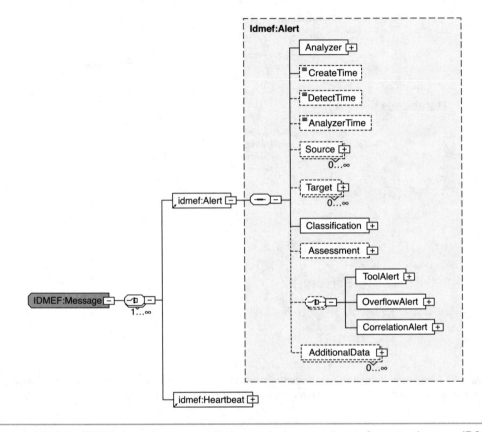

Figure 5-23   The IDMEF alert structure provides a standard way to share information between IDSs and TVA.

ATTACK PREDICTION AND RESPONSE

When intrusion alarms are generated, attack graphs provide the necessary context to correlate and prioritize them. First, you can place a high priority on alarms that lie on vulnerability paths through your network. You can prioritize them further based on their graph distance to given critical assets. In other words, events that are close to critical assets (in terms of next attack steps) are given a higher priority compared to resources buried deep in the infrastructure.

This kind of attack graph analysis is highly precise and takes all relevant facts into account. You determine not only whether a host is vulnerable to a given attack, but whether the attacker can traverse through firewalls to reach the host's vulnerable port and whether that attack can lead to subsequent network compromise. Thus, your prioritization also serves as an advanced form of false-alarm reduction, restricting alarms along critical paths.

It is important to model network vulnerability because multistep alarm correlation do not take real network vulnerabilities into account often.[34] Precomputing vulnerability-based attack graphs in advance of an attack has the additional advantage of rapid correlation, which means that it's faster than an IDS can generate them.[35,36]

Furthermore, the predictive capabilities of attack graphs enable you to correlate intrusion alarms based on attack causality. A set of seemingly isolated events might in fact be shown as multiple steps of incremental network penetration. Also, the context provided by these attack graphs enables you to predict potentially missed events (false negatives), which helps mitigate inaccuracies in your defense posture.[37]

To illustrate some of these ideas, consider Figure 5-24. This is the same residual attack graph shown in Figure 5-21, but with relevant protection domains expanded to show additional details. This attack graph provides considerable insight for correlating and prioritizing any alarms generated for this network and for responding to these potential attacks.

For example, suppose an alarm is raised for an attack between two machines in the DMZ (say, from DMZ_1 to DMZ_2). From just a single alarm in the DMZ, you might wait before responding. On the other hand, if an alarm is raised from Internet into DMZ, followed by an alarm within the DMZ, it is a stronger indicator that the attack might be a real security breach. Remember that false alarms are common with intrusion detection, and erroneously blocking traffic in response to false alarms is a denial of service.

From an alarm within the DMZ, another approach might be to block traffic from DMZ_3 to DB_1 and DB_2. Because of the possibility of denial of service, such an action is not usually taken. But you can limit the blocking to the vulnerable ports on DB_1 and DB_2 only, specifically from DMZ_3, so that any nonvulnerable services on those machines can remain unblocked. You might then keep traffic from DMZ_3 into Servers_1 machines unblocked, because those machines are one less attack step (three steps) from critical machine DB_4. In other words, you can wait to see if an alarm is raised from the DMZ into Servers_1, at which point you block the vulnerable paths from Servers_1 to Databases.

An even more aggressive response to an alarm within the DMZ is to block outgoing traffic from the DMZ to vulnerable services in Servers_1 and Databases. Again, there is the potential for denial of service, but you still limit your response to vulnerable connectivity. Without attack graph analysis, the only response to a serious attack is to block all

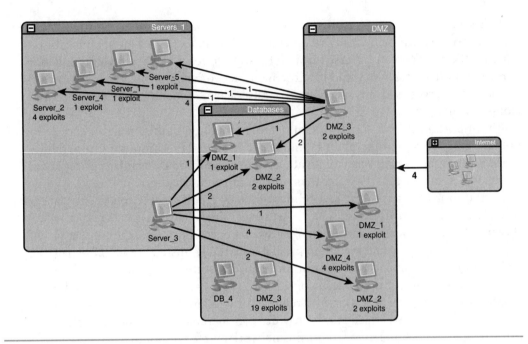

Figure 5-24 Attack prediction and response allows analysts to better determine risk

traffic from the DMZ, not just vulnerable connectivity. Furthermore, you can surmise that an alarm in the DMZ is follow-on from a missed intrusion from the Internet into the DMZ. This can guide further investigation into traffic logs into the DMZ looking for missed attacks, especially against the four vulnerable paths into the DMZ.

If an attack was detected within Servers_1 (such as from Server_1 to Server_2), a similar set of responses is indicated. As a precaution, you could block traffic from Server_3 to vulnerable ports on DB_1 and DB_2. But, blocking traffic from Server_3 into the DMZ is less indicated because it leads away from the critical Databases domain. Similarly, any alerts from Server_3 into the DMZ are lower priority, especially if they are not against vulnerable DMZ services.

Thus, provides a range of reasonable responses, ranked by severity or actual likelihood of attack. Here, severity is in terms of lying on critical vulnerability paths, especially close to critical assets, and its likelihood increases by causal correlation of alerts. Multiple options are available that enable you to fine tune responses as potential attacks unfold, based on proactive response plans.

SUMMARY

TVA attack graphs map all the potential paths of vulnerability, showing how attackers can penetrate a network. TVA identifies critical vulnerabilities and provides strategies for protecting critical network assets. This enables you to take a more proactive stance, hardening the network before attacks occur, handling intrusion detection more effectively, and appropriately responding to attacks.

TVA models the network configuration, including software, their vulnerabilities, and connectivity to vulnerable services. It then matches the network configuration against a database of modeled attacker exploits for simulating multistep attack penetration. During simulation, the attack graph can be constrained according to user-defined attack scenarios. From the resulting attack graphs, TVA computes recommendations for optimal network hardening. It also provides sophisticated visualization capabilities for interactive attack graph exploration and what-if analysis. TVA attack graphs support numerous metrics that quantify overall network security (for trending or comparative analyses).

By mapping attack paths to the network topology, you can deploy intrusion detection sensors to cover all paths using a minimum number of sensors. Attack graphs then provide the necessary context for correlating and prioritizing intrusion alerts, based on known paths of network vulnerability. Standardization of alert data formats and models facilitates the integration between TVA and IDSs.

By mapping intrusion alarms to the attack graph, you can correlate alarms into multistep attacks and prioritize alarms based on distance from critical network assets. Furthermore, through knowledge of network vulnerability paths, you can formulate the best options for responding to attacks. Overall, attack graphs offer powerful capabilities for proactive network defense, transforming raw security data into actionable intelligence.

ACKNOWLEDGMENTS

This material is based on work supported by the Homeland Security Advanced Research Projects Agency (ARPA) under the contract FA8750-05-C-0212 administered by the Air Force Research Laboratory/Rome; by the Air Force Research Laboratory/Rome under the contract FA8750-06-C-0246; by the Federal Aviation Administration under the contract DTFAWA-04-P-00278/0001; by the Air Force Office of Scientific Research under grant FA9550-07-1-0527 and FA9550-08-1-0157; and by the National Science Foundation under grants CT-0716567, CT-0627493, and IIS-0430402. Any opinions, findings, conclusions, or recommendations expressed in this material are the author's and do not necessarily reflect the views of the sponsoring organizations.

ENDNOTES

[1] S. Jajodia, S. Noel, B. O'Berry. "Topological Analysis of Network Attack Vulnerability." *Managing Cyber Threats: Issues, Approaches and Challenges.* V. Kumar, J. Srivastava, A. Lazarevic (eds.). Kluwer Academic Publisher, 2005.

[2] S. Jajodia, S. Noel. "Topological Vulnerability Analysis: A Powerful New Approach for Network Attack Prevention, Detection, and Response." *Indian Statistical Institute Monograph Series.* World Scientific Press, 2007.

[3] R. Deraison. *Nessus.* www.nessus.org. Last retrieved June 2008.

[4] R. Ritchey, B. O'Berry, S. Noel. "Representing TCP/IP Connectivity for Topological Analysis of Network Security." *Proceedings of the 18th Annual Computer Security Applications Conference (ACSAC),* 2002.

[5] eEye Digital Security. *Retina Network Security Scanner.* www.eeye.com/html/Products/Retina/index.html. Last retrieved July 2008.

[6] Foundstone. *FoundScan.* www.foundstone.com/us/index.asp. Last retrieved September 2008.

[7] MITRE, CVE: *Common Vulnerabilities and Exposures.* http://cve.mitre.org/. Last retrieved October 2008.

[8] Security Focus. *Bugtraq Vulnerabilities.* www.securityfocus.com/vulnerabilities. Last retrieved October 2008.

[9] Centennial Software. *Discovery Asset Management.* Last retrieved September 2008.

[10] Symantec Corporation. *Symantec DeepSight Threat Management System.* https://tms.symantec.com/Default.aspx. Last retrieved August 2008.

[11] L. Wang, S. Noel, S. Jajodia. "Minimum-Cost Network Hardening Using Attack Graphs." *Computer Communications,* 29(18), 3812–3824, 2006.

[12] D. Zerkle, K. Levitt. "Netkuang: A Multi-Host Configuration Vulnerability Checker." *Proceedings of the 6th USENIX UNIX Security Symposium,* 1996.

[13] R. Ritchey, P. Ammann. "Using Model Checking to Analyze Network Vulnerabilities." *Proceedings of the IEEE Symposium on Security and Privacy,* 2000.

[14] L. Swiler, C. Phillips, D. Ellis, S. Chakerian. "Computer-Attack Graph Generation Tool." *Proceedings of the DARPA Information Survivability Conference and Exposition II,* 2001.

[15] O. Sheyner, J. Haines, S. Jha, R. Lippmann, J. Wing. "Automated Generation and Analysis of Attack Graphs." *Proceedings of the IEEE Symposium on Security and Privacy,* 2002.

[16] P. Ammann, D. Wijesekera, S. Kaushik. "Scalable, Graph-Based Network Vulnerability Analysis." *Proceedings of the 9th ACM Conference on Computer and Communications Security (CCS),* 2002.

[17] S. Noel, J. Jajodia. "Understanding Complex Network Attack Graphs Through Clustered Adjacency Matrices." *Proceedings of the 21st Annual Computer Security Applications Conference (ACSAC),* 2005.

[18] R. Lippmann, K. Ingols, C. Scott, K. Piwowarski, K. Kratkiewicz, M. Artz, R. Cunningham. "Validating and Restoring Defense in Depth Using Attack Graphs." *Proceedings of the MILCOM Military Communications Conference,* 2006.

[19]S. Noel, S. Jajodia. "Managing Attack Graph Complexity Through Visual Hierarchical Aggregation." *Proceedings of the Workshop on Visualization and Data Mining for Computer Security (VizSec)*, 2004.

[20]W. Li. *An Approach to Graph-Based Modeling of Network Exploitations.* Ph.D. dissertation. Department of Computer Science, Mississippi State University, 2005.

[21]S. O'Hare, S. Noel, K. Prole. "A Graph-Theoretic Visualization Approach to Network Risk Analysis." *Proceedings of the Workshop on Visualization for Computer Security (VizSec)*, 2008.

[22]S. Noel, M. Jacobs, P. Kalapa. S. Jajodia. "Multiple Coordinated Views for Network Attack Graphs." *Proceedings of the Workshop on Visualization for Computer Security (VizSec)*, 2005.

[23]A. Jaquith. *Security Metrics: Replacing Fear, Uncertainty, and Doubt.* Addison-Wesley, 2007.

[24]*The Systems Security Engineering Capability Maturity Model.* www.sse-cmm.org/index.html. Last retrieved November 2008.

[25]M. Swanson, N. Bartol, J. Sabato, J Hash, L. Graffo. *Security Metrics Guide for Information Technology Systems.* Technical Report 800-55. National Institute of Standards and Technology, 2003.

[26]G. Stoneburner, C. Hayden, A Feringa. *Engineering Principles for Information Technology Security.* Technical Report 800-27 (Rev A). National Institute of Standards and Technology, 2004.

[27]Forum of Incident Response and Security Teams (FIRST). *Common Vulnerability Scoring System (CVSS).* www.first.org/cvss/. Last retrieved June 2008.

[28]L. Wang, A. Singhal, S. Jajodia. "Toward Measuring Network Security using Attack Graphs." *Proceedings of the ACM Workshop on Quality of Protection*, 2007.

[29]S. Noel, S. Jajodia. "Optimal IDS Sensor Placement and Alert Prioritization Using Attack Graphs." *Journal of Network and Systems Management*, 2008.

[30]Internet Engineering Task Force (IETF). *The Intrusion Detection Message Exchange Format (IDMEF).* www.ietf.org/rfc/rfc4765.txt. Last retrieved November 2008.

[31]ArcSight. *Enterprise Security Management.* www.arcsight.com/. Last retrieved October 2008.

[32]SourceForge. *Snort IDMEF Plugin.* http://sourceforge.net/projects/snort-idmef. Last retrieved July 2008.

[33]Sourcefire. Snort: *The De Facto Standard for Intrusion Detection/Prevention.* www.snort.org/. Last retrieved September 2008.

[34]P. Ning, Y. Cui, D. Reeves. "Constructing Attack Scenarios Through Correlation of Intrusion Alerts." *Proceedings of the ACM Conference on Computer and Communications Security*, 2002.

[35]S. Noel, E. Robertson, S. Jajodia. "Correlating Intrusion Events and Building Attack Scenarios Through Attack Graph Distances." *Proceedings of the 20th Annual Computer Security Applications Conference (ACSAC)*, 2004.

[36]L. Wang, A. Liu, S. Jajodia. "Using Attack Graphs for Correlating, Hypothesizing, and Predicting Network Intrusion Alerts." *Computer Communications*, 29(15), 2006.

[37]S. Noel, E. Robertson, S. Jajodia. "Correlating Intrusion Events and Building Attack Scenarios Through Attack Graph Distances." *Proceedings of the 20th Annual Computer Security Applications Conference (ACSAC)*, 2004.

Network Flows and Anomaly Detection

Today, network security engineers face a myriad of daunting conditions. They are tasked with protecting today's most critical asset—information—facing every possible threat and vulnerability while operating in a landscape of constant change. The business needs change, the network topology changes, the compliance regulations change, the threats change. Modern networks that are highly segmented and decentralized pose serious challenges to monitoring and securing your network the traditional way (with log analysis, SNMP/RMON probes, firewalls, and intrusion detection/prevention probes). Will it scale to provide the same level of coverage tomorrow as it does today while maintaining the same level of cost and manpower? How do you cover internal and external segments and not create a Frankenstein of its own in the process? What about the rest of that questionable server's traffic directed at or in your network? *It's usually what you don't see that gets you.* Today's security analysts immediately need the answers to these questions. With ever-increasing frequency, analysts, architects, engineers, and policy makers are turning to network flows to find the answers. Data flow has been said to provide the answers for the "Who? What? When? Where? and How?"

Expert systems, such as Intrusion Detection System/Intrusion Prevention System (IDS/IPS) probes, sort through the mountains of data they collect off the wire and do a good job detecting known threats. But, by nature, probes provide microanalytical data and can fail to provide the proper context, or broader view, of the problem (such as recognizing which computers the infected computer touched), which can lead to faster incident resolution. This chapter looks at network flows and the value they provide to help secure your network. Network data flow and its collection for network security analysis, specifically an emerging field called anomaly detection or behavioral analysis,[1] is also discussed.

Network flows and behavioral analysis are *not* meant to completely replace traditional IDS technologies; they fill the gaps that currently exist by monitoring their blind side. First, this chapter discusses flow technology and analyzes the different flow formats, their characteristics, respective datasets, and key fields. Next, it looks at device performance, data flow collection strategies, and how flow is used in the virtual environment. Finally, you learn about the usefulness of data flow for security and a new field called Network Behavior Analysis (NBA), which detects abnormal or anamolous traffic or host behavior on the network. This chapter ends by comparing flow-based monitoring versus traditional IDS/IPS, ending with a technology matrix that compares the three major sources of security event or telemetry data: IDS, syslog, and NetFlow/Internet Protocol Flow Information Export (IPFIX). The practical uses and benefits of network flows used for security are as follows:

- Near real-time network monitoring for troubleshooting and flow visualization
- Top talkers for any given time period
- Total network/application usage by user
- DoS, DDsS, worm, and botnet detection and mitigation
- Rich dataset of forensics data
- Threshold and policy-based rules and alerts and mitigation

IP DATA FLOWS

Just what is a network flow? An IP data flow is a unidirectional group of packets that share common characteristics. At its most basic level, a data flow contains source/destination Internet Protocol (IP) addresses, source/destination transport layer ports, IP, the ingress interface, and the Type of Service (ToS) field. Network flows, and NetFlow in particular, provide data that is macroanalytical in nature. Network data flow is metadata about a network transaction. This network-centric data is analogous to a cell phone bill; you see information about all the conversations without seeing their detailed transcripts.[2] The small but powerful data set (Netflow records are about 30 bytes each) offers a more multidimensional traffic analysis that is easier than what is accomplished with traditional probes or telemetry sources. As such, many network security practitioners are heavily relying on NetFlow to see which resources are communicating with each other.

At this time, Cisco Systems has, by far, the largest presence in the market because of its enormous install base and NetFlow's success. Cisco is so dominant that the underlying technology in NetFlow Export version 9 is on a standards track under the auspices of the IP Flow Information Export (IPFIX) Working Group, which is a member of the Internet Engineering Task Force (IETF). In addition to the standard data flow definition of a group of packets that share common attributes, the group further defines an IP data flow as "a set of IP packets passing an observation point in the network during a certain time interval" (RFC 3917, "Requirements for IP Flow Information Export"). Although flow technology has generally adapted to include modern functionality, such as Internet Protocol Version 6 (IPv6), Multiprotocol Label Switching (MPLS), quality of service (QoS), and multicast support, current flow technologies only account for IP-based traffic. Support for other protocols and future enhancements are provided with the extensibility of IPFIX/Flexible NetFlow.

These companies' devices support network data flows:

- **Cisco Systems**. NetFlow
- **Extreme Networks**. CLEAR-Flow and sFlow
- **Foundry Networks**. sFlow
- **Huawei Technology**. NetStream
- **Juniper Networks**. J-Flow, cFlowd (NetFlow v5)
- **Bluecoat Systems**. Packeteer-2

NOTE

In the spirit of objectivity, product manufacturers are only mentioned when their solutions are germane to the subject. For example, NetFlow is, and has been, a fundamental part of the Cisco Internetwork Operating System (IOS) for more than 10 years. Any discourse regarding that technology must necessarily include the company's name.

NETFLOW OPERATIONAL THEORY

NetFlow operations begin when an IP packet ingresses the interface of a NetFlow-enabled device, such as a router or Layer 3 switch. A metering process in the router captures the packet header and evaluates it for uniqueness against a common set of properties: the seven key NetFlow fields. If there is a match to an existing flow, the metering process generates a time stamp, applies any predefined input filters, and updates packet and byte counts in the associated flow record. If information in the packet header is unique, the metering process makes a new entry in the flow cache, based on the original set of properties. At this point, the new packet stream exists as a flow record in the cache shown in Figure 6-1.

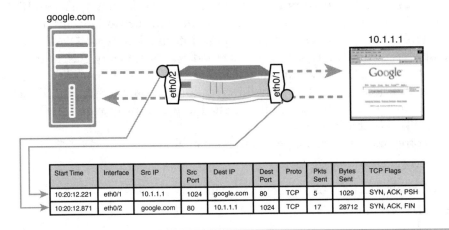

Start Time	Interface	Src IP	Src Port	Dest IP	Dest Port	Proto	Pkts Sent	Bytes Sent	TCP Flags
10:20:12.221	eth0/1	10.1.1.1	1024	google.com	80	TCP	5	1029	SYN, ACK, PSH
10:20:12.871	eth0/2	google.com	80	10.1.1.1	1024	TCP	17	28712	SYN, ACK, FIN

Figure 6-1   Netflow record in cache

Records in the cache are subject to continued monitoring by the metering process and are expired according to a set of timers. An inactive flow timer triggers expiration when the flow is idle for a default setting of 15 seconds, and the active flow timer expires records that have been active for a default setting of 60 minutes. For legitimate network transactions that last more than 30 minutes, flow records are recreated after expiration to capture the continuing packet stream. Flows that expire are not dropped; they are exported to a collector in a compatible data format for report creation and storage. Long flows never expire, because they are kept in the active cache until a FIN bit is seen or, in the case of User Datagram Protocol (UDP), the conversation represented by the flow expires. Active flow caches can be dumped (expired and exported) if using aggregation caches or if undesirable performance conditions develop on the exporting device. The exporter function traditionally uses the nonreliable UDP transport protocol to push records to a collector. The export function is represented in Figure 6-2.

As always, realization of certain benefits depends on whether a device has the correct hardware options and IOS release. An example is the MPLS feature set, which offers MPLS-aware NetFlow and MPLS egress NetFlow. They provide accounting and analysis functions at MPLS ingress and egress points, respectively. Because they are not available

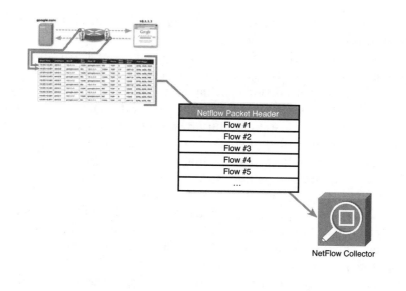

Figure 6-2 NetFlow export to flow collector

in all router models, plans to deploy this functionality might lead to unexpected financial costs in hardware and software upgrades. Always perform your due diligence audit when planning to deploy an enterprise-wide flow-based monitoring solution.

A MATTER OF DUPLEX

The Merriam-Webster Online Dictionary defines "duplex" as "allowing telecommunications in opposite directions simultaneously." This reference to full-duplex communication is a good way to explain that a single data flow (unidirectional) is one-half of a network conversation, which cannot characterize network activity or performance.[3] When unidirectional records unintentionally appear in a database that supports performance analysis, the validity of reports is questionable. Usage-based billing reports can still be valid, but only if the direction of collected data flows is uniform (in cases where the intended purpose is to monitor only at ingress or egress points). The more serious concern is in the realm of network security, where data flows can be used for anomaly detection. The unidirectional data flow attribute is an important concept to keep in mind when the goal is to understand the nature of network conversations. Deduplicating flows into unique host conversations for reporting and analysis requires correlation by special software. Depending on the system architecture, this function is performed by a collector or flow analyzer.

Flow-based monitoring in an enterprise network environment can, and will, produce multiple records (or flows) of a conversation as it traverses the network. This is practically unavoidable and not necessarily a bad thing, as long as the duplicate traffic is a small percentage and does not cause congestion on the network or flow collector. The flow collector or flow analyzer must deduplicate the superfluous flows from the entries it makes into its database(s). This is not a trivial task. Outside of the analysis algorithms, the deduplication function is the most important processing task for a flow collector or flow analyzer. If it is not done accurately, the fidelity of the entire dataset is in question. In short, it's garbage. It does not reflect what is actually going on in your network right now. Any security analysis performed on non-deduplicated data is a waste of time.

Some commercial flow analysis products also perform the additional step of combining the unidirectional flows into a data structure that represents the full two-way conversation. The level of efficiency in deduplication and creating bidirectional traffic streams is a critical component of data flow analysis tools. This step can also improve system performance and response time, because this extra processing step does not have to be performed each time a user queries for data flow. Even simple algorithms and analysis can take longer to complete because the correlation of the unidirectional flows must happen every time. This functionality can also negatively impact a solution's capability to scale. One true benefit of flow analysis is that it is passive and so lightweight that you can monitor your entire network with a small number of appliances. Consumers of commercial data flow analysis systems must evaluate software products carefully, with an eye toward features that address duplicates and other potential performance issues.

CISCO IOS NETFLOW AND FLEXIBLE NETFLOW

Cisco Systems devices currently switch packets from inbound interfaces to outbound interfaces by one or more of several methods: process switching, fast switching, Cisco Express Forwarding (CEF), and distributed CEF (dCEF). Monolithic NetFlow was also in competition as a path-switching and accounting technology. The CEF technology eventually was favored, but during this period, Cisco engineers recognized the value of the records created during the forwarding process, and NetFlow was reborn as an accounting technology. Since its inception in 1996, NetFlow has gone through several iterations of improvements and has been released in versions 1, 5, 7, 8, and 9. (Table 6-1 provides a brief summary of its versions.) NetFlow version 9 offers full extensibility with Flexible NetFlow, which means that the technology can capture almost any piece of desired network telemetry: traditional flows, device information, packet headers, flags, and even payload. Network data flow export is now so prevalent that it is offered on other Layer 3 network devices, such as firewalls, gateways/proxies, wide are a network (WAN) accelerators, and even some applications, such as VMWare.[4]

Table 6-1 NetFlow Export Formats

Export Format	Description
Version 9	Partial list of new and enhanced technology support and features: MPLS, Border Gateway Protocol (BGP) next hop, BGP autonomous system (AS), multicast, and QoS/Diff Serv fields.
	Flexible or Extensible NetFlow: All version 9 fields plus extensibility, which is the capability to define new fields. Templates, Layer 7 data, and even Packet Section Export for Deep Packet Inspection offer enhanced visibility.
Version 8	Export from aggregation caches, including a subset of version 5 data.
Version 7	Support for Catalyst 6000 Multilayer Switch Feature Card (MSFC).
Version 5	BGP AS information and flow sequence numbers introduced.
Version 1	The initial format. Not recommended for use today.

NetFlow is a free software application that performs packet monitoring, cache management, and data export in Cisco networking devices. It is embedded in the Internet Operating System (IOS) and is based on IOS path-switching technology.

NetFlow has the following key components:

- **NetFlow Cache Size**. Timeout values, sampling rate, and more
- **Flow Record**. Has definitions for NetFlow Key Fields and Non-Key Fields
- **Exporter**. Has the export destination, transport protocol, and export format
- **NetFlow Export Format**. Most current release is version 9

Cisco uses a seven-tuple model for out-of-the-box fields and, with the release of Flexible NetFlow, it offers an additional set of Non-Key Fields that are configured according to unique requirements. Flow records are created with key fields, while nonkey fields are simply added to the record for export. Enhancement work has provided an ample amount of new fields to identify, track, and export records for Layers 2–7 of the OSI Model. Table 6-2 describes NetFlow Fields.

Table 6-2 NetFlow Fields

Field	Usage Examples
NetFlow Key Fields	
1. Source IP Address 2. Destination IP Address	In addition to detailed host conversations and top talkers reports, source-destination pairs enable aggregation of multiple flows into a single report. For example, a report can be created to show utilization levels for the entire source or destination network.
3. Source Port 4. Destination Port	Transport layer protocol information can be aggregated to report network transport types by an entire source or destination network.
5. Protocol Type˙	A field in an IP header that describes the next level protocol. It is defined by the Internet Assigned Numbers Authority (IANA) codes for registered protocol types. Some examples are 1 (ICMP), 6 (TCP), 17 (UDP), and 88 (IGRP). Numbers 140–252 are unassigned as of April 18, 2008. Packet and byte counts can be tallied to create utilization reports by IP-based protocols.
6. ToS Byte (DSCP)	ToS information can measure service levels for data, voice, and video traffic.
7. Router or Switch Input Interface	The logical interface description from the SNMP object ifIndex. A major benefit to this field is that, in reports, it associates an interface name that is recognizable with values from other NetFlow keys fields.
NetFlow Non-Key Fields	
1. Time Stamp	Determines packets/bytes per second.
2. Source IP Address 3. Destination IP Address	Source and destination IP address of the next-hop AS.
4. Source IP Address 5. Destination IP Address	Source and destination IP address of the next-hop router.
6. TCP Flags	Flags examine TCP communication.

˙Some documents list this as the Layer 3 Protocol Type, which is somewhat ambiguous.

Network and device performance are also important considerations for the collection part of an analysis strategy. In many cases, acquisition of source data happens over WAN links on a scheduled basis, with the exception of real-time alerts. This is another area where data flow excels, because of its light footprint of 1.0–1.5 percent additional network overhead. However, when calculating an acceptable amount of network-management overhead, the answer is unique to each network. The best scenario is where baseline statistics—response times, capacity, and traffic types—are analyzed in light of business goals.

Furthermore, data-collection requirements differ according to the type of network and objectives under consideration. Internet Service Providers (ISPs), who usually have little control over the sources of network utilization, are less likely to use RMON-like[5] data than their colleagues in enterprise network management. Exceptions exist, most notably for network security, but it is unusual for ISPs to restrict the use of legitimate application traffic. This is not so for the enterprise network manager, who can keep the highly sensitive servers containing confidential information from running certain potential nefarious applications or port usage; for example, unauthorized connections to access the subnet where your ESX servers use VMotion. VMotion is the unencrypted data communication that ESX servers pass back and forth to optimize network efficiency. Currently, VMotion cannot be encrypted at any level and is, therefore, the target of many attacks.

sFLOW: MORE DATA, BUT LESS FREQUENCY

sFlow is an embedded packet-sampling technology that has its origins in Hewlett Packard (HP) switching products. In the early stages of development, HP partnered with a company called InMon Corporation on a large-scale network-integration project that was the result of a corporate merger. As the story goes, HP had the basic technology and InMon had the network analysis expertise, so the two companies agreed that InMon take the lead in a multivendor initiative that would put the technology to work in the industry at large. Other vendors that support sFlow are Alcatel, Allied Telesis, Dlink, Extreme Networks, Foundry Networks, HP, NEC, and Hitachi.

The description of sFlow as an '"embedded" sampling technology is important because it points out one of the main differences between sFlow and NetFlow: sFlow is a hardware-based solution, and NetFlow is a software-based solution. sFlow is considered a hardware product because the protocol is programmed into application-specific integrated circuit (ASIC) chips during the manufacturing process for switches and routers. sFlow generation is performed by an ASIC in hardware rather than at the device operating system (OS) level; therefore, overhead computing power typically is not a threat to cause performance degradation on the device. InMon licenses the technology for free, which is why so many Cisco competitors support it. Like NetFlow, generating sFlow data for export is easy; the challenge is to collect it in a network-friendly manner and then create meaningful reports through comprehensive correlation and analysis. There is no doubt that InMon Corporation, who sells analysis products, saw that at an early time (hence the free licensing).

Besides being hardware-based, sFlow and NetFlow have other differences that are noteworthy for security monitoring. sFlow provides more detailed packet data but is almost always sampled. sFlow provides the full headers, the TCP flags, and up to the first 80 bytes of the payload. Having TCP flags and payload allows expert systems to perform analysis that is more like deep packet inspection, such as deciphering OS information and detecting tunneling of applications or applications running across nonstandard ports. As Table 6-3 shows, sFlow's key fields comparatively map to NetFlow's to include such data points as source/destination Layer 2 and Layer 3 addresses, AS next hop, VLAN tags, and MPLS labels.

Table 6-3   sFlow Key Fields

Source/Destination (Src/Dst) MAC Addresses	NAT Translation	802.1X User Name or RADIUS/TACAS User ID
Src/Dst VLAN (802.1q and 802.1p)	Sampling process parameters (rate, pool)	Interface statistics (SNMP)
Src/Dst IPv4 addresses	Physical input/output ports	Snippet of captured packet (payload)
Src/Dst IPv6, IPX, or AppleTalk addresses	Src/Dst prefix bits and next-hop subnet	Communities and local preferences
MPLS labels, Tunnel data, and other information	Source AS, source peer AS, and destination AS path	URL information

The issue of network management overhead exists for sFlow implementors, just as it does for shops that use other data-collection tools. Cisco has made NetFlow available in hardware on certain devices, but it remains mostly a software solution with several compensating mechanisms. For example, NetFlow can aggregate certain flow records on the device before export to save resources. NetFlow also uses statistical sampling to reduce the number of records that are exported. sFlow does not perform aggregation at the device level, but it does include statistical sampling techniques for data management. sFlow has two methods for sampling: packet-based sampling and time-based sampling, which can be usurped by code that the ASIC manufacturer might have included. A more in-depth discussion of sampling comes later in this chapter.

INTERNET PROTOCOL FLOW INFORMATION EXPORT (IPFIX)

Network data flow analysis has become so pervasive that the IETF has adopted the NetFlow framework as a proposed standard. RFC 3917 defines a new flow format called Internet Protocol Flow Information Export (IPFIX). IPFIX offers numerous improvements, such as an option for a reliable transport mechanism while ensuring future relevance of the technology through extensibility. Table 6-4 lists a brief comparison of NetFlow and IPFIX terminology.

Table 6-4   NetFlow and IPFIX

Cisco Name	IPFIX Name	Description
Switching Path	Observation Point	Interface ingress (or egress) point.
NetFlow Monitor	Metering	Packet header capture, time stamps, flow record maintenance, timer values, and sampling rate.
NetFlow Key Fields	Information Model Uses the words "attributes" and "properties" interchangeably to describe model components.	Matching specifications: Source/destination IP addresses, source/destination transport layer port numbers, IP, ToS byte, and input logical interface. The IPFIX specification (RFC 3917) does not differentiate key fields and nonkey fields. The reference says that compliant implementations must somehow meet all specifications.

Table 6-4   NetFlow and IPFIX

Cisco Name	IPFIX Name	Description
NetFlow Export Format version 9	Data Model	NetFlow Export: IP, UDP, and NetFlow header information; flow record format. The IPFIX specification (RFC 3917) states only that the Data Model must be extensible.

IT'S A VIRTUAL WORLD

One of the most exciting developments in IT is virtualization. Although existent in mainframes and supercomputers for some time, virtualization is becoming mainstream and is transforming the datacenter in drastic ways. Widespread adopters of virtualization technology see substantial savings in operational costs and use the speed of reviving a server by using snapshots (such as a disaster recovery plan). But if not carefully planned, designed, and implemented, virtualization can be a nightmare in the loss of visibility and the subsequent complexity of troubleshooting workflows where traditional tools and methodologies don't work as they once did. How do you obtain the same level of visibility into your virtual environment as you have in your physical environment? Where do you now draw the boundaries for organizational responsibilities and separation of duties? Many traditional approaches to information security simply do not smoothly transfer to the virtual world. However, in the virtual world, NetFlow provides the visibility to help solve these problems.[6]

A physical network of any size usually has several good chokepoints for inspecting traffic. This makes it fairly easy to deploy probes. This is not true of virtual networking, which typically has multiple physical network interface cards (NICs), virtual switches, and virtual NICs, as shown in Figure 6-3.

One option is to monitor traffic egressing the NICs of the physical server onto the physical network. This might be acceptable depending on your expectations and requirements, but it's possible that you see only a small portion of the actual traffic that your virtual servers create: the ones that exit the physical server. What about the traffic that is internal to the physical box? How do you monitor virtual machine (VM)-to-VM traffic or traffic that is internal to the physical server and never gets to the *physical* network (see Figure 6-4)? Chances are this is the bulk of your traffic, especially if tiered applications are virtualized in the same physical host. Today, visibility into virtualized server traffic is a big problem for security practitioners.

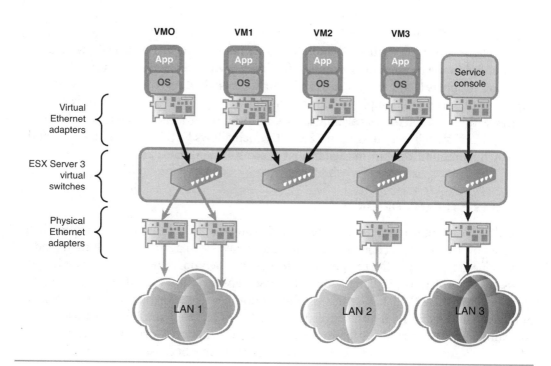

Figure 6-3 Standard virtual environment

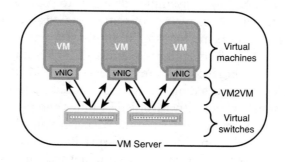

Figure 6-4 Internal communication between VMs

Exporting flows at the virtual switch layer is a simple solution to this problem. It provides full visibility into all the traffic that traverses the virtual switch but stays inside the same physical server as well as the traffic that egresses the physical NIC onto the physical network. The other plausible options are either implementing an IDS deployment in a virtual environment or virtual firewalls, both of which still have the same drawbacks experienced in the physical environment. Beginning with ESX Server version 3.5, VMWare supports NetFlow export from its virtual switches. As with traditional NetFlow export, configuration is simple—identify a few global configuration commands and turn on the feature on each interface you want to monitor. Integration of the Cisco Nexus 1000V virtual switch is an option in ESX 4.0, which allows NetFlow configuration (and all switch configurations) from the familiar Cisco IOS command line.

ENDLESS STREAMS OF DATA

Global views of Internet traffic have repeatedly shown at least one common reality: Not all data flows are created equal. Dozens of studies have been performed to understand how to measure and predict the performance of so much nondeterministic data. IP data flows are slightly more predictable on enterprise networks, and even that depends on several factors. The IETF has dedicated many resources to performance measurements, and has shared its findings and suggestions in RFC 3432, "Network Performance Measurement with Periodic Streams," and RFC 2330, "A Framework for IP Performance Metrics." These documents (and others) address sampling, because it is a critical factor in managing network data collection.

Traffic streams vary in duration, and usage patterns can demonstrate extreme variances in utilization levels. Adding nonsampled data flow to your production network typically adds an additional 1.5–2.0 percent of traffic. Analysis products must account for all traffic patterns with some mechanism for limiting the amount of data that is collected, which is an issue that affects both syslog message forwarding and NetFlow data export. Algorithms for expiring records from the flow cache add an additional level of protection from sudden, unexpected increases in monitored traffic. The key difference is that log message transmission is mostly throttled by filters and priority levels, while data flow collectors depend on sampling as part of the packet-monitoring function. Different sampling methods are available on different platforms. Random sampling collects one of every nth packet off an interface. Deterministic sampling accounts for one in every nth packet. Depending on the network architecture and the objectives at hand, sampling is often done on core and distribution devices and augmented with full flow capabilities from the edge devices. This reduces the overall amount of monitoring overhead on the network and provides as much fidelity of data and network visibility as possible. The trade-offs between the visibility provided by the data flow and the cost of acquiring it are best analyzed in light of business goals, objectives, and any technical obstacles that exist.

As previously mentioned, a carefully chosen sampling method and a good overall design ensures that network resources are not overwhelmed by increasing demands. The idea is to capture a sample dataset that closely represents the entire population of network flows and accordingly scale the devices. Sampling reduces network-management overhead and keeps device internal resource usage at acceptable levels. It also minimizes hardware specifications for collectors that might otherwise require more disk space and more robust system resources. Skeptics who doubt the validity of reports that are based on sampling must note that statistical sampling is not unique to collecting network metrics.[7] For example, during U.S. presidential elections, pollsters interview about 1,200 people in a demographic group to characterize a population of millions of registered voters. The important thing is using a method to select the sample in such a way that it represents the population. In the case of voters, random sampling methods are used. In the case of network traffic, representative data can be obtained more easily by simply collecting data at regular times.

Figure 6-5 and Figure 6-6 show examples of the impact of sampling. Figure 6-5 is based on SNMP polling of a router interface for utilization statistics. Each line represents the percentage of available bandwidth used at specific moments in time over a 31-day period. The rate of data acquisition, also called a polling or sampling interval, is equal to the display rate in the graph. To produce this graph, samples were read every minute, which is a highly granular interval by most standards. The total number of records in this example is 44,640.

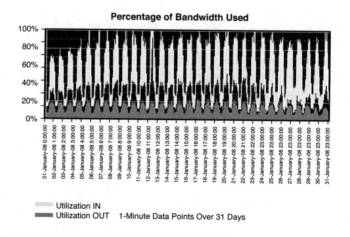

Figure 6-5 Data points in one-minute intervals

Figure 6-6 is for the same interface and time frame, but the sampling interval is hourly. The base calculation is the same for both graphs, which is that the system uses the delta value between the current and last sample to create an average rate of utilization for that data point.

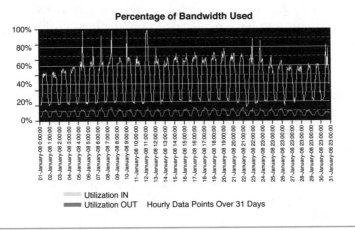

Figure 6-6   Data points in hourly intervals

An network engineer can tell by the hourly averages that this is a busy circuit and that further investigation is appropriate. The total number of records in this example is 744. In this scenario, the main issue is the different amounts of network overhead and device resource usage (memory) that were required by each method. Sampling works well to minimize resource contention while retaining the value of the data for analytical purposes. Most default sample rates in sFlow-capable equipment range from 1:2048 to 1:8096. This is acceptable for capacity planners, but obviously not for a security practitioner. Studies and mathematical calculations show that sample rates as high as 1:512 typically provide enough analytical value to be deemed worthy of the expense of collecting it. Sample rates as low as 1:128 can still be accurate for detecting threats, malware, and misuse, while keeping monitoring overhead at acceptable levels. Choose your sampling rate in light of supporting business goals and within the technical constraints of your network.

BEHAVIORAL ANALYSIS AND ANOMALY DETECTION

Network behavioral analysis is sometimes called Network Behavior Anomaly Detection (NBAD) and is broadly defined as a multidimensional statistical and behavioral analysis of a host's activity (or *behavior*) on the network and correlation/comparison to historical data. Implied in this type of analysis is the notion of prior activity, or baseline, of "normal" host activity. Historical flows are stored, and current flows are analyzed within the context of historical host activity. Behavioral anomalies are detected as current host activity is gauged and compared to a statistical baseline, or threshold, of known historical activity for that host. Also implied in this type of analysis and detection are protocol anamolies. Enterprise-quality commercial NBAD products also perform algorithms to ensure compliance with defined RFC protocols and applications.

Behavioral analysis does not depend upon reverse-engineered bit-matching pattern signatures and, thus, it excels at detecting zero-day threats for which a signature is not available. In addition, the multidimensional, data-mining nature of NBAD technologies also excels at detecting worms, viruses, and botnets. When data flow is stored in relational databases, it can be mined to quickly produce an audit trail for forensic or real-time investigations. In Figure 6-7 (from Lancope StealthWatch), data flow quickly determines the source and extent of a worm outbreak.

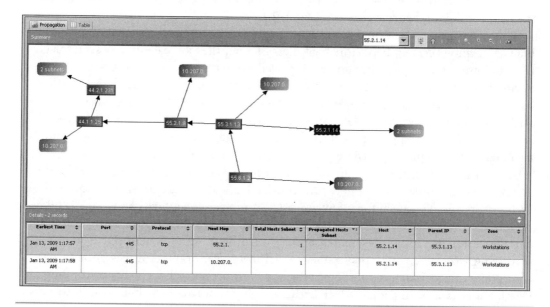

Figure 6-7   Lancope StealthWatch shows a worm outbreak.

Data flow can also easily produce "top talkers" for a given time period or provide detailed forensic analysis of previous activity. Data flow goes a step further than traditional SNMP polling for top talkers, because data flow lets an operator drill down to see the nature of the conversation—what ports are in use, how much data is being transferred, even which ports carry the traffic and what class of service (CoS) it is in. This typically can result in faster problem resolution. Because of the macroanalytical nature of data flow, flow analysis can be performed more quickly and efficiently than with packet capture data, and it is more comprehensive in the data it provides. No other telemetry technology in use today can match the "bang for bit" that data flow provides.

In commercial products, data flow builds behavioral profiles or baselines of "normal" behavior. A baseline needs to include as many relevant datapoints as possible, but it typically includes observations of the amount of traffic, ports used, number of clients connected, number of servers connected, and even high and low traffic periods. Policies can then be set to allow for threshold-based alarming. This permits an alarm to generate whenever a host's behavior exceeds a certain percentage relative to its previous activity or an absolute threshold set by an administrator. The top graph in Figure 6-8 shows a host's traffic patterns over the last 14 days, whereas the bottom graph in Figure 6-8 shows the same data extrapolated to the alarm settings for that host or group of hosts. The shaded area shows the threshold allowed for this behavior. (This host would have alarmed for the traffic spikes on February 25 and March 2.)

This detection type is valuable for detecting both internal and external threats. Most malware exhibits certain behaviors regardless of what they are called; they scan for victims and use random ports or tunnels over well-known ports to ultimately deliver a payload that contains malicious or stolen data. Behavioral analysis can detect this, because these activities are not normal for the host in question. As for an insider attempting to access sensitive data, anomaly detection systems also detect this type of activity. Behavioral analysis can detect even the smallest changes in a host's behavior. In a changing threat landscape, these capabilities are a huge asset.

As mentioned in Chapter 3, "Intrusion Detection Systems," denial of service (DoS) attacks are the Achilles' heel of network security. DoS attacks are most common against Web servers and have been for many years. (Although a DoS attack can victimize all servers, the most infamous attacks target high-profile Web servers, including online e-commerce and gambling sites, banks, and even Domain Name System [DNS] root servers.) A DoS attack attempts to starve a victim's server of its resources. Attacks are commonly categorized as either logic attacks or resource attacks. The historical Ping of Death is an example of a logic attack because a ping is normally 64 bytes, but it was discovered that, by sending a computer a specially crafted ping with a packet size of 65,535 bytes, the target computer crashed. Sending a ping packet of that size is illegal in traditional networking protocol standards, but if the packet is fragmented and then reassembled

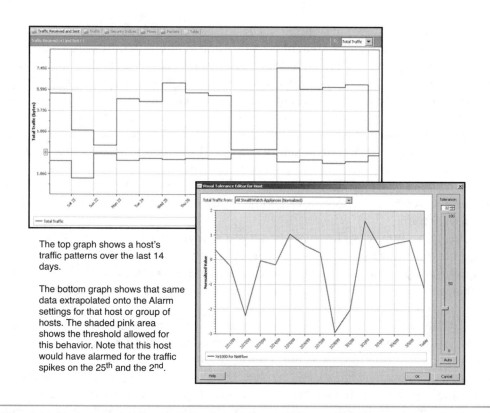

The top graph shows a host's traffic patterns over the last 14 days.

The bottom graph shows that same data extrapolated onto the Alarm settings for that host or group of hosts. The shaded pink area shows the threshold allowed for this behavior. Note that this host would have alarmed for the traffic spikes on the 25th and the 2nd.

Figure 6-8   Lancope StealthWatch's alarm settings

by a victim, is creates a buffer overflow that causes the system to crash. A resource attack saturates the victim by sending large numbers of requests to overwhelm the CPU, memory, or bandwidth in an attempt to lock out the machine from legitimate use or cause it to crash. A distributed DoS (DDoS) attack uses many source machines to bombard a target at once. A distributed reflected DoS attack (DRDoS or RDDoS) is a variation of the DoS attack.

NOTE

DRDoS attacks are outside this book's scope, but I am geekishly fascinated by it and, therefore, want to throw it in for good measure.

The DRDoS attack typically involves sending some type of forged requests to a very large collection of real computers that responds to the requests. (Any response legitimately helps, even if it is a port-closed response.) The attacker spoofs the source IP address in the forged requests and sets it to that of the unwitting victim. After the initial request launches, the responses are directed to the target, and it begins to flood the target with true responses. The term *true responses* is used because, typically in a DoS attack, the source IP addresses are spoofed. Typically, when an attack is spoofed, the defensive strategy is easy: Blackhole all IPs that cannot provide reverse path. That might or might not be possible in the time that it takes for the attack to reach a victim's threshold of processor power or bandwidth. Reverse path forwarding (RPF) attempts to guarantee that all traffic can be legitimately translated back to a valid network (meaning there is a computer on the other side of the conversation). DoS attacks that use SYN, UDP, and ICMP are the protocols where IP spoofing is used because the lack of a three-way handshake found in TCP traffic.

In fact, a DDoS attack can bring down not just a single server, but entire networks, or even an entire country's Internet access if enough traffic is sent. On April 27, 2007, a sophisticated, well-orchestrated, and "alleged" Russian DDoS attack targeted the country of Estonia, crippling some of the country's most notable IT sites, including banks, parliament, ministries, and newspapers.

Although most people think DoS attacks exclusively aim for Web servers, DoS attacks are most harmful when they target essential network devices and services, such as DNS servers, routers, and firewalls. Detecting a resource-exhaustive DoS attack against a server can usually be done fairly easily by checking the server's performance counters and noticing any abnormally high utilization issues. Typically, a server can report service request numbers, and when those peak to levels where performance is impacted dramatically, a DoS attack or the slashdot effect must be suspected.

Stateless packet filtering (whether a router or a firewall) is ineffective in halting DoS attacks, because the filter itself is overwhelmed by the attack. It does not have the capability to dissect the packets and find a distinguishing difference between good and bad traffic. A stateful packet filter (whether a router or firewall) that is resilient can drop obviously malformed or illegitimate packets and help survive short-term and low-intensity DoS attacks, but even these filters get overwhelmed in a well-orchestrated attack, especially when bandwidth becomes a limiting factor. To survive a DoS attack, you must plan in advance. Plans can include the following items:

- Reserving an alternate block of IP addresses for critical devices and enabling them to be switched when an attack is detected
- Separating routing systems for key servers or network devices
- Providing the capability to reroute legitimate traffic
- Implementing excessive load balancing capabilities

- Praying that your bandwidth pipe is bigger than the attacker's and can sustain the attack while maintaining normal business
- Working intimately with your ISP to identify and quickly blackhole possible DoS attacks
- Deploying anti-DDoS attack appliances
- Purchasing an ISP or datacenter's service offering for DDoS defense

Most of these strategies are self-explanatory except for, possibly, the final two. Cisco offers an anti-DDoS appliance called CiscoGuard, which diverts suspicious traffic to itself for "cleaning." For the device to adequately clean traffic, it must learn what normal traffic is and differentiate it from abnormal traffic, so the device must undergo a learning process. CiscoGuard can either be initiated manually or by an activation alert from a network attack device (such as the Cisco Traffic Anomaly Detector). Depending on the circumstance, there are three protection levels: Analysis Protection, Basic Protection, and Strong Protection. Analysis Protection simply monitors the traffic seeking out the malicious DoS attack. After it encounters anomalous traffic, it escalates to either Basic Protection or Strong Protection. Basic and Strong Protection ultimately work the same by authenticating traffic sources to eliminate antispoofing and antizombie traffic, but as their names imply, they just denote intensity levels. The previously mentioned cleaning process is the application of traffic filters, including User Filter, Bypass Filter, Flex-Content Filter, and Dynamic Filter.

Nearly every ISP or datacenter that I have worked with offers some comparable DDoS-defense service. As expected, the service caters to companies, institutions, and agencies that require high availability when downtime is catastrophic to their bottom line. Datacenters commonly rely on a combination of two technologies to guarantee their DDoS defensives, including anti-DDoS sensors and NetFlow. (Apologies for this tangent from network flow, but an elaboration on DoS was worthwhile and conveniently circles back to data flow.) The monitoring of ingress/egress traffic through a reasonably substantial datacenter requires extremely powerful appliances because of bandwidth capacity. Only a handful of vendors offer tools of that magnitude, and they are tremendously expensive. Arbor Network offers an appliance called PeakFlowSP (SP stands for service provider) that includes the capability to handle said traffic. After an attack is identified, the datacenter tries to cleanse the traffic to mitigate the attack or simply reach back and designate more bandwidth to "ride out the storm." Between the two technologies, datacenters and ISPs can usually avoid experiencing extensive downtime.

Organizations of every size can start using data flow. The flows themselves are usually a free feature of your Layer 3 device. Several good freeware tools are available today that you can use. *Flow-tools* is a free NetFlow collector that can provide a great starting point for readers interested in flow-based monitoring. Many commercial vendors allow free downloads of trial software for 30-day use. In addition, utilities can mimic the flow-cache generation functionality in the Layer 3 devices. Utilities such as *ntop* and *nprobe*[8] can generate NetFlow from nonflow-capable equipment from a network tap or SPAN port. This is great starting point to familiarize yourself with what flow monitoring looks like, because you can begin to comprehend the NetFlow metering process and the nature of the data flow itself. After you understand this, it makes sense to look at the many powerful commercial flow-based solutions on the market today, if you have a need beyond the capabilities. Many vendors now exist in this space, and their product offerings, price points, and capabilities vary. It does not make much sense to invest a lot of money in a solution until you fully understand what you get in return.

COMPARE AND CONTRAST

Syslog, IDS, and NetFlow techniques all share the ultimate end goal—to protect your network from malicious or inappropriate traffic—but each has its own specialty. This section focuses on the differences between each intrusion detection technology, and this chapter finishes with a definitive back-to-back-to-back matrix.

IDS AND NETFLOW

Today, businesses and organizations operate in an unpredictable world. Network operations and security teams operate in a complex and rapidly changing environment. They need to robustly support a mobile workforce, Voice over IP (VoIP), encryption, and Web-facing applications.

NOTE

IDS and encryption don't mix well. Host-based IDSs usually have no problem with encryption because, at the layer the IDS monitors traffic, the encryption has been unencrypted. Network-based IDSs (NIDS) typically cannot monitor traffic because, as you expect, the traffic is encrypted. The exception is if the NIDS owner loaded all the defended hosts' certificates on the NIDS, giving the device the proper decryption keys. Although this exception does exist, it is rarely configured as such. The SnortSSL project is working on a SSL decryption plug-in (www.ssltech.net/sfssl/index.html).

Yet, security teams are expected to keep everything secure and rapidly roll out new services, all while watching what's around the corner. Making matters worse (in the context of this chapter) is the inadequate performance of IDSs in combating changing attack vectors. The problem is twofold: threat signature updates and IDS resources.

SIGNATURE UPDATES

IDS threat signature updates cannot keep up with the amount of new threats, a situation that is worsening with the rapid growth of Web-facing applications. On most days, anyone can see the problem firsthand by navigating to a security Web site that has updated information for threats and signatures.[9] The exercise is simple: Observe the RSS feeds that show the latest threats and navigate to feeds that show the latest signatures (normally listed by technology and vendor). It is not unusual to see a delta of three or four days in favor of the threats. That is not the product manufacturer's fault; it is simply a technology limitation. Screenshots of a popular security Web site by Computer Network Defence, Ltd. (United Kingdom) are examples in Figure 6-9, Figure 6-10, and Figure 6-11.

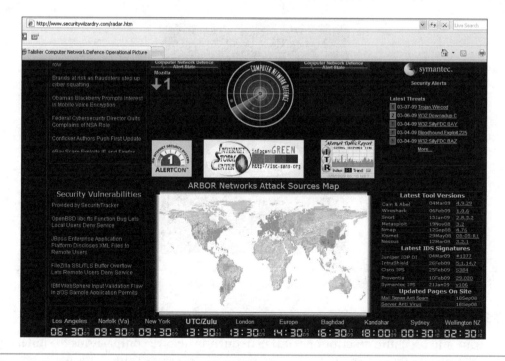

Figure 6-9 Computer Network Defence operational picture

Figure 6-10   Symantec security alerts

Latest Tool Versions		
Cain & Abel	02Jul08	4.9.16
Wireshark	30Jun08	1.0.1
Nmap	28Jun08	4.68
Snort	16Jun08	2.8.2.1
Kismet	29May08	08-05-R1
Nessus	12Mar08	3.2.1
Metasploit	27Jan08	3.1
Latest IDS Signatures		
Juniper IDP DI	01Jul08	#1202
Cisco IPS	02Jul08	S342
IntruShield	26Jun08	4.1.29.3
Symantec IPS	12Jun08	v97
Proventia	10Jun08	28.070
Updated Pages On Site		
Recruitment		12 Dec
Network Access Control		23 Sep
Endpoint Device Security		23 Sep

Figure 6-11   Latest security tool versions and latest IDS signatures

IDS SYSTEM RESOURCES

Magazine and brochure descriptions of IDS frequently involve comparisons to sniffers or RMON probes because, to a point, they are essentially the same thing. This is a good analogy for getting the connectivity concept across to a technical audience, but they do not always elaborate. In pure sniffing mode, sniffers basically just watch the data pass until an engineer commands it to capture something. RMON probes, and sniffers with RMON capabilities, do more; they actually periodically sample the data and then drop the samples into buckets to be polled by a network-management system. In other words, the probe makes the data available, but some other intelligence does the hard work. IDSs also monitor the data, but they are constantly looking up perceived threats in a resident signature database—that adds an extra load on system resources. Sometimes, legitimate threats fail to make it that far because, during heavy traffic periods, packets are dropped on the inbound side.

Installing multiple IDSs can mitigate hardware limitations to a certain degree, although that is usually done to address concerns about not monitoring all the important circuits. This brings up another possible shortcoming, because not all management systems can correlate events that are related, but on separate links. Some network managers rate-limit traffic on the wire to get around IDS limitations, but from the user's perspective, this can adversely affect performance.

By contrast, NetFlow does not suffer the effects of decoding and parsing superfluous packets as they traverse the network, and it does not rely on signature updates. That does not mean that using NetFlow for intrusion detection is entirely without hurdles. For example, the switching fabric in a router is capable of monitoring heavy traffic flows because that is what it is designed to do, but that can translate into huge volumes of data for exporting and storage. The solution is to configure a sampling interval so that the NetFlow monitoring function only inspects, and subsequently, exports a representative sample of traffic flows.

Short-term, highly granular data collection with a subsequent change to sampling is a standard technique for developing a baseline for future comparison. After a 30-day baseline period, the NetFlow analyzer[10] (Cisco or third-party) has enough data to have "learned" what is normal on the network and what is not. This anomalous behavior is seen from a global perspective without overtaxing bandwidth or collector resources. Furthermore, a good implementation strategy has baseline data collection done on a round-robin schedule to prevent concurrent demands for large sums of data.

IDS and NetFlow technologies also differ where network impairments are concerned. For various reasons, a certain amount of occasional packet loss and other error conditions are expected over time. Error conditions, particularly those that result in dropped packets, can cripple defense technologies, like IDS, that must compare data streams with known threat signatures. With the possible exception of a sustained circuit outage, NetFlow, as a defense technology or for managing performance, is not affected by the occurrence of network impairments.

With the release of NetFlow Export version 9, Cisco now offers features specifically designed to support MPLS networks. MPLS-Aware NetFlow and MPLS Egress NetFlow are feature add-ons that offer enhanced analysis functions. This is another area where IDS technology can fall short, especially for service providers or enterprise managers who build and maintain their own MPLS networks. Customers who purchase MPLS services from a provider are in a different situation, because MPLS terminates at the customer edge (CE) router. In that situation, placing an IDS between the local network and CE router is an acceptable solution.

The passive monitoring technology that IDS appliances employ has proven its worth over many years, owing much success to talented industry engineers who use it to solve complex problems. But, the proliferation of MPLS services means that IDSs have more data to parse, so there is an increase in demand for local platform resources. As an IP packet is switched through an MPLS network, up to six labels can be added to packets that IDSs must inspect. That same packet adds nine non-key fields for NetFlow monitors to process. Experience in the user community shows that IDSs do not handle MPLS labels well, which show up in product performance. Through the use of templates for non-key fields, and by the nature of its design, NetFlow monitoring and export functions show little or no performance degradation as MPLS and other features are added.

Things that might cause performance problems for both products—IDS and NetFlow—would create a constant new issue for IDS technology and an occasional issue for NetFlow. This again relates to the microview of traditional passive monitoring (IDS) and the macro-view of flow-based monitoring.[11]

Figure 6-12 shows a basic intrusion detection architecture with other types of network-management instrumentation. The associated labels (numbered 1–3) outline related concepts.

Figure 6-12 shows connectivity for a theoretical company that deploys a double firewall configuration and an intrusion detection appliance. The firewall at position 2 is a router that supports firewall services and was chosen as part of the security plan, because most attacks come from inside. The concern was for production devices in the demilitarized zone (DMZ) and instrumentation that is on the same LAN. The devices are a Cisco Security Monitoring, Analysis, and Response System (CS-MARS) and a NetFlow collector, which, for this example, also provides the analyzer function.

The CS-MARS unit serves as a collector for IDS events and, if permitted through the private side firewall, for other IDSs and syslog collectors. The MARS takes data from numerous sources, including third-party syslog collectors, as long as log messages are sent in a compatible format. Both the MARS and the NetFlow collector have the capability to send alerts to a network security management (NSM) appliance that are based on data collected from their respective sources. For this particular design, if the IDS detects an anomaly, it forwards events to the MARS, which processes the data and then sends an alert to the NSM. The same is true for the NetFlow collector, which likely sends a

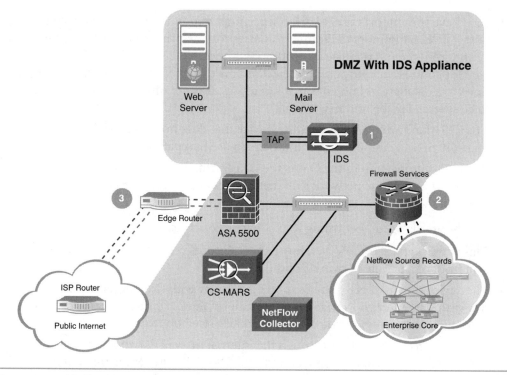

Figure 6-12 NetFlow for intrusion detection

legitimate alert before the MARS, because its data source—NetFlow Export Records—is not dependent on threat signatures. It would still be less active because it is not prone to false positives, as is the case for IDS monitoring.

The firewall and IDS architecture shown in Figure 6-12 have three components for review:

- **Position 1**. DMZ connectivity for an IDS system
- **Position 2**. Path of NetFlow record source data
- **Position 3**. Public-side connection to the Internet

The style of review for the components in Figure 6-12 is a simple statement of facts that either refute or support subjective comments about each technology. Equipment in the position labeled 3 is referenced in notes for positions 1 and 2.

View the area labeled 1 regarding the following concepts:

- In keeping with its basic design principle, the IDS at position 1 is only monitoring the connection to which it is physically attached (in this case, by a hardware tap).

- IDSs have two important network connections: a monitoring port and a control port. The IDS monitors the traffic from users on the private network (near position 2) and from the Internet (near position 3). The IDS is either using its historical database for comparison purposes to detect anomalous traffic patterns or is comparing flows to a database of known threat signatures. It is not unusual for threat signatures to be several days behind new threats.

- The IDS monitoring port is a passive device that does not have an IP address, which makes it virtually impossible for attackers to use that path to access the IDS platform.

- Because of its location in the DMZ, the IDS system cannot be used to support devices on the private network side (near position 2) except for traffic destined for a server in the DMZ.

View the area labeled 2 regarding the following concepts:

- This path is typical of how NetFlow Export Records reach a collector or analyzer that is in front of a private network firewall.

- The device shown directly adjacent to 2 is a router with firewall services. If UDP datagrams are blocked, NetFlow cannot support anomaly detection for data flows entering from the public side of the ASA 5500 (one hop from 3).

- If NetFlow records can pass through the internal firewall (2), they can be used for anomaly detection on the connection to the DMZ. The benefit is that potential anomalies are compared to historical global data flows, which makes NetFlow-based detection more accurate than signature-based IDS detection.

SYSLOG AND NETFLOW

NetFlow analysis reports and syslog messaging can be considered as complementary, particularly if the goal is to track device and network performance. Although NetFlow is network-centric, syslog messages are more event-oriented and device-oriented. They are source data for reports that describe a range of operational status information. But, the nature of syslog-based reports depends largely on the originating device type, and it is the job of an expert system to parse and correlate this data with other events to provide the proper context. The more correlation, the better, but this requires smart, distributed software agents or a lot of processing power. Among the most valuable reports for log messages are those that originate from security devices, such as the Cisco PIX firewall. Cisco advertises that PIX log files can be used for network troubleshooting and forensics, but the reality is more akin to security analysis for network connections.

In general, syslog messages are not particularly useful for data flow analysis purposes or for characterizing basic network performance. From an architectural standpoint, designing and implementing syslog devices, relays, and collectors on an enterprise-wide scale is inherently more difficult than implementing NetFlow on the same scale. Except for firewalls and other security devices, and if the granularity of syslog messages is not a requirement, a better complementary approach might be to use router-initiated events for proactive notifications, and NetFlow for analysis and anomaly detection.

Cisco network management best practices suggest the value in syslog messages, but they are clear that SNMP and RMON event generation and alerting need to be in use on all infrastructure devices. Neither type of internal router monitoring uses an excessively great amount of system resources or generates any significant network overhead. This is because there is no pulling or pushing of information at scheduled intervals. A huge benefit to this strategy is a reduction in database management and maintenance, and it complements NetFlow and syslog products. However, syslog messages and SNMP polling of network infrastructure remain valuable as feeds into an expert system, like a Security Incident Management (SIM/SIEM) system such as Cisco MARS or Arcsight.

The main challenges to SIM technology are providing near real-time visibility and scaling to process 100,000+ events per second. Syslog—and SNMP to some extent—remain too vendor-specific to allow for cost-effective scaling beyond these limits. The SIM must quickly parse intelligence from syslog feeds from many devices, in slightly differing formats, while trying to sustain a high processing rate and a low error rate. This is not an easy task. (These two SIMs in particular can also receive NetFlow as a source of data.)

Organizations that choose to use both NetFlow and syslog messaging in support of the same network need to know that they support messages for some of the same events. Table 6-5 shows a list of redundant syslog-NetFlow messages.

Table 6-5   Redundant NetFlow and Syslog Messages

Syslog Message	Description	NetFlow Event ID	NetFlow Extended Event ID
106100	Generated whenever an ACL is encountered.	1. Flow was created (if the ACL allowed the flow). 3. Flow was denied (if the ACL denied the flow).	0. If the ACL allowed the flow. 1001. Flow was denied by the ingress ACL. 1002. Flow was denied by the egress ACL.
106015	A TCP flow was denied because the first packet was not a SYN packet.	3. Flow was denied.	1004. Flow was denied because the first packet was not a TCP SYN packet.

Table 6-5   Redundant NetFlow and Syslog Messages

Syslog Message	Description	NetFlow Event ID	NetFlow Extended Event ID
106023	When a flow was denied by an ACL attached to an interface through the access-group command.	3. Flow was denied.	1001. Flow was denied by the ingress ACL. 1002. Flow was denied by the egress ACL.
302013, 302015, 302017, 302020	TCP, UDP, GRE, and ICMP connection creation.	1. Flow was created.	0. Ignore.
302014, 302016, 302018, 302021	TCP, UDP, GRE, and ICMP connection deletion.	2. Flow was deleted.	0. Ignore. > 2000. Flow was deleted.
313001	An ICMP packet to the device was denied.	3. Flow was denied.	1003. To-the-box flow was denied because of configuration.
313008	An ICMP v6 packet to the device was denied.	3. Flow was denied.	1003. To-the-box flow was denied because of configuration.
710003	An attempt to connect to the device interface was denied.	3. Flow was denied.	1003. To-the-box flow was denied because of configuration.

TECHNOLOGY MATRIX

One characteristic that is clearly shared by IDS, syslog, and network flow is their modular nature, particularly for reporting and analysis. All three technologies mainly serve as data sources that rely on third-party or manufacturer platforms to collect and format data for presentation. An exhaustive search might likely yield some document or Web page where there are claims of reporting capabilities not included here. For example, there is an extensive list of reports in the Cisco User Guide for Cisco Security MARS Global Controller, Release 5.3.*x*, that can cause confusion if a reader is accustomed to working with flow-based and RMON products, where Top *N* reports are commonly used. The Top Reporting Devices report in the MARS User Guide is a report based on device events and has nothing to do with traditional Top *N* Talkers reports, which are based on RMON or NetFlow data.

The Technology Matrix shown in Table 6-6 only includes features and functions that physically operate over networks and are related in some fashion to data flow analysis. It is based on standard industry practices for performance management and network analysis, and with any potential impact to performance and security in mind. The notation Not Applicable (N/A) is avoided, where possible.

Table 6-6   Technology Matrix

Technology Matrix	IDS	Syslog	Network Flow
Top Host Conversations	X	X	✓
Top Network Talkers	X	X	✓
Network Applications Report	X	X	✓
Network Protocols Report	X	X	✓
Packet Filtering	X	✓	✓
Reliable Transport	✓	✓	✓
Event-Driven Export	N/A	✓	✓
SNMP Alerts	✓	✓	✓
Network Flows Visualization	X	X	✓
User Account Security	✓	✓	✓
Encrypted Payload	✓	✓	✓
Network Capacity Planning	X	X	✓
Usage-Based Accounting	X	✓	✓
Network Forensics	✓	✓	✓
Configurable Record Export	N/A	✓	✓

Of the three listed technologies, network flow was specifically designed for these purposes and clearly fits into the description. IDS and syslog are included as products with overlapping functions. As such, the technology matrix is not an apples-to-oranges comparison; it is an informational tool for a concerned technical community.

SUMMARY

Data collection and reporting systems generally have several things in common, even if their end use differs or the underlying technologies are dissimilar. At a rudimentary level, network flow, syslog, and IDSs are simple data-collection tools that share the same basic vulnerabilities while exhibiting technology-specific limitations. Where applicable, all three technologies address vulnerabilities with encryption for moving report data from one point to another and user authentication protection for appliances and servers.

Unauthorized access to source data devices covers a wide range of concerns, such as hackers using them to launch attacks, which can involve using collected source data, or stealing information. In the context of network security and performance, the source of syslog and network data flow is the infrastructure itself, specifically routers, switches, and management servers.

Processes that secure potentially sensitive information and govern access rights to network infrastructure devices should include data monitors and collectors. Research through any manufacturer's support mechanisms does not show that there are more vulnerabilities in their network flow, syslog, and IDS products than in their routers, switches, and firewalls. The larger question might involve the performance aspect of collecting statistics for data flow analysis. Network overhead traffic needs to be understood before and during its time on the wire, and redundancies in the functions that management systems perform must be discovered and eliminated.

Network data flow in general, and NetFlow in particular, is mature and praised as a critical data source for network security and performance monitoring. The proposed IPFIX standard and associated work by the marketplace will continue to build on NetFlow's utility and promises to merge the best aspects of RMON, SNMP, and probe technology into one single platform. One of the main obstacles to its success is creating and exporting all that great telemetry data while keeping up with blazing wire speeds. The other is the amount of intelligence and correlational capabilities that can be built into an expert system and delivered cost effectively by vendors in the market.

Today's dynamic threat landscape and business challenges require a flexible, lightweight monitoring solution and telemetry. They also need a more holistic or network-centric view into the network ecosystem to quickly spot problems and quickly solve them *before* users are impacted. In depth, multidimensional flow analysis provides the platform for NBAD and has many uses for traditional network operations teams. In its current most widely deployed usage, flow analysis is also the best near real-time comple-ment to perimeter IDS/IPS systems, but provides more network-centric type reporting and analysis, in a more efficient, scalable, and sustainable model.

ENDNOTES

[1]Anomaly detection and behavioral analysis are used interchangeably in this chapter.

[2]This is not completely true of sFlow, which can provide up to 80 bytes of payload data. However, flow telemetry is still a smaller and more uniform data set than any other telemetry technology can provide.

[3]Performance in the sense of end-user response times during normal transactions.

[4]VMWare is partially owned by Cisco, and it offered trial support of the NetFlow v9 export in its ESX Server 3.5 version.

[5]"RMON-like" is a common way to describe application, protocol, and host traffic reports, regardless of the underlying technology.

[6]At this time, VMWare supports NetFlow only, because Cisco owns approximately 10 percent of VMWare.

[7]An excellent paper on this subject is available at http://pages.cs.wisc.edu/~estan/publications/elephantsandmice.html.

[8]For more information, visit www.ntop.org.

[9]Try www.securitywizardry.com/radar.htm.

[10]NetFlow collector and analyzer functions can be on the same server or on separate hardware platforms.

[11]Cisco advertises NetFlow as a passive monitor in spite of its export function, but the term is historically associated with appliances and software agents that inspect the entire data flow.

Web Application Firewalls

7

The Internet redefined how we communicate and interact with each other. Thanks to high-speed, always-on connections, businesses and consumers can instantly connect and share resources on a level that mirrors what local area networks (LANs) provided a decade ago. In addition to a broadband connection, this new model for sharing data requires a Web server running Web applications that process and deliver requested resources.

Although traditional network-based Intrusion Detection System (IDS) solutions can detect and protect against generalized threats that target Web servers, they cannot be depended upon to expertly understand attacks against a Web application. It is important to note this difference. As a result, the Web Application Firewall (WAF) concept was devised to fill the gap between the security threats associated with operating a Web server and the capabilities of an IDS and the programming team to quickly repair buggy code. This chapter examines why WAFs are beneficial to a comprehensive security solution (assuming there are Web applications and despite any development lifecycles that might exist) and discusses some of the key elements you find in a WAF.

"When you know nothing, permit-all is the only option. When you know something, default-permit is what you can and should do. When you know everything, default-deny becomes possible, and only then."

Dr. Dan Geer, Economics and Strategies of Data Security

WEB THREAT OVERVIEW

Before you can understand the value of a WAF, you must have a general working knowledge of how malicious hackers can attack a Web site and the more common threats/risks associated with this genre of application. This section outlines the format of a typical Hypertext Transport Protocol (HTTP) request, where in the process an attacker can inject his own data, and the top ten Web application threats defined by the Open Web Application Security Project (OWASP).

In a normal situation, a Web user makes a request, via her browser, to a resource located on a Web server at a remote location. This request is either a simple uniform resource locator (URL) or a more complex POST or GET request that contains variables that the server can parse out and use to create dynamic content to be delivered back to the browser. Because this process needs to work across a wide range of devices, operating systems (OSs), browsers, and programs, the request format is highly standardized into a collection of protocols (for example, HTTP, XML, HTTPS, and so on).

In the case of a typical HTTP request, only a few items are required, as the following code illustrates:

```
GET / HTTP/1.1
Host: www.google.com
```

However, by no means is this all that an HTTP request can include. The following are the full headers requested by Firefox:

```
GET / HTTP/1.1
Host: www.google.com
User-Agent: Mozilla/5.0 (Windows; U; Windows NT 5.1; en-US; rv:1.9.0.5)
Gecko/2008120122 Firefox/3.0.5 (.NET CLR 3.5.30729)
Accept: text/html,application/xhtml+xml,application/xml;q=0.9,*/*;q=0.8
Accept-Language: en-us,en;q=0.5
Accept-Encoding: gzip,deflate
Accept-Charset: ISO-8859-1,utf-8;q=0.7,*;q=0.7
Keep-Alive: 300
Proxy-Connection: keep-alive
Cookie:
NID=19=LWH0mZNAX517tLm1zQBdKc55MBOkXjxTfHcxEdwH9NTJaWLgYfGglP2Ji16h45r76aDJcqrKluXxr_X
zJETi1Zm45jVw_mQ1RiZp8dFji1SOigJ-HulNC9MBpOSG_RVO;
PREF=ID=3caba30d3a03f500:TM=1232592795:LM=1232592795:S=b3Yz2CoeVFRPz-fm
```

In this request, note that numerous header fields and associated values contain data that might be processed by the Web server at Google. With this many variables coming to a Web server or Web application, what are the chances that there might be an exploitable bug?

The question then becomes this: How can an attacker gain control over the data passing from a Web browser as it passes to and from the target Web application? The most popular method to do this is via a proxy program that runs on an attacker's local system. A commonly used proxy program that is useful for this type of in-process data massaging is Burp.

Burp allows someone to capture a request of any properly configured Web client (such as a browser) and pause it before it is sent to the intended destination. With the HTTP request held momentarily, an attacker can alter various pieces of information within Burp. For example, he can modify form field values passed as POST variables or header information, such as cookie contents (see Figure 7-1).

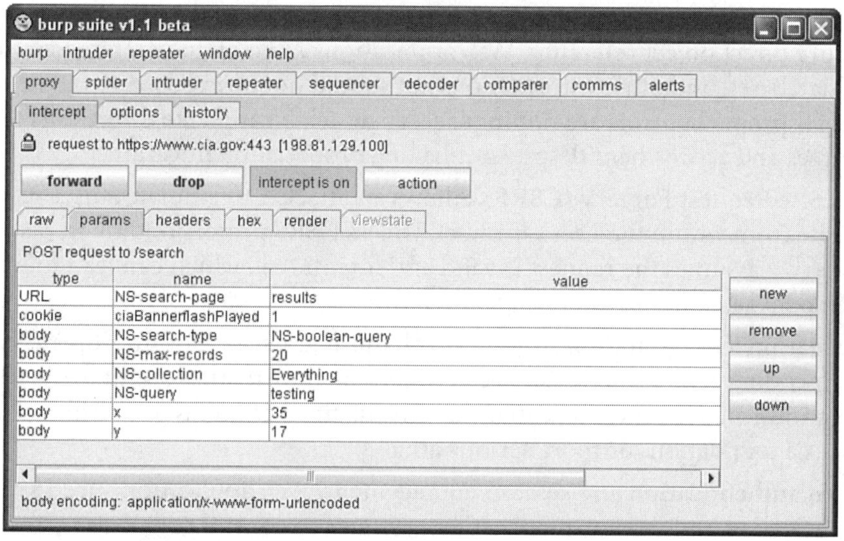

Figure 7-1 Burp capturing request to CIA.gov

Figure 7-1 shows the Burp proxy in action. Each field listed can be easily altered, and fields can be added or removed. The point is that an attacker can easily place himself in between the browser and the Web application, thus giving him unfettered control over what is passed to and from the Web server.

The final question becomes this: What can an attacker do with this kind of control? To answer this question, refer to the 2007 OWASP top-ten list. Although this is in no way comprehensive, it provides you with a starting point and an overview if you are unfamiliar with the many threats facing Web applications:

- **Cross Site Scripting (XSS).** Occurs when unfiltered data is accepted by the Web application and then returned as HTML/JavaScript to the target's browser, which then parses the content as if it was a valid part of the request's results. Common abuses are session hijacking and site defacement.

- **Injection flaws.** Most common attack is through SQL injection attacks, which target unfiltered SQL requests that include one of the variables passed to the Web server. Common abuses are data theft, account insertion, and authentication bypass.

- **Malicious file execution.** An improperly programmed Web server can be tricked into including code or data from remote servers. This gives an attacker the ability to execute his own code on the Web server, which can grant him access to the file system and more.

- **Insecure direct object reference.** Web applications often include references to local files, databases, and other information that should not be exposed to public direct access. If proper controls are not in place, an attacker can make direct calls to the resources and access them despite not having proper authentication.

- **Cross Site Request Forgery (CSRF).** Allows an attacker to emulate a user request to a Web site from within the user's browser. Unless CSRF protections are in place, the Web server assumes the request is valid and intentional, which can lead to hijacking of personal accounts, privacy theft, and more.

- **Information leakage and improper error handling.** Because of improper configuration or coding errors, applications can often leak information about file location, system information, and more that can give an attacker access to sensitive data or serve as a foundation for more serious attacks.

- **Broken authentication and session management.** Web applications need strong authentication and session-management systems to control resources. An attacker can exploit logic flaws, poor encryption schemes, or improper system configurations to gain unauthorized access to other users' sessions and their data.

- **Insecure cryptographic storage.** Web developers often fail to properly secure incoming data, such as sensitive user information. Attackers can find and bypass poorly implemented encryption schemes to access this sensitive data.

- **Insecure communications.** By default, all HTTP traffic is passed as plaintext data, which can be viewed by anyone with a sniffer. Unfortunately, Web developers do not realize this or take the threat seriously.

- **Fail to restrict URL access.** A Web server's resources need to be accessed with the correct URL. It is common for Web developers to rely on this form of obfuscation to hide sensitive parts of a Web site.

This list summarizes the top ten threats as defined by the OWASP 2007 list. Many other threats exist, all of which are the focus of the WAF. You can be sure that any WAF vendor worth his weight knows these threats in some detail.

WHY A WAF?

A traditional IDS examines packets as they enter a network and uses various pieces of information from these packets to determine if a potential threat exists (see Figure 7-2). Typically, this process involves monitoring for anomalies in traffic flow and/or pattern matching the packets against a known database of threat patterns. Although this functionality is great, it is usually not enough to properly protect a Web server running complex Web applications.

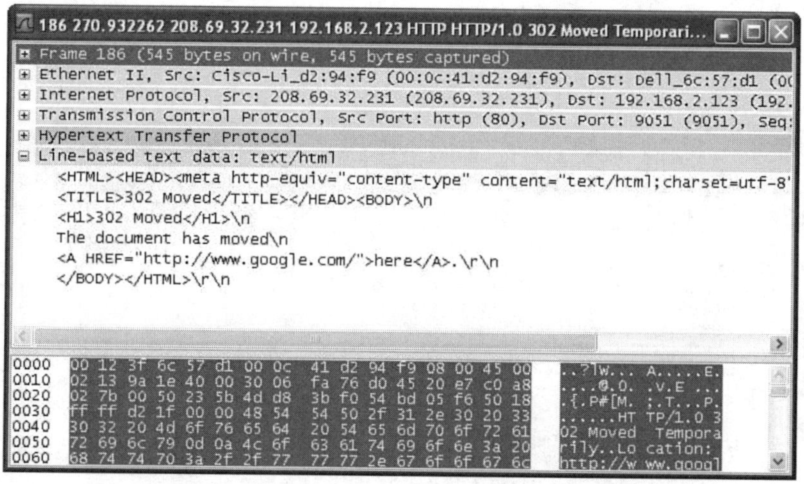

Figure 7-2 Packet as plain text

A Web application represents a scary situation for any administrator because it potentially combines sensitive information, internal access, and custom application code that tend to not be thoroughly tested for security problems. Given such statistics as "there is one bug per thousand code lines," it is not surprising that an estimated nine of ten Web sites have a security vulnerability. Compound this with the fact that Web applications are constantly updated makes them a moving target to properly test and validate. Overall, it can be a security nightmare.

Although an IDS deals with known generalized patterns, such as some XSS and SQLi strings, your average Web application can be completely unique and, as such, the IDS has no known patterns, for your proprietary application logic and associated security threats. For example, your Web application might be sensitive to the input received in the userid URL parameter; how could an IDS know that www.example.com?userid=65535 is acceptable, but www.example.com?userid=65536 causes an out-of-bounds array access and leads to an application crash?

Second, many Web applications pass information over a secure and encrypted connection by using the Secure Sockets Layer (SSL) protocol (see Figure 7-3). Given that many administrators do not have in-depth knowledge of SSL public/private keys, chances are that even if an IDS can see the traffic, it won't parse the data because it is encrypted. Although this protects valid traffic from sniffing, it also provides an attacker with the perfect tunnel through which she can send her attacks. A WAF, on the other hand, sits between the decryption process and the resource request, which gives it full access to the unencrypted content.

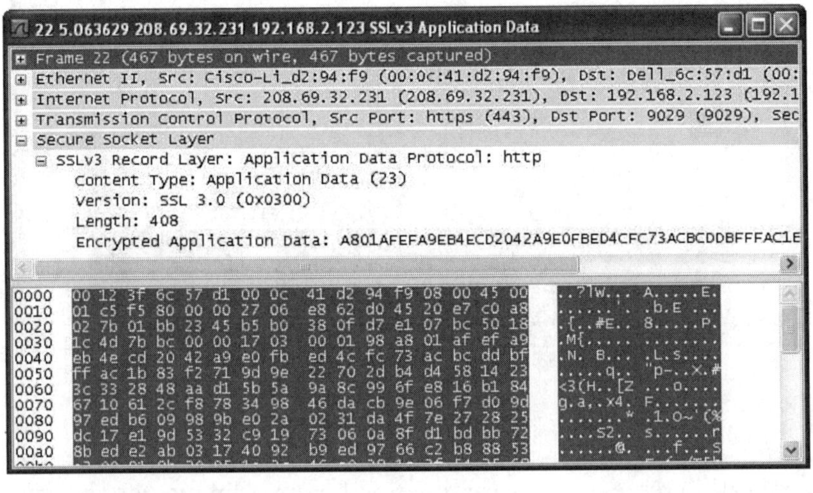

Figure 7-3   Same packet protected with SSL

In summary, a WAF is a valuable security solution because Web applications are too sophisticated for an IDS/Intrusion Prevention System (IPS) to protect. The simple fact that each Web application is unique makes it too complex for a static pattern-matching solution. A WAF is a unique security component because it has the capability to understand what characters are allowed within the context of the many pieces and parts of a Web page. Combine this with SSL encrypted data, and a network-based IDS/IPS is essentially worthless to protect the applications running on a Web server.

WAF PROTECTION MODELS

A WAF solution is like IDS/IPS that is designed to only detect and protect against a specific threat. By designating all the WAF's resources to two main protocols (HTTP/HTTPS), the solution can ignore everything but Web-related threats. This includes OS level attacks, third-party application vulnerabilities, and more that slow and complicate network IDS management. Second, because a WAF is more focused on a particular problem, it can be designed in several ways that give it more power and insight into to what is actually happening on the Web server. As a result, with regard to Web traffic, the heuristics and intelligence of a typical WAF is sophisticated.

To properly navigate its way through the many types of requests that enter a Web server, a WAF can take several modeled approaches to filtering traffic: user permission-based access control, centralized authentication, negative security, positive security, virtual patching, and output filtering. Each approach has its strengths and weaknesses, as the following sections detail. Fortunately, many WAFs permit combining these models into a custom solution that meets the specific and unique needs of a Web site operator.

POSITIVE SECURITY MODEL

Web applications are complex programs. Combine this with the fact that the typical Web server has several Web applications operating at any one time, and an attacker's landscape is broad. A positive security approach attempts to protect these applications by creating a fingerprint of what is acceptable; it essentially allows only "known good" traffic to pass. These fingerprints are built either statistically over a period of time or by performing a more direct benchmark to create direct fingerprints of acceptable requests.

This solution has many advantages and many disadvantages. First, a WAF designed to use this approach is fairly accurate when it comes to detecting an attack. However, at the same time, such a solution is more likely to generate false positives, especially as the WAF learns what is acceptable. To put it another way, a WAF running a positive security approach is like a paranoid security guard who automatically assumes that everyone he doesn't recognize is malicious.

Ironically, this paranoia also means that such a solution is bound to catch previously unknown (or zero-day) attacks. For example, it is highly likely that a positive security approach will detect a SQL injection worm, such as the one that infected hundreds of thousands of sites between 2006 and 2008. Because SQL statements do not look like valid application values received from users (hopefully), the following example is flagged as malicious even though the majority of the SQL command is encoded:

```
/search.asp fldSearch=12;DECLARE%20@S%20NVARCHAR(4000);SET%20@S=CAST(0x4400450043004C0
0410052004500200040005400200076006100720063006800610072002800320035003500290020C0040004
3002000760061007200630068006100720028003...%20AS%20NVARCHAR(4000));EXEC(@S);--
```

In fact, there are several characteristics to this real, truncated SQL injection attack that a positive security WAF might flag as suspicious: the length might be excessively long for that URL parameter, the inclusion of special characters that were not expected, and the overall data not fitting the expected pattern for data to that particular URL parameter.

Finally, a positive security WAF does not need to be updated in the same sense as an IDS. No updates are needed if a new exploit is found, and it does not need to regularly have its signature file updated. However, as previously mentioned, the positive security model requires extensive training to make it effective, which takes much up-front time and energy.

NEGATIVE SECURITY MODEL

By far, the most common system used to detect malicious code is the negative security model (also called the "block known bad items" approach). Antivirus programs, fire-walls, and IDSs all use this method to prevent known malicious code and/or known suspicious connections from passing through its filter. The reason for this is that creating a program to monitor for and detect known problems is relatively easy, because (by definition) everything is already known. For the most part, it is a matter of scanning data and alerting a user when a match is found, which is similar to the IDS signature-matching operation.

Although these systems are easy to develop, several other features of the negative security model can be seen as positive, depending on who you are. First, they help promote the subscription as a service model and all but guarantee that a company can continue to earn income by offering a product. This helps keep your vendor in business and, as a result, keeps your WAF up to par. For example, it is possible to create an antivirus program that works without subscriptions but, at the same time, after that product saturates market share, repurchasing is useless, thus killing the income flow.

Second, false positives are uncommon. This is because each signature can be tested thoroughly and a collision between a string of bytes in a file and a well-selected signature is fairly rare.

However, the relatively minimal disadvantage of relying on signatures is that someone must create them, and they must pass through each device that hosts the software. In addition, a negative security model does not detect unknown threats. If an attacker derives a new version of a malicious attack or exploit, the filter might not detect the malice because the new version does not match any of the known fingerprints in the filter's database. (That being said, the negative security model solution quickly spots known attacks and behaviors.)

VIRTUAL PATCHING MODEL

Over the last decade, a slow shift has occurred in how security bugs are reported and resolved. Early on, security researchers decided that software and hardware vendors had little interest in quickly fixing their problems. To help pressure these vendors into spending more time keeping their customers safe, the same security researchers started to publically post information on these bugs. (The process has been dubbed full disclosure.) This action worked, and it is the system currently in place. Although many believe this resulted in more secure software, a side effect is that everyone knows about the bugs, including malicious attackers. Because the public details often contain enough information to exploit a bug, it is trivial for an attacker to create an exploit program and use it against unpatched systems. Often, attackers create and use these exploit programs before organizations fully deploy the patch for a bug (assuming that a patch is available); thus, many security professionals feel that fully disclosed security problems give attackers the upperhand.

Therefore, to remedy this situation, a unique solution was developed: virtual patching. This concept allows an IDS/IPS administrator to install a custom filter to prevent an unpatched system from being exploited by tweaking the incoming/outgoing data as configured. After a patch is released and installed, the custom filter can be removed.

Unfortunately, and just like a traditional IDS/IPS, virtual patching requires an administrator to have the exploit code to properly test the solution, or the patch has to be generic. Ironically, for as much as having the exact code to test the bug out with is valuable, using a generic patch can be more effective, especially if the server/application might have other similar bugs. For example, if you install a patch to block all strings with `DECLARE%20@S%20NVARCHAR(4000)`, which is part of one particular SQL injection attack payload, the filter also catches all other SQL attacks that use those limited characters. In this case, installing a generic virtual patch can provide a longer lasting benefit than a carefully constructed targeted patch.

OUTPUT DETECTION MODEL/CONTENT SCRUBBING

The three other detection models all examine incoming requests for potentially malicious content. This prevents an attacker from ever getting his malicious request to the
Web server. However, given the shortcomings previously mentioned with the other models, it is completely possible that an attacker can subvert the filters and protections with
an unknown exploit or by encoding/obfuscating his attack so it does not match any
known attack fingerprints. This is where the output detection approach can be valuable.

Specifically, output detection filtering scans all outgoing data for suspicious content as
it leaves the Web server. Things such as credit-card numbers, social security numbers,
raw/unexecuted application source code, bulk database table dumps, and other sensitive
data are detected and blocked, which mitigates the exposure. This is similar in operation
to data leakage protection (DLP) systems. In addition to these sensitive pieces of information, output filters can detect error messages, which normally provide attackers with
clues that aid them in successfully attacking the Web application. For example, SQL
injection attacks typically involve an apostrophe, which can be encoded in the attack
request several different ways:

- `'`
- `%27`
- `Char(39)`
- `&apos;`
- `&#39;`
- `\\'`
- `&#0000039`

If a WAF fails to detect one of these variations, and the Web application is vulnerable
to SQL injection in a manner exploited by that variation, the application can produce an
error message that resembles the following:

```
DataLayerAPI error '80040e14'
Unclosed quotation mark after the character string ''.
```

If an output detection system is in place that is configured to detect this specific error
message, it prevents the error message from returning to the attacker. In addition, it
might rewrite the response to make it look like the error never happened. Hiding the
error messages removes the visual confirmation that an attacker or automated tool
might look for to know if their exploit worked or the application is vulnerable. Without
confirmation, they might conclude that the application is not vulnerable. However, note

that output detection does not actually prevent the exploitation of the security vulnerability—it just hides the results. For certain types of "blind" attack methods, visual confirmation of the results are not necessary. Therefore, output detection does not significantly mitigate vulnerabilities by itself; it is useful only as an additional layer of defense when combined with one of the other models.

WAF POLICY MODELS

After a WAF is placed on a network, it must be tuned to the details and behaviors of the Web applications that will be protected. Unlike traditional IDSs, which solely rely on a prepopulated general threat signature list, WAFs provide some other options when it comes to creating a signature/behavior database that is exclusive to the protected Web applications.

LEARNING

As previously stated, a WAF solution is tied to the particular Web application it protects. Because subscription-based services are out because of the impracticality of a third-party knowing the specific application details, the WAF must rely on another source of information. Ultimately, there is no better or more reliable source of obtaining a rule set than by placing the WAF in a secure environment and letting the software monitor create a database of what constitutes acceptable behavior. In other words, a WAF can learn by watching trusted activity from a trusted source.

VULNERABILITY ASSESSMENT FEEDBACK

Even if a WAF builds a comprehensive rule set from a trusted learning session, chances are high that something will be missed. For this reason, it is best to use information gathered from a vulnerability assessment (VA). Basically, an automated tool, professional service, or manual assessment can run against the Web application to find vulnerabilities, and you can use the resulting information to configure the WAF to protect against known problem areas in the application.

MANUAL ENTRY

There will always be a case where a developer or Web site operator wants to proactively restrict access to a specific resource. This might be access to an entire subdirectory, subdomain, file type, or any number of other files, folders, or situations. As a result, manual configuration is a valuable method of creating rules and policies for any WAF. Manual modification of autogenerated rules is also common, because often, the autogenerated rules must be tweaked to loosen or restrict the rule's coverage and sensitivity.

MODSECURITY

According to Forrester, ModSecurity is the most widely used WAF. It is open source, stable, documented, tenured, and it is fairly simple to install and work with. It also is integrated into numerous other WAF solutions. Simply put, your chances of encountering ModSecurity in the real world are high.

ModSecurity was created by Ivan Ristic, who simply (as he puts it) wanted a program to "...monitor what's going on in my [Web] applications." From there, it grew and Breach Security eventually acquired it. Although it has been commercialized, Breach Security pledges that it will keep ModSecurity open source and continue to add resources, which it has done to date.

Currently, ModSecurity is an add-on module for the open source Apache Web server. Although this generally means ModSecurity is running on/inside the Web server, it is possible to use Apache's reverse-proxy capabilities to leverage ModSecurity as a standalone WAF gateway to protect other Web servers. Because it is tied to Apache, most ModSecurity installations are on some flavor of UNIX. However, it is also possible to install special versions of Apache and ModSecurity on Windows.

ModSecurity provides four main functionalities: IDS/IPS, logging, virtual patching, and application hardening. Although ModSecurity comes with several prepackaged rule sets, it was designed to be extremely flexible and customizable. According to its philosophy, Breach Security wants to help users help themselves and ensure that, by having extensive and objective documentation, users are not unpleasantly surprised.

MODSECURITY RULE SETS

ModSecurity is 100 percent customizable by a user; however, most people are not familiar enough with all the various details of every Web attack vector to feel comfortable creating their own rule sets from scratch. To assist with this, Ofer Shezaf created a Core Rule Set that provides a generic and broad level of protection against most known attacks and exploits. This section outlines these attacks so you can see what ModSecurity can do and get a feel for the general landscape of attack vectors that can be used against Web applications.

Protocol Violations

HTTP is a set of standards with which Web servers and browsers are expected to comply. The result is that it is possible to have a wide number of browsers that can all communicate with a wide range of Web servers. Because all the software is written to comply with HTTP, it should work as expected. However, attackers often alter the data in a request that breaks protocol and might also break the Web application. ModSecurity recognizes the following protocol violations:

- **Request smuggling.** It is possible to wrap an HTTP request inside another request. The end result is that an HTTP device/application WAF or reverse proxy sitting between an attacker and Web server can be tricked into caching an object (B) with the identity of another object (A). Future viewers then think they get object A, but instead get object B.

- **Malformed content.** The body of an HTTP request might contain content that is malformed, unreadable, or malicious.

- **Numerical content length.** The content length header of an HTTP request is always supposed to be a number. However, if an attacker modifies the header data, she might include incorrect length information or nonnumeric characters, which could potentially crash or exploit systems.

- **GET and HEAD requests with bodies.** GET and HEAD requests should not have any content in their bodies. All data is passed through the URL.

- **POST request length.** A POST request does have content in its body. If a POST request is received with no content, something is wrong.

- **Unknown transfer request encoding.** According to the HTTP specifications, it is possible to chunk the body of a request into smaller parts. ModSecurity does not accept this type of encoding.

- **URL and UTF unicode encoding.** It is possible to encode the request using unicode, UTF, or URL encoding. Numerous attacks take advantage of encoding, or even encoding errors. ModSecurity can block these requests.

- **Proxy use.** Apache can be configured as a proxy server, which can allow someone to access the network. Although a properly configured Apache server blocks the request, ModSecurity provides a backup if it is improperly set up.

- **Evasion tricks.** Numerous odd characters can be sent to a Web server that are not readable. Although it is possible to change the default settings in ModSecurity, it only blocks NULL characters by default.

Protocol Anomalies

Not every HTTP request will be within standards. To accommodate this, ModSecurity includes an anomalies configuration file to deal with unusual requests. This includes items such as old (or nonexistent) versions of HTTP, missing header variables (such as User Agent), or requests to an IP address instead of a host name.

Request Limits

HTTP requests often include GET or POST data that the Web server processes. However, there is a reasonable limit to the amount of data that a user should send. By default, ModSecurity blocks any request with more than 255 URL request parameters. Other size-limiting options exist, such as URL length, total request size, and uploaded file size, but these inspection options are not enabled by default.

HTTP Policy

Almost all HTTP requests have a limited number of characteristics. ModSecurity recognizes and uses this to build a layer of protection between what HTTP can do and what it normally does. It does this by limiting what file types, HTTP version, request methods, and folders are available or restricted via positive and negative security models. Anything with an unaccepted request value is rejected.

Bad Robots

When you Google a phrase to search for related Web sites, you are provided with a list of pages with your desired search term. Google creates this list, which runs programs that scan the Internet for content and cache the results in its database. These programs, called robots or Web crawlers, provide a valuable and necessary part of giving you the ability to find information online. However, specialized Web robots can be abusive and can find vulnerable applications and content that should not be online.

Detecting these bad robots is easy; it only involves checking the User Agent for known values (such as Webtrends security analyzer) and other pieces of the header to detect that a robot is making the request.

Known Attacks

A WAF includes some blacklist negative filtering aspects to detect and prevent against known attacks. This section looks at a collection of attacks detected by ModSecurity. This is a fairly standard list of attack signatures that any and all WAFs should include:

- **Session fixation.** To track a user from page to page challenges a Web site because there is no constant connection between a browser and server. However, maintaining a visitor's state is essential, especially if the site is stateful. To accomplish this, the concept of a session was developed and implemented. To track the session, the browser must pass a unique identifier each time it requests a page. Although this is often done via a cookie, it is also possible to pass this information via a GET/POST request. Unfortunately, it is possible for a remote attacker to trick a user into accessing the site with a preknown unique identifier (UID). This enables the attacker to set the victim's UID, and when he logs into the site, the attacker uses the same identifier and gains access to everything in the user's account.

- **SQL injection.** SQL injection vulnerabilities are one of the biggest threats to the Internet. Not only are they rampant, but they give an attacker access to database contents, which often includes credit-card information, user credentials, and even the capability to interact with the file system. The general idea is that an attacker can append his own SQL commands on to the end of a dynamically created query that is submitted to the SQL server backend. Without proper sanitization, a malicious SQL query can be easily created. To compound the issue, certain databases contain powerful functionality that can give an attacker direct access to the operating system. For example, if an attacker can access the power of the xp_cmdshell stored procedure, they can execute system level commands on the target system. With this power, an attacker can add users, read sensitive data, delete data, and much more.

- **Cross Site Scripting.** Called XSS because CSS already established meaning in the Web world, this essentially gives an attacker the power to execute JavaScript in a victim's browser within the context of another Web site. With this capability, the attacker can steal the session cookies, access any sensitive information displayed on the Web page, download content to the computer, and more.

- **File injection.** Many Web applications include the capability to upload files or dynamically fetch files stored on a Web server. Without proper controls, an attacker can trick the application to accept or fetch arbitrary files on the Web server or other Web servers. This might even cause the arbitrary execution of application logic.

- **OS command injection.** It is common for a Web application to provide a frontend to system-level function. These functions are triggered by a Web request. If the request process is not properly coded, an attacker can twist the request into an alternate and more dangerous command that can give an attacker access to sensitive data or system commands.

- **ColdFusion/LDAP/SSI/PHP injection.** Although not as common as SQLi attacks, all these backend components have been found to suffer from the same kind of attack. Specifically, an attacker can provide unexpected input that the backend then processes to obtain data, perform undesired functions, inject files into the code/returned Web page, send spam, and more.

- **Universal PDF XSS.** Certain versions of Adobe PDF software were found to be vulnerable to an XSS attack. This is as simple as appending `#foo=javascript:<JS Code>` on the end of a request.
- **HTTP response splitting.** Each HTTP response separates the header from the body with a carriage return (CR) and line feed (LF) value. However, if an attacker can inject his own CR/LF characters into the header, he can trick the browser into thinking that the header content is complete. This enables the attacker to inject JavaScript or HTML after the false CR/LF, which is processed by the browser.

Trojans

Most online Web servers either support the PHP, ASP, or .NET programming languages, which are used to create Web applications. Although the normal program accesses data and displays it to an end user, attackers have created numerous malicious programs that can be placed onto a server and give them the power to read files, upload data, execute system level commands and more. Because these scripts are normally in plaintext, it is trivial to detect their presence by matching a pre-determined signature.

Outbound

The previous filters/configuration options all monitor incoming traffic. However, as discussed earlier, there is no 100 percent foolproof way to prevent all potentially malicious code from hitting the Web application. If an attacker finds a way to the server, the last line of defense is to prevent him from knowing it. To do this, ModSecurity includes support for outbound filtering:

- **Errors.** When a Web application receives unexpected data that causes it to crash, the results are typically an error message. An attacker can use these error messages to deduce the reason for the crash and sometimes help him find a vulnerability. By removing the error messages, the attacker never knows if he successfully found a bug, much less be able to deduce information from the crash.
- **Information leakage.** Improperly configured Web servers are notorious for being a valuable resource for information that should not be leaked to the public. Documentation, unexecuted Web application source code, directory content listings, default pages, default file locations, and so on are subtle indicators that can give an attacker all he needs to know about what Web server is running, how it is configured, how many people visit, what OSs they use, and more. Internal-only or sensitive office documents "hidden" in unknown locations on the Web site can have their location guessed and thus recovered.

VA+WAF

If a WAF protected a static Web site that never changed, it would only be a one-time effort to set the WAF up and create the policies to protect the Web site. However, most Web sites are constantly updated to fit new user needs, offer new features, and so on. As a result, new code is introduced to the Web application, and that can introduce a new security vulnerability. For the WAF to remain effective, it needs to be told about these changes and newly introduced security vulnerabilities.

To remedy this situation, a marriage between VA tools and WAFs was created. By combining the coverage and feedback obtained by automated VA scanning with the flexibility and power of virtual patching provided by a WAF, a solution can be created that both locates and intelligently prevents a Web application vulnerability from being exploited until it is fixed.

VA+WAF Example: WhiteHat Security and F5 Networks

Let's look into one commercial VA+WAF solution to illustrate how this concept operates.

As previously discussed, a VA+WAF combination is not typically a single vendor solution; it's more of a cooperative combination of products whose sum is greater than its individual components. In this particular combination, WhiteHat Security and F5 Networks team up so F5 Networks' Application Security Manager (ASM) WAF can use WhiteHat's Sentinel VA data.

Specifically, the solution works as follows:

1. The F5 Networks ASM WAF is installed and preconfigured to protect a target Web site.
2. WhiteHat's Sentinel service scans the target Web site and finds confirmed security problems.
3. The Web site administrator operator is notified and given the option to virtually patch the vulnerability.
4. With a single click, the virtual patch configuration information is passed from Sentinel to the ASM WAF.
5. After the virtual patch is in place, the Sentinel program provides the administrator with the option to retest the vulnerability to ensure that the virtual patch sufficiently mitigates the problem.
6. The process continually repeats back to Step 2.

Figure 7-4 depicts this solution.

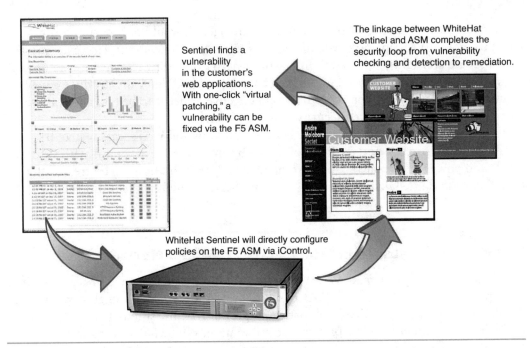

Sentinel finds a vulnerability in the customer's web applications. With one-click "virtual patching," a vulnerability can be fixed via the F5 ASM.

The linkage between WhiteHat Sentinel and ASM completes the security loop from vulnerability checking and detection to remediation.

WhiteHat Sentinel will directly configure policies on the F5 ASM via iControl.

Figure 7-4   WhiteHat Sentinel + F5 ASM integration flow

The key to this solution is that it parallels the software development lifecycle used to create enterprise-level Web applications. This is a key point, because it ensures that the regular changes to the application do not go unscanned. Without a cyclic approach, changes to the Web application can introduce vulnerabilities that might go unnoticed, undetected, and unprotected.

One other element of this particular solution is that WhiteHat verifies the bug before notifying the Web site operator. In other words, the false positive factor that afflicts many WAF solutions does not affect users of this service. Because it has access to a large database of scan results, WhiteHat can systematically rule out many false or duplicate positives. If a result is either not considered a false positive or is not automatically considered a threat because of its characteristics, WhiteHat employees manually verify the vulnerability. Regardless of the solution you might select, adding this service-oriented aspect is a major bonus for any customer because it saves him countless wasted hours of trying to weed out the false positives and testing/fixing/testing the issues.

Although automated scanning has its benefits, even WhiteHat's CTO understands the limits of automated scanning. For the best security, a combination of automation and manual labor is required.

WAFs AND PCI COMPLIANCE

Many Web sites that accept credit-card payments are required to meet the Payment Card Industry's (PCI) standards of security compliance relating to how that credit-card information is received, used, and stored by the Web site/application. PCI compliance is meant to confirm a certain level of security due diligence by the Web application owner; the requirements are enforced via the use of monetary fines if an application does not comply. Compliance is generally demonstrated in one of the following two ways:

- Undergo application scanning and code review by an application security specialist
- Install a WAF in front of the Web-accessible applications

Although a general WAF deployment will meet compliance requirements, note that using a VA+WAF solution will exceed the requirements. In addition, it a good idea for a company to demonstrate its willingness to operate above and beyond the minimal compliance level mentioned in the PCI standards, because the fines increase according to the proven level of negligence of the application owner at the time a security incident occurs. Thus, exceeding compliance requirements need to be considered as an insurance investment toward the losses experienced because of a potential future security incident.

WAF REALITIES

Given the previous discussion and the many options and methods that are available to WAF users, it appears that WAF would be a top priority for any company with a significant Web presence. Unfortunately, this is not so. WAF can be difficult to implement and properly maintain. Any WAF vendor that indicates his solution can stop *all* the bad guys is suspect and needs to be scrutinized.

IDS/IPS != WAF

A big problem is that many IDS/IPS vendors are adding minimal Web application security features into their products and selling the solution as comprehensive WAF alternative. Unfortunately, these IDS/IPS approaches are typically known-threat and signature based (like the rest of the product) and miss zero-day attacks or attacks that are strictly unique to that application. In addition, IDS/IPS solutions do not often have the capability to see into SSL encrypted traffic, which enables secure tunneling of attacker traffic to and from the server. Last but not least, Web application attackers typically gain unauthorized access to sensitive information by modifying parameter data in a proxy such as Burp (see Figure 7-5). Because a proxy server gives an attacker full control over the data coming from the browser and vice versa, it is trivial to change details of the requests to probe the application. The typical IDS/IPS does not know enough about the application layer traffic to recognize a threat, even if it sees it.

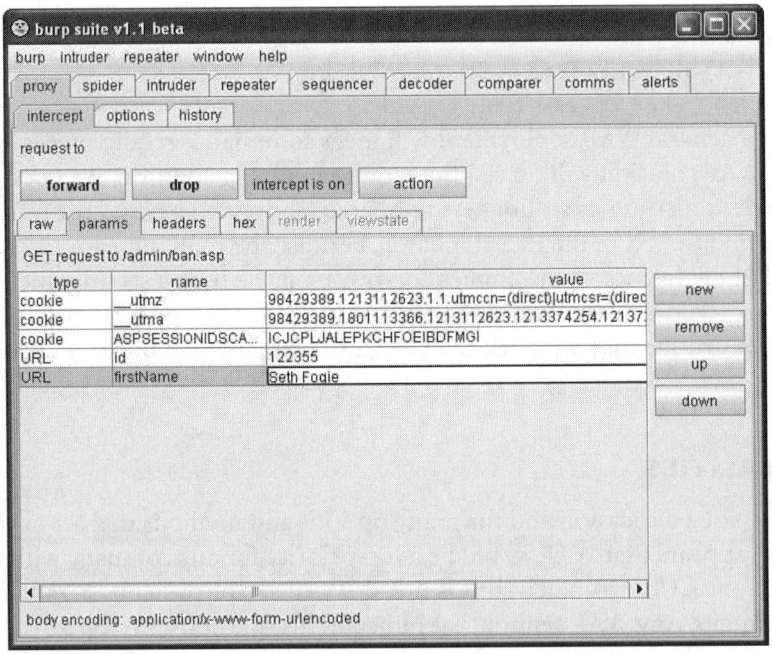

Figure 7-5 Burp: Modifying data on the fly

FALSE POSITIVES

Like IDS solutions, false positives are a huge problem for WAFs. For example, the presence of a single apostrophe might indicate an attacker probing for a SQL injection vulnerability, or it might just be part of someone's proper name (for example, Bill O'Reilly). Fortunately, this is where WAFs tend to provide more benefit than IDS/IPS solutions, because WAFs can be configured to differentiate between which input fields might normally see a single apostrophe (such as a name or address field), versus which fields are unlikely to contain such a character (phone number or postal code fields). Typically, a normal IDS alerts the basic presence of the single apostrophe regardless of the field within which it is present.

MISCONFIGURED WAFs

To properly protect a Web service, a WAF must be directly inline with the computer(s) hosting the Web applications. If the positioning of the WAF on the network is not correct, it can potentially allow an attacker to access the Web site via a network route that bypasses the WAF. In addition, a WAF is a specialized solution with only one main function: to detect and prevent Web application attacks. It does not provide any protection for non-HTTP network services running on the same Web server(s). Finally, it is common for WAF operators to make exceptions for internal IP addresses that allow them to do things that are not permitted by the public. The value of this is undeniable, because it can help streamline development; however, this "backdoor" becomes a serious liability if the internal machine is ever compromised by traditional, or even JavaScript, malware through which an attacker can relay requests to the Web application.

WAFs DO NOT FIX BAD LOGIC

Typically, a WAF does a good job at detecting specific malformed data or parameter manipulation attacks, such as SQL injection, XSS attacks, and session hijacking. These attacks are instigated by an attacker as he attempts to take advantage of a code flaw that can make the Web server do something that it isn't supposed to. However, application logic flaws are vulnerabilities caused by problems in how the application fundamentally operates and are not necessarily caused by malformed or manipulated data. For example, look at the following code:

```
User=request.querystring("username")
Pass= request.querystring("password")
If (user= "admin") OR (pass="strongpassword") then
```

```
      setupLoginSession()
end if
```

In this case, the programmer mistakenly typed in an OR instead of an AND. This means that anyone using the username admin can access the application without knowing the proper password. Incidentally, this is a real-world example. It is highly unlikely that a WAF can detect an attacker taking advantage of this bug, because nothing malicious needs to be passed in the request. Yet, an attacker can still gain full control of the site that this authentication scheme was trying to protect.

WAFs != Bad Code Patch

Unfortunately, a WAF often becomes a patching engine for vulnerable code. In other words, if a vulnerability is found in an enterprise-level application, it is often easier to install a virtual patch than it is to fix the bug. For example, if every single page in a 1,000 page Web site is vulnerable to a SQL injection attack, it is much easier to specify a ruleset to block the particular combination of characters that exploit the SQL based vulnerability than it is to fix the 1,000 pages.

This is an extreme example, but it emphasizes the point that a WAF must not compensate for poor code; yet, some vendors are practically using this as a selling point. If a operator Web operates this way, he will end up with a long list of rules on the WAF that will eventually create conflict.

I consider permanent patching in the WAF as bad practice. But the solution like the VA+WAF F5 fosters this behavior. In the end, WhiteHat Sentinel measures the WAF configuration and not the quality of the Web application. From my experience, it is better to do the testing with a disabled WAF to really feel the Web application. However, this cannot be done in a production environment.

Summary

WAFs are a hot topic for the Web application security community. For as many people who find value in them, there are as many who feel WAFs make the situation worse. There is no doubt that a WAF can be a valuable resource if you want to prevent an attacker from finding and exploiting the more general flaws that plague most Web sites; however, relying on a WAF to help secure a Web site is dangerous because it doesn't fix the problem; it only covers it up.

As this technology develops, expect to see WAFs become a bigger player in the security landscape. The reality is that firewalls are getting better and the bad guys are having a harder time getting into a network. As a result, they are shifting their focus to the Internet and letting vulnerable Web servers do their dirty work for them by injecting malicious code into valid sites that are in turn fed to the real victims: Web site visitors. Although the value of a WAF is debatable, you have to wonder: Would the 100,000 of sites attacked by automated bots would have remained uninfected with ModSecurity in place?

REFERENCES

www.owasp.org/index.php/Top_10_2007

www.businessweek.com/magazine/content/05_19/b3932038_mz009.htm

www.darkreading.com/document.asp?doc_id=149213

www.forrester.com/Research/Document/Excerpt/0,7211,39714,00.html

www.modsecurity.org/documentation/ApacheCon_Europe_2008-Web_Intrusion_Detection_with_ModSecurity.pdf

www.modsecurity.org/documentation/ModSecurity_The_Open_Source_Web_Application_Firewall_Nov2007.pdf

www.pcisecuritystandards.org/pdfs/infosupp_6_6_applicationfirewalls_codereviews.pdf

www.whitehatsec.com/home/assets/WP_WAF061708.pdf

http://portswigger.net/proxy/

Wireless IDS/IPS

Until this point, the book has focused on the traditional idea of an Intrusion Detection System/Intrusion Prevention System (IDS/IPS). This typically involves performing an in-depth analysis of captured data frames, determining what constitutes a threat, and then parsing the traffic for any predefined threats. Although this concept works well in a traditional networked environment, the twenty-first century is redefining the reality of where data goes and how it gets there. This chapter focuses on the wireless perspective and examines the technology needed to analyze the airwaves for threats specifically associated with this communication medium.

NOTE

Unless otherwise stated, this chapter's contents apply to 802.11-based wireless networks.

WHY A WIRELESS IDS?

As we mentioned in Chapter 3, "Intrusion Detection Systems," a traditional wired network has two main types of IDSs. The first consists of a product you install on the PC, known as a host-based system. Because the product resides on a computer, it can analyze all traffic passing through its technologies implementing the layers of the Open System Interconnection (OSI) Model and use its own processing power to detect and prevent potential threats from causing harm. The second type is a network-based IDS that basically sits on a segment of the network and monitors all traffic for indicators that something is wrong. This solution can examine some application layer data, but generally, it detects threats that are found in the data link layer or network layer of the information passing through the network.

Both types of solutions have their own strengths; however, they are useless when it comes to detecting threats that affect wireless networks. This is because an 802.3 Ethernet frame is not an 802.11 wireless local area network (WLAN) frame. Because most vulnerabilities that affect wireless users are a result of some design flaw within the 802.11 protocol, by the time that wireless frame is reassembled by the access point (AP) and stripped of its headers, any indication of an attack underway is most likely going to disappear. Figure 8-1 and Figure 8-2 provide you with a detailed look at a basic Internet Control Management Protocol (ICMP) packet. Figure 8-1 includes the 802.11 header information, and Figure 8-2 illustrates what happens to the frame after the AP reassembles it.

From these figures, it is easy to see that the typical 802.11 frame contains plenty of data that never shows up in the 802.3 frame. Of interest, numerous attacks affect the physical layer of wireless networks that never show up as actual data, which means there is nothing for the traditional analyzer to detect!

As a result of the limited value a network/host-based IDS provides with regard to the 802.11 network, a special and targeted solution must be deployed to detect and prevent potential wireless security threats. This is why the Wireless Intrusion Detection System/Wireless Intrusion Prevention System (WIDS/WIPS) is a necessary component of a comprehensive security solution. Without a WIDS, your wireless network can become the target of an attack with no one the wiser. By the time a network-based analyzer scans the data that an attacker passes into the network, it looks like it came from an authorized user.

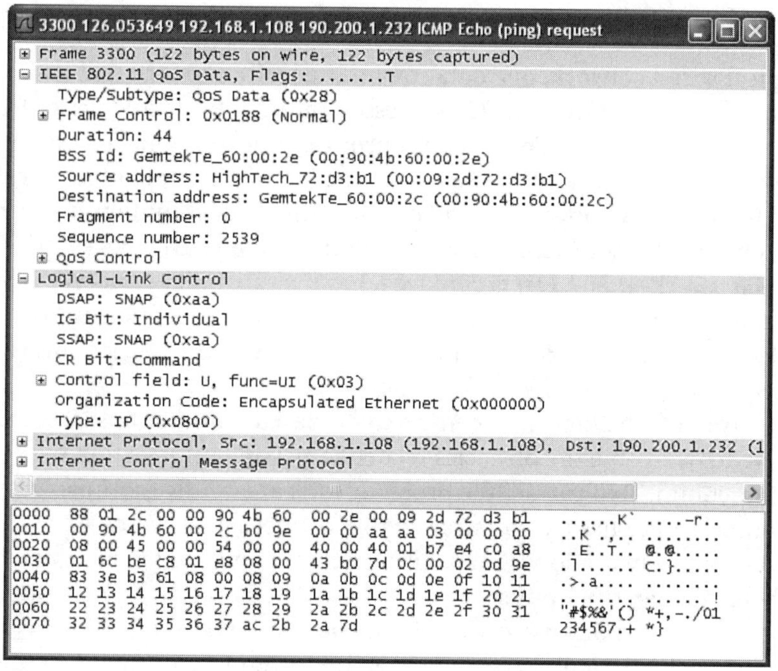

```
3300 126.053649 192.168.1.108 190.200.1.232 ICMP Echo (ping) request
⊞ Frame 3300 (122 bytes on wire, 122 bytes captured)
⊟ IEEE 802.11 QoS Data, Flags: .......T
    Type/Subtype: QoS Data (0x28)
  ⊞ Frame Control: 0x0188 (Normal)
    Duration: 44
    BSS Id: GemtekTe_60:00:2e (00:90:4b:60:00:2e)
    Source address: HighTech_72:d3:b1 (00:09:2d:72:d3:b1)
    Destination address: GemtekTe_60:00:2c (00:90:4b:60:00:2c)
    Fragment number: 0
    Sequence number: 2539
  ⊞ QoS Control
⊟ Logical-Link Control
    DSAP: SNAP (0xaa)
    IG Bit: Individual
    SSAP: SNAP (0xaa)
    CR Bit: Command
  ⊞ Control field: U, func=UI (0x03)
    Organization Code: Encapsulated Ethernet (0x000000)
    Type: IP (0x0800)
⊞ Internet Protocol, Src: 192.168.1.108 (192.168.1.108), Dst: 190.200.1.232 (1
⊞ Internet Control Message Protocol

0000  88 01 2c 00 00 90 4b 60  00 2e 00 09 2d 72 d3 b1   ..,...K`....-r..
0010  00 90 4b 60 00 2c b0 9e  00 00 aa aa 03 00 00 00   ..K`.,..........
0020  08 00 45 00 00 54 00 00  40 00 40 01 b7 e4 c0 a8   ..E..T..@.@.....
0030  01 6c be c8 01 e8 08 00  43 b0 7d 0c 00 02 0d 9e   .l......C.}.....
0040  83 3e b3 61 08 00 08 09  0a 0b 0c 0d 0e 0f 10 11   .>.a............
0050  12 13 14 15 16 17 18 19  1a 1b 1c 1d 1e 1f 20 21   .............. !
0060  22 23 24 25 26 27 28 29  2a 2b 2c 2d 2e 2f 30 31   "#$%&'() *+,-./01
0070  32 33 34 35 36 37 ac 2b  2a 7d                     234567.+ *}
```

Figure 8-1   An 802.11 ICMP frame

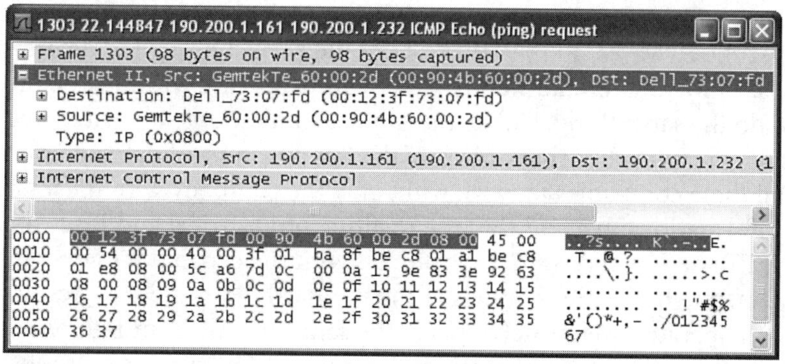

```
1303 22.144847 190.200.1.161 190.200.1.232 ICMP Echo (ping) request
⊞ Frame 1303 (98 bytes on wire, 98 bytes captured)
⊟ Ethernet II, Src: GemtekTe_60:00:2d (00:90:4b:60:00:2d), Dst: Dell_73:07:fd
  ⊞ Destination: Dell_73:07:fd (00:12:3f:73:07:fd)
  ⊞ Source: GemtekTe_60:00:2d (00:90:4b:60:00:2d)
    Type: IP (0x0800)
⊞ Internet Protocol, Src: 190.200.1.161 (190.200.1.161), Dst: 190.200.1.232 (1
⊞ Internet Control Message Protocol

0000  00 12 3f 73 07 fd 00 90  4b 60 00 2d 08 00 45 00   ..?s....K`.-..E.
0010  00 54 00 00 40 00 3f 01  ba 8f be c8 01 a1 be c8   .T..@.?.........
0020  01 e8 08 00 5c a6 7d 0c  00 0a 15 9e 83 3e 92 63   ....\.}. .....>.c
0030  08 00 08 09 0a 0b 0c 0d  0e 0f 10 11 12 13 14 15   ................
0040  16 17 18 19 1a 1b 1c 1d  1e 1f 20 21 22 23 24 25   .......... !"#$%
0050  26 27 28 29 2a 2b 2c 2d  2e 2f 30 31 32 33 34 35   &'()*+,- ./012345
0060  36 37                                              67
```

Figure 8-2   An 802.3 ICMP frame

Wireless Intrusion Detection/Prevention Realities

On your typical wired network, one data stream is usually unencrypted and offers full access to Media Access Control (MAC) addresses, Internet Protocol (IP) addresses, port numbers, and usually even application-level protocol information. For example, an IDS can easily recognize AOL Instant Messenger traffic because it is plaintext, formatted as HTML, and is passed over only a handful of ports, the most common of which is 5190.

Now, imagine an IDS solution that can monitor up to 36 networks (A/B/G), plus an additional 39 networks if 802.11n is deployed, has the capability to decrypt data on the fly, and reassemble fragmented frames in an orderly manner, not to mention examine the frames for anomalies and known attacks. Although this might seem overwhelming, this is exactly what your typical WIDS solution does.

The core reason for the increased complexity is based on the simple fact that wireless networks have to overcome the obstacles related to passing information over a radio frequency (RF) medium. To illustrate the problem, look at an office complex from 1995. In this scenario, each office has its own firewall that connects to a switch or router. From here, the rest of the network looks much like a web of connected devices and computers. Although there are many computers, each one is isolated on its own network because the wires do not enter neighboring offices. Now, if you fast forward to 2009, the office environment looks much different. Each suite is set up for Ethernet using the same wiring from 1995, but now, many devices are laptops and PDAs instead of static PCs.

To maintain connectivity to the core resources, each office is set up with at least one AP that receives and transmits data into the airwaves in the form of radio energy. Because it takes both a receiver and transmitter set to the same frequency to successfully send data over the airwaves, all the office's computers must be able to detect their company's signals. Unfortunately, numerous other companies are within close proximity and are trying to do the same thing. Unlike the physical limitations of a wired network, a wireless signal enters neighboring offices. If the 802.11 protocol defined only one frequency for all these companies to work with, only the company with the loudest radio could send information. To avoid this, the Institute of Electrical and Electronics Engineers (IEEE) designed the 802.11 protocols with the capability to operate on different frequencies, much like the channels of the standard FM radio. As a result, numerous companies can operate wireless networks in the same area without interference.

Although all these channels and options are valuable for creating a productive wireless network, they cause huge problems for any solution that attempts to monitor a wireless network for attacks. The reason is because of the simple fact that a comprehensive solution must track all active clients and APs on all channels while simultaneously decrypting and examining data passing over these networks.

To further complicate issues, the 802.11 protocol is not fully developed. As a result, there are 802.11 Frequency Hopping Spread Spectrum (FHSS), 802.11b, 802.11g, 802.11a, and 802.11n networks that all pass information over the same frequency range in different and incompatible ways. In addition to the numerous protocols, the IEEE manages to ratify a new standard every few years, which alters everything and ends up creating a completely new way to transmit information. This means that any WIDS solution you purchase might be rendered obsolete in three years. For example, any 802.11/b/g WIDS device never detects an 802.11n-based rogue AP if it is operating in Greenfield mode, which locks the actual transmission/reception into high performance mode out of view of the legacy 802.11a/b/g WIDS. Needless to say, Ethernet-based IDS solutions do not deal with the same level of obstacles and frustrations that WIDS vendors must overcome!

TYPES OF WIRELESS IDSs/IPSs

Not all WIDSs operate in the same way. Like any solution, expect to find different layers and features, depending on what kind of product you use and how much it costs (which does not always indicate features). Regardless of the internal details of any solution, a WIDS falls into only three main categories: overlay, combined AP/WIDS, and total AP/AM solution. This section breaks down the details, advantages, and drawbacks of each type.

OVERLAY

An overlay WIDS typically takes the form of a dedicated device that constantly monitors the airwaves around its location. This solution typically either has a self-contained Web application server that provides the user with constant feedback about the issues it detects in the area, or it feeds into a central processing and analyzing server solution on the host network.

Because the overlay solution only passively monitors the local airwaves, it is generally not too expensive and can be placed almost anywhere and in any configuration. In addition, because this type of solution is passive, it does not create interference issues if it's placed close together. Finally, an overlay solution is an excellent choice if a business does not want to use wireless technology but wants to have the capability to detect rogue APs, signal hijacking, or other related attacks that do not require a wireless infrastructure.

The downside of using an overlay solution is that these devices do not have as deep an understanding of the wireless traffic as a device that is integrated into the network. This is particularly true if the local wireless network being monitored is encrypted. Although a passive device can be programmed to decrypt static Wireless Encryption Protocol (WEP) protected traffic, WPA/WPA2 or IPSec protected traffic cannot be decrypted because each and every client has a unique key that a monitoring device does not know. As a result, anything in those 802.11 frames is ignored.

Combined AP/WIDS

To help overcome the limitations of a passive monitoring solution, vendors created a more powerful and flexible solution that provides the usefulness of an AP, but includes the monitoring features of a WIDS. These devices cost more and have more beef than a monitoring-only solution. However, they have the added benefit of serving as a functional component to the network.

Other than having the capability to serve as an AP, which helps increase the solution's functionality, a combined AP/WIDS device can gain a better understanding of the attacks that might be occurring in the surrounding area. Unlike a passive device that has no intrinsic knowledge of the wireless users, the fact that the AP handles authentication, association, and encryption of users means that it can get deeper inside the communications and detect a greater number of risks. For example, if an attacker used a stolen or cracked WPA key to perform an ARP-based man-in-the-middle (MITM) attack, the overlay monitoring device has no idea about it. However, an AP/WIDS combo can decrypt the data on the fly and have access to the content, which allows it to detect and block any attack occurring between the wireless clients.

Although a combined AP/WIDS provides a more solid detection/prevention vantage point, they are isolated devices with limited resources. As a result, they miss some attacks that might show up in larger wireless networks. For example, many businesses use an access control list (ACL), based on wireless network interface card (WNIC) and MAC addresses, to prevent unwanted wireless networks from getting on the network. However, because a MAC address can be spoofed, it is simple to emulate a valid user, as long as they aren't online. If a series of AP/WIDS are set up, but they aren't centrally managed or communicating with each other, an attacker can capture the MAC address of a client associated to one AP and simply move to another AP and use the borrowed MAC to bypass the ACL.

COMBINED AP/WIDS/ACCESS CONTROLLER

For the best protection, functional use, and management features, the only option is an AP/WIDS with an access controller. This solution combines the monitoring capability with a centrally managed collection of APs that pass off all the identity-based authorization, encrypted session details, and intrusion detection to a powerful device that sits between the APs and the rest of the network.

Although the features vary between vendors, the heart and brains of this system reside on the controller. With the capability to manage thousands of APs and tens of thousands of users, it is no surprise that the device must be a power house. However, thanks to the resources, the access controller can receive data from the remote APs/monitoring devices and consolidate it into a single stream from which further analysis is performed.

In addition to analyzing and managing protection schemes, the controller also ensures that users do not lose their connection as they move about the covered area. Known as roaming, the controller has to use signal strength indicators and other pieces of information to track where a user is located, with regards to the closest AP. Although this is useful for the controller to help maintain connectivity for clients, this feature also provides valuable information about the location of an attacker. For example, if an attacker was using NetStumbler to locate APs in a densely covered area, a controller can detect the movements of the attacker as he passes from one AP to another. This, in essence, shows an administrator how an attacker is moving, which can then be used to catch him.

Finally, because the data is consolidated to one device, the IDS can include analysis tools for networks threats and wireless attacks.

WIRELESS IDS EVENTS

All IDSs, whether network, host, or wireless, operate in a reactive world. They must capture data, analyze it, and use a preexisting set of signatures to determine if the activity is a recognized threat. Currently, roughly 100 vulnerabilities and about 70 exploits/attack programs are registered in the Wireless Vulnerabilities and Exploits database (http://wirelessve.org). Although this adds up to a significant list of threats for a WIDS to sort out, you can narrow the entire list to three different categories: unauthorized activity, active cracking, and denial of service (DoS). This section describes these categories and lists the typical signatures on which the standard WIDS needs to detect and report.

UNAUTHORIZED ACTIVITY

Wireless networks are notorious for attracting unwanted attention. Although the majority of the attention comes in the form of freeloaders, other forms of unauthorized activity are not so benign. The following lists the typical threats for which a WIDS looks:

- **Unauthorized AP/client**. Any time a new wireless device point enters into a protected area, it is classified as unauthorized. Depending on the policies, the device might be isolated and a warning sent to the administrator. If an enterprise WIDS is in place, numerous monitors can use location-aware technology to determine where the client/AP is located. This increases the reliability of classification, because wireless devices can easily be spoofed. By using the Received Signal Strength Indicator (RSSI) value to get a rough idea of location, a virtual shell can be created around the authorized area. If a device enters that shell and it is unauthorized, IPS measures can keep it disconnected from the network.

- **Rogue AP**. Typically installed by well-meaning departments who want wireless access to the network. However, attackers use rogue APs to look for a remote backdoor into a network. Regardless, they are a serious threat. To determine if an AP is rogue, the WIDS (or third-party application) must perform a test to see if it can locate the device on the local network. Figure 8-3 shows the freely available Paglo RogueScanner in action as it scans and locates the DD-WRT AP on the LAN.

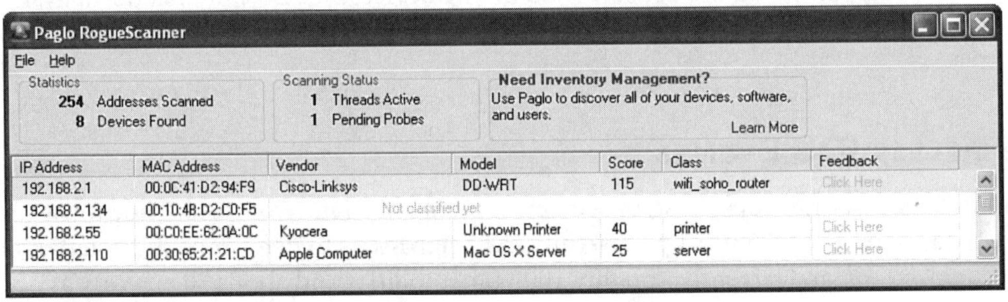

Figure 8-3   RFprotect rogue AP discovery component

Typically, this test is accomplished by having the WIDS connect to the RogueAP and attempt to connect back to itself or a central controller. If the test is successful, the AP can be assumed to be connected to the local network.

- **Unauthorized connections**. An unauthorized device is not a serious threat in and of itself. Neighboring APs, ad-hoc devices, laptops with broadcasting network cards, and so on are all part of the wireless landscape. However, this all changes after a connection is established between the unauthorized and the authorized. Because of the inherent risk of the unknown, a WIPS wants to prevent all such connections from occurring.

- **Insecure AP**. All APs, with the exception of public hotspots, should use encryption. Most WIDS detects the existence of unencrypted traffic or networks using insecure encryption algorithms (such as WEP) and warn that an AP is insecure. Other potential issues include the transmission of SMB and/or plaintext traffic and default settings (for example, BSSID of Linksys).

- **Ad-hoc activity**. Not all 802.11 traffic requires an AP. Laptops, PDAs, and desktop computers can also create an ad-hoc network of connected computers that can be used to share files or perpetuate an attack.

- **Broadcast Secure Set Identifier (SSID)**. By default, APs are configured to emit broadcast beacons that contain the name of the wireless network. Some companies might want to turn off this broadcasting feature. This doesn't necessarily make a wireless network more secure, but it can help obfuscate its existence.

- **Spoofed AP**. An attacker can easily detect the SSID and radio's MAC address with a sniffer. Using this information, he can set up his AP to emulate an authorized device and trick clients into connecting. The result is that the attacker can now control all aspects of the traffic passing through the device, to the point where encrypted data can be compromised.

- **Soft AP**. AP running from a computer. Typically, this is a Linux-based laptop with a wireless card. Attackers often use these to set up MITM attacks and spoof valid APs.

ACTIVE RECON/CRACKING

A WIDS must be able to detect unauthorized or insecure wireless events; however, a good attacker can passively monitor the airwaves and preconfigure his wireless devices to bypass any unauthorization flags. After this occurs, the WIDS has to detect the attacker based on the fingerprint of attacks used to access sensitive data.

NetStumbler

NetStumbler is the tool responsible for helping countless IT professionals understand that wireless security is important. It single-handedly spawned the creation of a new term, war driving, which is the activity of driving around to collect statistics on wireless networks. This program, and others like it, sends out probe requests to the surrounding area and listens for any probe responses. According to the 802.11 protocol, any AP that is configured to broadcast its SSID replies to a request with its SSID information. Because the requests occur rather frequently, it is trivial to detect war-driving tools, such as NetStumbler. For example, in the Snort-Wireless package, the following entry from the snort.conf file tells the IDS to send an alert if there are more than 90 probe requests in a 30-second time period:

```
preprocessor antistumbler: probe_reqs 90, probe_period 30, expire_timeout 3600
```

Figure 8-4 shows a NetStumbler probe request.

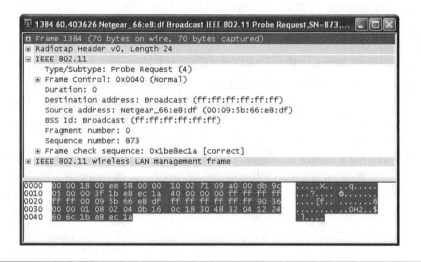

Figure 8-4   NetStumbler probe request packet

WEP Attacks

WEP is a broken protection scheme used to encrypt the data of many wireless networks. Just its existence alone should create an alert in most WIDS. However, several active attacks against WEP create unusual-looking data on a wireless network. For example, it is possible to use fragmentation and injection attacks to insert valid frames into a WEP protected network, thus creating traffic that can be used in a statistical attack by which the shared key can be deduced. Each part of this attack has a fingerprint that can indicate when an attack is underway.

For example, Figure 8-5 shows a frame sent during a fragmentation attack. In a normal healthy network, there is no reason to fragment data, so any frame with the fragmentation bit (highlighted in Figure 8-5) set should be cause for concern.

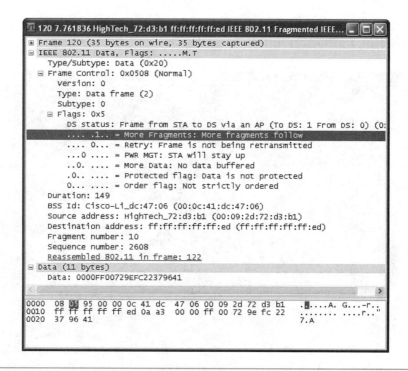

Figure 8-5 The fragmentation bit being set is cause for concern.

Replay/Injection Attacks

Unprotected and WEP-protected wireless networks have no internal mechanism to detect a replayed frame that is injected into the air. As a result, it is trivial to capture data and insert it back into the network at a later date. A WIDS can detect this type of attack by examining the sequence number tied to each wireless frame (for example, 2608 in Figure 8-5). These sequence numbers typically help a receiving device keep the frames in their intended order and detect missing frames.

Although the sequence number helps keep a network running smoothly, a complete session can be reinserted at any time. A WIDS can detect the abrupt change in sequence numbers, which might indicate foul play.

Driver Attacks

One of the latest and most significant threats to arise in the wireless world is a direct attack against wireless drivers. These attacks are particularly devastating because they require no knowledge of encryption passwords, only take a few seconds to perform, and typically exploit the target computer in the kernel space, Ring 0. As a result, if successful, a driver attack can have full control of the targeted device. Figure 8-6 illustrates Metasploit during an attack against a DLink device.

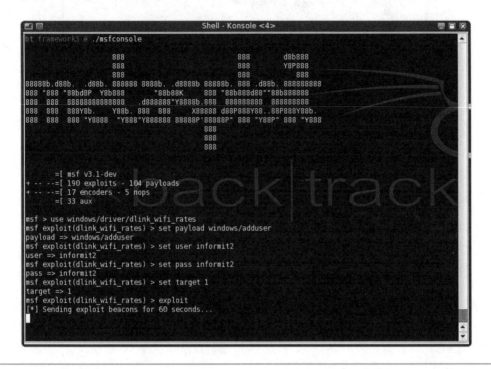

Figure 8-6   DLink driver attack

Note that because these attacks are quick and the typical WIDS has to hop from channel to channel, there is a high chance that the exploit's fingerprint goes unnoticed.

MITM Attack

It is fairly trivial for an attacker to set up a fake AP that is configured to look like a real one. For example, if an attacker wants to create an AP that emulates one with the BSSID of ACME, all he needs to do is run a sniffer for a few seconds to detect the MAC address of a valid ACME AP, configure his wireless card with that MAC address by using `ifconfig wlan0 hw ether 00:11:22:33:44:55`, and then turn the wireless card into an AP by using the command `iwconfig wlan0 channel 2 essid ACME`. With this setup, the attacker only has to put a powerful antenna on the wireless network card to overwhelm the valid RF energy and steal valid devices from the network.

In an attacker's perfect world, this much interaction with the network would not draw attention to itself, but performing this attack causes sequence numbers to jump, RSSI values to change, traffic to disappear from internal networks, and more—all of which are detectable and provide a good fingerprint for this attack.

DoS ATTACKS

Wireless networks are vulnerable to DoS attacks. Not only are they susceptible to protocol-related issues, but the simple fact that wireless networks are exposed to anyone with an antenna means it is possible to inject raw RF energy into the airwaves and completely block out valid traffic. The following outlines the details of each type of attack.

RF Attacks

Wireless networks communicate over specific radio frequencies (RF). As a result, it is trivial to create a device, or even a program, that emits raw RF energy that can create a serious interference issue that effectively shuts down the network. To detect this type of attack, a WIDS must be able to determine the difference between interference related to channel overlaps and a real threat. Figure 8-7 illustrates the results of an RF attack using a testing function of the hostap drivers. Keep in mind that this same attack can be done from a PDA or even a smaller dedicated RF jammer. The solid area on the left indicates a heavy and constant flooding of channel 2 while the larger area on the right indicates a normal AP with light traffic. If there was an AP at channel 1-3, the amount of constant RF energy created by the DoS attack would render it useless.

Authentication/Association Attacks

To connect to a wireless network, every client must first authenticate and then associate with a wireless network. This is performed via a two-stage process. The first stage, authentication, is typically as simple as the client sending an authentication frame to the AP, which replies with "OK." The only time this changes is if the wireless network has shared the enabled authentication. The second stage of a wireless connection is association, which connects the client to the AP.

An authentication/association flooding attack takes advantage of the fact that most APs are resource-limited devices. As a result, if they are overwhelmed with numerous requests that require internal processing, they overload and crash. In addition to overwhelming the AP, certain devices can only hold a small list of clients that are associated. If an attacker submits numerous associations, it can fill up this list. Depending on the AP, the results can cause the AP to reboot or to freeze. Fortunately, detecting this type of attack is easy, because it is highly irregular to experience numerous authentication/association requests in a short time period.

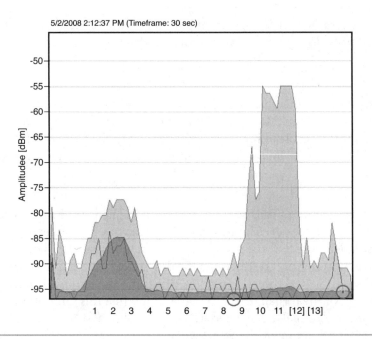

5/2/2008 2:12:37 PM (Timeframe: 30 sec)

Figure 8-7   Results of RF attack

Deauthentication/Disassociation Spoofing Attacks

When a client or AP is going to reboot or leave the area, the polite process is to send out a deauthentication frame so the communication session can be cleanly broken. This is accomplished through management frames, which are not authenticated by any 802.11 device. As a result, it is trivial for an attacker to spoof a frame that looks like it came from the AP that tells all connected devices to deauthenticate. Most attack tools simply inject numerous deauthentication frames to accomplish this, which can be detected and, in some cases, blocked.

CTS Flood/NAV Attack

For a wireless network to be functional, only one device can be transmitting at a time; otherwise, there is a virtual shouting match and only the loudest or strongest signal wins. To facilitate the transmission of RF energy in an orderly basis, it is possible to enable a request to send/clear to send (RTS/CTS) system by which a client must first ask the AP for permission to speak. This lets the AP control which device is allowed to send data and for how long it can control the airwaves. To do this, a CTS frame is sent to all listening devices that includes this information. Unfortunately, it is possible to spoof this frame and increase the timer to a long value. The end result is that all listening devices on the network do not emit any data because they were told to sit and be silent. A WIDS can detect these malicious frames and possibly take appropriate action to correct the problem.

EAPoL-Related DoS

Extensible Authentication Protocol (EAP) is an integral part of a secure enterprise solution using WPA2. The first stage of the EAPoL authentication process consists of an EAPoL-Start frame that the AP processes. By sending a flood of these frames to the target AP, an attacker can use up the resources and crash the device (see Figure 8-8). In addition, EAPoL is also vulnerable to a spoof attack by which an attacker can inject EAPoL-LogOff frames to the AP by pretending to be a wireless client. This causes the AP to disconnect the valid client, thus breaking service (see Figure 8-9).

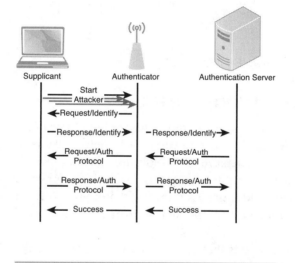

Figure 8-8 EAP-Start DoS

802.11n

Although the protocol is still mostly untested, there are already several DoS bugs that have shown up. For example, the Block ACK DoS attack takes advantage of a protocol-based vulnerability that tells the receiver to ignore all packets outside a specified sequence number range. If an attacker injects a spoofed packet with an Add Block Acknowledgment containing a starting sequence number well outside the current range, the receiver essentially rejects all valid packets while waiting for packets containing the proper sequence number.[1]

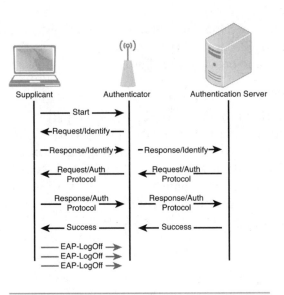

Figure 8-9   EAP-LogOff DoS

INTRUSION PREVENTION TECHNIQUES

A wireless network is a much more complex technology to protect when compared to the typical wired network. Not only do you have to detect problems that directly impact your network, but a comprehensive WIDS solution also has to look out for rogue APs, users with WNICs enabled but not connected to anything, other wireless networks in the area, interference issues, and more. As if this isn't enough, a WIDS must essentially track of all these problems for some 32+ possible networks at one time, thanks to channel distribution.

Because many of the threats that affect wireless users are actually off the network and outside physical control, wireless security vendors had to figure out how to prevent these external threats from impacting the internal users. This section illustrates a few tricks that wireless engineers have devised to control the chaos.

LIMITATIONS

Not all wireless attacks and threats can be prevented; this is a reality that comes with the territory. First, all wireless data can be encrypted and nothing can be done to prevent it from occurring. The only option WLAN users have is to encrypt the data, which needs to be implemented for various reasons.

Second, a WIDS can only prevent attacks within a fairly defined range. As a result, if a user leaves her wireless card enabled but not connected to a network, she can be protected while within the coverage area of the monitoring device. However, after the user moves outside of that area, she is susceptible to attack. To complicate this more, the 802.11 protocol puts a lot of emphasis on the strength of a signal, which typically correlates to quality. As a result, if an attacker's signal is stronger than the WIDS, there is a great chance that the IPS techniques are useless.

Third, the main IPS prevention technique takes advantage of an oversight in the 802.11 protocol that the IEEE wants to correct in the form of the 802.11w protocol. Once ratified, this update slowly gets integrated into the wireless devices, which neutralizes the IPS' weapon of choice.

Finally, as previously indicated, WIDS prevention methods are often very closely related to the attack techniques that malicious hackers use. As a result, launching the IPS attacks against a legitimate network might result in legal action if a valid service was inadvertently disrupted. For example, it is easy to imagine a scenario where a neighboring business sets up a new wireless network that an IPS perceives as a rogue AP. If configured properly, the IPS might take preventative measures against that AP and perform a DoS attack against the neighbor.

ISOLATION

Most WIDS solutions have a whitelist/blacklist approach to determine if a detected device is acceptable. This is determined by capturing the MAC address on the frame and other information that might be available. When an unauthenticated address appears, many WIPSs allow an administrator to isolate that device until further details are learned.

Although this is called isolation, in reality, the WIDS device essentially attacks the rogue device. If the target is an AP, the WIDS simply sends out spoofed deauthentication frames, which causes any device connected to the target AP to disconnect. If the target is a client, the same technique can be used in a targeted deauthentication attack to ensure that the client never establishes a reliable connection to another device.

As previously discussed, if used in the wrong way, this isolation method can have some undesired legal consequences. In addition, this kind of protection assumes all acceptable devices are truly valid. In other words, if an attacker changes his MAC address into one that is on the whitelist, the IDS does not flag it and, as such, the IPS technologies are of no value.

Figure 8-10 shows the AirTight Networks SpectraGuard Sentry's Intrusion Prevention Policy screen. The Policy options allow the device to determine when to launch automatic intrusion prevention. Fortunately, AirTight makes it difficult to accidentally perform a DoS attack against an innocent party.

In addition to configuring the autoprotection policies, this device also lets you determine how aggressive it should be in keeping unwanted communication from occurring. Because this device has only one NIC, it can only scan for and prevent intrusions on a limited number of networks/channels. You can see this at the bottom of Figure 8-10, where the administrator can select what prevention type to use. If the device is expected to block all traffic, it must focus on one channel. If the IPS hops off to another channel for even a second, there is a chance that an attacker can slip through and gain a foothold into the network.

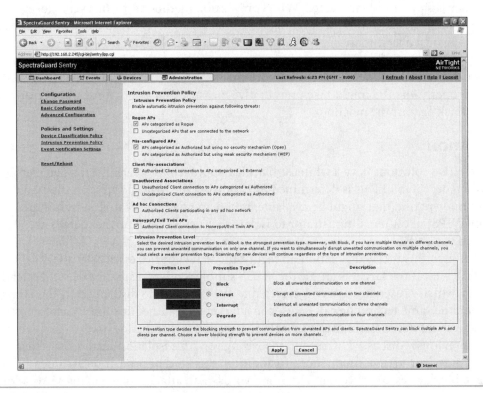

Figure 8-10   AirTight SpectraGuard Sentry intrusion prevention screen

Figure 8-11 shows an isolation in action. Note the deauthentication frames that are performing the actual isolation. The moment a wireless client detects one of these, it assumes that the AP sent it and disconnects itself from the wireless network. Under normal circumstances, APs use deauthentication frames to warn connected clients that it is about to reboot, which gives the client a chance to smoothly break away from its current AP and hopefully find another one in the area to which it can quickly connect. However, because the deauthentication frame can be spoofed without the client ever suspecting that the request is fake, it is trivial for an IPS to inject frames into the airwave and cause all clients to disconnect from the target AP.

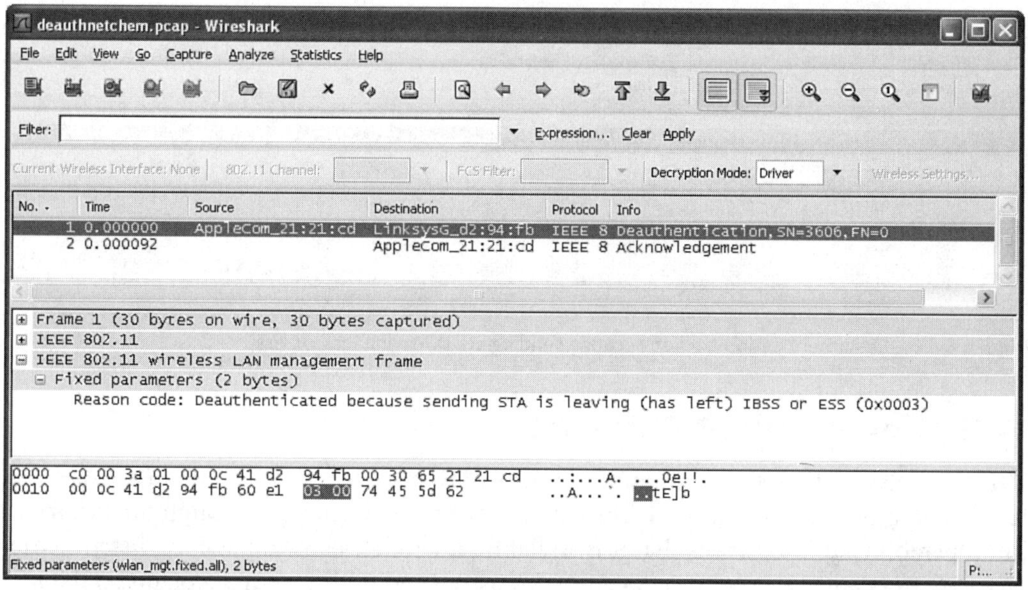

Figure 8-11 Rogue client isolation

In Figure 8-12, you can see what appears to be a valid deauthentication request. The client Netgear card appears to send the AP a deauthentication notice. The specified reason in this frame is that the station is leaving the area and politely says, "Good bye." This causes the AP to then transmit a deauthentication statement to the Netgear device that says the previous authentication is no longer valid. On the surface, this appears valid, except we know that the IPS actually spoofed the original deauthentication frame in lieu of the valid Netgear device that is being isolated. The AP simply assumes that the frame is valid, and it responds accordingly with a deauthentication command to the valid Netgear device, which then disconnects because the AP said it was to do so and, as such, the isolated device can't remain online.

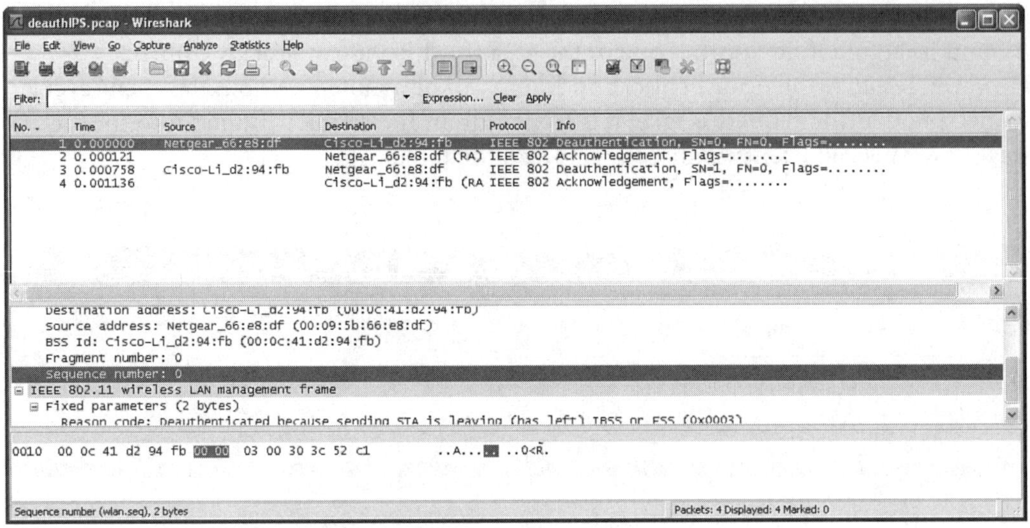

Figure 8-12 Deauthentication packet because sending sta is leaving ibss or ess

WEP CLOAKING (WEP CHAFFING)

802.11 wireless networks use a standard protocol to pass data over the airwaves. As a result, one vendor's equipment works with another's equipment. Although this promotes interoperability, it also means that it is trivial for a wireless card to passively listen to the airwaves and capture data. To reduce the risk associated with capturing plaintext data, the 802.11 protocol includes several options to enable data encryption. One of the first options available is called WEP.

WEP is broken and, as a result, the shared key used to set up a WEP-protected network can be cracked in minutes. In summary, the reason is that, over time, the WEP-protected frames statistically leak enough information to allow someone to guess the key used to encrypt the network. Although it used to take up to five million frames (a lot of data) to successfully extract the key, that number has been reduced to as little as 10,000 frames, which can be obtained in under a minute on a busy network.

Unfortunately, many devices and business still use WEP-protected networks. The reasons vary from ignorance that WEP is broken, to having no choice because of the existing legacy devices that cannot use anything more complex or powerful. To help rectify this situation, some WIDSs/WIPSs have implemented a technology known as *WEP cloaking* to protect networks using the insecure protection scheme.

Because using WEP is dangerous, one IPS vendor worked out a way to provide a level of protection against WEP cracking attacks. Although the value of such a solution is debatable, it is a clever idea and worth understanding, because it can make a difference in IPS choice.

Specifically, cracking WEP is only possible if a person can collect enough data from a target network—assuming the collected data is all encrypted with the same key. WEP chaffing interferes with this possibility by injecting frames that appear to be valid to any would-be sniffer, but in reality, it causes the entire WEP-cracking process to fail. Because a key is cracked by exposing a statistical flaw in WEP, injected frames alter the statistics and, as a result, cause any analysis to deduce the incorrect value.

Although this appears to be a potential solution on the surface, note that many wireless security experts do not find this to be a truly valuable and reliable solution. For example, because WEP cloaking involves injecting frames from a statically placed IPS solution, an attacker can focus on the RSSI value and either only include data from known clients (whitelist) or block data from questionable sources (blacklist). Other possibilities include monitoring channels, sequential numbers, only using expected results from injected frames (ARP frames always same size), and a bunch of other tricks. In fact, the most popular WEP-cracking tool available (aircrack-ng) includes some built-in features to detect and avoid chaffing techniques. The point is this: WEP cloaking/chaffing is valuable, assuming the user understands that it is not foolproof and can be bypassed. Plus, any user of this IPS solution must realize that WEP has numerous other vulnerabilities that cannot be covered with any chaffing/cloaking system.

LOCATION DETECTION

According to the IEEE 802.11 standard,

> The RSSI is an optional parameter that has a value of 0 through RSSI Max. This parameter is a measure by the PHY sublayer of the energy observed at the antenna used to receive the current PPDU. RSSI shall be measured between the beginning of the start frame delimiter (SFD) and the end of the PLCP header error check (HEC). RSSI is intended to be used in a relative manner. Absolute accuracy of the RSSI reading is not specified.

What does this have to do with WIDS systems? Well, because of the built-in capability to determine received signal strength, a WIDS can physically map out where a threat might be located. Because the WIDS device must have a listening radio, it can deduce the RSSI value for each frame/client that it detects. By monitoring and recording the increase and decrease of this value, a WIDS can determine if an attacker is getting closer or moving away. When combined with the RSSI information from other WIDS in the area and using it to deduce an estimated distance, it is possible to create a fairly accurate guesstimate as to where the attacker is located.

Figure 8-13 illustrates how this works. As an attacker attempts to connect to internal resources, its signal is detected by all APs/AMs in the area. Upon detection, the devices figure out how far away the device is located and consolidate this information. Because AP4 determines the signal is about 60 inches away, and AP3 determines it is 27 inches away, the controller can deduce that the signal is coming from a north direction, which puts it outside the protected area. The input from the other APs serves to further solidify this deduction.

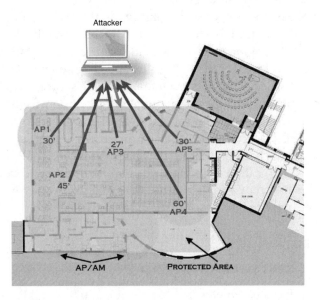

Figure 8-13   Using RSSI to deduce location

Although this capability is a nice feature, it is not always accurate, depending on the vendor and complexity of the solution. Wireless signals are affected by everything from a human body to electronics...even the weather. As a result, RSSI information fluctuates even if there is no movement. This throws off the calculations and, as a result, places an attacker in a false location. However, if the solution supports the creation of an RF benchmark by performing a preanalysis of the area and border that is to be protected, the results are fairly accurate.

HONEYPOT

A *honeypot* is a simulated environment meant to attract, distract, and engage attackers in an effort to both learn about their methods and keep them focused on a fake network to keep them away from a valid one. Although the traditional network-based honeypot includes common services and vulnerabilities, such as a Windows XP system with no updates, it is possible to create a wireless honeypot that focuses on issues completely related to the 802.11 protocol. This section outlines the ways to accomplish this.

Fake AP

Fake AP is a script that emits spoofed probe responses into the air in an effort to mislead any war drivers. The script essentially ties into the wireless card of a computer and dynamically changes the SSID, MAC address, channel, signal strength, and protection type to make it look like numerous wireless networks are operating in the area. Figure 8-14 illustrates what NetStumbler experiences when it's exposed to Fake AP. Attackers use these types of scripts to confuse clients; it is also possible to use this technique to confuse people looking for an AP. This technique is not useful for more skilled hackers who can recognize the method and easily focus in on the valid network.

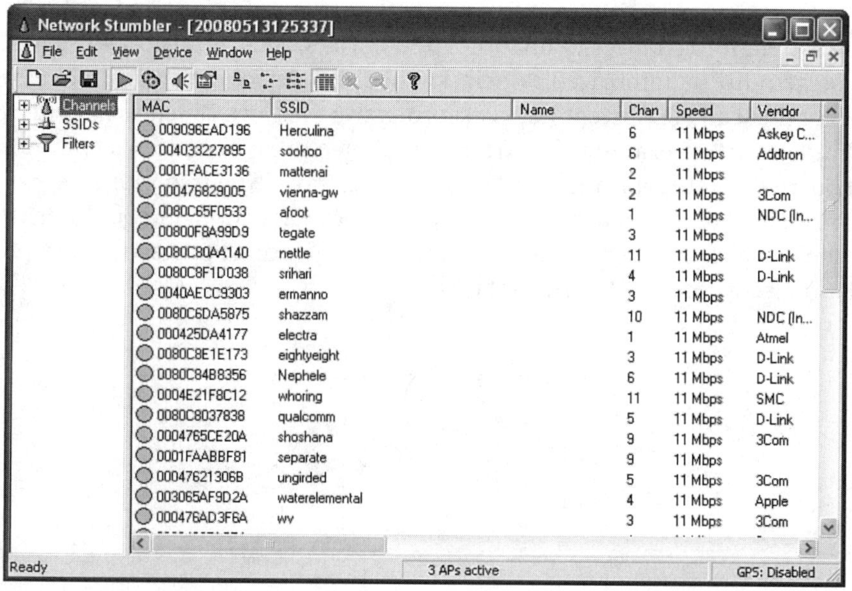

Figure 8-14 Fake AP

Wireless Honeypot

A wireless honeypot (see Figure 8-15) takes the noninteractive Fake AP approach one step further and creates a seemingly valid environment that looks and acts like a real wireless network, yet gives an attacker nothing but practice. Such a honeypot includes APs, emulated client traffic, monitors for data collection, and maybe even a valid infrastructure if the honeypot owner wants to collect data on deeper penetration techniques.

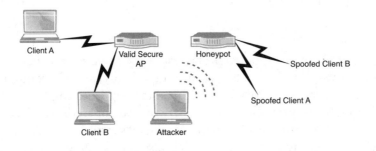

Figure 8-15   Wireless honeypot

Tarpit

Unlike a honeypot, a tarpit is meant to capture the attention of internal authorized clients that attempt to connect to unauthorized devices, such as an attacker's AP. A tarpit can also prevent the unauthorized association of client devices in an ad-hoc network (see Figure 8-16) that can circumvent network-protective measures, such as network access controls and more. For example, it is trivial to set up a proxy server on a computer with an unauthorized wireless ad-hoc interface and an authorized wired interface. Unauthorized clients can then connect to the ad-hoc connection and get Internet access through the network via the proxy server, thus bypassing most protection and preventative measures a corporate network contains.

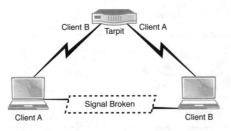

Figure 8-16   Tarpit preventing unauthorized ad-hoc connection

OTHER WIRELESS THREATS

When the subject of wireless security arises, most companies understand and respect the problems associated with operating a safe and secure 802.11-based WLAN. However, several other threats need to be addressed when discussing wireless technology. This section overviews the technology and what can be done to mitigate any associated risks.

LEGACY WIRELESS TECHNOLOGY

Wireless networking has been available long before the 802.11 standard was released. Since the early 1990s, it has been possible to transmit data over the 900MHz frequency range, and you can still purchase WLAN technology that is not based on the 802.11 protocol. This is important to recognize because WIDS solutions do not have the capability to detect or analyze traffic passing over non-802.11 networks. As a result, an attacker can easily put in a rouge AP and gain remote access to the network with no one the wiser.

BLUETOOTH

Bluetooth technology is typically associated with communication devices, such as phones, headsets, and keyboards. In addition, most people consider the threat of Bluetooth as a minor issue because it doesn't carry far—30 feet. The result is that Bluetooth is ignored by most companies and is not detected by most WIDS systems. However, Bluetooth is a real attack vector. Not only can an attacker set up a rogue Bluetooth-based AP, but he can also hijack Bluetooth conversations from distances of more than a mile.

SNIFFERS

Wireless sniffing is next to impossible to detect. As a result, it is also impossible for a WIDS to prevent an attacker from passively monitoring traffic for offsite analysis. Many companies try to mitigate this threat by directing the signal internally and controlling the strength of the energy emitting from the transceivers. Although this can help contain the WLAN for a typical user, the reality is that an attacker can easily overcome any weakened signal by employing a larger antenna. For example, a satellite dish can provide a 31dBi gain, which essentially takes the weak signal and drastically amplifies it. With such an antenna, an attacker can easily sit outside a company's intended wireless perimeter and capture all its traffic.

SUMMARY

This chapter looked at wireless intrusion detection/prevention and provided a detailed look at what a WIDS/WIPS solution needs to provide. It also examined the many challenges that wireless technology creates when it comes to protecting and defending against attacks. Finally, although numerous 802.11-based solutions can assist in the monitoring of a WLAN, all wireless administrators must ensure that they understand that RF energy can transmit data outside the 802.11 protocol. In addition, wireless communications can easily be disrupted and monitored. In short, there really is no such thing as a 100 percent safe wireless network.

A special thanks to Joshua Wright for the insight, knowledge, and feedback during the research and writing of this chapter. The security community, as a whole, greatly benefits from Joshua's continued work, so thanks, Joshua!

ENDNOTE

[1] See www.wirelessve.org/entries/show/WVE-2008-0006.

Physical Intrusion Detection for IT

Many organizations have desires to integrate components, curb redundant functionality, and stop data isolation. It is strange to see organizations consider only traditional IT department systems, components, and processes as candidates for these lofty goals. Sometimes, integration opportunities lie outside the borders of IT. For example, if I were to describe a "team of security professionals responsible for 24x7 monitoring of security violations and attacks, supported by networked systems of security sensors, and responsible for maintaining a security audit trail," your first thought might be that I was referring to the IT security team or a Network/Security Operations Center (NOC/SOC). Truthfully, I didn't refer to IT at all; I was referring to the physical security team. The similarities to IT security are undeniable: There are essentially two groups, IT security and physical security, that enact the same processes, use parallel technologies, and offer the same organizational risk management function.

Because the physical security team mirrors IT security is the reason why many corporations want to converge those resources to have more holistic risk protection and streamline operating budgets. After all, who wants to pay for two security monitoring centers, two security teams, two sets of intrusion detection controls, and so on? This chapter discusses the background of physical security, the parallels between physical and IT security, and some of the advantages that organizations (specifically IT security) can gain by cooperating or converging with their physical security counterparts.

ORIGINS OF PHYSICAL SECURITY

Physical security is an ancient practice compared to logical security. Although the theories and components of logical security were created in the late twentieth century, the use of locks for selective physical access control can be traced back to ancient Egyptian times. Common historic physical security elements include castles, drawbridges, fences, and moats. If you are envisioning a medieval warfare scene, you are definitely justified: Plenty of physical security technology is born out of the battlefield, or from other nation-state needs. That is typically because nation-states tend to have unique security needs that are important enough to make it worth investing the money necessary for research. Keep in mind that the Internet grew out of the original ARPANET project, which was military based, and designed by the Defense Advanced Research Projects Agency (DARPA).

Look at a recent example of federal needs bringing forth physical security innovation. In 2005, the U.S. Department of Homeland Security (DHS) enacted the Secure Border Initiative (SBI). The SBI called for multiple enactments; one in particular was the more thorough policing of U.S. borders to thwart illegal immigration and smuggling.[1] To monitor the 6,000 miles of land borders, a sensor and surveillance network is scheduled to be deployed by 2010. This sensor network, SBINet, has demands that are not typical for today's physical security use cases. To pull off SBINet, the folks at Boeing and the other technology partners are innovating with the latest camera and sensor technology. When all is done, SBINet will be the first use of some of these new long-range sensor and camera inventions; however, expect that same technology, once vetted by SBINet, to trickle down to other federal needs and eventually wind up in the commercial market.

Homeland Security Presidential Directive #12 (HSPD-12) is another example of a large-scale federal-security initiative that has yielded derivative private-sector advantages. HSPD-12 is basically a federal mandate for physical and logical security convergence. The details of HSPD-12 are so topical that the section, "HSPD-12: Convergence Trial by Fire," is devoted to it.

ASSUMED, YET OVERLOOKED

Physical security is often assumed by normal network security professionals. After all, how many network security professionals routinely leave a system containing sensitive data in a public location, confident that the logical security components of the device will keep it safe? Many network security folks assume the use of a secure datacenter or dedicated server closet location, often with specialized door locks, to keep their systems physically secure. It is becoming commonplace to include laptop security cables as standard issue with all organization laptop requisitions (see Figure 9-1).

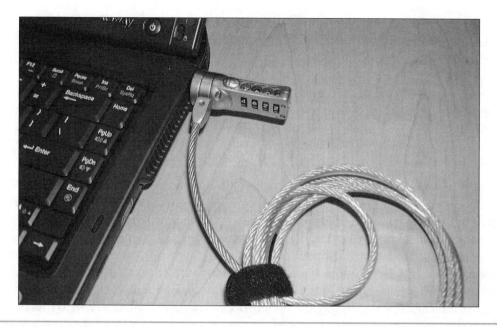

Figure 9-1 Laptop security cables, like this one, are becoming standard issue within organizations.

FULL-DISK ENCRYPTION: A LOGICAL SECURITY SOLUTION TO AID IN PHYSICAL SECURITY PROTECTION

Nowadays, laptops containing mountains of sensitive user data are being stolen left and right. Some notable examples are the August 2006 theft of 16,000 VA clinic records; the January 2008 theft of 2,500 NIH patient records; and the August 2008 false-alarm theft of 33,000 TSA Clear-enrolled travel records from a San Francisco airport office. Many people are re-evaluating how they can securely and safely store sensitive information on their computers.

The emerging solution is encryption in the form of full-disk encryption. Basically, most or all the contents of the system's hard drive are encrypted and require a password or hardware key to use them. Even the operating system (OS) files are encrypted; the only unencrypted part on the disk is the software necessary to perform the decryption operations. Certain systems offer an embedded TPM hardware module and BIOS hooks to facilitate secure password storage and disk encryption, and some OSs are even natively including encryption capabilities. Linux has been including cryptoloop and dm-crypt support for years; Mac OS X

10.3 and later includes FileVault; Windows NT and thereafter has included file-based encryption (EFS) within its NTFS filesystem; and Windows Vista now ships with BitLocker full-disk encryption. Beyond the OS, many commercial and free third-party software packages provide disk-encryption capabilities, including TrueCrypt, PGP, SafeBoot, SecureDoc, SafeGuard Easy, and Pointsec. A handy product matrix is available at www.full-disk-encryption.net/Full_Disc_Encryption.html.

Many network security practitioners believe physical access to a server is a "game over" scenario—meaning that the logical security functions of a device can be compromised or impacted if an attacker can physically manipulate it. Physical attacks can range from simple denial of service (DoS) situations to complex data or system compromises. For example, a DoS is possible by simply unplugging the power cord, disconnecting the network cable, or rebooting the server with the standard Ctrl, Alt, Delete sequence. Many OSs and network devices allow a specialized administrative mode via the local physical console, typically by interrupting the boot process; attackers gaining access to this administrative mode can potentially compromise the system. An attacker can reboot the system into a substitute OS via a Linux bootable CD, such as Knoppix, and mount the hard drives for direct disk access. This typically bypasses file system access control lists (ACLs) in the process. Attackers with local access can also remove media from the system, such as pulling out hard drives mounted in removable cages and taking backup media sitting in peripherals. A hardware-based key logger can be shimmed onto a keyboard cable of a system or Keyboard Video Mouse (KVM) switch (see Figure 9-2).

KEY LOGGERS + LONDON BANK = U.S. $420 MILLION

In 2005, a group of would-be thieves attempted to steal U.S. $420 million from the London branch of the Japanese bank Sumitomo Mitsui.[2] Although not publicly confirmed, it was rumored that key loggers installed on bank computers were a component of the heist. Fortunately, the British Hi-Tech Crime Unit got wind of the plot and foiled the robbery, but the entire situation has been branded as the largest attempted computer crime ever.

At the most extreme, there are sophisticated and complex physical attacks for recovering all in-memory system information, including encryption keys and other system secrets. One attack involves flash-freezing the RAM of a running system to preserve its

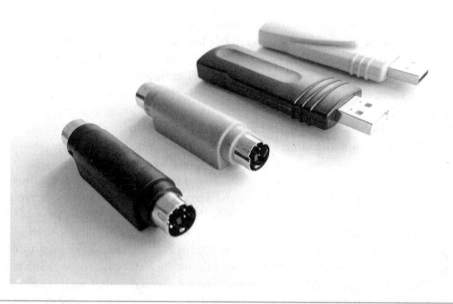

Figure 9-2   Assorted commercial USB and PS/2 key loggers (Courtesy: http://keyghostkeylogger.com/)

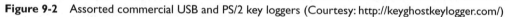

contents for recovery. In February 2008, some folks at Princeton, EFF, and Wind River Systems published a security research paper detailing how the memory remnants in DRAM can linger longer by lowering the temperature of the DRAM chips ("cold boot" attack). In other words, blasting system memory chips with freezing air/liquid can cause them to remember their data values even if power is temporarily removed from the chips. If you quickly reboot the system (after freezing the memory) into a special-purpose OS designed to quickly record all data in memory, you might find, in certain conditions, full-disk encryption keys can be recovered. The research team successfully used this method to defeat many software-based full-disk encryption security applications.[3]

A PARALLEL UNIVERSE TO IT SECURITY

Physical security is not much different than IT security. The overall goal is to manage risk and protect assets, although assets include employees/people in the physical world. Physical security is enacted by deployed access control mechanisms (locks, biometric readers), monitoring sensors (cameras, motion detectors, smoke alarms), often connected via a network to one or more central monitoring stations and manned by monitoring personnel. Like IT security, personnel must deal with false positives, nuisance alarms, and evaluate alarm alerts to determine the most appropriate course of action.

In typical non-high-security locations, physical security is usually most robust around the exterior of the facilities and relatively lax on the inside. This is similar to protecting the perimeter of an intranet with firewalls and virtual private networks (VPNs), but being relatively open once inside the network. Occasionally, a special area, such as a telecom closet, datacenter room, or CEO's office, might warrant additional access control. This protection can range from strong mechanical door locks to proximity cards and/or biometric reader locks. This is similar to how certain critical IT systems might require an additional authentication layer, such as S/KEY or other one-time password (OTP) measures.

Although only larger corporations typically have a dedicated SOC staffed with round-the-clock security analysts, it is more common to find 24x7 physical security monitoring stations on many premises. Unlike typical SOCs, the composition and purpose of the physical security monitoring station can drastically vary, depending on the level of necessary security and whether the physical security team is dedicated to the organization or is part of a service inclusive to a multi-tenant building. The station can be as simple as an outsourced security guard watching for the occasional video or other security alarm, all the way to sophisticated centers with video surveillance matrices and video-analytic systems steered by a fleet of physical security analysts. In the IT security world, this is like having one network engineer running Nagios or WhatsUpGold versus having a SOC armed with a dedicated staff reviewing all IDS sensor and system log alerts in real time. Regardless of whether the task of physical security is entrusted to a single outsourced night watchman or to a crack force of ex-military veterans armed with the latest security surveillance and enforcement equipment, the overall objectives are the same:

- Monitor and control the movement of people and assets into, out of, and within a location
- Account for people during and after an emergency situation
- Ensure the safety of all occupants and assets

One significant difference between physical access controls and logical access controls is that physical access controls are often better thought of as deterring or delaying an attacker. Although logical access controls are not perfectly infinite (for example, encryption can always be brute forced if given enough time, even if that time period is measured in eons), it still takes notably more time to crack a fairly strong encryption key than to saw through a door or ram a vehicle through a wall. Although physical access controls can be negated by the overzealous use of high explosives, there is generally not an equivalent circumvention situation for logical access controls.[4]

Do not forget the biggest challenge faced by any security mechanism: user subversion and coercion. Physical security teams encounter the same user tendencies to work around a security control that proves too inconvenient to deal with directly. IT security worries about password-laden Post-It notes stuck to monitors, and physical security teams worry about doors being propped open when users step outside for a smoke break.[5] Of course, users can be coerced by a menacing attacker to provide keys and passwords.

Lastly, there are the privacy concerns. No one likes the idea of IT security staff reading personal e-mails or instant messages, and no one likes the idea of a physical security staff watching his every move on a camera. But, these human factors can be dealt with by the judicious use of corporate policy and human resources (HR) involvement.

PHYSICAL SECURITY BACKGROUND

At first glance, physical security seems fairly straightforward: Access to items or sensitive areas is controlled by the use of various access control mechanisms, such as locks and barriers. But there is more to physical security than just doors, keys, and locks. Physical security encompasses the security and safety of all occupants and items; this often includes fire detection, emergency response, disaster evacuation, internal environment maintenance, structure fortification, and so on.

In a way, IT security teams have a relatively easier job than their physical security brethren. Physical access control systems (PACS) have specific requirements that can complicate or even negate the security benefit of the physical access controls. For example, during the event of a disaster, the deployed physical access control mechanisms must "fail open" to appropriately allow the speedy evacuation of occupants. Any physical security mechanism that impedes the safe movement of individuals during a crisis is more of a liability than an asset. This, of course, poses an interesting paradox: The physical access controls are supposed to maintain an appropriate integrity of controlled access, but that integrity must be immediately disabled during an emergency situation. Such a situation is unheard of in IT security; there is little reason to ever warrant the immediate removal of all access control mechanisms from a network, leaving it wide open.

Other constraints on physical access control mechanisms can further complicate matters. Certain physical security mechanisms might not be appropriate for use in accessibility-required locations. Americans with Disabilities Act (ADA) requirements often call for special design or consideration of physical security mechanisms to achieve an appropriate balance of security and accessibility for handicapped individuals. In addition, general construction building codes require physical security mechanisms to conform to architectural and installation requirements. Often, PACS components need Underwriters Laboratory (UL) approval to meet fire department guidelines or insurance carrier requirements.

Traditionally, physical security is handled by the same group in charge of the building facilities. After all, the building facilities group is in charge of the building and internal structure elements, and aren't doors and locks part of the building's structure? The previous paragraph regarding ADA requirements, building codes, and fire department considerations sure make it seem so. Once upon a time, this all made sense, because physical security had most to do with the building's premises and shared little with the rest of the organization. Physical security could be, and often was, isolated from the rest of the organization. Or it might not be a part of the organization at all, if you lease or rent your facilities, or your facilities are multi-tenant. In such cases, it is often common, and perhaps even required, for a third-party to manage the physical security of the facilities or at least its exterior aspects. An unaffiliated facility's security group can maintain security control over all external entrances of the building and mediate visitor access on behalf of all tenants. Optionally, the tenants can oversee their own physical security needs within their leased space.

Unfortunately, physical security is not infallible. Physical controls can be compromised: Doors can be propped open, locks can be picked, and cameras can be blinded, covered, or disabled. Thus, some element of human monitoring is essential to ensure that the overall physical security system and its controls are operating at peak capability and providing their respective control capabilities.

In some ways, the physical security universe is not just parallel to IT security, it is colliding with it. Nowadays, physical security components are leveraging commodity technology that has long had an established presence in IT. PACS components and video cameras can be retrofitted or include native capability to speak over TCP/IP networks. The majority of PACS control systems now run only on the ubiquitous Microsoft Windows platforms. PACS headend systems and data stores can interface with Microsoft Active Directories or off-the-shelf LDAP directories. Some PACS platforms include SOA-style capabilities, including SOAP endpoints, XML data exchange mechanisms, message queuing, and the use of commodity databases, like Oracle and Microsoft SQL Server.

COMMODITY TECHNOLOGY EXAMPLES: BRIGHTBLUE AND BLUEWAVE

The BrightBlue line by Schlage is a great example of a physical security vendor designing physical security components using commodity technologies. The BrightBlue access controllers are essentially embedded Linux systems that run on ARM processors—the same type of processor frequently used as the brains in PDAs, cell phones, and small office/home office (SOHO) networking devices. A USB flash drive is used for data storage, and the system runs a Web server for remote management over an Ethernet/IP network. The controller interfaces with up to 32 PACS devices over an RS-485 bus.

BlueWave is another physical security vendor that sells locks and door controllers specifically designed to be accessible over Ethernet or Wi-Fi (802.11) networks.[6] It offers standalone locks that can be deployed anywhere within range of a wireless access point (AP); the lock's built-in 802.11b radio logs the lock onto the wireless network and makes it remotely accessible.

COMMON PHYSICAL ACCESS CONTROL COMPONENTS

Physical security systems often involve a large array of components necessary to achieve all the desired security protections. The list includes

- **Environmental monitoring components.** Fire/smoke, humidity, temperature, and motion sensors
- **Access control components.** Identification credential readers, door locks, door/window open detectors, and window shatter detectors
- **Surveillance camera systems.** Cameras, displays, DVRs, and video-analytic servers
- **Interconnectivity and processing systems.** Wiring, access control panels, and event monitoring systems

Figure 9-3 depicts an example deployment of all these items.

Let's start with the most fundamental access control mechanism: locks. Locks are a staple of physical access control. They range from simple mechanical key locks, like those found outside of typical homes, all the way to complex electronic locks controlled by biometric authentication devices, such as fingerprint readers.

The use of mechanical key-based locks is not extremely practical in environments beyond a small office, simply because the ongoing management of physical keys starts to become cumbersome beyond a few dozen individuals. Ignoring master-key and multimaster-key setups for the moment, a key-based lock is essentially based on a shared symmetric key—each user's key is identical. Because all the keys are the same, there is no accountability to match the use of a specific key with a specific person. Mechanical push-button combination locks, where everyone shares the same combination, are similar in fashion. Certain master-key and multimaster-key setups allow for a certain number of different keys to operate the same lock; however, the numbers of key permutations are still limited and are still not practical for giving many users a different key.

To gain user accountability, you must be able to provide different keys to each user. Key use can be directly associated with the assigned user of the key, thus providing an audit trail. The only way to achieve such a system beyond a few users is to use an electronic lock where users are given an identification credential that an electronic lock/reader device interrogates. The lock/reader, or an attached controller, receives the identification credential from the user and decides whether to allow access to that resource for that specific credential.

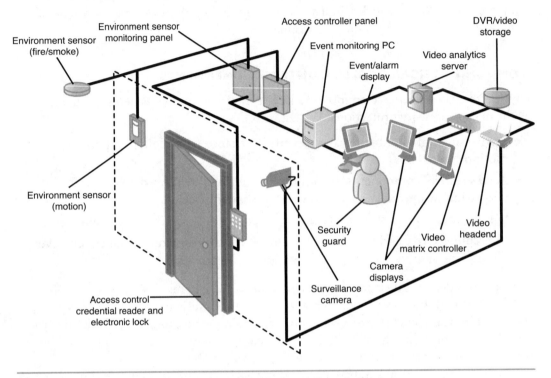

Figure 9-3   Generalized illustration of commonly deployed physical security components

NOTE

Electronic locks used in doorways are often times electromagnetic in some way, whether it is a powerful electromagnet that holds the door closed directly or a smaller electromagnet indirectly operating a mechanical latch that normally prohibits the door from opening.

The exact method used to look up whether an identification credential can access a resource varies, but it usually can be classified by two system deployment types. The first type is called a *standalone* system, which couples a small access controller, identification credential reader, and access control mechanism (such as an electronic lock) into a single self-contained unit. The unit internally maintains a database of all possible identification credentials valid for that specific resource. A standalone lock is fairly simple to deploy and operate with a small number of static users, but it does encounter scalability issues. Most standalone locks can only maintain a database of a few thousand individual users, and making frequent changes to the database can require notable overhead time, especially if you must repeat the change process on multiple standalone locks throughout the premises.

The second type is a *networked* system, which allows multiple credential readers and access control mechanisms to communicate and share resources (see Figure 9-4). Networked systems can range from single specialized embedded controllers to large-scale multicontroller installations. The networked systems can remotely interconnect via proprietary or Ethernet networks. They use a central access control user database or interface to external user data stores (for example, via LDAP).

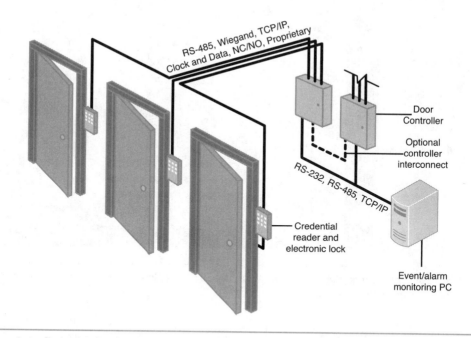

Figure 9-4 Example of multiple doors, controllers, and their associated interconnect networks

PACS use numerous interconnect technologies. Identification credential readers tradi-tionally use Wiegand, RS-485, clock and data, TCP/IP, or proprietary protocols to talk to door controllers. Electronic locks usually operate on a simpler normally close/normally open (NC/NO) wiring scheme that is common in simple burglar alarm systems. Controllers can sometimes be linked by using TCP/IP, RS-485, or proprietary protocols, and the controllers often communicate to management PCs via RS-232, RS-485, or TCP/IP.

Until now, the term "identification credential reader" has been used. The identifi-cation credential is merely something the user uniquely possesses. The credential reader is designed to receive the appropriate information from that identification credential. Common identification credentials include magnetic stripe cards, smart-cards, proximity cards or fobs, PIN or combination numbers, or biometrics (see Figure 9-5).

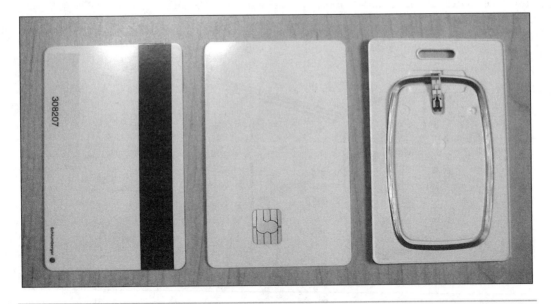

Figure 9-5 Common identification credential cards: magnetic stripe, smartcard, and radio frequency iden-tification (RFID) (with cover removed)

Magnetic Stripe Cards

Magnetic stripe cards are identical in composition and similar in function to a common credit card. When you swipe a magnetic stripe card through a reader, the reader interprets the data encoded onto the card's stripe as data; that data identifies who you are by your name, an account number, and so on. Unfortunately, it is relatively trivial to create or clone a magnetic stripe card using off-the-shelf magnetic stripe card writers commonly sold on eBay, as shown in Figure 9-6. This is generally why the magnetic stripe card is becoming extinct, at least for use in physical security applications.

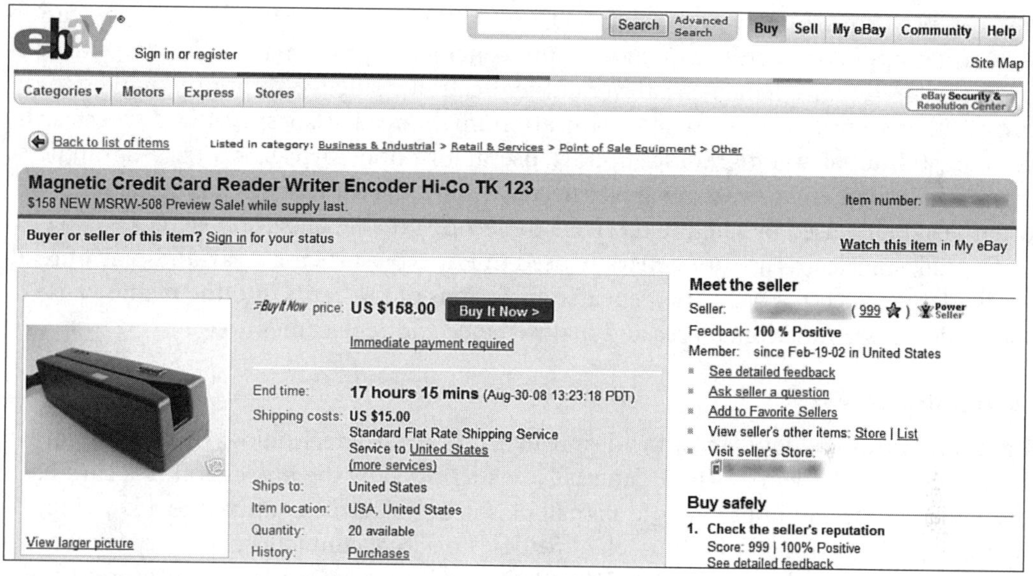

Figure 9-6   Magnetic stripe cards can easily be created or cloned with a writer, which can be purchased from various locations, including online e-tailers like eBay.

These materials have been reproduced with the permission of eBay Inc. © 2009 EBAY INC. ALL RIGHTS RESERVED.

Smartcards

Smartcards are a well vetted and widely deployed technology. To slightly overgeneralize them, smartcards are essentially a tiny microprocessor, complete with RAM and flash memory, embedded onto a card similar in dimensions to a typical credit card. The card contains an exposed area of metal contacts on one side; when inserted into a smartcard reader, the reader connects with these contacts to interface with the card's electronics.

Smartcards widely vary under the hood. Some not-so-smart smartcards function only as a data storage medium (think USB flash drive, albeit much smaller storage space), and specialized variants have a write-once memory capability used for disposable prepaid card applications where the "data" on the card represents money and the write-once operation permanently removes the "money value" from memory as the card is used. Some smartcards add a security protection gateway in front of the storage memory, such that the memory cannot be accessed unless an appropriate PIN or strong password is first supplied to the card. This type of card can be used to store X.509 certificates. At the high end, smartcards contain a full CPU and specialized virtual machine that is capable of running Java or .NET applications. These applications are often referred to as cardlets and can perform arbitrary processing on the card. This enables a vendor or organization to load the applicable cardlets of choice onto general-purpose smartcards; the cardlets can be tailored to implement whatever authentication challenge/response, single sign-on, or other security processes an organization might need. Also, specialized smartcards contain additional cryptographic support, useful for public/private key cryptographic operations where the private key never needs to leave the card, or stream decryption often seen being used by satellite receivers to decode satellite television signals.

Overall, smartcards are not generally used in PACS because the wear-and-tear of readers is a large concern. Over time, repeated insertions of the cards into the reader cause the reader to malfunction, increasing maintenance and replacement costs.

Proximity Cards

Proximity cards are popular and widespread access control technology. Proximity card technology, also known as RFID, can easily be identified by the possession of a card or *fob*, which is a term used to denote a small plastic bobble usually affixed to a key ring, that is waved in front of a wall-attached reader; no actual contact is necessary for the reader to access the data on the fob. What happens is that the reader is continuously sending out a small field of energy in the form of radio waves; when the proximity card enters that field, it absorbs just enough power to power up and transmit data. Proximity technology is considered ideal for access control applications because the noncontact nature of the technology negates physical wear and tear on the reader and the card. Figure 9-7 shows some examples of RFID technology.

Two types of common proximity access control technologies are in use: legacy 125kHz systems and newer 13.54MHz systems. The number specified indicates the radio frequency used to communicate between the card and reader; however, that is not the only difference.

Figure 9-7 Some examples of RFID readers owned by the author. Clockwise from left: a commercial Motorola standalone controller with integrated RFID, an RFID reader out of an electronics experimenter's kit from qkits.com, and the internals of a PCProx reader sold by RFIdeas.com

Legacy 125kHz systems are simpler in operation. After the proximity card enters into the reader's field, the proximity card transmits a fixed ID number hard coded into the microchip in the card. The reader consults the database to see if that ID number is allowed access and, if found, it opens the lock. The process might seem fishy, and rightfully so: The number transmitted by the card is always the same, and nothing else is necessary to gain access. The card essentially tells the reader, "I am ID #31337," and the reader simply decides whether ID #31337 is allowed to pass. The million dollar security question is this: What prevents an attacker from fabricating an RFID circuit or otherwise encoding a proximity card so that the new card also identifies itself as ID #31337? Historically, the technology and skill required to do so was generally felt to be high enough to not be a practical threat. However, today's proliferation in tech-savvy individuals and significant advances in the RFID space have lowered that bar almost to the point of being flat on the ground. You can now even find numerous locations on the Internet that offer free electronic schematics of circuits that can clone or emulate legacy RFID tags. Such schematics can build homemade RFID tag emulators, like the one shown in Figure 9-8.

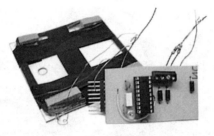

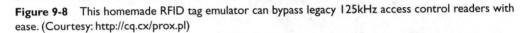

Figure 9-8   This homemade RFID tag emulator can bypass legacy 125kHz access control readers with ease. (Courtesy: http://cq.cx/prox.pl)

NOTE

There is still a significant existing installed base of PACS using legacy 125kHz proximity/RFID technology. It must be said: The security capabilities of this technology have been compromised. If your organization still uses legacy proximity cards for access control, you need to run (not walk) to a physical security vendor and get an upgrade solution now.

The 13.54MHz proximity technology solves some of the shortcomings of the legacy 125kHz systems. Generally speaking, 13.54MHz cards are a hybrid union of smartcards and RFID, which is why they are often referred to as "contact-less smartcards," although you might also hear references to the brand names MIFARE or iClass. Like legacy proximity technology, the contact-less smartcards receive their power from an energy field that the reader creates; however, 13.54MHz proximity technology enables bidirectional communication between the reader and the card. This enables the reader to use multi-step authentication methods with the card, such as a challenge/response authentication process. Overall, 13.54MHz technology conceptually provides the power of smartcards combined with the practicality of proximity cards, which makes it the ideal technology for access control. They provide wonderful converged/dual-use access control capabilities, because you can leverage existing smartcard-based logical access control solutions while also extending that investment to include physical access control. ISO standard 14433 has emerged to cover certain 13.54MHz RFID technologies.

Despite the great promise of the 13.54MHz proximity technology, some of the actual implementations leave something to be desired. We have previously discussed how smartcards can widely vary under the hood, ranging from nonsmart storage mediums to virtual minicomputers. It turns out that the contact-less variants of smartcards are not much different in that respect. In fact, some vendors ran off and implemented their own versions of this technology before the ISO 14433 standard emerged. As it turns out, they are now paying the price: Many of these nonstandard implementations are being debunked and considered insecure. The most recent example is the fall of the MIFARE Classic card.

MULTIPLE FACES OF MIFARE

MIFARE is a brand name of NXP Semiconductors (formerly Philips Semiconductors) and its 13.54MHz RFID technology line. It has branded numerous technologies as being in the MIFARE family, using a secondary subname to distinguish the actual technologies. For example, you can find MIFARE Classic/Standard, MIFARE DESFire, MIFARE UltraLight, MIFARE ProX, and so on. To make matters worse, the underlying technology differs enough to make them all incompatible with each other, and only a select few are actually ISO 14433 compliant. Thus, when someone uses the general term MIFARE, stop and ask exactly to which flavor they are referring. A handy description of each is available at http://en.wikipedia.org/wiki/MIFARE.

The MIFARE Classic cards use a proprietary encryption and authentication process called Crypto-1 between the cards and readers, which differs from the ISO 14433 standard. It turns out that this proprietary process, much like other vendor-proprietary encryption processes offered in security products, involves more obfuscation than actual vetted encryption. Various researchers found that it is possible to compromise MIFARE Classic cards, clone them, and so on. Unfortunately, the system security was not proven insufficient prior to the worldwide adoption and deployment of hundreds of millions of MIFARE Classic cards in transit system applications found in many cities and countries. Here is a short list of the cities and country transit systems affected (courtesy Engadget.com):

- London (Oyster Card)
- Boston (MBTA)
- Netherlands (OV-Chipkaart)
- Minneapolis/St. Paul
- South Korea (Upass, T-money, Mybi)
- Hong Kong

- Beijing
- Milan
- Madrid (Sube-T)
- Australia (Smartrider)
- Sao Paulo (Bilhete Unico)
- Rio de Janeiro (RioCard)
- Bangkok
- New Delhi

As a result of this insecurity, NXP Semiconductors has introduced the MIFARE Plus line, which is a backwards-compatible derivative of MIFARE Classic with stronger encryption, courtesy of the standard AES algorithm, bringing it more in line with the ISO 14433 standard. Despite having an upgrade route to fix this security oversight, countless localities have collectively invested billions of dollars into MIFARE Classic technology only to discover they have to spend many more millions to upgrade their systems to the new MIFARE Plus technology and phase out all MIFARE Classic cards.

NOTE

You can watch an online video presentation about the insecurities of MIFARE Classic cards at www.hackaday.com/2008/01/01/24c3-mifare-crypto1-rfid-completely-broken/.

Of course, we are not telling you all this to make you believe proximity technology, as a whole, is suspect. In fact, the story of proximity technology's history in access control has provided a great moral: The security value of proprietary and closed vendor technologies cannot be guaranteed; if you have to choose, choose open standard technologies that have been better scrutinized and accepted for their security value. Proximity technology based on ISO 14433 standards is robust and provides demonstrable security value.

PIN/Combination Numbers

The use of a personal identification number (PIN) or combination number, entered via a keypad, is still fairly common in PACS, but not as the sole authentication method. By themselves, PINs are weak; they can be easily recovered by looking over one's shoulder and infinitely copied merely by knowing the number. At least the use of a physical identification credential, such as a smartcard, proximity card, or magnetic stripe card, conceptually limits reproduction because you must physically possess the identification credential or fabricate a physical clone. Of course, theft of the physical identification credential still causes the same problems, which is why the combination of using a physical identification credential (something you have) along with a PIN (something you know) increases the overall system security. Such a setup is often referred to as *two-factor authentication.* You encounter this system every time you visit an ATM.

As previously mentioned, shoulder surfing is a practical way to learn a person's PIN. This problem can be solved with certain low-tech approaches, including user education and privacy shields around the keypad area. Unfortunately, truly determined attackers can use a high-tech method to recover the PIN after a user leaves the area: thermal imaging. Specifically, an attacker can use a thermal camera to view the latent heat print left behind after touching the keypad keys. A keypad key is warmed by a user's finger upon contact, even if the contact is brief. A constant cooling rate by all keys also allows someone to literally see the order that the keys were pressed, because the recent keys are hotter than the previous ones, as shown in Figure 9-9.

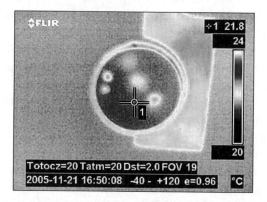

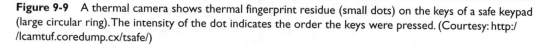

Figure 9-9 A thermal camera shows thermal fingerprint residue (small dots) on the keys of a safe keypad (large circular ring). The intensity of the dot indicates the order the keys were pressed. (Courtesy: http://lcamtuf.coredump.cx/tsafe/)

To counter thermal cameras, high-security facilities can use scramble keypads. Scramble keypads are essentially digital keypads where the numbers randomly rotate before every use. This makes it significantly more difficult to recover a user's PIN just by monitoring which keypad key/location the user pressed. Hirsch Electronics, who came up with the original idea, and Schlage are popular scramble keypad manufacturers.

Biometrics

Biometrics is when someone uses some physical attributes of a user to identify the user, such as her fingerprint. The term itself implies the measurement of a live characteristic of a person. Common biometrics used for identification include the following:

- **Fingerprints**. The unique pattern of lines and ridges on the ends of your fingers
- **Hand geometry**. The size and shape of your hand
- **Retinal**. The unique pattern of blood vessels seen in your eyes
- **Facial**. The shape and distance between facial features
- **Voice**. The frequency and patterns of the sound you make when you talk

Overall, biometrics adds the "something you are" type to the established list of the "something you have" and "something you know" types of security credentials, which provides an even greater level of nonrepudiation.

Biometrics are quickly becoming a standard as a second or third authentication factor for use in security-sensitive applications. The popularity is because of two significant advantages: users cannot lose/forget the body part being measured, and attackers cannot easily steal the body part from a user. For example, users will always have their fingers at hand whenever they encounter a biometric fingerprint reader, and an attacker is incapable of stealing the user's finger (that is, without the user noticing). For high-security requirements, biometrics solves the issue of accountability because the identification credential shares a strong relationship with the user possessing the credential. A normal password or ID card does not actually identify its possessor.

Biometric fingerprint readers are the most common type of biometric-based authentication in use today. In fact, biometric fingerprint readers are quickly gaining ubiquitous status—you can find them built into many laptop models, such as the one shown in Figure 9-10. Hand geometry also has a notable presence, although some security integrators indicate that the current crop of hand geometry readers did not prove to be as accurate as you might hope when deployed in large environments. The same integrators also indicated that retinal and facial are not popular because users have reservations about sticking their face in front of an eye/face scanner.

GUMMY BEARS, SILLY PUTTY, AND SEVERED FINGERS

The early days of biometrics had vendors making many promises about the robustness and integrity of biometric readers. Needless to say, early implementations left a lot to be desired. In 2002, Tsutomu Matsumoto created fake fingers using ingredients similar to those found in gummy bears and Silly Putty, and tested a battery of commercial fingerprint readers. Overall, the gummy-bear gelatin finger proved successful at fooling 80 percent of the tested biometric readers; the Silly Putty variant was not successful. The variance is attributed to a special feature of fingerprint biometric readers: the capability to gauge the capacitance of the finger being presented for authentication. Dead tissue (such as from a severed finger) reacts differently to electric currents than live tissue, and it just so happens that gelatin exhibits a capacitance similar to live skin. This contributes to its success in fooling the readers. For a more comprehensive look at over-the-counter materials and their success at fooling fingerprint readers, read www.washjeff.edu/users/ahollandminkley/Biometric/index.html.

Figure 9-10 A fingerprint reader (horizontal bar located beneath Fn and Ctrl keys) found on the author's Gateway laptop

THIS IS NOT YOUR FATHER'S CCTV

When you hear of a closed-circuit television (CCTV) camera security, you might conjure up images of one or more security guards sitting in front of several glowing TV monitors, diligently trying to watch all of them for any suspicious activity. In this setup, the cameras' video signals are just data feeds that terminate at the security guards' eyeballs, and those security guards must make sense of what they see. In other words, the humans do all the video analysis and provide the intelligence. They are truly are the brains of the operation.

This situation might have been common in CCTV's prehistoric times, but it is far from today's CCTV capabilities. The historic setup of running analog coaxial cable between cameras and a video headend controller is slowly being replaced by cameras that transmit video over IP/Ethernet networks. Digital video recorders (DVRs) are replacing the use of time lapse and slow-running VCRs to archive video streams. In the old days, video feeds were often fed into a video matrix switcher, which displayed the various video images onto multiple monitors so that surveillance personnel could watch it. Nowadays, video monitors are being complemented or replaced by a video-analysis server capable of analyzing the video feeds for humans.

Video analytics, the analysis of video feeds and images, has a well-established and yet continuously growing presence in the video security space. In fact, video-analytic features now often come as standard in CCTV packages, although they can require additional license keys to enable.

What does video analytics entail? Well, it entails a lot more than just the mundane "something seems to have moved in the field of vision" variety. Common video-analytic capabilities found in current marketplace products include the following:

- **Crowd counting.** Being able to determine how many people are present in a group
- **Virtual fences.** Capability to define a specific area or boundary within the field of vision, and warn whenever an object crosses/comes in contact with that area/boundary (for example, an invisible fence that no one should cross)
- **Forbidden paths.** Detecting when an object moves in the wrong direction, such as trying to move into an exit-only doorway
- **Loitering detection.** Determining when someone is hanging around a certain area for too long
- **Target tracking.** Following a target across multiple cameras
- **Target differentiation.** Automatically determining the difference between different target types (such as a person and an automobile)
- **Camera positioning.** Automatically adjusting the position of movable cameras to ensure a moving object remains in view

Video analytics are not just for security applications; many capabilities are being expanded and applied to other uses. For example, video analytics can monitor grocery store aisles to determine the product sections that people frequent more often or whether certain aisle endcaps are receiving more attention than others.

Many capabilities of modern video analytics come about by huge advancements in CPU speeds. Basic motion detection can be a computationally expensive process. Yet the market for video analytics is so hot that even CPU vendors are adding video-analytic-centric instructions to their processors. For example, Intel's latest SSE4 processor extensions, found in its high-end CPUs, feature new CPU instructions that are specifically aimed to speed up common motion-detection algorithms. Basically, the CPU has been somewhat optimized for video analytics, which means that more processing can be done in less time, further opening the doors to more complex algorithms that provide deeper analytical capability.

In fact, a lot of video surveillance advancements are actually trickling down to the consumer level. There are a number of SOHO offerings of DVRs, IP-enabled video servers, and IP-enabled surveillance cameras complete with motion detection features (see Figure 9-11). All these can be found at your local computer megastore. Of course, do not expect any of these under $100 video cameras to rival the quality and features you find on a professional CCTV camera that is 20 times the price. These are great toys for a home user, but they do not generally meet the requirements for professional use in an organization with true security risks.

Figure 9-11   Examples of video surveillance devices available to home users. Clockwise from top: IP-enabled video camera, a two-camera DVR with built-in motion detection, and a TCP/IP network video server that supports four analog cameras/video sources. All items retail for less than U.S. $150.

CISCO SYSTEMS: A FAMILIAR FACE IN THE SURVEILLANCE SPACE

Yes, the 800-pound gorilla of IT networking space also is strongly competing for presence in the physical security markets too. Previous acquisitions of SyPixx and BroadWare jump started Cisco Systems' video-surveillance-over-IP offerings. However, the presence of Cisco in the IP-enabled video security surveillance market is not that surprising; Cisco's outward mission has been to provide the platforms necessary to carry an enterprise's communications, which is comprised of data, video, and audio. It does not matter if the network video data is from a Web cast, YouTube, or a security surveillance camera...it is all just video data on the wire. Because Cisco already had a significant investment in its video communication platform, targeting the security surveillance market is just repurposing what it has already developed. The acquisition of SyPixx and BroadWare gives Cisco a few key endpoint technologies that enables an enterprise to bridge existing analog video surveillance feeds onto digital networks and additional technologies to manage the video.

That said, Cisco also has physical security offerings beyond just IP-enabled video surveillance; it has a basic lineup of IP-enabled door controllers and gateways, along with a software solution to manage all of it. These components are discussed later in this chapter.

How does this apply to intrusion detection and analysis? Beyond the obvious benefits of detecting physical intrusions, video analytics is converting CCTV camera feeds from analog signals processed mostly by human eyeballs into contextual digital data. Once it is in digital form, the data can be indexed, searched, and datamined, just like any other log file. IT professionals already understand the capabilities and benefits of ongoing network packet and flow logging, network traffic pattern analysis, and network anomaly detection. Now, these principles can be applied to CCTV data feeds, because the video data is finally in a format that is easily applied to these methodologies. Imagine...you can now Splunk your video surveillance data!

SPLUNK

Never heard of Splunk? Splunk (www.splunk.com) is essentially a search engine geared toward log files, and it provides phenomenal log analysis capabilities that you can use for both logical and physical security log analysis needs. If you are not already using Splunk in your enterprise, it is worth a look; after all, free versions of it are offered.

OLD HABITS DIE HARD

The proliferation of Ethernet-equipped and IP-enabled physical access control components can lead you to assume that the days of separated PACS versus IT networks are in the past. As it turns out, this might not be the case. The consensus of many vendors and integrators seems to be that many organizations, particularly when constructing a new building, still opt to create separate network drops and backbones for the PACS and IT networks (assuming PACS is using an IP network). This is usually at the insistence of the IT department, because it does not specifically know how the PACS traffic impacts the overall IP network bandwidth/performance. There might be much truth to this, especially when dealing with IP-enabled CCTV cameras. Real-time, continuous high-resolution streaming video coming from 100 IP-enabled CCTV cameras can definitely impact network bandwidth! That is not to say the separate PACS and IT networks won't ever talk to each other—a router placed between the two networks still lets them communicate. But, the idea of using a single shared network for all IT and PACS needs might not be as ubiquitous as you might think.

Fortunately, IP-enabled CCTV camera vendors are hearing the plea. They are rethinking how IP cameras send video data over a network. Traditionally, the camera just sends a continuous video feed to a headend receiver, where it is fed into a video matrix switcher, DVR, and/or video analysis system. Many times, the camera sends a relatively uninteresting feed of nothing out of the ordinary. Thus, vendors are moving some of the DVR and analytical functions into the camera, so that the camera can store the video locally, analyze it, and only send the portions of the video stream that contain something interesting. This can significantly save bandwidth. VideoIQ is heavily marketing its iCVR series based on this reasoning. By moving portions of the DVR into the camera, it also means that the camera is fault tolerant; if the network and/or the connection to the far-end DVR goes down, no video is lost. For large-scale IP-enabled camera deployments, this type of technology can make a significant amount of sense. One potential downside to this arrangement, however, is that any on-board DVR video data is lost if the camera is damaged/destroyed.

Hesitation in moving toward convergence is not just coming from the IT department. The physical security team has its fair share of concerns, too. Because of the value of the lives of the people that the physical security team protects, physical security systems have critical needs for availability and uptime. The availability and uptime requirements for physical security systems are often stricter than traditional IT components. For example, an IT department achieving a 99.99 percent availability/uptime measurement for a given year might be seen as exceptional; however, a physical security system achieving a 99.99 percent availability/uptime over the course of the year means that there were 52 minutes (the .01 percent) when fire alarms and surveillance were unavailable and door locks allowed anyone into the premises. That is a significant concern and can have ramifications with the fire department, insurers, and so on. Simply put, physical security system downtime can be life threatening.

It is not that IT networks have a guaranteed aspect of unreliability; there is just no way to predict all events that affect a network's availability ahead of time. IT and physical security teams have different perceptions and expectations of downtime. If you ask an IT person when the last network/system outage occurred, whether planned or otherwise, you might get an answer measured in days or weeks; if you ask a physical security person when the last PACS outage occurred, you are likely to get an answer measured in months or years. As much as IT tries to design resilient networks and systems, flukes and unpredictable occurrences—often caused by security threats—can cripple a network with little or no warning. SQL Slammer and other worms of yore are a great example: Many enterprises had one of these digital pests slither into their intranet, and from that point, the network became swamped with traffic that impacted IT operations. Today, you have to worry about things like users getting infected with Trojans and botnets during his Web surfing, or even just network saturation because many users are checking out the latest viral YouTube flick. That does not even take into account the ever-increasing complexity of the systems often found in IT environments; sometimes, it is amazing that these systems can achieve even a modest uptime at all!

It is worth mentioning that these arguments are not unique; environments taking the voice over IP (VoIP) plunge have probably encountered concerns from the telecom group about network congestion affecting telephone operations. In particular, it is of grave concern if people cannot dial 911 in an emergency simply because network congestion caused there to be not enough bandwidth.

CONVERGENCE OF PHYSICAL AND LOGICAL SECURITY

Why should the risks of an attacker walking into a building and an attacker logging into a network be categorically separated and handled by different organizational units? Why should an organization pay for two security monitoring centers, two security teams, two sets of intrusion detection controls, two access control credentials deployed to every user, two access control education campaigns, and so on? We have effectively entered the age where operational streamlining and budget stretching is not just a necessity, but an actual business tactic to remain competitive. As such, businesses can no longer afford to overlook the redundancy between physical and logical security operations.

But, the drivers for convergence are not just monetary. We are also in an age where both risk and corporate liability are high. We can identify risk silos, analogous to data silos, that are overseen by different organizational champions:

- **Personnel risks.** VP/director of HR
- **Financial risks.** CFO
- **Physical risks.** COO, facilities manager, physical security officer
- **Logical risks.** CIO, CSO
- **Legal risks.** General counsel, CFO

This scattered approach, separating risk under the proper organizational department, makes it difficult to gauge an organization's overall risk index. An organization's executive committee or board of directors would have to consult a half-dozen organizational figureheads to gain their limited risk perception, and even then, the big picture is not immediately evident without additional work to stitch together those perceptions.

This is why many organizations embrace an Enterprise Risk Management (ERM) strategy, championed by a chief risk officer (CRO) or chief risk management officer (CRMO). This new executive position is accountable for governing all organizational risk, regardless of whether the risk is strategic, reputational, operational, financial, or legal/compliance-related. This provides a single oversight of risk throughout an enterprise, but the quality of that oversight largely depends on how well the CRO can gather the necessary risk perceptions and data from various parties (CFO, CSO, and so on). A converged environment significantly aids a CRO in gathering an accurate picture of organizational risk for all physical and logical threats.

HOW CONVERGENCE WORKS

The technical definition of convergence varies, depending on who you talk to and what his agenda is. To some, convergence is just the use of a single identification token for both physical and logical access. An example of this is a contact-less smartcard used to open proximity-based door locks and to log into a smartcard-capable PC.

But is that truly converged? Sure, it is one access token to the user, but the functions of the token are essentially unrelated and unknown to each other. Communication occurs with separate, disparate systems. If an IT administrator revoked all privileges from a user's account, the user is prevented from using her smartcard to log into her PC, but would it prevent her from opening the building doors? Or is that under the control of a separate PACS maintained by the physical security group? It might look and feel like a glorified single sign-on situation, but actually, a dual-use token is really just two separate tokens fused into one physical form factor. The only thing that is converged is a minor aspect of the overall user experience.

Overall, convergence just measures how well these historically separate security systems work together. Convergence can provide operational benefits in multiple ways:

- Consolidate the number of access control tokens (proximity or swipe cards, USB dongles, smart cards, and so on) into a single physical token
- Simplify the user enrollment and identity-maintenance process
- Centralize access control information for users
- Unify access control reporting and threat detection

What technologies are involved in a converged environment? Access tokens, usable for both physical and logical access, are a given. In nonconverged environments, legacy proximity card technology has been the traditional reigning champion for physical access tokens, although it is still common to find magnetic swipe cards. Traditional logical access tokens are being replaced by contact smartcards and USB keyfobs, or password-derived solutions (such as OTP tokens). For converged environments, contact-less smartcards are quickly becoming the de-facto standard.

Keep in mind that the most popular application of smartcards, contact or contact-less, for access control purposes involves a stored X.509 certificate unique to a user and usually protected by a PIN/password or biometric authentication mechanism. This makes the smartcard act like a small vault, containing the security credential of a user protected by an additional authentication factor.

Wait, how does the X.509 certificate on a user's smartcard relate to the rest of the environment? The answer is a three-letter acronym that has long been a controversial topic in IT: PKI. Yes, most converged security infrastructures are built on a public key infrastructure (PKI). PKIs often carry a negative connotation because of overhyped marketing efforts and widespread implementation disasters in the late 1990s. Part of the problem is that the technology was not as mature as everyone hoped, and the caveats and implementation "gotchas" were unknown. Fortunately, all those past implementation failures served as a learning experience for both enterprises and vendors. As a result, today's products are more capable; that is not to say that PKIs are not still complicated environments requiring an elevated level of diligence, commitment, and finely tuned system orchestration.

Various recommended business processes are specific to a converged security environment. The first, and most important step, is credential enrollment. A user must be furnished with his access control token, and that token must be populated with all appropriate identifying information, X.509 certificates, and so on. That token must also be entered into all appropriate identity-based databases. In a truly converged environment, this should be only a single location, typically in an identity management system (IDMS). In loosely converged environments sharing only the access control token in common, a user needs to be enrolled into HR systems, IT logical control directories (such as Active Directory), and the PACS user store. Depending on the reuse of the card, other system enrollments might be required; for example, some companies use their access control tokens as a method for cash-less cafeteria transactions. In this case, a user sets up the necessary vending account information. For biometric-capable environments, the user's biometric data—fingerprints, retina pattern, and such—is taken and stored.

This process seems straightforward, but all this relies on a fundamental assumption: The person present for the enrollment is the intended person to be enrolled. If Malory learns that Alice is becoming the new global CTO of a corporation, Malory can potentially walk in to the enrollment department, present herself as Alice, and be enrolled with substantial privileges. Therefore, the enrollment process needs to incorporate some sort of identity verification. Depending on the security requirements of your organization, this can range from simple photo ID verification (using a driver's license) to a more thorough background check with known photo verification.

After a user is enrolled, she can then proceed to use the physical premises and the computers/networks. Physical access is granted by waving the contact-less smartcard in front of card readers stationed at various access control points. In high-security environments, there might be the additional requirement to enter a PIN on a keypad or to use a biometric sensor that is built into the card reader. The user's identification information flows through the reader, over a chain of PACS components (door controller, access controller headend, and so on) and is eventually compared against identification and policy information in a centralized IDMS. Using a computer is similar; a user waves the contact-less smartcard in front of a smartcard reader attached to the computer. Authentication components installed into the OS reads the user's identification data from the card and translates it into a final identification credential usable to log onto the system.

During the course of a user using the physical premises and computers, all audit and log information of her use is transmitted from her appropriate PACS or IT system sources into a centralized event manager. A security operations team monitors all alerts from all systems, both physical and logical. At any point in time, the team can recount a user's full activity, where she went in the building and what she did on the network.

When it comes time for a user to leave the organization, HR makes a change in the personnel system to indicate that the user is no longer with the company. The IDMS immediately picks up that change and then disables all access privileges for that user, effectively locking the user out of the building and the network.

Sound great? It sure does! But, all this assumes that the various systems necessary to support a converged environment are able to communicate and understand each other...and as they say, the devil is in the details.

PHYSBITS

The Open Security Exchange, founded by Computer Associates International, Gemplus, HID Corp, and Software House, has championed the Physical Security Bridge to IT Security (PHYSBITS) specification. PHYSBITS is a vendor-neutral framework and data model for integrating physical and logical/IT security systems. The capabilities provided by the specifications are aimed toward ERM requirements, leading to the capability of seeing a complete picture of organizational security. Version 1.0 of the specification was released in April 2003.

PHYSBITS is touted as achieving three primary goals:

- **Data auditing.** The PHYSBITS framework has a unified and common format for all security-related events, which allows for central storage, searching, and analysis of all audit data sourced from multiple security systems.
- **Strong authentication.** The PHYSBITS framework is built around the use of a strong unified authentication credential.
- **User rights management.** The PHYSBITS data model can represent a consolidated view of a user's rights across multiple access control systems, offering a centralized manner to truly manage access control permissions.

The significant hurdle to creating a converged environment is the creation of a central identity store. This can be a dedicated IDMS or some other database that holds a superset of all necessary identification records. Surprisingly, this is usually the biggest hurdle for organizations. A naïve approach would be to assume IT's active directory or the HR personnel system has all the necessary user records. In fact, the physical security teams routinely deal with people that are often not given actual logical computer accounts: visitors, janitorial staff, utility repairmen, delivery personnel, etc. Often a superset database is created by importing and merging existing records in multiple organizational databases (HR, active directory, PACS, and so on).

HSPD-12: CONVERGENCE TRIAL BY FIRE

In August 2004, U.S. President George W. Bush released Homeland Security Presidential Directive #12 (HSPD-12). In eight brief paragraphs,[7] the president set forth a policy requirement for a common identification standard for federal employees and contractors. The basic idea is to ensure federal personnel can be easily and consistently identified and authenticated in a manner that is not subject to forgery. But, do not be fooled by the brevity of the directive; the policy is actually a landmark in security history.

HSPD-12 does not actually contain any technical details on how to achieve the required common identification standard; those details are left up to the National Institute of Standards and Technology (NIST). NIST followed up by creating Federal Information Processing Standard 201 (FIPS-201), which details the technical requirements for the identification card. The Office of Budgets and Management (OMB) oversees the overall execution of the directive. The OMB set October 27, 2008, as the deadline to have all federal agencies perform the necessary background checks and issue the new identification cards to all employees and contractors.

DÉJÀ VU FOR THE DoD

Prior to HSPD-12, the Department of Defense (DoD) had its Command Access Card (CAC) program. The CAC program supplied smartcards to military personnel and other DoD employees/contractors. By the time FIPS-201 starting gaining traction, the DoD had issued 13 million CAC cards since the program inception in 1999. Needless to say, the CAC program was large, but HSPD-12 was going to be much larger. Fortunately, many lessons learned from the CAC program were incorporated into the new HSPD-12 initiative and FIPS-201 standards.

The FIPS-201 requirements call for a contact-less smartcard that is used for both physical and logical access control. The card is used in combination with a biometric fingerprint reader, which provides two-factor authentication. The FIPS-201 standard describes mundane details of the card, such as what must be printed on it, where it needs to be printed, the size of the font, the colors of the background, and so on. If all goes accordingly, the card will contain all the necessary visual-identification data for inspection by security guards, with the same information embedded onto the smartcard, along with the user's biometric data for electronic readers.

FIPS-201 covers only the aspects of the identification card and its issuance; details of how it could be used for access control needs will be specified in a later standard. This makes the effort more digestible—first, work toward getting everyone a common identification card, and then worry about how to use that card later. Of course, it is not entirely practical to specify the details of the identification card without forward-thinking about how it will be used. But, a certain level of freedom is left to the individual agencies to be creative; now that every user has a common credential, the agency is in a better position to leverage that common credential for its localized needs.

If your organization does not have federal ties, FIPS-201 and HSPD-12 are not applicable to you. However, private-sector organizations should not overlook two advantages: the U.S. government, by way of its potential purchasing volume, is causing many security vendors to quickly innovate and create convergence-capable products to sell. Additionally, the U.S. government is absorbing all the early adopter risk of these new products and technologies. By the time the dust starts to settle on FIPS-201 deployments, private-sector organizations will find a suite of certified products that have already been tested, vetted, and deployed in real security-sensitive environments. This alone significantly jump starts private-sector convergence efforts by streamlining the product evaluation phase, which saves both money and time.

A LOOK AT SOME VENDOR OFFERINGS

The physical and logical security convergence market is relatively young and full of many first-time offerings that have not been well vetted yet and are constantly changing shape as convergence needs become clearer and more standardized. However, a handful of specific products are worth highlighting because their vendors are significant players in today's convergence efforts or are unique and forward-thinking companies that are finding new ways to use the converged environments of tomorrow.

Lenel OnGuard

Lenel is an established security access control solution vendor that is considered to be a pioneer in openness and convergence. Its OnGuard platform is a software-centric solution that integrates with hardware from many different vendors and Lenel's own line of physical access control devices. OnGuard was one of the first PACS that allowed for external communication and integration with traditional IT components and technologies. Nowadays, it is common to find both IT and PACS point-products that come with the necessary modules to integrate with OnGuard. Lenel actually does not provide much in the way of logical access control; instead, it has teamed up with companies like Imprivata and ActivIdentity to integrate its logical access control products into the

OnGuard platform. Once integrated, the OnGuard CredentialCenter can use a single contact or contact-less smartcard for all access control needs. OnGuard typically runs on a Windows-based system and uses a Microsoft SQL Server or Oracle database for storage. It offers native LDAP and Active Directory integration.

One of OnGuard's key convergence capabilities comes from the DataConduIT toolkit, which enables IT systems to bidirectionally interact with the OnGuard platform. This enables IT systems to trigger events in the OnGuard system for purposes of synchronization, and so on. The DataConduIT is based on the Windows Management Instrumentation (WMI) platform provided natively by Microsoft Windows. OnGuard also has the capability to integrate with components over OLE, SNMP, and XML exchange.

ArcSight ESM

There is a collection of security-related log/event collection and analysis acronyms:

- **SIM.** Security Information Manager/ment
- **ESM.** Enterprise Security Manager/ment
- **SEM.** Security Event Manager/ment
- **SIEM.** Security Information and Event Manager/ment
- **USM.** Unified Security Manager/ment

Regardless of what acronym you use, these sorts of systems generally have the same capabilities: process security audit logs and events while providing various levels of analysis and correlation for greater threat understanding and risk management. To that end, ArcSight ESM is a strong player in this market and has already been adapted for physical security.

Traditionally, ArcSight ESM has been used to process log, event, and audit information from IT components and systems. All this information is correlated and analyzed to provide a big-picture view of security happenings in the enterprise. ArcSight ESM is natively intelligent enough to track a user as he moves through an enterprise's IT systems.

Therefore, it is no surprise that ArcSight ESM can be readily adapted to handle physical security system information as well; after all, a user logging into a PC or passing through a controlled doorway can both be distilled down to fundamental authentication events. Thus, the only real trick is to export the audit log information from the PACS into a meaningful format that ArcSight ESM can import, preferably in real time. It sounds simple, but it can actually be much more difficult than expected. Legacy PACS designed and installed decades ago are still present and working at many locations. The design standards of that era did not include real-time data export in a standardized way.

After all, this was an era where it was not a common requirement for PACS to be networked and integrated into other external. Where would the PACS send this real-time information if it was the only one that cared about it? Most often, the only real-time device supported to receive PACS events was a line printer. Every time someone swiped a door, the printer printed a time-stamped line to indicate the user and door IDs, creating a paper audit trail.

Brian Contos from ArcSight passed along a story from one of his customer encounters: The customer had a PACS that he wanted to integrate with ArcSight ESM. After analyzing the relatively old PACS, it was determined that the best route to retrieve real-time event information was through capturing the data sent to the printer. With a little bit of cleverness and some LPR/LPD network print service redirection, ArcSight was able to reroute the printer output to another system waiting to receive and import it into ArcSight ESM. Ironically, after all that work, the resulting event information was found to be so nonspecific that it provided little actual correlation value. This illustrates another point: Not only do you need to get the data out of the PACS, but the data must also contain the right pieces of information to begin with...otherwise, data exportation is a moot point.

CoreStreet and Kaba Card-Connected Locks

The innovating PKI-esque technology vendor CoreStreet has teamed up with physical security vendor Kaba Access Control to produce a new generation of locks using CoreStreet's Card-Connected technology. The Kaba E-Plex 5900 is the first commercially available lock to use this technology.

CoreStreet's Card-Connected technology is truly unique, to say the least. CoreStreet has devised a way to use standalone electronic locks/controllers in a manner that still allows the devices to behave as if they were networked and, thus, had access to current policy information. The entire solution uses a "miniaturized PKI" approach that involves storing global data destined for all locks on each individual's contact-less smartcard identification credential.

The process flow is as follows:

1. A user presents his smartcard at the main building's entry door.
2. After access to the main door is confirmed but still while the user is initially presenting his smartcard, the user's smartcard is loaded with an access control ticket (similar in concept to Kerberos), which is valid for 8 hours; a list of data that is equivalent to a PKI Certificate Revocation List (CRL); and a list of global policy changes.
3. The user proceeds to another standalone lock inside or outside the premises and presents his smartcard.

4. The lock validates the access control ticket on the user's smartcard to ensure that it is not expired, downloads the CRL and policy changes from the card, and stores them in local memory (thus updating itself). The lock also uploads an audit log of all lock events back onto the user's card.

5. Assuming the access control ticket on the user's smartcard is valid and allows him to access this lock, the lock opens.

6. Eventually, the user presents his smartcard at the main building's entry door the next day, or some other centralized access point reader on premises.

7. Any lock audit-log information put there during Step 4 is transferred off the user's smartcard and loaded into a master audit database; then, the process continues at Step 2.

The entirety of the technology essentially turns users and their smartcards into a form of "sneaker net" on behalf of the locks. Another way to look at it is to imagine the lock configuration data as a virus. When the user first presents his smartcard at the beginning of the day, the card catches the "virus" from the initial control lock; then, as he encounters other locks throughout the day, the new locks are infected with the same "virus," causing it to spread. Of course, the "virus" is actually policy data related to access control policy changes.

To make the entire thing secure, a lot of public/private cryptography, the core of a PKI infrastructure, is necessary to ensure the authorization and integrity of the data that the users' cards are transporting to the offline locks. The system assumes a minor amount of initial lock provisioning and configuration to inform the lock of the necessary certificate authority (CA) data and other global lock policies, such as what groups are allowed to access this lock. The advantages to such a system are unique: mobile assets such as shipping containers and vehicles can use these offline/standalone locks without any required lock configuration upkeep, yet still take advantage of recent access control policy changes. The only shortcoming to the system is when a user's privileges are revoked after his card is given the period access control ticket; the card continues to be valid against locks until the access control ticket time period expires, the user presents his card to a master control lock (causing the access control ticket to be updated and revoked), or the same locks are used by someone else who has encountered the master control lock sometime after the target user has been revoked (thus transferred the updated CRL to the locks). Yes, a user might have a short period of time where he can still operate locks that they are no longer entitled to operate, but that time period can now be measured in hours or less, rather than days, weeks, or months.

A CoreStreet Card-Connected system would be fairly easy to deploy in a converged environment already using contact-less smartcards. The only necessary changes would be to use CoreStreet C5 systems to control the RFID readers on certain centralized location points to populate user cards with all the necessary information.

Cisco and ASSA ABLOY Hi-O Locks

ASSA ABLOY, a large security vendor that owns popular security brands like HID and Sargeant, has a new generation of locks dubbed with the Highly Intelligent Opening (Hi-O) moniker. These locks connect with and use a controller area network (CAN) (sometimes called CAN-bus or DeviceNet). The immediate benefits of using a CAN-bus approach is that the locks can have autodiscovery capabilities as soon as they are plugged into the network, which makes them conceptually self-aware. The necessary wiring for a CAN-bus network is also simple compared to other interconnect technologies. The Hi-O lock capabilities include many types of self-diagnostics and status-report broadcasting, which makes it easy to learn when a lock is malfunctioning or sabotaged.

Cisco has partnered with ASSA ABLOY to make IP-to-CAN-bus gateways. The Cisco Physical Access Gateway can control up to 15 CAN-bus devices and can store 250,000 user credentials and 150,000 events on the gateway itself. A Cisco Physical Access Manager system controls and manages the gateways.

The partnership between Cisco and ASSA ABLOY provides all the pieces to a workable solution: ASSA ABLOY provides the access control devices while Cisco provides the controller's gateways and management infrastructure. Because the gateways are smaller and functionally light-weight compared to traditional door controllers, the overall PACS deployment is simplified and significantly moves toward a plug-and-play environment.

CAN-bus Instead of IP/Ethernet

A long-term benefit of using CAN-bus for access control devices is that CAN-bus is a strongly established standard. If/when physical access control manufacturers decide to take the CAN-bus plunge, facilities that already have CAN-bus wiring can (theoretically) seamlessly interchange different vendor components with ease. Many believe that the use of CAN-bus technology for access control devices makes more sense than using IP/Ethernet networks, because IP/Ethernet carries a heavy overhead in terms of the digital components necessary to interface with Ethernet, the nonshared Ethernet wiring drops required to each device location, and the administrative requirements to assign the devices a proper network address.

INTRUSION DETECTION EXAMPLES IN A CONVERGED ENVIRONMENT

A truly converged security environment provides holistic risk-management opportunities and capabilities not previously present in a dual/separate physical + logical security environment. From a business perspective, a single entity now manages all business risk.

What are the benefits to an intrusion analyst? There are now more data points available for threat correlation, which allows the analyst to see a much bigger picture. Because risks can be blended between physical and logical threats, having a converged environment is the only way to identify the risks.

Let's start with a simple example. Converged LLC runs a fully converged security environment where all PACS, IT, and surveillance events and data are fed into a central ESM, and surveillance video is stored on a network-accessible DVR. One evening, the security monitoring and operations team of Converged LLC receives an event alert that someone is trying to log into the root account via the console of the UNIX DNS server located in the datacenter. Upon displaying the alert, the ESM also pulls up records of all individuals and their photos that entered the datacenter in the past five hours and queues the DVR to display video of the KVM console desk area at the time of the detected login event. By comparing the user photos to the video of the person sitting at the console at that time, the security team quickly determines it was Charlie, the database administrator, trying to log in as root. Further investigation can be started to determine if this was an innocent policy violation by directly logging into a privileged, shared administrative account or something more malicious, such as an "inside job."

If that example seems too good to be true, you might be surprised to hear that you can do much of this today. ArcSight ESM can already perform most of the operations, including fetching a snapshot from an appropriate IP-enabled camera at the time of an event. Interfacing to a DVR, assuming that the DVR is IP accessible and convergence friendly, is only a small leap.

Let's try another example. On a given day at NonConverged, Inc., the logical security group notices in the logs that Alice, Joe, and Charlie all logged into the company's wireless network. Separately, the physical security group notices that Alice and Charlie used their badges to enter into the building today. As far as each group is concerned, all is well. But is it? Now, look at the same scenario at Converged LLC, where it has a fully converged security environment. Alice, Joe, and Charlie have logged into the wireless network, and Alice and Charlie used their badges to enter the building. Fortunately, the converged reporting and cross-correlation of physical and logical access control data can clearly identify that Joe is logging into the wireless local area network (WLAN), but did not enter the building; thus, it is likely that an intruder operating from a nearby distance is impersonating Joe (see Figure 9-12).

Because Joe is not physically present in the building, it is highly suspicious that he is accessing the wireless network. The security monitoring team of Converged LLC catches the intruder before anything goes wrong, but the security monitoring team of NonConverged, Inc., never knows what happened until, most likely, it is too late.

The inverse scenario also applies: Converged LLC can detect when Bob is present in the building and when he is accessing the teleworker VPN, as shown in Figure 9-13. Of

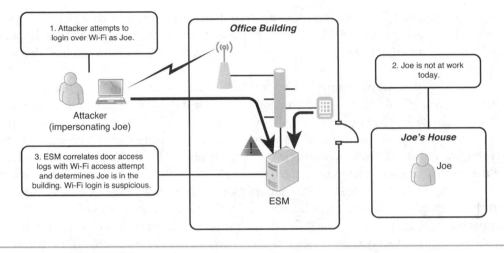

Figure 9-12 Detection of a Wi-Fi imposter in a converged environment

course, both cases assume that WLAN and VPN access can occur with simple passwords, rather than by the user of the access control token possessed by Bob. But, the potential benefits are obvious. Actually, ESM and similar products available today can perform these correlations, although the use of a converged environment makes them significantly easier to deploy.

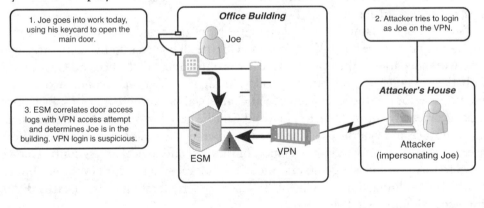

Figure 9-13 Detection of a VPN imposter in a converged environment

Let's look at another interesting scenario. NonConverged Inc., stores a lot of data on various storage network devices—and that means a lot of data to back up. It maintains mountains of backup tapes scattered around the facilities in various server closets. What the company does not realize is that, periodically, an unscrupulous janitor has been pilfering an occasional tape and selling it to NonConverged, Inc.'s competitors. With so many backup tapes, who knows if NonConverged Inc. will ever notice that one has gone missing—until it's time to restore from the backup.

Eventually, the unscrupulous janitor becomes unsatisfied with his minor side income and decides to take a janitorial position at Converged LLC to attempt the same shenanigans to boost his financial bottom line. All is going well during the janitor's first attempt to steal a backup tape—that is, until he passes down a common hallway. What the janitor does not know is that all of Converged LLC's backup tapes have RFID tags embedded into them, and the common hallway contains RFID readers that sense the presence of the backup tape. A security team is quickly alerted to the in-progress theft. Generically, this is not much different than trying to walk out of a store with unpaid merchandise; the anti-theft sensors that blanket the doorways can sense the anti-theft tag on the item and sound an alarm. However, with the extra advantage of RFID, the security team knows not only that a tape is being removed from the facility, but also exactly what tape it is, what data is on it, how old that data is, and so on. The readers can also sense the janitor's RFID physical security badge, so his identity is immediately linked to the theft. The information capabilities provided by the RFID tags provide better overall information to assess the risk of the situation.

Seem far-fetched? Imation does not think so. It is currently adding RFID tags to its backup cartridges (current product is Imation DataGuard rf VolSer labels), and it plans to embed RFID tags into the cartridges by 2011. A similar setup is already deployed in some U.S. hospital maternity wards: To prevent newborn baby theft, newborns are given an RFID anklet/bracelet that corresponds to a matching one that the mother wears. Sensors at the perimeter of the maternity ward can detect when a newborn is being removed from the facility without the additional presence of its mother. Other facilities are already using a similar deployment to detect the wanderings of Alzheimer's patients.

Using an ESM/SEM/SIM solution, such as ArcSight ESM, can potentially offer a way for an organization to experiment and receive converged security and intrusion analysis reports without actually having a converged environment. Even if the physical and logical access control systems are completely separate, the audit logs and event data can be taken from each[8] system and virtually stitched together by the ESM to still provide a bigger picture. After all, that is what the ESM does in the first place, right?

Well, kind of. Conceptually, this will all work, but it overlooks one crucial nuance provided by a converged environment: a universal identifier for each user used by all systems. In a nonconverged environment, your PACS might report that swipe card #31338 opened the datacenter door, and your Windows event log might report that user JForristal logged into the Exchange server. The ESM has no way of knowing that physical access ID #31338 and logical access ID JForristal are the same person, and thus those two events should be correlated. Solutions, such as Imprivata, can tackle this challenge, but there is always the possibility of using ESM's capabilities to create a basic minimal mapping for the purposes of experimenting. The size of this endeavor will largely depend on the number of users needing to be mapped and whether the PACS and IT user databases share any common pieces of information, such as user's full name, to speed up the mapping process.

SUMMARY

Hopefully, this dive into physical security provided you with proper background information on physical security systems and common components to participate in meaningful physical and logical security convergence discussions. The highlighted vendor offerings give you some starting points for technology evaluation, and the example scenarios show how physical security can directly aid intrusion detection efforts run by IT. Those simple scenarios are still far ahead of the current capabilities of typical organizations. As time passes and more converged environments start to exist, you will see new and novel ways where intrusion detection and prevention efforts are enhanced by these new converged technologies.

ENDNOTES

[1] Read more at www.dhs.gov/xnews/releases/press_release_0794.shtm.

[2] One rendition of the story is available at www.eweek.com/c/a/Security/ Police-Foil-420-Million-Keylogger-Scam/.

[3] You can find the details at http://citp.princeton.edu/pub/coldboot.pdf

[4] Some might consider zero-day exploits a potential high explosive equivalent for logical access controls, depending on the nature of the associated vulnerability and the widespread deployment of the vulnerable access control. However, zero-day exploits/vulnerabilities are specific and selective; they are not a general-purpose solution to all circumvention needs similar in nature to physical explosives against physical access controls.

[5] These can technically be countered by the use of one-time passwords and "door held open" alarms, respectively.

[6] Did BlueWave see the recent article discussing the scalability challenges of wireless networks? Introducing security-critical components, like door locks, onto a wireless network seems to be a cause for general concern in more ways than one (www.networkworld.com/news/2008/082808-wireless-lans.html).

[7] Read the entire directive at www.whitehouse.gov/news/releases/2004/08/20040827-8.html.

[8] This assumes that the PACS has a practical way to extract the log and event data, as discussed previously.

Geospatial Intrusion Detection

Geospatial intrusion detection (GID) is a cross-pollination of network security and Geographic Information Systems (GIS). The resultant composite enhances situational awareness in ways that existing solutions do not. This is because GIS applications and services are not new, a fact that is evident in global marketplaces. A notable exception is the network security field, which has been riding the coattails of more financially motivated sectors, including credit-card fraud, online target marketing, and digital rights management. But, network security initiatives have not been a major factor in the drive to associate IP addresses with geographic locations, which is a process called *geocoding*. As is the case with most technological wonderments, the driving force is commerce.

   This chapter conveys the relevance of geospatial technology to network security management (NSM). The goal is to demonstrate that geocoding the source Internet Protocol (IP) address of a network alert is an exceptionally powerful piece of information, especially when defending against highly motivated attackers. This chapter's topics compose a technique for successfully coupling GIS with traditional security mechanisms. The technique starts with a representation of data on a geographic map, which is not a new concept in itself, and then adds a layer of GIS intelligence. Although it is not plenary in its defense capabilities, it fills in more pieces of the security puzzle to determine whether an alert is a false positive or a genuine threat. Because this book's target audience is network security professionals, many of whom do not have GIS experience, a considerable amount of this chapter is dedicated to GIS concepts and definitions.

GID is most effective when it is used to preempt professional attacks rather than the "smash and grab" ones that an amateur might launch. It involves a correlation of events that appear to be independent, but are actually parts of an expertly coordinated attack. This is not trivial, and it is difficult to achieve with traditional security systems alone, particularly on complex network environments. Intrusion detection systems (IDS) and intrusion prevention systems (IPS), for example, pinpoint the final execution of an attack, but they do not see the bigger, and more serious, threat.

NOTE

This chapter applies this technique to IDS alerts but it can also be applied to any network security mechanism that extracts/produces source IP addresses to provide a deeper level of analysis, including Web logs, firewall logs, and so on.

Current network-wide event correlation engines in the form of NSM, security event monitoring (SEM), and security information monitoring (SIM) are helpful when dealing with alert types, severity ratings, time stamps, and previous attack history. However, they miserably fail against professional attacks that are stealthfully distributed over several zombie machines. Real global defense assurance requires information from the source IP address of network alerts, which is probably the most overlooked piece of information in IDS analysis. Historically, correlation engines have only used the source IP address for indexing attack history. However, knowing the approximate geographic source location of an attacker can potentially amount to significant threat avoidance. Security analysts can immediately react and, depending on the identified threat severity, decide whether to blacklist the source IP address at the perimeter or simply focus on traffic to and from that address. To put things in perspective, reliable geographic intelligence about dozens of such attackers—on a concurrent basis—creates an extremely powerful defense posture for Security Operations Centers (SOCs).

The three-dimensional visualization shown in Figure 10-1 was produced by a software called VisNet, which is a product of the Electronics and Telecommunications Research Institute (ETRI). ETRI is a nonprofit, government-funded research organization that was founded in 1976 in Korea.[1] This particular executive-level view is, in my opinion, among the best in the industry, a fact that is not lost on SOC security analysts who are responsible for critical network elements.

Figure 10-2 is a 24-hour historical view of global statistics produced by Arbor Networks PeakFlow solution.[2] Among other things, the tool does modeling as part of its Network Behavior Analysis (NBA) intelligence. NBA is a proactive defense mechanism that supports analyst decisions within corporate networks. This example, which shows

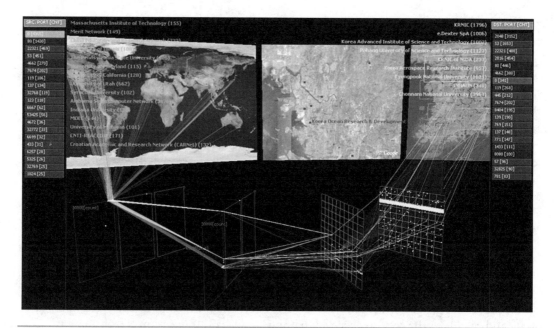

Figure 10-1   VisNet application by ETRI

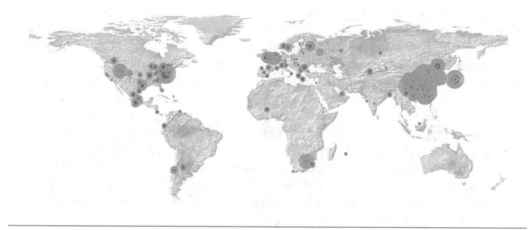

Figure 10-2   Arbor Networks 24-hour statistics

holistic Internet attack patterns for the past 24 hours, lacks the level of intelligence required for true defense assurance because the Internet is too dynamic to baseline.

VisNet and Arbor's global views prove that displaying geographic locations of network attacks is a current network security technique that enables analysts to evaluate the "bigger picture" of their network data communications to help identify suspicious connections. However, the downfall of these applications, and others like them, is the lack of historical geointelligence to discover and alert based on geographic patterns often left behind by professional attackers who slowly probe their next victim over several days, if not weeks.

The main topics in this chapter include current uses of geocoding, an introduction to GIS, Spatial Point Pattern Analysis, the dynamics of a professional attack, geolocation intelligence vendors, and a case study in GID.

CURRENT USES OF GEOCODING

As previously mentioned, georeferencing plays a major role in other industries, including the prevention of credit-card fraud, online target marketing, and digital rights management. For example, before an e-commerce transaction is finalized, a geointelligence vendor compares the source geographic location of the IP address with the ship- or bill-to city and/or state and calculates the confidence level that the credit-card translation is legitimate.

Internet-based marketing intelligence is responsible for a large part of a multibillion-dollar advertising industry that anticipates nothing less than vertical revenue growth. In developed countries, virtually every home is connected and active at speeds that deliver eye-catching animations, interactive communications, and more entertainment choices than ever before. GIS technology delivers valuable intelligence about the online shopping and browsing habits of consumers in those connected homes. Automobile manufacturers, for example, have access to data that shows whether a potential customer will pass a competitor's dealership on the way to their own. Armed with this information, they might choose to invest marketing resources within the most opportune radius. Internet advertising played a bigger role in the 2008 presidential election than ever before. By June 2008, combined Internet campaign expenditures exceeded the staggering amount of $350,000,000![3] Because political campaigns have turned to comical satire and the Internet to appeal to younger voters, it has become essential to create a larger economic footprint on the Internet to target certain Internet ad campaigns to specific geographic areas where the candidate is trailing in the polls.

Digital Rights Management or Content Rights Management is most commonly known to safeguard against movie and music pirating, but it can extend a bit closer to "IT home" as it ensures Export Encryption Laws are upheld. U.S. and NATO allies have regulated the export of cryptography to protect national security interests and have made it illegal to transfer cryptographic forms to some foreign sovereigns. Given the massive impact cryptanalysis has had in past wars, it was abundantly clear that denying enemies access to cryptographic systems is invaluable to better ensure that opponents were unable to decrypt allied sensitive communication lines while simultaneously guaranteeing that allies could still break the opposition's encrypted communication. Currently, this regulation is used by a major network device manufacturer of routers, switches, firewalls, and so on, to better guarantee that its advanced encryption-algorithm devices located in "enemy" countries or territories cannot upgrade its firmware. Even Tenable Security, who created and support the Nessus vulnerability assessment (VA) application, displays this Export Notice on its download Web page after a registered user logs into his account:

> These technology and/or software were licensed in accordance with the US Department of Commerce, Export Administration Regulations (EAR). Diversion contrary to US law is prohibited. No physical or computational access by nationals of tier 4 countries (Cuba, Iran, N. Korea, Sudan, or Syria) is permitted.

INTRODUCTION TO GEOGRAPHIC INFORMATION SYSTEMS

Professionals in virtually all modern scientific disciplines communicate by speaking their own languages. Although outsiders can listen and understand much of the dialogue, becoming an actual participant requires an interpreter. Because the GIS field is not an exception to this rule, all terms, including basic, intermediate, and advanced concepts, receive an equal amount of attention in this chapter. Although this is largely addressed within the body text, tables (such as Table 10-1) provide a summary at the beginning of each section. If you want to bypass the GIS introduction and continue with network security concentration, skip this section and go to the following section, "*Dynamics of a Professional Attack.*"

Table 10-1 Key GIS Terms and Definitions

Term	Definition
ArcGIS	Desktop GIS for visualizing spatially referenced data.
ESRI Vector Shapefile	Proprietary file format of the Environmental Systems Research Institute that holds nontopological geometry and attribute information.
GeoRSS	Graphic encoding standard for associating maps with the Really Simple Syndication (RSS) Web feed format.

Table 10-1   Key GIS Terms and Definitions

Term	Definition
Geospatial	Something that occurs or exists both in space and on Earth.
GeoTIFF	A version of the raster graphics tagged image file format that offers superior compression to support spatial metadata.
Global positioning system (GPS)	Orbiting satellites continuously transmit images of Earth ground locations to mobile and stationary receivers. Positioning information becomes increasingly accurate with each additional signal received.
Vector Keyhole Markup Language (KML)	Google Earth file format for displaying geographic data.
Spatial	Existing in space; not necessarily "outer space."
Web Mapping Service (WMS)	Standard specifications for how GIS Web clients request maps.
UTM spatial grid coordinates	Universal Transverse Mercator (UTM) is a project coordinate system that divides the world into 60 north and 60 south zones that are 6 degrees wide. The UTM Grid was derived from the Military Grid Reference System (MGRS).
Raster	A spatial data model that defines space as an array of equally sized cells arranged in rows and columns. Each cell or group of cells contains an attribute value and location coordinate(s) [Wade, 175].
Vector	A coordinate-based data model that represents geographic features as points, lines, and polygons. Each point feature is represented as a single coordinate pair, while line and polygon features are represented as ordered lists of vertices. Attributes are associated with each vector feature [Wade, 224].

A GIS is an integrated collection of computer software and data used to view and manage information about geographic places, analyze spatial relationships, and model spatial processes. GIS provides a framework for gathering and organizing spatial data and related information about a specific geographic location so that it can be displayed and analyzed. Information that is collected and processed in this manner is considered spatial, geospatial, or georeferenced. Practitioners also describe GIS as including the procedures, operating personnel, and spatial data that go into the system. Conceptually, GIS data is organized as a stack of spatial layers, as shown in Figure 10-3. Structuring data by location and viewing it in relation to other layers is the basis for spatially explicit analysis. The power of a GIS is in its analytical capabilities; those analytic capabilities allow you to answer the questions of "where," "what," "when" (historical imagery overlaid with present day imagery), and "who" (geocoding along with other data, like imagery, parcel vector layers, and so on). Based on that information, you can begin to ask the "how," "why," and "what if." Naturally, the answers to the questions are keyed by location.

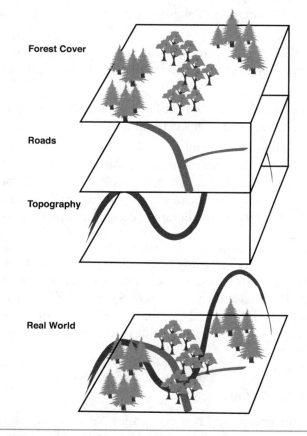

Figure 10-3   GIS stack of spatial data layers

GIS BASIC FUNCTIONS

The basic functions of GIS include the following: information retrieval, entry, display, and analysis. Terms, such as entry and display, are self-explanatory and do not need clarification. However, information retrieval and analysis within the GIS environment can take many different forms. For example, analysis itself can be broken down into specific kinds of analysis, including topological modeling, linear networks, or overlay. The following list elaborates on their meanings:

- **Information retrieval.** Access information based on location. This can take numerous forms, from personal interaction to highly automated transfers. For example, information can be accessed by viewing a map on a desktop GIS with a graphical user interface (GUI), initiating a database query language, or by making a request over the Internet.
- **Topological modeling.** Recognize and analyze the spatial relationships among mapped phenomena. A GIS can compute conditions of adjacency, containment, and proximity.
- **Linear networks.** Facilitate the study of flow and transport along constrained paths. Examples include stream runoff calculations and vehicle traffic modeling.
- **Overlay.** Stack and potentially combine different datasets on the same area for further analysis. Overlay is the quintessential GIS capability, because it superimposes one geographic layer over another, which makes it easy to reach conclusions. For analysis, disparate datasets must be of a common scale and registration for the results to be valid. For display, cartographic design principles apply to create accurate visualizations.

Different software products, including commercial products ESRI ArcGIS and Google Earth PRO, and the open source projects, including Geospatial Data Abstraction Library (GDAL), Geographic Resources Analysis Support System (GRASS), Earth Resource Data Analysis System (ERDAS), and the ever-popular Google Earth free version, offer these services in varying degrees. Each service provides different levels of complexity that far exceed the scope of this section.

FRAMEWORK FOR COOPERATION

GIS can encourage cooperation and communication between organizations. Sharing analysis results as maps or sharing geographic datasets provide a common reference system for collaborators. Standard GIS formats ease the exchange of digital information among the users of different systems. Sharing or serving spatial data is now commonplace;

a flat text or database file might tag each record with latitude and longitude commonly represented as *x, y* coordinates or by using UTM spatial grid coordinates.

NOTE

For a more in-depth look into the workings of x, y coordinates, visit www.csu.edu.au/australia/latlong/coord.html. For a more in-depth look into spatial grid coordinates, visit www.fgdc.gov/usng/how-to-read-usng.

MAP PROJECTION

GIS transforms digital maps from different sources to a common projection. *Projection* is a mathematical means to transfer information from the three-dimensional, curved surface of Earth to a two-dimensional medium—namely, paper or a computer screen. The fundamental problem with projection is that it is extremely difficult to accurately represent an ellipsoid object (such as Earth's shape) in a two-dimensional medium. The easiest and most common way to explain this is to visualize Earth and split it along the equator with a hypothetical piece of paper. If you lift up the paper, pulling Earth with it, you get a two-dimensional representation along the polar axis. This technique is commonly referred to as the planar projection or transverse azimuthal, depending on the skillset of your audience, and it is shown in Figure 10-4.[4]

Figure 10-4 Planar projection

There are two other types of projection: oblique and equatorial. The category of projection is determined by the position of the imaginary piece of paper. Oblique is defined as at some angle that is neither parallel nor perpendicular to the plane of the equator.

Equatorial is defined as perpendicular to the plane of the equator. Note this is the exact opposite as most rational thinking as most people would associate the equatorial to be running along the equator when in fact it means perpendicular to the equator. Figure 10-5 offers a better visual representation of this.[5] Conical and cylindrical identify the shape of the piece of paper (whether a cone or cylinder).

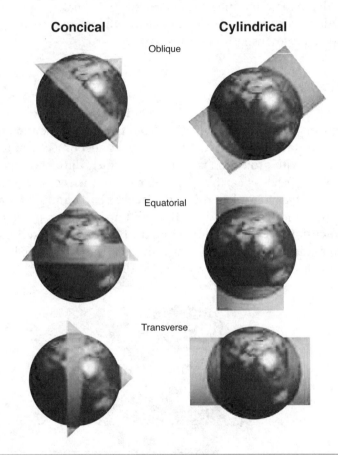

Figure 10-5 Three primary map projections (oblique, equatorial, and transverse)

Deciding which map projection to best represent the reference datum (dataset) determines the level of distortion of the area being mapped. Four key factors determine which is ideal: distance, direction, shape, and area. Unfortunately, with most map distortions, a GIS analyst can only truly preserve one of these characteristics. Common projection techniques include Mercator Projection, Lambert Conformal Conic, Miller

Cylindrical Projection, Goode's Homolosine Equal Area Projection, Sinusoidal Equal Area Projection, Gall-Peters Projection, Mollweide Projection, or Robinson Projection (which is used in this chapter's case study). Figure 10-6 provides a visual association to the projections mentioned.[6] For a more in-depth look at map projections, visit http://egsc.usgs.gov/isb/pubs/MapProjections/projections.html.

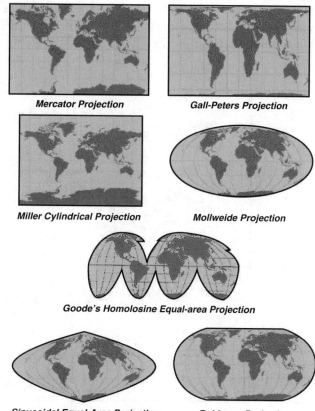

Mercator Projection   Gall-Peters Projection

Miller Cylindrical Projection   Mollweide Projection

Goode's Homolosine Equal-area Projection

Sinusoidal Equal-Area Projection   Robinson Projection

Figure 10-6   Example of common map projections

RASTER VERSUS VECTOR

The two data structures in GIS are *raster* and *vector*, which are shown in Figure 10-7. The raster data model consists of rows of uniform cells (similar to a grid) that are coded by data values. An elementary example of a raster image can be best explained in digital photography. Each photograph is a collection of pixels which are uniform in size and each displays a color (or data value). On the other hand, vector data represents features as points, lines, polygons or areas. For example, a GPS receiver that collects exact point locations or altitude measurements of specific coordinates and then translated to a map would represent a vector image. Vector representations can approximate the appearance of more traditional hand-drafted maps. Choosing which particular data model, raster or vector, is primarily determined by the source and type of data, as well as the intended use of the data. In this circumstance vector mapping is better suited for the GIS analytical procedures and raster images are better for the correlation component.

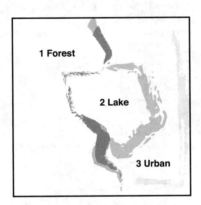

1	1	3	3
1	2	2	3
1	1	2	3
1	1	3	3

Figure 10-7   Vector (top) and raster (bottom) data models of the equal land cover classification

VECTOR DATA MODEL

Vector data represents the world using points, lines, and polygons that are defined by beginning and end points, which meet at nodes. The locations of these nodes and the topological structure are usually stored explicitly. Features are defined only by their boundaries. Curved lines are represented with intermediate points in a line, referred to as vertices.

Some important vector data model concepts include the following:

- **Data representation.** In the vector-based model, geospatial data is represented by a system of coordinates. In vector data, the basic units of spatial information are points, lines, and polygons. Each unit is composed simply as a series of one or more coordinate points. For example, a line is a collection of related points, and a polygon is a collection of related lines.

- **Coordinates.** Pairs of numbers that express horizontal distances along orthogonal axes, or triplets of numbers measuring horizontal and vertical distances. Conceptually, coordinates are n-numbers along n-axes expressing a precise location in n-dimensional space. Coordinates generally represent locations on Earth's surface relative to other locations.

  A latitude and longitude pair is a coordinate, but it represents a location on the surface of a sphere. A GIS can store data in latitude and longitude (sometimes called geographic coordinates), but it must project that data to display it. Most spatial analysis takes place in a projected coordinate space such that distance and areas can be computed in two-dimensions. Geographic data can be explicitly converted to a single projection when imported to GIS, or it can be projected and unprojected on the fly.

- **Point.** A zero-dimensional abstraction of an object represented by a single x, y coordinate. A point normally represents a geographic feature too small to be displayed as a line or area; for example, the location of a city on a broad scale map, or the location of a building on a medium scale map.

- **Line.** Synonymous with arc. A set of ordered coordinates that represent the shape of geographic features that are too narrow to be displayed as an area at the given scale. It also refers to linear features with no country-boundary lines.

- **Polygon.** Represents areas. A polygon is defined by the lines that make up its boundary. A polygon might have holes and might be disjointed, having more than one separated section. The topological definition of a polygon defines which areas are inside the polygon and which rings define a hole within it.

SPATIAL POINT PATTERN ANALYSIS

Spatial Point Pattern Analysis, otherwise known as Spatial Statistics, is about the study of spatially referenced data and associated statistical models and processes. Why do spatial statistics matter? According to Bailey and Gatrell (1995), the major distinction between spatial statistics and nonspatial statistics is that recognition of the spatial dimension might yield different and more meaningful analysis results than those obtained without reference to the spatial dimension.

An excellent example of Spatial Point Pattern Analysis is the well-known spatial analysis that Dr. Snow used in 1854, shown in Figure 10-8, when he overlaid and analyzed the outbreak of cholera deaths and the geographic location of water pumps throughout London. The results supported the direct relationship between the two and established how the disease spread. In the figure, the numbers of deaths are represented by horizontally stacked bars. The water pump is labeled "pump" and is identified by a solid circle.

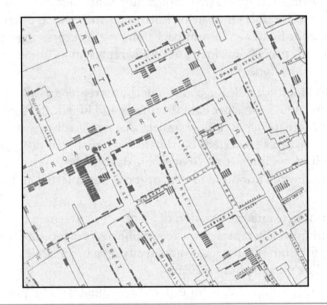

Figure 10-8 Map of cholera outbreaks in London

"Spatial statistics is not a monolithic subject, so it is critical to identify the correct subdomain for our area of interest" (Ripley, 1981). Although some readers might think that Ripley's comment amounts to stating the obvious, it really reinforces the practice of clearly defining objectives. A stated purpose and specific focus on data characteristics is critical to analysis efforts in this complex technical discipline. In keeping with such principles, Bailey and Gatrell (1995) organize spatial analysis problems into classes. Each Spatial Analysis class is defined in the next section to provide you with background on the initial approach GIS analysts apply when they exam a raw and untouched dataset. Again, the first round of analysis is applied to the dataset, and then a more granular approach is necessary to evaluate the specific data points. The secondary round of analysis consists of point intensity and point process statistics, because both approaches scientifically evaluate the exact locations of the data points identified by the Spatial Analysis classes.

To put this into geek speak: When a security analyst is given a large Nessus VA report and is told to prioritize the findings to determine what order the hosts will be patched in, the analyst needs to apply several sorting passes to the report before he has a true prioritized list. The first technique the analyst might apply is to sort the alerts by severity, similar to applying one of the classes of spatial analysis. As you know, a security analyst cannot truly evaluate the host patching order based on a single pass of sorting and must apply a secondary sorting pass. The second pass might be to sort the dataset by host. By correlating the alert severity by host allows the security analyst to prioritize the classified servers containing sensitive data to be patched first. It makes more sense to patch servers holding confidential data within the "trusted network" before servers in the "untrusted network," which are less mission critical. This secondary pass is similar to applying either a point intensity or point process technique.

CLASSES OF SPATIAL ANALYSIS

The classes of spatial analysis include the following:

- **Area.** The analysis goal for this class is to understand any existing patterns and the relationships between units, which are organized in sets by country, census zone, or zip code.

- **Spatially continuous.** This analysis is concerned with the measure of variables at given points. The goal is to understand how they are created and then estimate values where points are missing. Examples of continuous data are temperature, surface elevation models, and soil contamination levels.

- **Point pattern.** This class defines the overall manner of point location configuration and, in some cases, might include unique attributes for each point. Examples of point data are police crime databases, car accident locations, GPS-collected tree locations in a forest, and locations of computers that are connected and communicating over the Internet.

- **Spatial interaction.** An analytic technique that estimates the number of interactions occurring between an origin and destination locations.

POINT INTENSITY

Point intensity describes the pattern identification, analysis, and classification of meaningful points within a dataset. Point analysis is a function in which points in a space represent a specific pattern in an arbitrary space. Several primary algorithms are used for point intensity analysis, including quadrant count and kernel estimation.

Quadrant Count

A simple way to summarize patterns is by performing a quadrant count. Areas are partitioned into equal subregions, and then the events in each of the quadrants are counted. The frequency of events becomes an intensity measure for the area and indicates changing process. Figure 10-9 shows the distribution of redwood tree locations. If a two-meter square grid is applied, a quadrant count can be obtained, as shown in the bottom of Figure 10-9. The intensity of each quadrant is calculated by dividing the count by the quadrant area.

The major limitation of the quadrant count method is that the result is sensitive to the quadrant size. Moreover, selecting quadrant size is empirical. A GIS rule of thumb is to determine the appropriate size of a quadrant be approximated as twice the size of the mean area per point over the study area.

Kernel Estimation

Kernel estimation is a tool commonly used to obtain smooth estimates of univariate or multivariate probability densities from a sample of observations. The basic idea is similar to a moving window method and attempts to overcome limitations of the quadrant count method. The moving window estimates intensity by counting the number of points within each window and also ignores the distance of each observation from the center of the window. By contrast, kernel estimation uses three-dimensional functions to assign a weight to the distance from the center where the intensity is being estimated (see Figure 10-10).

Kernel intensity estimations show different results given different bandwidths. It is therefore important to select an appropriate bandwidth to pick up the spatial pattern characteristics of interest. Figure 10-10 represents kernel intensity estimates based on different kernel bandwidths.

POINT PROCESS STATISTICS

A determination of whether points are clustered or randomly distributed is gained by analyzing point process statistics. Where clustering does exist, insight is available into the degree of departure from complete spatial randomness (CSR). Figure 10-11 demonstrates

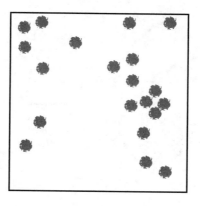

3	1	1	1
1	0	3	1
1	0	1	4
1	0	0	2

Figure 10-9   Event locations and quadrant counts

a progression from CSR to a cluster. A Poisson point process, which exhibits CSR, can be employed to test a known set of event's departure from CSR.

Poisson Process Model

The Poisson process model is basic, yet it is commonly used to develop point pattern models. It is defined by the following criteria: n points are placed in a region where each possible location for a point is equally likely to be chosen, and the location of each point is independent of the location of any other point. That is, in no way does the selection of a location for one of the points bear on the selection of a location for any other point. Thus, a Poisson process can be used to analyze datasets that exhibit CSR or clustering.

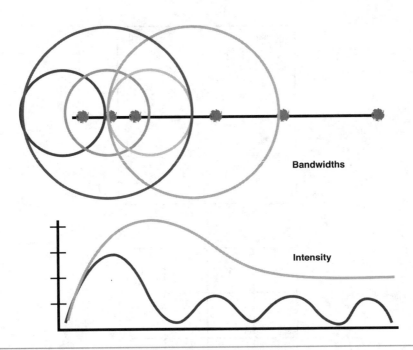

Figure 10-10   Kernel estimation and point pattern intensity at different bandwidths

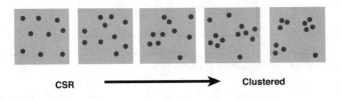

Figure 10-11   Progression from CSR to clustered events

Quadrant Test

Testing the observed dataset's departure from a random distribution is a simple method
to test for clustering. A quadrant grid can be generated for the study domain and quadrant counts performed to calculate observed intensity in each dataset. Also, a Poisson
process can generate a random point distribution over the same quadrant domain. In a
CSR pattern, the point counts for each quadrant over the entire area are expected to follow a Poisson distribution. The *chi-square goodness of fit* test can test the fit between the
observed dataset and the Poisson distribution.

Nearest Neighbor Test

Calculating the nearest neighbor distance (the distance between two points) is a simple and convenient measurement among a set of points. In general, there are two types of distance measurements between points:

- **Event-event distance** is the distance between a randomly selected event point and its nearest neighbor event point.
- **Point-event distance** is the distance between a randomly generated new point and the nearest event point.

Take the example of a police database of crime locations for a particular city. Then event-event distance is the distance from a randomly selected crime location to the nearest neighbor crime location (event). In contrast, a point-event distance selects any point in the city (it does not have to be a crime location) and measures the distance to the nearest recorded crime location.

There are various methods to detect departure from CSR using either event-event distance or point-event distance. Calculations vary between the methods, but they share a similar idea to compare the observed distance from CSR.

K Function Test

One of the major limitations of the nearest neighbor distance method is that it only considers the closest events, limiting the scale to its smallest. The *K* function test is an alternative tool that provides more accurate information about the spatial dependencies of a wider range of scales. Ripley's (1981) *K* function counts the cumulative number of points within a circle of a certain radius. The count might be made at multiple radii so that the concentration can be compared at different scales.

This concludes the introduction to GIS and the techniques and theories used in the industry. The deeper dive into the geospatial fundamentals provides you with the necessary GIS knowledge for this chapter's case study, because it addresses the cross-pollination of network security and GIS to better identify professional attacks. Now, take a break from GIS and look at the dynamics of a professional attack.

DYNAMICS OF A PROFESSIONAL ATTACK

In today's world, many people consider blackhat hackers to fall into three broad groups: inexperienced, moderately experienced, and professionals. These rankings are derived directly from their skill levels and motivation. Inexperienced attackers, who are the most lacking in these attributes, typically do not have the patience to adequately hide their reconnaissance activities within normal traffic, and they are quickly identified. Their initial attacks, in the form of port scans, are easily identified because they trigger a high number of alerts and can be categorized as noisy port scans. Experienced security analysts frequently ignore this type of alert and categorize it as "the big, bad Internet doing what it always does."

NOTE

Transient "smash and grab" alerts are indicators of suspicious activity, so analysts cannot always blacklist[7] the offending source IP address. Google spiders that index Web pages can trigger reconnaissance signatures, because the high rate of page requests exceeds what a human can manually execute. This is typically a false positive and can be tagged accordingly. If the malicious traffic continues, an analyst can re-evaluate countermeasures to determine the best course of action.

By current standards, moderately experienced attackers are the majority of the crowd and, although they might have the skills to exploit a vulnerability, they might be easily discouraged when challenged by a relatively secure network. It is interesting to note that, in some cases, intrusion attempts are executed for "legitimate" purposes, at least in the mind of the perpetrator, by security or network analysts who use the Internet as an evaluation testbed for offensive security tools and tactics to research better ways to defend their own networks. This type of nefarious activity, commonly referred to as grayhat hacking, is still considered illegal but, in the scope of the Internet, the probability of prosecution is slim to none.

Professional adversaries are the minority of network criminals, but they possess the intellect, tools, and motivation to successfully infiltrate the most secure networks. However, they are selective in their choices of targets and tend to remain under the defensive radar at all times. To put it in context, imagine a sniper whose only duty is to stealthily eliminate a specific target. Snipers do not develop skills by practicing with a machine gun or rocket launcher, because they never take their jobs/training lightly. They train by repetition with the same weapon that they will use in the field and prepare themselves by knowing as much about the enemy as possible, including normal daily routines, defensive posture, and points of weakness.

Professional attackers are often motivated by financial gains and can bypass defense mechanisms by extending port scans over long periods of time, usually from multiple zombie machines. A *zombie* is a computer that a hacker compromises to launch attacks while deflecting suspicion from his own computer, ultimately a computer already under their control. Separating port scans into smaller segments on multiple zombie sources makes reconnaissance virtually impossible to isolate for three reasons:

- Security analysts cannot easily correlate multiple port scans from different sources among the volume of network alerts. (SIM/NSM/SIEM packages do not even attempt this level of correlation.)

- Adversaries reduce the speed and aggressiveness of their port scan to avoid a network defenses' port scan alert thresholds and, therefore, the scans do not trigger an alert.

- In an attempt to drastically reduce alerts, security analysts sometimes disable port scan signatures or modify the signature thresholds to an unrealistic level.

NOTE

Many inexperienced security analysts have the impression that professional attackers guarantee complete anonymity by always IP spoofing their attack's source IP address. This is a common misconception, because IP spoofing is only successful when launching DoS, DDoS, or RDDoS attacks because the attacker does not need any return communication. Professional attacks that target the process of stealing sensitive information, including credit-card information, identity-theft information, and proprietary information, require the data stream to return with the information and therefore require a true source IP address (mind you, usually an address of a zombie computer). If the attacker spoofs the source IP address to one *not* under his control, the return data stream containing the sensitive information would never occur.

CORNERSTONE THEORY

In the process of assembling zombie computers, professional adversaries use automated scanning tools to probe sequential IP addresses to find computers that are susceptible to attacks. Considering this particular tactic, it is reasonable to assume that attackers control zombie computers within a close geographic proximity of each other. Primarily because local Internet Service Providers (ISPs) are allotted a predetermined number of IP addresses to distribute them for both commercial and residential clients. As people register for Internet service, they are allocated a corresponding static or Dynamic Host Control Protocol (DHCP) IP address within that ISP's geographic region. When a sequential scan executes, the perpetrator unknowingly leaves a geographic cluster pattern of zombie machines that can be identified using GIS algorithms.

An efficient network defense enables a security analyst to visually identify the source location of an attacking node, which increases situational awareness and makes data available for analysis. Multiple network security alerts on a geographical map permit an analyst to assess pattern clusters to determine if attackers are working together or if a single blackhat hacker is in control of multiple zombies. The following section describes an all too familiar professional attack on a victim network.

EXAMPLE OF ATTACK STEPS AND METHODS

The following chronological steps mimic those of a professional compromise of a victim network. This methodology does not include the information-gathering phase, because there are numerous strategies for information gathering:

1. Select a target to attack. For commercial victims, this is usually driven by revenge or financial gains. For government victims, this is usually driven by financial gains or political retribution.

2. Use an open Internet access point (AP), such as those at coffee shops, public libraries, schools, or even a neighbor's unsecured wireless AP, to scan and take control of other unsecured residential computers (*not* the target determined in step 1), forming a collection of zombie machines.[8]

3. Immediately after gaining control of the host machine and making it a zombie, patch the entry point.[9] Install a rootkit on the system as a backdoor into the system for re-entry. Most rootkits have phone-home capabilities in case the zombie's external IP address is changed (usually by DHCP).

4. After the system is controlled, disconnect and do not connect to it again for 2 to 3 weeks to ensure that a backup is made; the backup provides a greater chance that either the original or hacker-constructed backdoor is still enabled. This step is usually only recognized if the zombie is a commercial computer, because most residential users are not advanced enough to make a backup image. This is not in conflict with the fact that attackers primarily target residential users, but it needs to be part of a security professional's thought process.

5. After the machine is fully compromised, repeat steps 2 to 4 until the required number of zombies is obtained. Prepare to target the main objective.

6. Using the zombies, begin the network reconnaissance stage by performing a "low and slow" scan of the target. Scans are used to learn the general network topology of perimeter devices and the services, applications, and ports that are enabled on each. This stage typically lasts between 2 to 4 weeks in order to avoid attention.

7. At completion of network and application reconnaissance and any necessary enumeration, analyze the results and narrow the possible vulnerabilities to evaluate the best attack vector to launch.

8. An additional layer of blackhat obfuscation is performed to guard against monitoring activities by security analysts; the true attack is camouflaged by an onslaught of

false ones from other zombies. These bogus attacks are directed to other parts of the target network, which takes attention away from the true target server.

9. Launch the exploit(s) from a zombie machine that most likely did *not* participate in the reconnaissance phase. This ensures that records of the attacking computers are not already in victim machine logs and is intended to thwart the efforts of security analysts who might be evaluating historical patterns.

10. As soon as the exploit is successful, the attacker works quickly to escalate privileges, if needed, and erase system logs that might expose the attack.

NOTE

An attacker inherits the privileges of the active user at the moment it executes the exploit. If a commercial employee user is logged in, who has minimal network privileges and accidentally initiates a Trojan, the attacker must escalate his privileges to a user with more rights. A common policy of commercial system administrators is that only users with escalated privileges can delete local system logs.

---

11. As with the residential compromise, patch the entry point and create a backdoor point for reentry.

12. Disconnect from the computer and do not reenter for 2 to 3 weeks to make sure that a backup runs; if the compromise is discovered later, the target company will likely restore a backup. Depending on the skill set of the company and its capability to find the entry point, backup data can still have the backdoor loaded or, more likely, the original vulnerability will still be in place.

NOTE PORT SCANNING: SMASH AND GRAB VERSUS LOW-AND-SLOW

A noisy port scan that most likely alerts security analysts is as follows:

```
nmap –sS 192.168.0/24
```

A low and slow `nmap` reconnaissance scan in the form of a script might look like the following:

```
for target in 192.168.1.0/24; do nmap —scan-delay 1155
—max-hostgroup 1 –f –g 53 –n –vv
-PS21,22,23,25,53,80,113,45943
-PA80,113,443,45943 $target; usleep 1075000; done
```

The descriptions of these identified parameters are as follows:

- —scan-delay 1155 tells nmap to wait 1.155 seconds between each probe it sends to a target host.
- —max-hostgroup 1 tells nmap to only scan one host at a time.
- -f tells nmap to fragment probes into up to 8 bytes of data in each fragment.
- -g 53 tells nmap to send the probes from the port specified (in this case, port 53).
- -n tells nmap to disable all reverse Domain Name System (DNS) resolution.
- -vv tells nmap to be verbose x2 (otherwise known as extra verbose).
- -PS21,22,23,25,53,80,113,45943 tells nmap to run a TCP SYN ping to the identified ports; the arbitrary port 45943 will help the attacker distinguish whether the firewall is only configured with default deny for ephemeral ports.
- -PA80,113,443,45943 tells nmap to run a TCP ACK ping to the identified ports.
- $target string variable represents the identified targets.
- usleep 1075000 delays nmap for 1.075 seconds between nmap calls, which comes into play when the last probe is sent to one host and the first probe is sent to the next host.

Two helpful nmap resources are Professor Messor's electronic nmap book[10] and a book by the creator of nmap, Gordon Fyodor Lyon, called Nmap Network Scanning: The Official Nmap Project Guide to Network Discovery and Security Scanning (Insecure Press, 2008).

As mentioned previously, when attackers look for vulnerable connections, they use automated scripts and applications that scan subnets in sequential order. Because ISPs are given preallocated static IP addresses, it is safe to assume that those sequential subnets are close together within the same geographic location. By expanding security resources to consider geographic location, security analysts can piece together distributed network reconnaissance from zombie machines using "shared situational awareness."

Another benefit of analyzing source geographic locations is learning the local time of source attackers. Although a zombie can be located anywhere in the world, a local time-of-day determination is beneficial because it adds another significant piece of the puzzle. An analyst might treat an alert differently if the local time is during nonbusiness hours versus business hours.

Correlating low and slow port scans is the key to mitigating professional attacks. A quote from a movie illustrates the theory perfectly: "I'm not afraid of the country with 20 nuclear bombs; I'm terrified of the rogue entity with 1." Professional attackers make it their business to stay under the network security radar. Many security analysts only capture the onslaught of scanning attacks rather than searching for the low and slow precursor of professional port scan reconnaissance. Therefore, port scan thresholds must be extremely sensitive. Although this logic increases the number of captured alerts by orders of magnitude, it might also give the target corporation a fighting chance against a professional attack. Most security analysts and security managers would refuse to implement this because of the amount of hard drive space required to handle this level of alerting. Fortunately, one process can make these huge numbers of alerts manageable: meta-alerting.

Meta-alerting is the process in which several alerts initiated by the same event are summarized into a single alert. For example, if a full port scan runs against a Web server, there is a possibility that each port can trigger an IDS alert! Of course, that is directly determined by the IDS configuration. Knowing there are 65,535 TCP and another 65,535 UDP ports on a server can lead to 131,070 alerts generated from one port scan possibly lasting less than 5 seconds from a single source. Imagine the possible alerts over 24 hours from multiple sources. Absolutely staggering! Meta-alerting takes that identified port scan and consolidates those 131,070 alerts into a single entry. This significantly reduces the total number of alerts to a manageable amount.

GEOCODING TECHNIQUES

The process of translating an IP address to latitude/longitude coordinates or UTM spatial address grid coordinates and utilizes several behind-the-scenes techniques described in this section. The six main geocoding procedures are as follows:

- Whois
- Autonomous system (AS)
- DNS LOC
- Traceroute
- Trilateration
- Strategic business partnerships

Whois

The Whois service is the most basic form of an Internet phone directory. It was developed in support of users as a way to obtain names, email addresses, postal addresses, and other pertinent pieces of contact information. As the World Wide Web grew exponentially, the Whois database became the main source for network information, administrative, and technical contact information for all Internet domains and IP addresses.

The following code displays the Whois database query for www.geosnort.com, which is one of my domains that is decommissioned, using a freeware network reconnaissance tool called SamSpade:

```
www.geosnort.com = [ 70.169.166.89 ]
(Asked whois.namejuice.com:43 about geosnort.com)
Registration Service Provided By: Domain Registry of America
Contact: support@droa.com
http://www.droa.com
Domain name: geosnort.com
Registrant Contact:
Ryan Trost
Private Registration
2316 Delaware Ave Suite 266
Buffalo
NY    14216-2687    US
866-434-0212
866-434-0211
privacy@droa.com
Administrative Contact:
Ryan Trost
Private Registration
2316 Delaware Ave Suite 266
Buffalo
NY    14216-2687    US
866-434-0212
866-434-0211
privacy@droa.com
Technical Contact:
Ryan Trost
Private Registration
2316 Delaware Ave Suite 266
Buffalo
NY    14216-2687    US
866-434-0212
866-434-0211
privacy@droa.com
Creation date: 2005-12-30
Update date: 2007-07-23
Expiration date: 2009-12-30
```

In 1992, the Integrated Network Information Center (InterNIC) was created as a five-year, joint project of the National Science Foundation (NSF) and Internet Assigned Names and Numbers (IANA) to maintain IP addressing and DNS information. At that time, the records and their accuracy were well maintained (www.iana.org).

Simultaneously, the Internet Corporation of Assigned Names and Numbers (ICANN) developed the Shared Registry System by setting the standards for accrediting Internet Domain Registrars (www.icann.org). The decentralization of records compromised the precision of the information. On November 25, 1998, ICANN assumed the responsibilities of the InterNIC and is still in control today. The InterNIC is still in operation and, although its nature has changed, is an active participant in managing the Internet. The organization manages a Whois database that is becoming increasingly decentralized, mostly to global registrars that handle data for their own geographic region, but in coordination with InterNIC custodians. In the previous example, the records point to Domain Registry of America (www.droa.com).

As the service has evolved over this relatively short time frame, the use of Whois records still plays a significant role. The primary function has deviated, because the service is now used to determine if a domain is vacant or not. Although it is the only source of contact information for proprietors of a domain or network, registrars have expanded services to include a level of privacy for customers. In the previous example, names for the registrant contact, administrative contact, and technical contact are really the registrant's contact information instead of the owner's information. It is yet to be determined if this stemmed from added security or a desire to make an extra buck.

The point is that Whois information is no longer verified for its accuracy. After someone purchases a domain from a registrant of his choice, he can just as easily put false information in the contact fields provided. As a result, absolutely nothing will happen, as long as the credit card clears. The repercussions of entering false information should be mentioned in full disclosure; for companies, it does not make sense to provide false information because, if an issue arises, an external party could not contact the company. The most common practice is that commercial companies take advantage of their registrar's privacy service and, if a problem arises, let the identifier call the registrant who, in turn, contacts the company.

Assuming that the Whois information is accurate, it contains a substantial amount of information, including city, state, zip code, and area code, that directly or indirectly suggests a geographical location. An important caveat is that Whois records that contain DNS ranges might encompass a company's entire subnet range, but the contact information represents a single physical location, usually that of the corporate headquarters. In cases like this, the true extent of office and other locations is not represented. For example, Google domains/IPs are all registered in Mountain View, California, which is one of many corporate locations Google maintains.

Clearly, the geographical data provided in the Whois database search is not conclusive and must be used in collaboration with the results produced by other techniques or at least as a secondary metric against which to check.

Autonomous Systems

Border Gateway Protocol (BGP) is the routing protocol that preserves the Internet topology in global autonomous systems (AS). It is used by major Network Service Providers (NSPs), including Sprint, Level3, Qwest, and others. BGP determines the loop-free path through AS networks, but it does *not* track the route through individual routers within an AS. An AS, by definition, is a collection of IP networks under control of a single entity, typically an ISP, a large organization, or an educational institute. Given an IP or host name, fixed orbits can find the relevant AS. Then, using a table of AS-number-to-name, additional information is available. AS numbers are authoritatively maintained by American Registry for Internet Numbers (ARIN), which charges a minimal fee for AS numbers to cover administrative costs. AS custodians can maintain multiple systems, but each system is independent with respect to BGP. Autonomous systems have a globally unique number to differentiate them from other systems. Figure 10-12 displays the relationship between three autonomous systems.

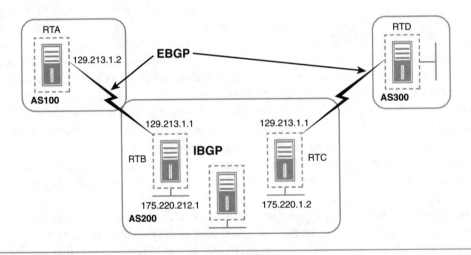

Figure 10-12   Example of interior and external BGP between autonomous systems

There are several ways to determine a router's AS number. The three described here use BackTrack, the IP to ASN Mapping Project by Team Cyrmu, and the nmap scripting engine.

BackTrack, as described in Chapter 2, "Infrastructure Monitoring," is an extensive collection of security tools that are used with both good and bad intentions. They include an application called Autonomous System Scanner, which can find the AS associated with a specific router. It was developed by Phenoelit within the Internetwork Routing Protocol Attack Suite (IRPAS).

The second technique is the IP to ASN Mapping Project by the specialized Internet security research firm Team Cymru.[11] Team Cymru uses four methods to find AS numbers: Whois, DNS, HTTP, and HTTPS.

The most common technique in use is the Whois daemon, which acts like a standard Whois server, but with added functionality. It accepts arguments on the command line for single Whois queries, and it supports bulk IP submissions when combined with GNU Netcat. Currently, Cymru has two Whois servers available for queries: v4.whois.cymru.com and v4-peer.whois.cymru.com. Figure 10-13 displays the command parameter syntax to use the IP to AS Mapping Project.

Figure 10-13 Cygwin commands to use Team Cymru's IP to AS Mapping Project

The third technique is the famous nmap utility tool which has a built-in AS query. The script works by sending DNS TXT queries to a DNS server, which then queries the Team Cymru services. The proper syntax is

```
nmap —script asn-query.nse [—script-args dns=<DNS Server>] <target>
```

An online list of all the autonomous systems can be found at www.cidr-report.org/v6/as2.0/autnums.html.

Autonomous systems play a complimentary role because they can often determine a general geographic locale. Most AS results can be extracted using other tools or by using other methods, but can provide unique information not located anywhere else. AS locating information is not a primary technique of translating IP addresses to geographic locations but, similar to whois, can assist to better validate the accuracy of other approaches.

DNS LOC

DNS LOC was proposed as an experimental RFC 1876[12] by integrating location information into current DNS records. Because the Internet does not have an authoritative power that enforces a uniform standard DNS format, the DNS LOC was never universally implemented. Although it can be found today, it is rarely practiced.

The anatomy of the DNS addition is shown in Figure 10-14, and it is followed by the data definition, which consists of seven different fields to express the geographical location. Even though the latitude, longitude, and altitude fields extend to multiple lines in the diagram, they are one unique field.

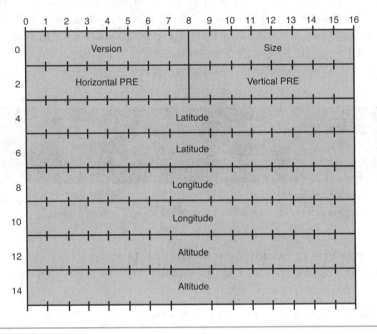

Figure 10-14   DNS LOC field layout

Source: www.faqs.org/rfcs/rfc1876.html

The seven fields include the following:

- **Version.** 8-bit field that represents the version number (which is always zero).
- **Size.** 8-bit field that represents the diameter of the sphere enclosing the entire network entity. Allowing two 4-bit unsigned integers ranging from 0 to 9 allows the size to range from < 1cm (0e0) to 90,000km (9e9).
- **Horizontal Precision (PRE).** 8-bit field that represents the potential size of the circle of error.

- **Vertical Precision (PRE).** 8-bit field that represents the potential size of the circle of error. An additional point to make is, depending on the altitude, the vertical precision might need to be adjusted.

- **Latitude.** The latitude of the center of the sphere described by the size field. Each field is a measurement of thousandths of seconds of an arc.

- **Longitude.** The longitude of the center of the sphere described by the size field. Each field is a measurement of thousandths of seconds of an arc.

- **Altitude.** A measurement from the center of the sphere. It is measured by centimeters from a base 100,000m below sea level. Because the Earth's surface is not flat, adjustments to altitude are common.

The LOC record is expressed in a file in the following format:

```
<owner> <TTL> <class> LOC ( d1 [m1 [s1]] {"N"|"S"} d2 [m2 [s2]] {"E"|"W"}
alt["m"] [siz["m"] [hp["m"] [vp["m"]]]] )
```

The parentheses are used for multiline data, as specified in RFC 1035, section 5.1, where

- **d1.** [0 .. 90] (degrees latitude)
- **d2.** [0 .. 180] (degrees longitude)
- **m1, m2.** [0 .. 59] (minutes latitude/longitude)
- **s1, s2.** [0 .. 59.999] (seconds latitude/longitude)
- **alt.** [-100000.00 .. 42849672.95] BY .01 (altitude in meters)
- **siz, hp, vp.** [0 .. 90000000.00] (size/precision in meters)

If omitted, minutes and seconds default to zero, size defaults to 1m, horizontal precision defaults to 10,000m, and vertical precision defaults to 10m. These defaults represent typical zip code area sizes, because it is often easy to find approximate geographical location by zip code.

The information provided in the DNS LOC resource record is an excellent solution to the problem of geographically locating, but proponents of its use might have had poor timing. In 1996, when the DNS LOC was introduced, there might have been a widespread need for the geographic locating of objects, such as IP addresses, equipment, assets, and resources, but the capabilities of mapping software were greatly lagging behind the technology. At that time, determining latitude and longitude coordinates required a significant investment from companies because there were few cost-effective means to calculate that information. Not to mention, because DNS LOC records were/are maintained by network administrators, this might have lead to inaccurate information. Most network administrators are not well versed in geological surveying, not to mention, how a network administrator would determine geographic coordinates in 1996. As time progressed, geographic intelligence gained more accurate tools, like Google Earth and/or GPS systems, such as the handheld Garmin GPS, that provide geographic coordinates with a high level of accuracy with little difficulty. Figure 10-15 provides an example of how easy is it these days to get accurate coordinates by street address for office buildings, courtesy of Google Earth. Notice the following coordinates are located in the lower left-hand corner:

Figure 10-15   Google Earth satellite image

- Latitude. 38°56';39.57"N
- Longitude. 77°18';53.99"W

Traceroute

Traceroute is a standard utility provided on all UNIX- and Windows-based systems (traceroute and tracert commands, respectively) to help system administrators and security analysts troubleshoot various network link issues. By showing a list of possible routers traversed, it enables the user to identify the potential path taken to reach a particular destination on the intranet or Internet. This can help identify routing problems or firewalls that might be blocking access to a site. Penetration testers also use traceroute to gather information about network infrastructure and IP ranges around a given host.

The Internet routes data communication using packet switching. However, even given two distinct communicating locations, the information path over routers can vary from packet transmission to packet transmission. A packet's typical lifespan works by modifying the Time to Live (TTL) field inside each packet transmission so, as the packet passes through routers en route to its destination, the TTL field decrements by 1. If a router receives a packet when the TTL field reaches 0, it returns a time-expired Internet Control Message Protocol (ICMP) error message to the original sending computer. A traceroute starts by a computer sending a single packet to the destination computer with the TTL field set to 1. The packet reaches the next router and decrements to 0, which generates the aforementioned error message. The original computer receives the error message and makes a list of the routers. As a result, it sends a second packet with the TTL field set to 2. The packet transverses the initial router and is passed forward, and as it reaches the second router, the TTL field again reaches 0, which generates another error message. This method is repeated until the destination computer is reached. The resulting list of router IP addresses represents the most feasible route along which the data packets traveled. Figure 10-16 illustrates this process.

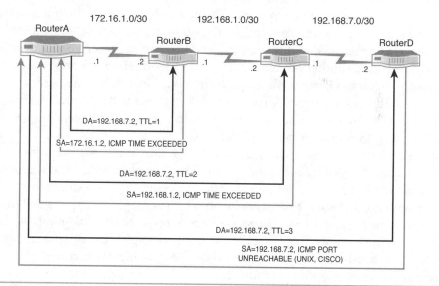

Figure 10-16 Visual representation of traceroute

The traceroute utility can offer geographic hints for external hops between source and destination nodes, as shown in the following example:

```
Tracing route to [216.148.xxx.xxx] over a maximum of 30 hops:
1     12 ms      9 ms     13 ms    10.7.0.1
2      9 ms      9 ms     11 ms    ip72-219-223-21.dc.dc.cox.net [72.219.223.21]
3     12 ms      9 ms     11 ms    mrfddsrj02-ge110.rd.dc.cox.net [68.100.0.149]
4     13 ms     11 ms     11 ms    att-level3-oc192.Washington1.Level3.net [4.68.127.154]
5     85 ms     79 ms     78 ms    tbr1.wswdc.ip.att.net [12.123.8.114]
6     81 ms     78 ms     78 ms    cr1.wswdc.ip.att.net [12.122.2.29]
7     80 ms     79 ms     84 ms    cr2.phlpa.ip.att.net [12.122.4.53]
8     80 ms     80 ms     79 ms    cr2.cl2oh.ip.att.net [12.122.2.209]
9     81 ms     78 ms     83 ms    cr1.cl2oh.ip.att.net [12.122.2.125]
10    89 ms     76 ms     79 ms    cr2.dvmco.ip.att.net [12.122.31.85]
11    80 ms     78 ms     77 ms    cr1.slkut.ip.att.net [12.122.30.25]
12    84 ms     79 ms     79 ms    tbr2.la2ca.ip.att.net [12.122.19.230]
13    79 ms     80 ms     81 ms    gar4.la2ca.ip.att.net [12.123.222.93]
14    91 ms     91 ms    idf26-gsr12-1-pos-7-0.rwc1.attens.net [12.122.255.142]
15    92 ms     87 ms     86 ms    mdf4-bi8k-2-eth-1-5.rwc1.attens.net [216.148.209.142]
16    94 ms     88 ms     90 ms    [216.148.xxx.xxx]
Trace complete.
Route: Washington DC → Philadelphia, PA → Cleveland, OH → Denver, CO → Salt Lake
City, UT → Los Angeles, CA → Middletown, NJ → San Diego, CA → Redwood City, CA
```

The routing device's primary and sometimes secondary domains provide hints that can locate the target's geographic location. The city codes found in the traceroute results do not have a unifying naming convention. For example, the District of Columbia area can be identified by dc, washington, dca, iad, and bwi, without mentioning case sensitivity. Airport codes are another popular router name identifier. In the previous example, dca translates to Ronald Reagan Washington National Airport, iad equates to Washington Dulles International Airport, and bwi represents Baltimore/Washington International Airport. The device's geographic hints are not guaranteed, but the routers are configured by ISPs that are geographically located. Having the location included in the naming convention assists them when a network issue requires troubleshooting.

Unfortunately, the routing codes are not always self-explanatory and occasionally require some additional research to identify device locations, as is evident from hops 14 and 15. In both hops, there are no easily identifiable geographic locations that indicate Middletown, New Jersey, and San Diego, California, respectively. Thankfully, with user-friendly traceroute software, like VisualRoute, it is easy to plug in both host names and rely on the embedded knowledge that led to both geographic destinations.

Traceroute represents a possible route that data packets might have traveled; it is not a guarantee. Routers use several algorithms to determine the best path to travel from the source node to the destination node. These paths can change unpredictably within milliseconds of having sequential packets pass, which ultimately sends the packets in two different directions, even though both packets are heading for the same final destination.

Trilateration

Trilateration is a bivariate technique that uses time and distance to determine the geographic location of an endpoint. By using the *round trip time* (RTT) functions of ping or traceroute, an analyst can estimate the geographic location of an unknown computer with a high degree of accuracy. RTT is the time it takes to receive a ping response from the target device. Trilateration relies on two key components: there are at least three source computers initiating the RTT and the analyst knows the geographic locations of the source computers initiating the RTT (also called landmarks), which are described later in this chapter. This technique is well known within the nautical industry because it is identical to a submarine using sonar to determine the position of an unknown submarine.

NOTE

Do not confuse trilateration with triangulation which is similar, but uses the distance and angle from two known locations to locate a node. In this day and age, *cellular triangulation* is probably the most familiar example of *triangulation*.

Trilateration uses three geographic source locations to find the suspicious asset. Multilateration uses the same technique, but uses four or more source locations to provide a more precise location and a level of redundancy in case one of the source locations is unavailable or is providing skewed information. For the remainder of this chapter, the technique is referred to as multilateration.

The approaches to determining geolocation from a packet's RTT goes by several different names, including Topology-Based Geolocation (TBG) (Katz-Basset, Ethan, et al., 2006) and Constraint-Based Geolocation (CBG) (Gueye, Gamba, et al., 2004). Although each method differs slightly from the other because they use different strategies to determine distance and time, the underlying methodology holds true. Traceroute and ping are the most obvious technologies to implement the methods because that is one of their primary uses; however, some papers outline other ways to calculate packet travel times. For example, technologies such as HTTP refresh, Telnet, Secure Shell (SSH), and Hypertext Transfer Protocol (HTTP) GET requests can also be used.

Espen Andre Fossen, a graduate student at the Norwegian University of Science and Technology, provided an excellent description of multilateration in his master's thesis, "Principles of Internet Investigations: Basic Reconnaissance, Geopositioning, and Public Information Sources." He states that multilateration is a way to estimate the position of an unknown point using the distance from a set of known points. Figure 10-17 shows trilateration from three landmarks (L1, L2, L3) to find the position of an unknown point.

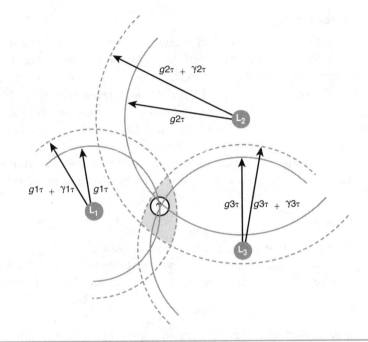

Figure 10-17   Trilateration with geographic distance constraints

Multilateration needs distances from multiple known points to calculate the approximate geographic location of the unknown point; these are called landmarks. To maximize the algorithm's accuracy, designated landmarks should be geographically distributed within a reasonable distance of the unknown host. A landmark typically consists of a router or server, but primarily, it is a device capable of performing a ping, traceroute, or similar network delay measurement command.

Geolocation   The geographical distance constraint $\hat{g}_{i\tau} = g_{i\tau} + \gamma_{i\tau}$ for each landmark is given by two factors: *real geographical distance* $g_{i\tau}$ and *additive distance distortion* $\gamma_{i\tau}$. *Additive distance* distortion puts the target location estimate within the grey area of Figure 10-15. The grey area is an intersection of the *geographical distance constraints* from each landmark Li to the target host τ. Given a set of K landmarks, it is possible to see this intersection as an order-K Venn diagram. Given K landmarks, the target host τ has a collection of closed curves $C_\tau = \{C_{1\tau}, C_{2\tau}, ..., C_{K\tau}\}$, and the intersection region where all circles intersect each other can be given by the equation

$$R = \bigcap_i^K C_{i\tau}.$$

To find the precise position of the target host, you must calculate the area of the region R which is the intersection points that belong to all circles . The area of the region with vertices can be calculated with this equation:

$$A_R = \frac{1}{2} \sum_{n=0}^{N-1} \begin{vmatrix} x_n & x_{n+1} \\ y_n & y_{n+1} \end{vmatrix}$$

The coordinates of the target host τ can be expressed as (C_x, C_y), where C_x and C_y are calculated as

$$C_x = \frac{1}{6A} \sum_{n=0}^{N-1} [(x)_n + x_{n+1}) \begin{vmatrix} x_n & x_{y+1} \\ y_n & y_{n+1} \end{vmatrix} \qquad C_y = \frac{1}{6A} \sum_{n=0}^{N-1} [(y_n + y_{n+1}]) \begin{vmatrix} x_n & x_{n+1} \\ y_n & y_{n+1} \end{vmatrix}$$

So, the mathematical equations are somewhat outside this book's scope and might be overwhelming; however, it proves multilateration has credible mathematical support and scientific consistency.

Confidence Region   The approximate location of the target host has been calculated using geographical distance constraints consisting of two factors: the actual geographical distance, $g_{i\tau}$, and the additive distance distortion, $\gamma_{i\tau}$. The additive distance distortion might be used to evaluate the confidence of results (see Figure 10-18). It is the small distance between the dotted circles and solid circles encompassing the landmarks (L1, L2, L3). The confidence region helps eliminate overestimation, underestimation, and mismatch, shown respectively in Figure 10-18(a), 10-18(b), and 10-18(c).

In his academic thesis, "Trilateration Utility for Locating IP Addresses: A Delay Base Solution for IP Geolocation" (Javed, 2003), Faran Javed identified several factors that must be taken into account when estimating geolocation:

- Capacity bandwidths differ by many orders of magnitude (for example, 1Mbps versus 10Gbps). For a 1Mbps link, the time to clock a 100-byte packet onto the link is about 0.8msec. This is roughly the time for light to propagate through 100 (~161km) miles of fiber. A canonical average delay per distance for packets traversing well-provisioned parts of the Internet is about a factor of two slower than this (for example, 1ms per 100km) because of nongreat circle routes, multiple hops, and so on. Therefore, it is not possible to have a single conversion factor from RTT to distance that works for all links for all distances.

- Cross-traffic results in queuing delays, which in turn affects the RTT. This is the reason for using the minimum RTT of multiple measurements, understanding that the faster times are by packets that were probably not affected by queuing issues.

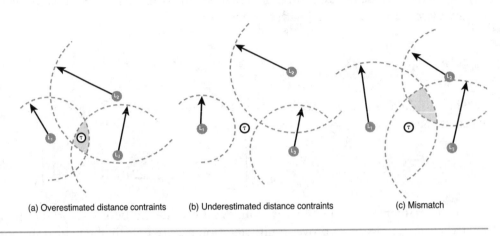

(a) Overestimated distance contraints   (b) Underestimated distance contraints   (c) Mismatch

Figure 10-18 Effects of geographic distance constraint calculations

However, if the queuing affects all RTT measurements, the minimum RTT will include a queuing interval and will not accurately reflect the distance.

- Routing policy is the path a packet takes over the network and depends on link/router availability and individual router policies. Extra hops in the path increase extra router and clocking delays, different hops have different delays, and different links have different capacities and distances. The route linking might be such that the route between a landmark and a selected host is not direct. For example, the route from one landmark in San Jose, California, to Mountain View, California (20 miles away), has a route that goes through New York. Therefore, a better approach requires that the analyst compare the results from a cluster of known landmarks.

- Bottleneck bandwidth is the saturation of link resources and might indicate a low-capacity or heavily loaded high-speed circuit in the path. Circuit utilization changes as a function of time, so the magnitude of a bottleneck and, possibly, link location will vary.

- Configuration errors in routers and switches can cause unexpected delays in the form of transient link failures. The problem is compounded if traffic is rerouted to an alternate path that is also heavily loaded.

- Traffic conditions might enormously vary as a function of time. For example, on Monday mornings, there is typically a surge in traffic as people come to work; also, there is usually more traffic during peak work hours compared to weekends and nights. Such increased traffic often leads to congestion, increased queuing, and thus increases in RTT.

Javed helped create a multilateration tool, called Tulip, that uses round-trip ping statistics from well-known, publicly accessible servers, mostly within academia, to geolocate a specific target machine. Figure 10-19 shows the visual output of a series of accuracy tests.

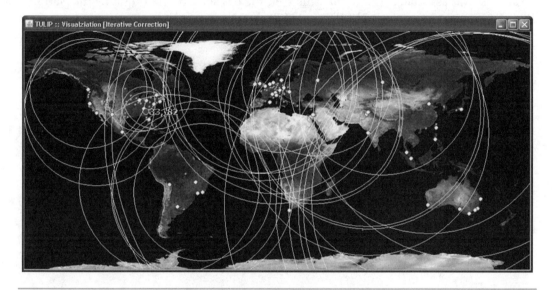

Figure 10-19   Tulip visualization of Web server tracking

Using multiple instances of the RTT method, which is evident in the multiple circles in the figure, improves the accuracy of the algorithm. The Tulip result, which displays a slightly larger dot labeled 33 and -82, indicates the location of the *unknown target* (URL or IP address). It appears to be located over Northern Georgia and is about 50 miles off target.

Strategic Business Partnerships

Strategic business partnerships are probably the most commonly used and beneficial technique for mapping IP addresses to geographic locations, mainly because the sheer volume of results enables a vendor to eliminate anomalous outliers. Web surfers unknowingly submit their approximate geographic location on a daily basis, whether through manual submission or automated processes. For example, Digital Envoy, a subsidiary of Landmark Communications Inc., reaped the query results from the highly popular Web site www.weather.com. Web surfers submit their street address/city and state/zip code (or any combination of the three) and the Web site displays the daily and/or weekly weather reports for their desired location. Digital Envoy, being affiliated with the primary custodian of the Web site, collected the submitted information and, in turn, accurately determined with which street address/city and state/zip code the source IP address was associated. (Note that this Web site has since been bought by the National Broadcasting Company [NBC].) Figure 10-20 shows a www.weather.com snippet.

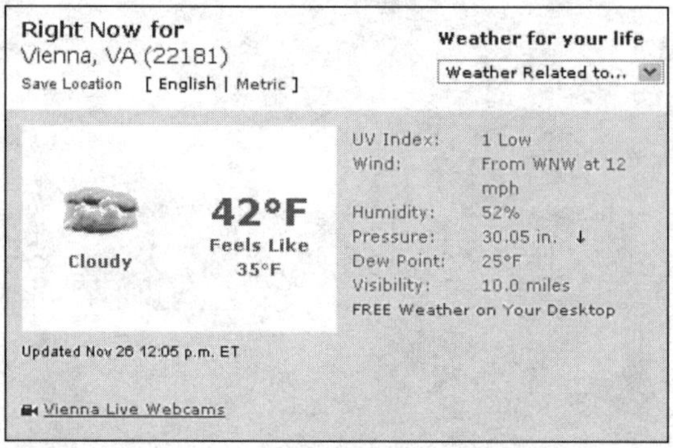

Figure 10-20   Weather.com

Of course, a Web surfer can just be researching the weather for an upcoming vacation or business trip, which gives incorrect information on the backend. However, this is where sheer volume quickly identifies these outliers and the erroneous information can be easily eliminated.

Think about how often Web surfers enter their own zip code or home address into a Web form to retrieve information without really thinking about it. Here are some examples of where that occurs:

- Weather sites or the automated client from WeatherBug
- Movie listings
- Real-estate listings
- Home Depot Web site (an example of surfing a specific store's inventory)

- Craigslist
- CarMax
- Job listings
- Mapping Web sites, such as MapQuest and Yahoo! maps (This is the scariest of all, because most inquiries include an exact street address.)

Most Web surfers are unaware that some Web site owners sell their collected information to firms that want it. Is this information somehow protected by privacy laws? That question is impossible to answer across the board, but it is unlikely because, depending on the Web site, the submitted information might be surrendered to custodians to do as they please.

Some techniques described in the previous list (weather sites, movie listings, and so on) should only be used for validation and should not be used as a primary geolocation data point. Some methods are accurate and, although they might require another level of verification, can provide a precise city-level representation.

GEOCODING LIMITATIONS

As with any technology these days, obstacles must always be overcome. In most cases, geocoding an IP address produces an accurate representation of where it is located. However, some technological components make tracing back to that location difficult. Anonymizing proxy servers were specifically designed to mask the source location of a user, usually to avoid detection while violating organizational Web surfing policies. Publicly accessible anonymizers are identifiable themselves, and most geolocation services maintain a database of these devices so they can be monitored.

America Online (AOL) is another more common limitation that stems from ISP legacy architecture. All AOL traffic is routed through its larger corporate facilities in Herndon, Virginia, and Mountain View, California, which results in an additional layer of obfuscation.

Satellite communications is another element that adds difficulty to determining source locations, because signals literally bounce all over the globe, creating a somewhat untraceable path (at least using any publicly available methods, which is my conspiracy theory).

Another common issue worth mentioning is how residential ISPs use DHCP. Theoretically, residential routers need to relinquish their external IP addresses every interval of time and request a new IP address from their ISP. Each ISP has its own policies and procedures, whether it occurs every 30, 60, or 90 days, and few publicly disclose this information. It might be nothing more than a way to ensure that residential users are not running Web servers at their houses without paying an extra fee for business-class services. However, the reallocation of a residential IP address does not diminish GID because the new IP address still provides ample information for geolocation.

Finally, as previously mentioned, Whois can cause an issue, because the information is not validated nor does it represent information for multiple locations. Whois records that contain DNS ranges might encompass a company's entire subnet range, but the provided information represents a single physical location (typically that of the corporate headquarters) and does not accurately depict the extent or locations of other offices, sites, and so on. Clearly, the geographical data provided in the Whois database search is not conclusive, and it should be used in collaboration with the results produced by other techniques or as a secondary metric.

ACCURACY

"How accurate is the geocoding of IP addresses to geographic coordinates?," remains the most frequently asked question at conferences and IT security focus groups. A multitude of external factors need to be considered before a precise answer can be provided. For example, if the target IP is using a satellite link, proxy server, or is being routed through AOL's infrastructure, those characteristics affect the level of accuracy. The silver lining is that most geocoding vendors recognize these obstacles and provide an accuracy rating (or confidence measurement) in addition to providing relevant information regarding target IP characteristics. This basically provides a security analyst with all the pertinent information to make an educated decision. Vendors publicly confirm that they typically use traceroute, trilateration, strategic business partnerships, and internal proprietary algorithms as primary data elements to create an accurate geographic location. As expected, they do not disclose any information regarding their internal algorithms. They validate the location with less accurate and less critical data elements, including Whois, AS, DNS LOC, or Geopriv, if it catches on.

NOTE

Geopriv is a working draft RFC 3693 that provides a secure geospatial protocol that protects the privacy of an individual, resource, or other entity and simultaneously provides location-based services. The past decade has seen a swarm of new geographical-savvy applications that require geolocation intelligence, including navigation applications, emergency services, management of equipment in the field, and other location-dependent services. At this time, it is unknown if the Geopriv protocol will become mainstream.

GEOLOCATION INTELLIGENCE VENDORS

Lackluster investment levels in GIS services by network security firms are becoming less of an issue, largely because of the efforts of some of their best innovators. Vendors such as Quova, MaxMind, and Digital Envoy have opened their IP intelligence technologies to industries that might benefit from the information-rich data. The richness is in the details, such as geographic coordinates, connectivity speeds, time zones, proxy server intelligence, ISP names, much of which are determined by proprietary algorithms. U.S. area codes, zip codes, and their foreign equivalents are also included and, perhaps most importantly, so are precision ratings that affect consumer provider choices. Currently, only a handful of geocoding vendors exist. Here is a brief summary of each vendor:

- **MaxMind.** Founded in 2002, MaxMind (www.maxmind.com) provides IP address geolocation and online fraud-detection tools. Located in Boston, Massachusetts, MaxMind provides geolocation solutions through its GeoIP product line and offers proprietary fraud protection with its minFraud service. minFraud helps merchants guard against fraudulent online transactions, and it includes proxy detection to uncover IP addresses that originate in anonymous networks. MaxMind offers IP-to-data configurations in either a comma separated values (CSV) download or an online query that includes about 2,700,000 records. Queries range from 1,250 for $5 to 25,000 queries for $100. The downloadable CSV file ranges in value, depending on the purchased data points with an additional monthly charge for updates. A key data point that MaxMind provides for an additional cost is an accuracy radius, which reflects the estimated average distance between the actual location of the source IP address and the location returned by its product. The accuracy rating is based on usage data collected over IP addresses and IP blocks and is largely dependent on the particular ISP. For example, Verizon DSL offerings in the Massachusetts area typically have accuracy radius of 5 miles. On the other hand, SBC Internet in California might have an accuracy radius of 50 miles, while SBC Internet in Texas might have 2 miles. As expected, MaxMind does not release the exact methods it relies on to collect and correlate its data, but has expressed openly that it relies on automated processes and datasets that are available to it through strategic business partnerships' datasets, with minimal, if any, human analysis. In 2006, MaxMind formed a partnership with SkyHook Wireless, a provider of Wi-Fi positioning systems and has integrated complementary products without exclusively playing in the wireless geolocation space. SkyHook uses an interface between a Garmin GPS locator and NetStumbler to produce a database that is gathered by mobile operators. In addition, MaxMind offers a binary data format that can directly be used with geoiplookup tools, as well as a plug-in (mod_geoip) for Apache, which allows Web site owners to analyze geolocations of Web visitors.

- **IP2Location.** A subsidiary of Hexasoft Development Sdn. Bhd. (HDSB), located in Penang, Malaysia, with a remote office in Florida (www.ip2location.com). Data points are supplied in CSV or binary format to maximize speed and are priced from free shareware to $1,399 per server each year for the DB18 containing 6,200,000 records. However, costs can potentially double depending on the required Application Programming Interface (API) needed. Of course, an in-house intermediary can be installed between the database and application. Database updates are provided monthly, free of charge, to ensure accuracy. IP2Location is an excellent source of IP intelligence information, because the Web site provides sample scripts, sample data, product line comparisons, data specifications, and an FAQ section.

- **Digital Envoy.** Founded in 1999 and is based in Atlanta, Georgia (www.digitalenvoy.com). To strengthen its position for acquiring geocoding business, the company separated into two business units: Digital Element and Digital Resolve. Digital Element (http://digitalelement.com/) targets online advertising, content localization, local search, geographic rights management, and enhanced analytics. Digital Resolve (www.digital-resolve.com) targets online fraud and identity-theft solutions for login authentication, customer acquisition, and transaction monitoring and fraud detection. The technology that GID uses is offered through a Digital Elements product line called NetAcuity, which focuses on IP intelligence. NetAcuity is offered as either a real-time online query service or a flat file, depending on application needs. Digital Element is also independently audited to ensure its advertised accuracy ratings hold true. Early in 2008, Digital Element engaged Keynote Systems to perform an accuracy rating of 2,400 computers and mobile devices in over 240 locations around the world of which 160 metropolitan areas. The audit evaluated the accuracy from a country, city, and, where applicable, state perspective. City results were graded for service locations that were within a 30-mile radius of the each city. The results yielded 100 percent match at the country level, 100 percent match at the state level, and 97 percent match at the city level. However, Digital Element could not elaborate on the techniques or methodologies that Keynote Systems used to perform the audit.

- **Quova.** Founded in 2000 and resides in Mountain View, California. It is an industry-leading provider of geolocation data points, offering businesses the added IP-intelligence layer of knowledge by specializing at geotargeting advertising and Web content, detecting card-not-present fraud and identify theft, managing digital download distribution, enhancing Web analytics, and ensuring regulatory compliance. Quova specializes in proxy detection by monitoring almost half a million anonymizing proxies as part of its weekly data updates. Quova also sets itself apart from most of its competition in three unique ways:

  - Independent auditing

- Incorporating wireless datasets
- Network Geographic Analyst (NGA)

PriceWaterhouseCoopers (PWC) performs annual audits to confirm that Quova's advertisement of 99.9 percent accuracy rate at the country level and 96 percent at the U.S. state level holds true. PWC uses a truth set to calculate the accuracy. A truth set, also known as a ground set, is a universal term and is not Quova specific, but it is defined as a dataset where the location of the IP addresses is known to the auditor but not the firm providing the geocoding translation. Quova extended its strategic partnerships by incorporating the wireless positioning capabilities of the Navizon product by Mexens Technology. Navizon is a wireless positioning system that triangulates signals broadcasted from Wi-Fi APs and cellular towers. It is a small snippet of Java code that interfaces with cell-phone transmissions and captures cell tower or GPS coordinates and reports back to a central repository. The final, and the most unique element, is the use of NGA: human analysis. Quova has two NGA teams (one in the U.S. and one in Amsterdam) that manually map Internet subnets to assess geocoding results. The unexpected, yet, extremely successful trait that is shared by NGAs is a lack of extensive knowledge of the GIS discipline (although it is a benefit, it is not required). Quova seeks candidates that are multilingual or have experience in multiple international markets. For example, Quova was mapping German domains, specifically router host names, and found that the naming convention was too cryptic for people who did not understand German common markets. A Quova employee with experience in that area determined that the naming convention mimicked the same geographic distribution as German license-plate lettering. In that context, consider the domain dtag.de in the Class C 62.153.47.0/24, specifically do-ag7.DO.DE.net.DTAG.DE (62.153.47.x).

The traceroute yields the following:

```
Tracing route to do-ag7.DO.DE.net.DTAG.DE [62.153.47.1] over a maximum of 30 hops:
1     8 ms      9 ms     8 ms   10.7.0.1
2    10 ms     10 ms    13 ms   ip72-219-223-21.dc.dc.cox.net
[72.219.223.21]
3    15 ms      8 ms     9 ms   mrfddsrj02-ge110.rd.dc.cox.net
[68.100.0.149]
4    12 ms     11 ms    11 ms   ashbbrj02-as0.0.r2.as.cox.net [68.1.1.232]
5    20 ms     22 ms    18 ms   nyk-bb2-link.telia.net [80.91.250.18]
6   140 ms     94 ms    90 ms   ldn-bb2-link.telia.net [80.91.248.253]
7    90 ms     90 ms    88 ms   ldn-b4-link.telia.net [80.91.251.17]
8    92 ms     91 ms    90 ms   62.156.138.53
9   112 ms    111 ms   110 ms   do-ag7.DO.DE.net.DTAG.DE [62.153.47.1]
Trace complete.
```

DO.DE.net.DTAG.DE is in Dortmund, Nordrhein Westfalen, Germany. Figure 10-21 shows other one, two, or three-letter acronyms that mimic German license plates.

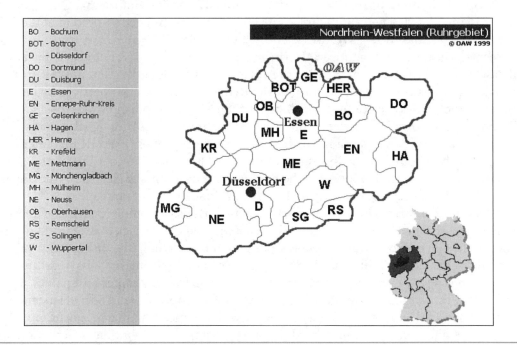

Figure 10-21   Acronym distribution of German license plates

CASE STUDY OF GEOGRAPHIC INTRUSION DETECTION

After several unsuccessful attempts to convince corporations/educational institutions to allow me to use their IDS dataset for this case study, I finally obtained a dataset to prove my GID model. I considered pulling my personal honeypot dataset; however, the chance that it had undergone a true professional attack was minimal. Unfortunately, in asking around, companies and network security professionals are extremely protective when asked to share their "live" IDS datasets, even for research purposes. Luckily, a friend that runs the network security department of a well-known organization agreed to share his dataset and assist with my case study as long as he (and the company's industry) remained absolutely anonymous. The IDS dataset used in this case study was donated by an entity that defends against thousands of daily attacks, some of which I will prove are professionally coordinated attacks. The pool of alerts consisted of a three-month set of Snort IDS logs from January 1, 2008, to April 1, 2008, and contained 341,268 alerts. In addition to its internal 24x7/365 security surveillance team tackling manual analysis and research, the company uses a mainstream SEM to assist with correlation and event escalation.

Each IP address in the alert database was geocoded by using a commercially available IP to latitude/longitude translation database, with the corresponding coordinates amended to the database. Figure 10-22 displays each georeferenced IP address from the database. To visually ease the global view of alerts, if more than one alert was from a single IP address, the point symbol was weighted by the total number of alerts originating from that IP.

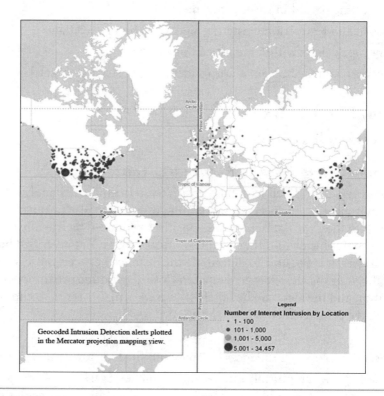

Figure 10-22 Each IP address geocoded to corresponding geographic coordinates

CASE OUTLINE

A high-level case outline is described here. Each point is more extensively discussed in a moment:

1. Eliminate friendlies to reduce IDS false positives:
   a. **Street address.** Geographically plot remote branches, small office/home office (SOHO), or business partner's locations by street address.
   b. **IP translation.** Geographically plot remote branches, SOHO, or business partner's location by static IP address.
   c. **IP translation.** Create an IDS alert that is triggered when a customer authenticates to a Web site and extracts its IP address; this is not bulletproof.
2. Plot rolling time period in weekly increments.
3. Run Poisson and K function clustering algorithm on plotted data.
4. Extract network alerts within identified hotspot.
5. Manually correlate the hotspot alerts to identify a professional attack.

BREAKDOWN OF THE STEPS

Let's closely look at each step in the process.

Step 1: Eliminate Friendlies to Reduce IDS False Positives

IDS datasets are usually riddled with false positives, so to efficiently apply this method in an optimal environment, it is necessary to eliminate as many false positives as possible. The first step is to filter the dataset for false positives produced by friendly facilities and locations. By geographically plotting remote branches, SOHO, and verified business partner's addresses, it is possible to determine the distance between those locations and the alert locations. If the alert was generated in close geographic proximity of the friendly location and the alert can be falsely triggered, it makes sense to eliminate it from the dataset. Three primary methods can be applied for this step:

- **Street address.** Geographically plot remote branches, SOHO, business partner's locations, or employees' residences compared to the location of IDS alert(s).
- **IP translation.** Geographically plot remote branches, SOHO, business partner's location, or employees' residences based on static IP addresses by geolocating the static IP address and comparing it to the location of the IDS alert(s).
- **IP translation.** Create an IDS alert that is triggered when a customer authenticates to a Web site and pulls his IP address, geolocates the IP address, and compares it to

the location of the IDS alert(s). This approach assumes attackers are *not* current customers, which is a potentially dangerous assumption.

To better illustrate this approach, here is a proof-of-concept to eliminate false positive alerts based on geographically plotting internal resources by street address. The street addresses of 65 assumed friendly facilities (15 corporate facilities and 50 employee home addresses) were georeferenced to latitude and longitude points and plotted on a map. If the source of an alert was within 1 kilometer (about .62 miles) of a friendly facility, it was removed from the alert database and considered a false positive. Figure 10-23 shows the elimination of a deemed false positive using the street address of a remote office as the identified friendly facility. Because the alert was within a reasonable proximity (approximately 100 yards) of the network alert, it was categorized as a false positive.

Figure 10-23   Display of mapping friendly facilities and network alerts

This step is optional, and performing it is risky, because there might be a professional attacker within close proximity of a corporate location, especially within a metropolitan area. Taking that into account, the distance was decreased to .5 kilometer (.31 miles) within metropolitan regions. Figure 10-24 demonstrates the close proximity of an employee's home address to a network alert. Given the specific network alert identified, it was categorized as a false positive and deleted from the IDS dataset. It is important to point out that, when evaluating the friendly locations and the triggered network alert, an analyst *must try not* to automatically disregard the alerts solely based on geographic proximity. The analyst needs to also consider the probability that the alert might be a false positive triggered by an external employee, client, or Web user. Some IDS signatures are more plausible to be false positives associated with friendly locations than other signatures. For example, in Figure 10-24, the identified employee #38 works in the accounting department, and because the dataset occurred over tax season, the employee was extremely busy remotely logging into his Deltek server running various budget reports at all hours of the night. Keeping that in mind, a network alert associated with Deltek failed login is a reasonable false positive. On the other hand, if the network alert was a Veritas Backup Exec root connection attempt using default password hash, there is absolutely no reason that an employee in the accounting department should trigger that alert and, therefore, the network alert would hold true and *not* be eliminated from the dataset.

Figure 10-24 Display of mapping friendly facilities and network alerts within a metropolitan area

Because the IDS dataset was historical instead of real time, neither of the IP translation strategies could be implemented to identify friendly connections. IP translation is using the same process (taking the source IP address of the alert, translating it to geographic coordinates, and plotting it on a map) to geolocate the source IDS alerts but is using it to geocode friendly locations.

The previous strategy identified was to create a Snort signature that would trigger after a user authenticated to the company's Web site (similar to entering a username and password to access banking information or a customer's online profile). After he authenticates and the custom IDS alert is triggered, just extract the user's source IP address and geolocate. This is helpful, because it allows the security team to potentially eliminate a large number of false positives triggered by users. A secondary benefit is having the immediate ability to visually locate your clients on a map. As previously mentioned, eliminating alerts based on customer authentication is risky, because it also assumes the professional attacker is not a customer. However, depending on the company's risk comfort levels, computing power, and capability to collect the information, this step can be eliminated.

In this instance, extracting and eliminating the identified friendly locations successfully reduced the network alert dataset by 10,401 alerts and, although that is a relatively small number, it is still substantial if all 10,401 alerts required manual analysis. Figure 10-25 displays the overlay of plotted network alerts and friendly locations.

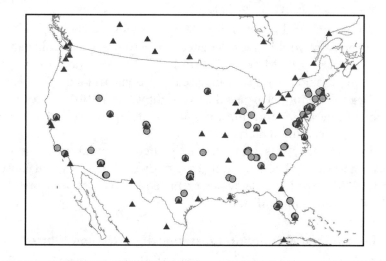

Figure 10-25   Overlay of network attacks and friendly locations

Step 2: Temporal Analysis: Plot the Rolling Time Period

As mentioned in the section, "Dynamics of a Professional Attack," a truly professional attack occurs over several weeks in order to not attract attention to the network reconnaissance phase. To be conservative, a 4-week rolling time duration was chosen for this particular case, the premise being that a professional attack from the starting network reconnaissance to the finishing launch of attack vectors would occur within that time frame. The number of weeks applied is a variable in the model and can be modified by the user, but a general rule of thumb is the interval for temporal analysis should be *at least 2 weeks*. The 4-week interval is a rolling daily parameter so, every 24 hours that passes, the temporal analysis extends another 24 hours. This might cause some confusion, so what follows is a conceptual representation:

- No (monthly):
  - January 1, 2008 to February 1, 2008
  - February 1, 2008 to March 1, 2008
  - March 1, 2008 to April 1, 2008
- Yes (daily):
  - January 1, 2008 to February 1, 2008
  - January 2, 2008 to February 2, 2008
  - January 3, 2008 to February 3, 2008
  - January 4, 2008 to February 4, 2008

The entire 3-month model resulted in 62 temporal subsets. The total subsets would have been 92 as each day would have calculated a new rolling temporal analysis subset (January = 31, February = 29, March = 31, April = 1); however, because this dataset ends at April 1, 2008, there is no reason to reanalyze the subsets over again inside the last 4 weeks. Applying a rolling model avoids the oversight where network reconnaissance starts at the end of one subset and continues into the following subset, therefore potentially severing the correlation of alerts.

The individual network alerts within the designated temporal subsets were extracted and continued on to step 3. The remaining case study uses the temporal subset identified from March 5, 2008 to April 1, 2008, which extracted 95,734 total network alerts stemming from 3,847 unique source IP addresses.

Step 3: Run Poisson and K Function Clustering Algorithm on Plotted Data

Applying the GIS algorithms to a subset of network alerts provides the new layer of intelligence and is the core of this GID model. Identifying clusters of network alerts within close proximity of each other provides the malicious geographic fingerprint needed to establish professional coordinated attacks.

The first issue encountered in this step was determining which GIS algorithm would lend itself to problem-solving and accurately identifying clusters. Based on the advice from three independent GIS consulting firms and a hefty proof of concept price tag, the Poisson model with K function was selected.

Creating GIS Layers To apply the Poisson process model, follow these steps:

1. Determine the number of network alerts and plot the equivalent number of Poisson points all over the globe.

   The Poisson process requires the number of Poisson points to be equivalent to the number of network alerts. It was also proper to require that all Poisson points fall on a land mass rather than in the oceans, because the test for CSR logically only applies to terrestrial area. Poisson points were created in GIS by computing random x, y coordinate pairs until there were 3,847 coordinate pairs that fell on Earth's land mass. In practice, an abundance of Poisson points were computed, and those not intersecting a landmass polygon were removed and coordinates were recalculated. Remaining terrestrial points were culled to leave 3,847 Poisson points. Figure 10-26 shows the randomly generated Poisson points throughout the world.

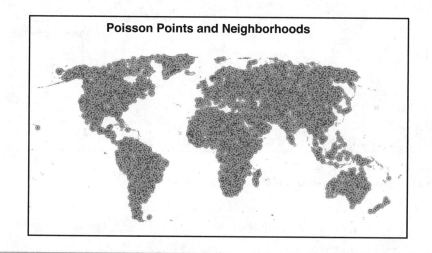

Figure 10-26 Global view of the Poisson points and neighborhoods

2. Determine a Poisson radius commonly referred to as the Poisson neighborhood.

   Poisson neighborhoods were created by buffering the Poisson points with a radius of 50km, about 31 miles. This radius was selected to capture a fair number of alerts in moderately dense areas, yet minimize overlap. The radius was determined as it represents a standard diameter that local ISPs will provide Internet services and distribute IP addresses. Figure 10-27 represents the Poisson radius; however, the radius was increased to 100km to make it easy to visualize the methodology of applying the Poisson neighborhoods. The center dots represent the Poisson point; the shaded radius represents the Poisson neighborhood, and the randomly offset dots represent network alerts.

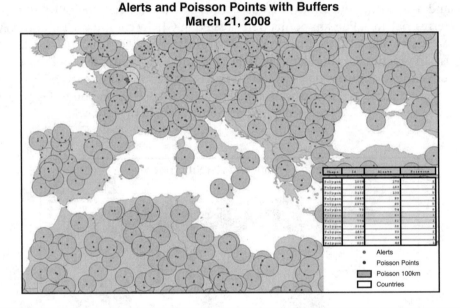

Figure 10-27   Poisson neighborhoods with 100km radius over Europe

3. Calculate the number of alerts that are located within each Poisson neighborhood.

4. If a threshold is met, it is reasonable to assume there is clustering.

Spatial Analysis   To determine if spatial clustering of attacks had been taking place, the case study implemented the test for CSR as a K function test at a fixed radius determined by a Poisson process model. The K function test was performed using the alert points, Poisson points, and Poisson neighborhoods, each as a GIS layer, as previously described. For each Poisson neighborhood, the number of alerts and the number of other Poisson points falling within the neighborhood were counted. The counting was performed in the GIS using a spatial overlay. First, attribute columns were created in the Poisson neighborhood layer to store the alert count and Poisson point count for each neighborhood. A script selected each Poisson neighborhood and overlaid it with the alerts layer first and then the Poisson point layer. The alert and Poisson point tallies were saved as separate attributes in the neighborhood layer. In that the Poisson neighborhoods were overlapping, an alert or Poisson point could be double counted as being in more than one neighborhood polygon.

Table 10-2 shows the alert count versus Poisson point count. For this dataset, most of the Poisson neighborhoods contained no alerts. A single Poisson neighborhood contained more than a thousand alerts. As expected, Poisson points were evenly distributed among Poisson neighborhoods. This concentration of alerts versus a relatively even background of Poisson points statistically confirmed that clustering was evident.

Table 10-2   Poisson Neighborhood Alert Count

Number of Alerts (Per Bin)	Frequency
0	3,244
<=10	65
<=100	27
>=101	510
>=1000	1

Step 4: Extract Network Alerts Within Identified Hotspot

A cartographic projection was needed in which to best display the alerts points, generate new Poisson points, and compute distances between neighboring points. The choice of coordinate space will distort the apparent density of alerts; different places on Earth are either more or less compressed by different map projections. Different map projections are better optimized to local, continental, or global scales of analysis. Alerts points would then be projected from latitude and longitude into the Cartesian coordinate system of the chosen map projection. Also, alert data could remain in latitude and longitude coordinates with the spatial point pattern analysis being computed on the surface of a sphere. The geographic origin of the alerts in this study spanned all six continents. For this global domain, the Robinson projection was chosen for its appealing display and its approximate preservation of area.[13]

The Robinson project worked great for applying the Poisson algorithm, but with the extraction of the determined clusters, the case study now transitions from GIS back to network security expertise. The geographical display that catered to exact location measurements needed by the GIS algorithms and performed by ESRI might not be sufficient for researching the network alerts within the clusters. By using Google Earth PRO, the elevation level is controlled better, which produces a more accurate situational assessment. For example, if the attacks traced back to a university rather than a farmhouse in Montana, it could affect the way alerts are viewed.

NOTE

Most educational institutions are clearly visible in Google Earth because of their close proximity to sports fields. An additional perk of using Google Earth PRO is the capability to extract street addresses, commonly known as address interpolation. When a user places the mouse over a desired destination and hits Alt + right-click, Google Earth PRO displays the street address of the location. Then, using a quick Google search, a security analyst can fairly easily determine the nature of that location. The result provides another piece of information to better determine the appropriate course of action.

Figure 10-28 shows an identified cluster of network alerts in Brazil. The IP addresses have been masked to respect privacy rights.

Results of the GIS application identified the following:

- 3,244 Poisson neighborhoods with no alerts
- 65 Poisson neighborhoods with <= 10 alerts
- 27 Poisson neighborhoods with <= 100 alerts
- 510 Poisson neighborhoods with >= 100 alerts
- 1 Poisson neighborhood with >= 1000 alerts

As mentioned in the introduction, this strategy is designed to identify professional attacks. The 510 Poisson neighborhoods with >=100 alerts and 1 Poisson neighborhood with >= 1000 alerts can be eliminated. It is either a DoS attempt, an extremely noisy network recon attempt, or traffic funneled from an AOL-like ISP; either way, this method is not practical for that case. The Poisson neighborhoods with no alerts can obviously also be eliminated. The majority of analysis involved dissecting the 65 Poisson

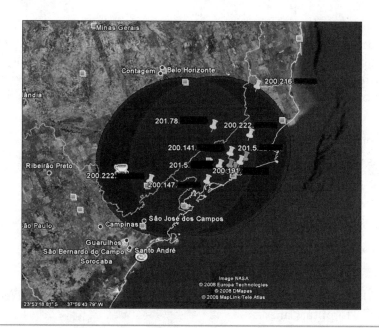

Figure 10-28   Google Earth visual display of an identified hotspot

neighborhoods with <=10 alerts. The 27 Poisson neighborhoods with <= 100 are not irrelevant, but manual analysis becomes tedious at this point.

Step 5: Manually Correlate the Hotspot Alerts to Identify a Professional Attack

Now that the clusters have been extracted, step 5 provides a final decision on whether the clustered events have a direct relationship with each other. The goal of this chapter is not to define a particular process for correlating IDS alerts, because the art of IDS correlation is developed as a result of training, experience, and a hint of intuition. After graciously bribing my friend, who provided the IDS dataset, and two of his security coworkers with Dunkin' Donuts coffee, Pepsi, an abundant supply of Red Baron pizzas, a tweaked version of Greg Conti's RUMINT tool, and a custom developed Java/Tomcat geospatial Web application, they agreed to help me manually comb through the alerts. Over two weekends, we dissected each identified cluster. Because they knew their network topology and were familiar with normal server communication flows, they were able to steamroll through most clusters. We ultimately separated the clusters into respective yes, no, and maybe piles, and as a collective group revisited the maybe and yes piles.

Of the 92 identified hotspots extracted in step 4, the manual correlation phase classified three potentially professional attacks. The remainder of this chapter focuses on one

of the three attacks that was later confirmed by the dataset owner as a flaw in the architecture and has since been remedied. The other two professional attacks targeted a legacy
application vulnerability and, as of this writing, had not been corrected, and thus, I was
not given permission to include it. The key factors for consideration are shown here and
are similar to traditional IDS analysis but are expanded to include geographic specific
information:

• Number of possible zombies within the cluster
• Alert classifications
• Time stamp correlation
• Distance between alerts
• Target(s) of the attacks
• Target ports of the attacks
• Attacker history (hence the temporal extraction)

The Snort IDS alerts in Table 10-3 are from an identified cluster in the New England
area, specifically Toronto, Canada.

Table 10-3   Snort IDS Alerts for the Identified Cluster in the New England Region

Signature	AM Time Stamp	Priority	Source IP	Dest. Port	User Attempt	Latitude	Longitude
Port scan	3/5/2008 8:26	3	70.xxx.xxx.125	1400 – 3390		43.3	-79.9
Port scan	3/5/2008 8:31	3	70.xxx.xxx.128	501-784		43.666698	-79.416801
Port scan	3/6/2008 8:16	3	70.xxx.xxx.128	260-458		43.666698	-79.416801
Port scan	3/6/2008 8:35	3	70.xxx.xxx.35	785-943		43.666698	-79.416801
Port scan	3/7/2008 8:27	3	70.xxx.xxx.125	459-500		43.3	-79.9

Table 10-3 Snort IDS Alerts for the Identified Cluster in the New England Region

Signature	AM Time Stamp	Priority	Source IP	Dest. Port	User Attempt	Latitude	Longitude
Port scan	3/7/2008 8:30	3	70.xxx.xxx.131	1000 – 1324		43.6833	-79.766701
Port scan	3/7/2008 8:30	3	70.xxx.xxx.131	9950 – 12032		43.6833	-79.766701
Port scan	3/9/2008 8:25	3	70.xxx.xxx.13	80; 8080		43.549999	-80.25
Port scan	3/9/2008 8:25	3	70.xxx.xxx.13	1 – 259		43.549999	-80.25
Port scan	3/9/2008 8:30	3	69.xxx.xxx.123	1434; 1433		43.25	-79.833298
Port scan	3/10/2008 8:23	3	69.xxx.xxx.123	444; 4010 - 4983		43.25	-79.833298
Port scan	3/11/2008 8:27	3	70.xxx.xxx.35	5003 – 6516; 100000		43.666698	-79.416801
Port scan	3/11/2008 8:28	3	69.xxx.xxx.245	6480 – 7501		43.25	-79.833298
Port scan	3/11/2008 8:28	3	69.xxx.xxx.245	7823 – 9123		43.25	-79.833298
SharePoint failed logon.	3/15/2008 8:26	3	70.xxx.xxx.94	80	Wsmith	43.666698	-79.416801
SharePoint failed logon.	3/15/2008 8:28	3	70.xxx.xxx.94	80	Wsmith	43.666698	-79.416801
SharePoint failed logon.	3/15/2008 8:29	3	70.xxx.xxx.100	80	Wsmith	43.6833	-79.766701

Table 10-3   Snort IDS Alerts for the Identified Cluster in the New England Region

Signature	AM Time Stamp	Priority	Source IP	Dest. Port	User Attempt	Latitude	Longitude
SharePoint failed logon.	3/15/2008 8:31	3	70.xxx.xxx.100	80	Wsmith	43.6833	-79.766701
SharePoint failed logon.	3/15/2008 8:37	3	70.xxx.xxx.100	80	Wsmith	43.6833	-79.766701
SharePoint failed logon.	3/15/2008 8:43	3	70.xxx.xxx.100	80	Wsmith	43.6833	-79.766701
SharePoint failed logon.	3/15/2008 8:55	3	70.xxx.xxx.94	80	Wsmith	43.666698	-79.416801
SharePoint failed logon.	3/15/2008 9:03	3	70.xxx.xxx.94	80	Wsmith	43.666698	-79.416801
SharePoint failed logon.	3/17/2008 8:03	3	70.xxx.xxx.100	80	Janderson	43.6833	-79.766701
SharePoint failed logon.	3/17/2008 8:03	3	69.xxx.xxx.247	80	Janderson	43.25	-79.833298
SharePoint failed logon.	3/17/2008 8:03	3	69.xxx.xxx.247	80	Janderson	43.25	-79.833298
SharePoint failed logon.	3/17/2008 8:04	3	70.xxx.xxx.13	80	Jkim	43.549999	-80.25
SharePoint failed logon.	3/17/2008 8:04	3	70.xxx.xxx.13	80	Jkim	43.549999	-80.25
SharePoint failed logon.	3/17/2008 8:04	3	70.xxx.xxx.13	80	Jkim	43.549999	-80.25
SharePoint failed logon.	3/17/2008 8:04	3	69.xxx.xxx.247	80	Jsmith	43.25	-79.833298
SharePoint failed logon.	3/17/2008 8:05	3	70.xxx.xxx.183	80	Jsmith	43.799999	-79.25

Table 10-3 Snort IDS Alerts for the Identified Cluster in the New England Region

Signature	AM Time Stamp	Priority	Source IP	Dest. Port	User Attempt	Latitude	Longitude
SharePoint failed logon.	3/17/2008 8:05	3	70.xxx.xxx.183	80	Jsmith	43.799999	-79.25
SharePoint failed logon.	3/17/2008 8:37	3	69.xxx.xxx.247	80	Janderson	43.25	-79.833298
SharePoint failed logon.	3/17/2008 8:37	3	69.xxx.xxx.247	80	Janderson	43.25	-79.833298
SharePoint failed logon.	3/17/2008 8:37	3	70.xxx.xxx.183	80	Janderson	43.799999	-79.25
SharePoint failed logon.	3/17/2008 8:38	3	70.xxx.xxx.183	80	Jsmith	43.799999	-79.25
SharePoint failed logon.	3/17/2008 8:39	3	69.xxx.xxx.247	80	Jsmith	43.25	-79.833298
SharePoint failed logon.	3/17/2008 8:39	3	69.xxx.xxx.247	80	Jsmith	43.25	-79.833298
SharePoint failed logon.	3/17/2008 9:05	3	70.xxx.xxx.183	80	Janderson	43.799999	-79.25
SharePoint failed logon.	3/17/2008 9:05	3	70.xxx.xxx.183	80	Janderson	43.799999	-79.25
WEB-MISC SharePoint Cross-Site scripting attempt.	3/25/2008 8:28	1	70.xxx.xxx.183	80		43.799999	-79.25
WEB-MISC SharePoint Cross-Site scripting attempt.	3/25/2008 8:32	1	70.xxx.xxx.183	80		43.799999	-79.25
WEB-MISC SharePoint Cross-Site scripting attempt.	3/25/2008 8:39	1	70.xxx.xxx.183	80		43.799999	-79.25

Table 10-3   Snort IDS Alerts for the Identified Cluster in the New England Region

Signature	AM Time Stamp	Priority	Source IP	Dest. Port	User Attempt	Latitude	Longitude
WEB-MISC SharePoint Cross-Site scripting attempt.	3/25/2008 8:39	1	70.xxx.xxx.183	80		43.799999	-79.25
WEB-MISC SharePoint Cross-Site scripting attempt.	3/25/2008 8:45	1	70.xxx.xxx.183	80		43.799999	-79.25
WEB-MISC SharePoint Cross-Site scripting attempt.	3/25/2008 8:48	1	70.xxx.xxx.183	80		43.799999	-79.25
WEB-MISC SharePoint Cross-Site scripting attempt.	3/25/2008 8:51	1	70.xxx.xxx.183	80		43.799999	-79.25
WEB-MISC SharePoint Cross-Site scripting attempt.	3/25/2008 8:58	1	70.xxx.xxx.183	80		43.799999	-79.25

Several indicators prove this cluster of events is a more sophisticated attack, including geographic proximity, time stamps, port analysis, advanced methodology, and patience. Because this chapter revolves around geographic proximity as a preliminary indicator of an attack, it is obvious to mention it first. The next level of analysis that steered us to determine it was a professional attack were the time stamps of the alerts within the cluster consistently occurred between 8 AM and 9 AM. The next level of manual correlation was to identify the initial network reconnaissance because that typically requires more network traffic; attack vectors themselves target specific vulnerabilities that can be much more elusive. Extracting the port scan alerts confirms our suspicions, because the coordinated attack is a "broken sequential port scan." Analysis of the dst_port column reveals the disjoined sequential scan. The segmentation of port scans target all the well-known service ports and a handful of the registered ports. Table 10-4 shows the port scan sorted by both destination port and time stamp. Destination port proves the distributed port scan when analyzed shows a sequential scan of most ports up to port 12032 (which is all the well-known reserved ports). The second column shows the port scan in chronological order, which shows the difficulty analysts or correlation engines have trying to find direct relationships of network reconnaissance over an extended time period. Keep in mind the time stamp column extends over six days, so in a real-world scenario, you would actually look at potentially hundreds, thousands, or millions of alerts instead of 12 alerts.

Table 10-4   Port Scans Sorted by Destination Port (Left-Hand Side) and Date (Right-Hand Side)

Port Scan Sorted by Destination Port	Port Scan Sorted by Time Stamp
3/9 :: 1 – 259	3/5 :: 1400 – 3390
3/6 :: 260 – 458	3/5 :: 501 – 784
3/7 :: 459 – 500	3/6 :: 260 – 458
3/5 :: 501 – 784	3/6 :: 785 – 943
3/6 :: 785 – 943	3/7 :: 459 – 500
3/7 :: 1000 – 1324	3/7 :: 1000 – 1324
3/5 :: 1400 – 3390	3/7 :: 9950 – 12032
3/10 :: 4010 – 4983	3/9 :: 1 – 259
3/11 :: 5003 – 6516	3/10 :: 4010 – 4983
3/11 :: 6480 – 7501	3/11 :: 5003 – 6516
3/11 :: 7823 – 9123	3/11 :: 6480 – 7501
3/7 :: 9950 – 12032	3/11 :: 7823 – 9123

Notable complex port scan techniques include all the port scans that occurred on the same day stemmed from six different source IP addresses, which is the disconnect the attacker was relying on to keep from being identified by an SEM or equivalent correlation system. So, not only did the attacker(s) expand the port scan to last several days but extended it to several machines. This also proves one or more of the following are possible:

- The recon is a coordinated attack among attack friends.
- The attacker has access to several machines. Mobile attackers basically extend their network recon over several days/weeks and use multiple open APs, including coffee shops, library, educational institution, or even a handful of wireless savvy fast-food restaurants.
- The attacker has control of zombie machines.

It is feasible for the attacker to jump open APs by using several open APs within close proximity of each other (think small shopping center with several open APs). However, we can discount the second bullet point because the attacks from the various locations occur at close time intervals – too close for that to be a feasible possibility. For the remaining part of this chapter, I reference the attacker(s) as "attacker," even though the analysis cannot support whether it is a group of friends working together or an individual controlling multiple zombies.

On three occasions, the attacker directed more exact network recon tools against ports 80, 8080, 444, 1434, 1433, and 10000. Those ports are used by relatively standard traffic, such as HTTP and MS SQL, but port 444 and 10000 are unique to specific applications including SharePoint Administration and Veritas, respectively. It appears as though a server response peaked the interest of the attacker, which is addressed shortly.

Correlating broken port scans can be tedious and, most of the time, considered mission impossible from the sheer number of port scans stemming from the big bad Internet. Piecing together possible random port scans really does not indicate a professional attack. However, the next component of the attack absolutely indicates a sophisticated approach and thought process. After the port scan, the attacker focused on the SharePoint installation. For readers unfamiliar with Microsoft SharePoint, it is a Web application that resides on an IIS Web server and is used as an information-sharing repository where employees, contractors, clients, or whoever can read, download, and upload documents or information. It is often found within companies on the intranet as it is an easy way to deploy, maintain, and share company information. My current company uses SharePoint as a departmental central repository to distribute current goals and objectives, important documentation that is being maintained by a committee (for example, business continuity plan [BCP]), organizational charts, and our corporate policy library.

The SharePoint attack methodology shown in Table 10-5 displays the sophistication and patience of the attacker.

I added the number of the attempt next to the username for ease of explanation. The company wrote a Snort rule to log when a user's SharePoint logon attempted failed. This is a custom signature the Security Department created that extracts the standard alert information and username.

Table 10-5 SharePoint Attacks

Signature	AM Time Stamp	Priority	Source IP	Dest. Port	User Attempt	Latitude	Longitude
SharePoint failed logon.	3/15/2008 8:26	3	70.xxx.xxx.94	80	Wsmith (1 attempt)	43.666698	-79.416801
SharePoint failed logon.	3/15/2008 8:28	3	70.xxx.xxx.94	80	Wsmith (2 attempt)	43.666698	-79.416801
SharePoint failed logon.	3/15/2008 8:29	3	70.xxx.xxx.100	80	Wsmith (3 attempt)	43.6833	-79.766701
SharePoint failed logon.	3/15/2008 8:31	3	70.xxx.xxx.100	80	Wsmith (4 attempt)	43.6833	-79.766701
SharePoint failed logon.	3/15/2008 8:37	3	70.xxx.xxx.100	80	Wsmith (5 attempt)	43.6833	-79.766701
SharePoint failed logon.	3/15/2008 8:43	3	70.xxx.xxx.100	80	Wsmith (6 attempt)	43.6833	-79.766701
SharePoint failed logon.	3/15/2008 8:55	3	70.xxx.xxx.94	80	Wsmith (7 attempt)	43.666698	-79.416801
SharePoint failed logon.	3/15/2008 9:03	3	70.xxx.xxx.94	80	Wsmith (8 attempt)	43.666698	-79.416801

NOTE

By default, failed SharePoint authentication attempts are logged into IIS, so ultimately, the custom signature was not actually necessary because the company just needed to ensure their SIM was pulling the logs from IIS. But IIS logs are maintained by a system administrator or system owners of the IIS machine rather than the security department, which does not help the security team protect the company; it leaves out a significant piece of information. SharePoint also inherits the same policy settings from Active Directory (AD). SharePoint and AD can be configured in any number of different ways. Internal users follow their same internal corporate policies. However, external users (clients and contractors) are given AD accounts but not Windows credentials, so the clients and contractors cannot log onto Windows machines if they are ever on location. Again, this is a single possible configuration.

These alerts had us scratching our heads, but we finally realized the attacker was evaluating the SharePoint authentication settings. Wsmith attempted to logon 4 times within 5 minutes and, on the fourth failed logon attempt, the account got locked out. Normally, if this was a legitimate user, the failed attempts would occur in a much smaller interval of time instead of 5 minutes. The fifth logon attempt occurred at 8:37 AM, exactly 6 minutes after the lockout attempt. The sixth logon attempt occurred at 8:43 AM, exactly 12 minutes after the initial lockout attempt. The seventh and eight logon attempts occurred at 8:55 AM and 9:03 AM, exactly 24 and 32 minutes after the initial lockout attempt, respectively. Concentrating on the time intervals after the initial lockout attempt (6, 12, 24, and 32 minutes), it seems like the attacker was testing the Group Policy (GPo) setting Reset account lockout counter after x minutes. The intervals the attacker was evaluating, most likely, are >5 minutes, >10 minutes, >20 minutes, >30 minutes. Although this AD setting can be set to any minute interval, most administrators maintain clean numbers: 5, 10, 15 minutes, and so on. After the attacker confirmed the AD setting was set to 30 minutes, the SharePoint logon attempts were ended.

Another interesting element of the attack that helped us link the second wave of attacks was the username, Wsmith. Using the last name Smith seems fairly generic, because it is one of the most common last names in North America. Keeping with this logic, the attacker is using the same methodology as the first name; the W could stand for William Smith. The combination of the two names has a high probability of existing within a large company. Again, it's a bit of a stretch, but it's worth considering.

After the attacker determined the reset time interval for the logon credentialing, the attacker stayed out of the IDS logs for two days. He was, most likely, plotting the next phase of the attack, which inevitably will target the SharePoint logon credentialing. On March 17 at 8:03 AM, the password guessing commenced. Table 10-6 presents the extraction of this wave of attack.

As previously mentioned, the time stamps remained between 8 AM and 9 PM, so that helps conclude the two SharePoint failed logon waves were connected. The failed attempts also indicate the attacker is maintaining the generic name logon using Janderson, Jkim, and Jsmith. The password guessing or brute-force logon attempts were wisely distributed between the three masqueraded users. It appears that, after the attacker reached the third failed logon attempt (one less than the account lockout threshold), he moved on to the next user account (in this case, Jkim and Jsmith) and circled back around after approximately 30 minutes to avoid locking the account and raising possible suspicion. The attacker made a critical error in the second wave of SharePoint attempts because of the port scan alerts mentioned earlier and the second wave of SharePoint logon attempts share a single IP address 70.xxx.xxx.13. This provides conclusive evidence that at least the port scan alerts and the second wave of SharePoint password guessing cluster of attacks are related.

Table 10-6 Next Wave of Attack

Signature	AM Time Stamp	Priority	Source IP	Dest. Port	User Attempt	Latitude	Longitude
SharePoint failed logon.	3/17/2008 8:03	3	70.xxx.xxx.100	80	Janderson	43.6833	-79.766701
SharePoint failed logon.	3/17/2008 8:03	3	69.xxx.xxx.247	80	Janderson	43.25	-79.833298
SharePoint failed logon.	3/17/2008 8:03	3	69.xxx.xxx.247	80	Janderson	43.25	-79.833298
SharePoint failed logon.	3/17/2008 8:04	3	70.xxx.xxx.13	80	Jkim	43.549999	-80.25
SharePoint failed logon.	3/17/2008 8:04	3	70.xxx.xxx.13	80	Jkim	43.549999	-80.25
SharePoint failed logon.	3/17/2008 8:04	3	70.xxx.xxx.13	80	Jkim	43.549999	-80.25
SharePoint failed logon.	3/17/2008 8:04	3	69.xxx.xxx.247	80	Jsmith	43.25	-79.833298
SharePoint failed logon.	3/17/2008 8:05	3	70.xxx.xxx.183	80	Jsmith	43.799999	-79.25
SharePoint failed logon.	3/17/2008 8:05	3	70.xxx.xxx.183	80	Jsmith	43.799999	-79.25
SharePoint failed logon.	3/17/2008 8:37	3	69.xxx.xxx.247	80	Janderson	43.25	-79.833298
SharePoint failed logon.	3/17/2008 8:37	3	69.xxx.xxx.247	80	Janderson	43.25	-79.833298
SharePoint failed logon.	3/17/2008 8:37	3	70.xxx.xxx.183	80	Janderson	43.799999	-79.25
SharePoint failed logon.	3/17/2008 8:38	3	70.xxx.xxx.183	80	Jsmith	43.799999	-79.25
SharePoint failed logon.	3/17/2008 8:39	3	69.xxx.xxx.247	80	Jsmith	43.25	-79.833298

Table 10-6   Next Wave of Attack

Signature	AM Time Stamp	Priority	Source IP	Dest. Port	User Attempt	Latitude	Longitude
SharePoint failed logon.	3/17/2008 8:39	3	69.xxx.xxx.247	80	Jsmith	43.25	-79.833298
SharePoint failed logon.	3/17/2008 9:05	3	70.xxx.xxx.183	80	Janderson	43.799999	-79.25
SharePoint failed logon.	3/17/2008 9:05	3	70.xxx.xxx.183	80	Janderson	43.799999	-79.25

Another giveaway is the logon attempts are recorded from different source IP addresses, which is highly suspicious, because realistically, that should never occur within the given small window of time. The troubling evidence of the compromise comes as the third series of attempts for Janderson stops at two (making eight total attempts). At that point, all attempts stop completely from Janderson and the other two masqueraded users. This typically indicates an attack vector was successfully executed.

Table 10-7 shows the final alerts identified within the dataset/subset of network alerts.

The SharePoint specific alerts surface again on March 25 at approximately 8:28 AM (eight days after the successful SharePoint attack) from the IP address 70.xxx.xxx.183, which looking back at the alert history, was also used during the SharePoint compromise. According to the IDS logs, the eight alerts generated were a WEB-MISC Share Point Cross-Site Scripting attempt signature. The Snort signature for that alert is as follows (this is not the exact alert from the dataset owner but is the default rule extracted from the Snort signature download):

```
alert tcp $EXTERNAL_NET any -> $HTTP_SERVERS $HTTP_PORTS (msg:"WEB-MISC sharepoint
cross site scripting attempt"; flow:to_server,established; uricontent:"/sharepoint/";
pcre:"/sharepoint[^\n]*\x22\s*\x29\s*\x3b/Ui"; metadata:service http;
reference:bugtraq,23832; reference:cve,2007-2581;
reference:url,www.microsoft.com/technet/security/bulletin/ms07-059.mspx;
classtype:web-application-attack; sid:12629; rev:2;)
```

A quick explanation of the alert shows that three conditions needed to exist for the alert to trigger:

- `flow:to_server, established;` indicates the malicious traffic was detected on an established TCP connection from the client to the server.

Table 10-7 Final Alerts

Signature	AM Time Stamp	Priority	Source IP	Latitude	Longitude
WEB-MISC SharePoint Cross-Site scripting attempt.	3/25/2008 8:28	1	70.xxx.xxx.183	43.799999	-79.25
WEB-MISC SharePoint Cross-Site scripting attempt.	3/25/2008 8:32	1	70.xxx.xxx.183	43.799999	-79.25
WEB-MISC SharePoint Cross-Site scripting attempt.	3/25/2008 8:39	1	70.xxx.xxx.183	43.799999	-79.25
WEB-MISC SharePoint Cross-Site scripting attempt.	3/25/2008 8:39	1	70.xxx.xxx.183	43.799999	-79.25
WEB-MISC SharePoint Cross-Site scripting attempt.	3/25/2008 8:45	1	70.xxx.xxx.183	43.799999	-79.25
WEB-MISC SharePoint Cross-Site scripting attempt.	3/25/2008 8:48	1	70.xxx.xxx.183	43.799999	-79.25
WEB-MISC SharePoint Cross-Site scripting attempt.	3/25/2008 8:51	1	70.xxx.xxx.183	43.799999	-79.25
WEB-MISC SharePoint Cross-Site scripting attempt.	3/25/2008 8:58	1	70.xxx.xxx.183	43.799999	-79.25

- `uricontent:"/sharepoint/";` indicates that /sharepoint/ was found in the body of the packet.
- `pcre:"/sharepoint[^\n]*\x22\s*\x29\s*\x3b/Ui";` is the Perl-Compatible Regular Expression (PCRE) that identified the cross-site scripting attack vector.

Because this is a cross-site scripting alert, it is safe to assume the attacker was trying to entice a legitimate user to click something to execute the exploit. (Unfortunately, I was not given permission to include the SharePoint posting that triggered this alert.)

Given the evidence of the professional well-orchestrated attack my friend and his colleague set out to validate our theory, they discovered that the AD OU was misconfigured, because the Password must meet complexity requirements was set to disabled. They approached one of their contractors, the SharePoint user that had his SharePoint identity stolen, and blatantly demanded he provide his logon SharePoint password to them.

Normally, it is forbidden to ask a user for his password, but in this case, there was no time to be polite and follow proper IT etiquette. He apprehensively surrendered his password to them: *qwerty123*. The infamous keyboard password strikes again! Sadly, I have seen the keyboard logic used in even the most secure environments. For those that do not know what keyboard logic is, it is choosing a password based on the ergonomic of keyboard patterns. *qwerty* is probably the most popular as it is the first six letters on the standard keyboard located directly below the number keys.

The company corrected its AD misconfiguration and, following my recommendation, extended its external SharePoint guidelines to include the arbitrary alphabetical letter x as a placeholder for the middle initial for all external users. For example, the user's new logon account name is Jxanderson. The methodology here is that middle names are easily discovered by using Google and other resources, like company directories and so forth. To counteract that, use a rare alphabetical letter, such as x or z. So, all external SharePoint users now have to log on with the middle initial of x. The company also included the SharePoint server in its monthly vulnerability scans, because Nessus would have identified the AD misconfiguration using admin-supplied credentials.

Fortunately, the final wave of alerts finish within the end of the IDS dataset provided for analysis. Afterward, it was confirmed that the well-known IDS SIM correlation engine the company is using did *not* identify the attacks.

SUMMARY

This chapter introduced you to GID and conveyed the underestimated power that geo-intelligence holds. The defensive technique has several powerful advantages, including correlating professional preemptive network reconnaissance, enabling less experienced security analysts to visually identify the geographic location of external data streams, and pinpointing the local timezone to help determine communication legitimacy. The capability to identify and be proactive against professional attackers is monumental in the network security industry. By correlating the source location of distributed network reconnaissance, a potential victim can take the proper countermeasures to successfully mitigate the final exploit. Those defensive countermeasures can range from configuring an ACL firewall rule to anticipating the attacker's next move and ensuring the potential victim server is fully patched, logging successfully, and has a successful backup. In real time, geocoding source locations provide less experienced security analysts the situational awareness to better assess suspicious network connections. A typical IDS alert contains crucial information, one piece being the source IP address. Experienced security analysts can look at the first octet and associate it with a general geographic location. For example, throughout my career, several infamous first octets have been burned into my brain, including 221 and 222 stemming from China, 125 and 220 from Japan, 85 and 217 from Iran, and 66 and 67 from the United States. By associating IP addresses to physical locations, an inexperienced security analyst can use that information in addition to the alert details to make a more educated decision about the nature of the connection.

Determining the local time zone of the attack is a significant clue. Given the type of industry your company is in can determine how significant but if you geolocate an IDS alert from Dublin, Ireland, and pinpoint that it is occurring at 2 PM local time, you might react completely differently if the same IDS alert was triggered at 2 AM local time. That is a primary reason why most SOCs have multiple clocks with variously displayed time zones. So, an analyst can associate a geographic location with a local time. (This is evident in the popular security Web site www.securitywizardry.com/radar.htm.) GID adds another layer of intelligence to network security. Current IDS vendors focus a majority of their attention on creating signatures, which is expected because that is from where their revenue stems. NSM/SIM vendors focus their efforts on making their solution compatible with as many logging technologies as they can to maximize client sales. Unfortunately, no industry body focuses its efforts on correlation of alerts. By implementing this new defensive technique, you give your network a fighting chance.

ENDNOTES

[1] http://amtrac.etri.re.kr

[2] http://atlas.arbor.net/worldmap/index

[3] http://tomokeefe.com/2008/06/24/the-political-web-barack-obama-vs-john-mccain/picture-6-2/

[4] http://geology.isu.edu/geostac/Field_Exercise/topomaps/map_proj.htm

[5] http://geology.isu.edu/geostac/Field_Exercise/topomaps/map_proj.htm

[6] http://geology.isu.edu/geostac/Field_Exercise/topomaps/map_proj.htm

[7] To blacklist an IP address means to add it to an ACL of a switch or router to block it from entering the network.

[8] Average residential users lack the understanding or patience to properly secure their home networks, which makes them unwitting targets. As speeds increase in residential areas, so does this nefarious technique because bandwidth capacity is a primary requirement for an ideal malicious zombie.

[9] Hackers are protective of their conquests.

[10] www.professormesser.com/secrets-of-network-cartography

[11] www.team-cymru.org/Services/ip-to-asn.html

[12]www.faqs.org/rfcs/rfc1876.html

[13]The Robinson projection is a pseudo-cylindrical projection (neither equal-area nor conformal, but a compromise) popularly used since the 1960s to show the entire world at once. See http://en.wikipedia.org/wiki/Robinson_projection.

REFERENCES

Bailey TC, Gatrell AC. *Interactive Spatial Data Analysis.* Harlow, Essex, England: Longman, 1995. p. xiv, 413.

Fossen, Espen. *Principles of Internet Investigations: Basic Reconnaissance, Geopositioning and Public Information Sources.* Department of Telematics. Norwegian University of Science and Technology, 2005, p. 66.

Gatrell AC, Bailey TC, Diggle PJ, Rowlingson BS. "Spatial Point Pattern Analysis and Its Application in Geographical Epidemiology." *Transactions of the Institute of British Geographers*, 1996, 21(1): p. 256–274.

Gueye, Gamba, et al. *Constraint Based Geolocation of Internet Hosts. International Conference on Microelectronics*, Sicily, Italy. October 24–27, 2004.

Javed, Faran. *Trilateration Utility for Locating IP Addresses: A Delay Base Solution for IP Geolocation.* National University of Sciences and Technology: Pakistan, 2003. p. 47.

Katz-Basset, Ethan, et al. *Towards IP Geolocation Using Delay and Topology Measurements.* International Conference on Microelectronics, Rio de Janeiro, Brazil. October 25–27, 2006.

Lyon, Gordon. *Nmap Network Scanning: The Official Nmap Project Guide to Network Discovery and Security Scanning.* Insecure Press, 2008.

Messer, James. *Secrets of Network Cartography: A Comprehensive Guide to nmap.* www.professormesser.com/secrets-of-network-cartography, 2007.

Ripley BD, MyiLibrary. *Spatial Statistics.* Wiley series in probability and mathematical statistics. New York: Wiley, 1981. p 252.

Wade, Tasha and Sommer, Shelly. *A to Z GIS.* ESRI Press, 2006.

Visual Data Communications

This chapter describes data visualization as it applies to several facets of IT, but it concentrates on how it relates to network security. The primary goal is to arm you with knowledge that supports the visual-data creation for your own particular domain. Although this chapter accomplishes that goal, you are encouraged to consider several related books by Edward Tufte, who has produced some amazing explanations on the subject of visualization. One of his most technical books, *Envisioning Information*, is particularly relevant to this chapter, but his complete works cover a range of topics that matter when the goal is to deliver accurate data quickly, not hastily. His examples meld nicely with the types of data that traverse a network, although they can sometimes convey a preference for abundance over representative samples "Data graphics should often be based on large rather than small data matrices and have a high rather than a low data density" (Tufte, 2007). Although this seems contrary to methods used by polling companies, whose results are based on samples rather than an entire population, it is not. The difference between Tufte's example and what pollsters do in public-opinion research is project a sweeping view of humanity directly to our senses, while the pollster extracts targeted information for a specific analysis effort. The different purposes served by Tufte's high data densities and a relatively small polling sample are a matter of using the right tool for the right job. One tool shows the big picture and the other tool reveals important details. The concept applies to visualizing networks, where technical managers must stay informed about the state of an entire network and have their engineers worry about the details.

Although Edward Tufte's contributions to the study of visualization encompass dozens of subjects, one specific area of IT has emerged as a cyber battleground that demands special attention: network security. Visualizing security data has already proven its worth in defending against attacks, thanks to the visionary work of several key individuals, including John Goodall, Greg Conti, and Raffael Marty.

SIGNIFICANT VIZUALIZATION CONTRIBUTORS

John Goodall is a contributor to the published proceedings of VizSec conferences and maintains its Web site at www.vizsec.org. He made his initial mark in the security field by developing the Time-Based Network Visualizer (TNV), which is a data-stream analysis tool that offers deep packet inspection and visually appealing reports. Currently, he works for Secure Decisions and is developing a network security and visualization product line called *MeerCat*.

Raffael Marty, author and Splunk chief security strategist, is considered to be an authoritative voice in the security visualization disciplines. In his book, *Applied Security Visualization* (Addison-Wesley, 2008), he guides readers from basic to advanced concepts in a way that maximizes the learning process, which makes it a must-read for security professionals. Much like his colleague John Goodall, Raffael is personally involved in the upkeep of his visually dedicated Web site www.secviz.org.

Greg Conti is the author of *Security Data Visualization* (No Starch Press, 2008), which explores ways to visualize network data through the use of tools, such as RUMINT (www.rumint.org). He developed RUMINT while working toward a doctorate at the Georgia Institute of Technology. In his book, Greg lays out a solid foundation of visual techniques and methods before diving into the security and visualization domain.

INTRODUCTION TO VISUALIZATION

Data visualization is the art of conveying meaningful and accurate information in an intuitive, graphical form. It needs to accommodate a diverse audience, at least within its intended discipline, and the underlying dataset must include all relevant facts. For the intuitive part, a good analogy is the purchase of a desktop spreadsheet program by an experienced Office product user. An intuitive interface for this type of product is one where the user can open a blank document, view the available commands, and produce a basic spreadsheet without using a help file or tutorial. This is possible only when the graphical interface is designed with human visual perception in mind.

NOTE

In this chapter, all forms of the word report describe security and business management-level presentations of information. Usage examples are *reporting strategy*, *report developer*, and *report author*. Reports might include charts, graphs, tables, and similar presentations of information, all of which are based on the same datasets that are used to visualize security events and other operational data. The purposes served by offering these concepts are to broaden the discussion to include important IT topics for a diversified readership, and to stimulate the creative thought processes and critical thinking of readers considering visual data communications for the first time.

The goal of data visualization is to provide an at-a-glance understanding of accurate and relevant statistics so that viewers can draw conclusions and appropriately act on them. Implicit in this goal for business users is the concept of an *ethical presentation of statistics*, which is the responsibility of report authors and presenters. All significant cause-and-effect factors must be included when presenting a visualized dataset (if not in the graph, then in an associated document). To avoid the appearance of manipulated statistics that support a specific outcome, a good practice is to make the source dataset available within the organization; a well-written narrative of how data was collected, aggregated, and otherwise processed adds credibility. Quantitative statistical presentations need to compare interesting data points with what is considered normal or acceptable. For example, reporting that a location experienced 5,000 security events in a month is only meaningful when the normal amount of 2,000 is included in the presentation.

Providing an accurate and true perception of data is essential. The fact that perception is not always reality comes from how the human mind gives special treatment to figures over other stimuli and has generated more than a little interest for educators and psychologists. For example, in June 2002, psychologists at the University of Iowa conducted eight experiments to assess "figure/ground discrimination" and the brain's natural preference for one region or another in a figure.[1] Figure/ground discrimination characterizes the ability to distinguish between a coherent figure in a visual display and the background. Experiment results, which were published in the American Psychological Association (APA) *Journal of Experimental Psychology*, uncovered an interesting phenomenon regarding human visual perception. Participants in each experiment usually considered the lower region of an image, the part below the "horizon," as the figure itself, even when it was not.

Figure 11-1 is a simple figure/ground display that psychologists use to test visual perception; the challenge is to identify the figure in the frame.

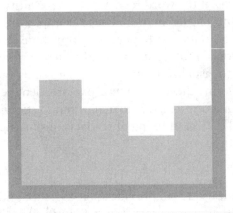

Figure 11-1   Example of a figure/ground display

Test subjects who envisioned something like a city skyline in the bottom of the frame were deemed wrong because the figure is actually at the top. After this phenomenon of visual perception was exhibited frequently, researchers began to consider possible causes. One theory is that the brain learns what natural shapes are supposed to look like from experiences in everyday life, and then offers an automatic response to observed images. Extending this thought process to a technical level, specifically in the networking field, brings to light some interesting points. At the very least, presenters of numeric datasets need to consider the "eye of the beholder" when working with graphical formats. This is especially true for visualizations that involve large datasets, a fact that has been known by experts for a long time.

Visualizing numeric data can be traced back to Rene Descartes, who is best known for his quote, "I think, therefore I am." In 1644, he considered what would later be called the Voronoi diagram, named after the scientist who expanded and enhanced its utility. A Voronoi diagram is a plane that is divided into regions, called polygons, from a set of points. Figure 11-2 shows a basic diagram of Voronoi regions and how, when each region is divided, a second set, called the dual, is created. The Voronoi Nodes and Regions part represents Voronoi nodes as dots in the center of each region.

Voronoi diagramming was the most important tool that physician John Snow used in his analysis of the famous London cholera epidemic of 1854, which is discussed in

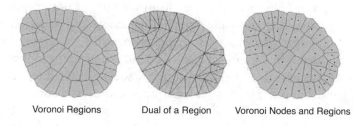

Voronoi Regions   Dual of a Region   Voronoi Nodes and Regions

Figure 11-2 Voronoi diagram

Chapter 10, "Geospatial Intrusion Detection." He was curious about the number of deaths in close proximity to a water pump on Broad Street, in spite of a common belief that the disease was spread through the air. The approach he took to this classic visualization scenario was to create a Voronoi map based on the distribution of water pumps throughout the city. He started by drawing a line between the pump in question and its nearest neighbor pump, labeling it the "boundary of equal distance between the Broad Street Pump and other pumps." He built on that, and the result was that each pump became a node in its own region, as defined by Snow's diagram. When death rates were represented in each cell, it became clear that more were occurring at the Broad Street pump.

Snow's methods included the use of time series graphs and various other visual displays, such as a timeline with stacked coffin icons to represent the number of deaths over time. The doctor's visualization of this morbid dataset fueled widespread interest in statistical analysis, and his conclusions are still a popular topic. As it turned out, Dr. Snow's fervent dedication to facts proved that his original hypothesis was correct: Tainted water from the pump was spreading the disease. More germane to this chapter is the skill he demonstrated in visualizing data, which in all likelihood expedited a solution.

Data visualization techniques are solidly embedded in the accounting and finance world, where profitability and stockholders demand the same expeditious clarity that Dr. Snow used to understand a life-threatening situation. There is an entire industry built around graphical statistical tools that track finances, earnings, and the stock market. These data types are similar to those found in computer networks for tracking performance, capacity, and operational statistics; both industries need to know if some value is changing and, if it is, the nature of the change. Proactive notifications are a good thing, but IT requirements go far beyond the need to manage network or server capacity, and they involve clearly defined technical disciplines, such as network security and fault management—areas that call for a prompt delivery of statistically accurate information.

Statistical analysis is used extensively by authoritative Internet bodies as they endeavor to understand the divergent properties of global traffic patterns. In addition to ensuring that the Internet is robust for the foreseeable future, their work strengthens the operational outlook for the long term. This benefit comes from volumes of nonproprietary analysis results and special reports that are made publically available and delivered in a comprehensive format, including visualizations. Information sharing, in turn, increases the knowledge base of cooperative technical resources and is an important part of the evolution of the Internet. For example, the Cooperative Association for Internet Data Analysis (CAIDA), a joint effort of government, research, and commercial entities, contributes by providing consulting services and developing tools that enhance analysis techniques. Its Web site[2] offers a wealth of information on topics ranging from bandwidth estimation to visualizing the global topology of the multicast backbone (MBone). CAIDA members are solid proponents of data visualizations and include them in projects. Raw datasets from various network activities are available for experimentation on select Web pages. To protect the privacy of certain groups, data files are organized in categories according to access level. At the time of writing, the categories are Freely Available, Available on Request, and CAIDA Visit Required.

Another major contributor to the evolution of the Internet is the National Institute of Standards and Technology (NIST), whose Information Technology Laboratory (ITL) makes advances in IT measurement sciences and technology standards. The Statistical Engineering Division (SED) of ITL provides consulting services to NIST labs and performs research. Its Web site[3] offers an abundance of information, which it openly shares with the public. Engineers with SED developed *Dataplot*, which is a graphical data-analysis program, and provided sample output in the Graphics Gallery on the Dataplot Web page. The *NIST/SEMATECH Engineering Handbook* and various other documents are also available there. Concepts in the handbook are not necessarily specific to Dataplot, which makes the book an excellent source for analysts and engineers. An electronic copy of *Exploratory Data Analysis (EDA)* complements the sample graphs and handbook. EDA is an analysis approach where engineers defer the choice of a statistical model to a later step in the process, opting instead to first view patterns in their natural state. EDA is distinguished from the classical approach by the basic sequence of steps, as shown in the following:

- **EDA.** Problem > data > analysis > model > conclusions
- **Classical Analysis.** Problem > data > model > analysis > conclusions

The EDA process puts the analysis step before the model is created and Classical Analysis is the reverse. This seemingly insignificant rearrangement of steps means that the data itself reveals the correct statistical model.

EDA and similar philosophies are in full keeping with visualization concepts, because they call for a visual analysis before modeling begins. Among other benefits, this gives an organization an opportunity to consider outliers early in the process. Outliers are data points that are well above or below mean values for time series data or noticeably separated from clustered points in multivariate data. In some cases, they represent suspicious activity and need to be investigated. Note that clustering occurs naturally in some data patterns, but there is also an analysis procedure that involves intentionally moving data points into groups, which are then called clusters. These, and other observations, are part of the procedures that are executed during a structured analysis process, such as EDA, leaving little or no doubt as to which graphical presentations are the best fit.

Any graph that quickly projects an idea—the right idea—upon being viewed is a superior analysis tool. The following two graphs, which are of the *performance management*[4] category, offer a fair example of how different pieces of information are seen, depending on the visual display. Although both graphs offer useful information, one seems to help you arrive at the answer to the question quicker than the other. In this example, the question is, "Who won the four-year sales award?"

Without lingering for more than a second, look for the answer in Figure 11-3, and then look at Figure 11-4.

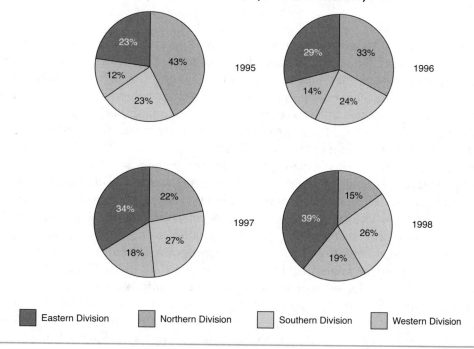

Figure 11-3 Comparative revenues (dollars in millions) pie chart

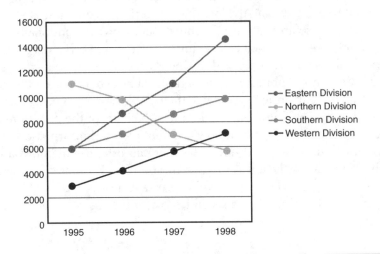

Comparative Revenues (Dollars in Millions)

Figure 11-4   Comparative revenues (dollars in millions) line chart

There are no correct or incorrect answers to questions of a subjective nature, such as which graph is better. However, it is likely that most readers immediately chose Figure 11-4 as the visual display that most expeditiously showed who won the award, the Eastern Division. The main reason that Figure 11-4 worked better has to do with human visual acuity, an attribute that has received a tremendous amount of attention by psychologists. Remembering the figure/ground example, there is empirical evidence that people have a natural preference for one region of an image or another. For images that present a real or perceived horizon, the most common preference is for the lower region. Although Figure 11-4 holds numbers for non-winners there, the result is a clear and immediate point of reference. In contrast, Figure 11-3 makes little distinction between regions, except a possible reduction from four, shown as calendar years, to two. But, the viewer then has to process at least four percentage values, which were used rather than raw numbers in an attempt to add clarity, before computing a solution. There is a definite place for percentage values in graphically displaying data, but in Figure 11-3's example, the author simply converted good data to extraneous information.

The descriptive statistics that Figures 11-3 and 11-4 are based on are basic and, with a little careful consideration of the intended audience, easy to visualize. A more challenging task is to present a complex dataset to the same audience. Visual perception and, unfortunately, attention spans do not improve simply because a report is more complicated.

Although many graphs never fit into the "create a reference point below the horizon" category, the psychology still applies. The face/vase illusion, shown in Figure 11-5, better challenges visual perception.

Figure 11-5   Face/vase illusion

The figure/ground ambiguity in the face/vase illusion plays tricks on the brain, because the viewer tries to decide whether the picture is a vase or two silhouettes facing one another. Although it is not likely that this illusion would be unintentionally created in a data visualization, graphical authors need to be aware of the concept as they address complex visualization challenges.

DEVELOPING A VISUALIZATION STRATEGY

The broad, long-range plan that is known as a *strategy* is a fundamental part of any business or government agency, but it is not something that is limited to the organization as a whole. Considering that information is valued as an intangible asset in business and government, a formal, written plan for IT data collection and reporting is appropriate.

Although this section addresses key technical aspects of a visualization strategy, recommendation #1 is that report developers, whether a security analyst, security manager, or compliance officer, seek guidance from their employers before developing a plan.

Considerations for a reporting strategy must be discussed in light of any formal strategy that management has in place, particularly regarding time tables and goals. Technology tends to change faster and with more frequency than many other business aspects, and obsolescence is a real threat. If a hardware platform needs a forklift upgrade after a year and the company amortizes assets on a three-year schedule, the impact to operations can be significant. Plan well, measure performance against goals along the way, and create visualizations that users view as an operational requirement.

A strategic visualization plan that is focused on security includes, but is not limited to, the following components:

- User audiences
- Statistical graphing techniques
- Technological considerations
- Security event visualizations

These components are discussed in the next four sections, which are followed by additional information to support strategic and tactical requirements.

USER AUDIENCES

The groups and individuals that visual authors prepare graphs for are called a *user audience* (or target audience, depending on local terminology or personal preference). Knowing your user audience is important, because several exist and they are delineated by job function, knowledge, and skills. The influence of a user audience on choosing the right graph is a critical starting point. For example, technical managers, who have to justify requests for budgetary dollars, know intuitively that what works for an analyst will not open the wallet of a chief financial officer (CFO). They further know that such requests must be supported by factual information that is presented to a busy, nontechnical audience. The task becomes daunting when the genesis of the request is in a detailed report that was submitted to the technical manager by staff security analysts. To move information further up the management chain, someone needs to translate volumes of log file output to a message of factual justification for the expenditure, and it must allow the CFO to think about finances, not message logs. Although that means a standard business report is appropriate, the CFO needs to see the information it holds before noticing aesthetics and formatting. This particular attribute applies to business reports and network data visualizations alike.

To be realistic about this scenario, assume that some amount of summarization will have occurred even before delivering the report to the technical manager. However, this might depend on the working definition of technical manager, which directly affects the amount of summarization needed.

Figures 11-6, 11-7, 11-8, and 11-9 depict a hypothetical situation where engineers confirm that security events in their area of responsibility, the company's Eastern region of the U.S., have increased more than other regions. Their goal is to claim a higher share of scarce budget dollars for sensor upgrades and additional router hardware for a failover and load-balancing architecture.

Security analysts first confirmed the validity of their request by analyzing medium and high priority events from a global database. They started with a baseline set of analysis results for their own region that was built as part of normal operations over the past year, and then added events from all other regions for comparison. Figure 11-6 shows the level of detail required for the effort.

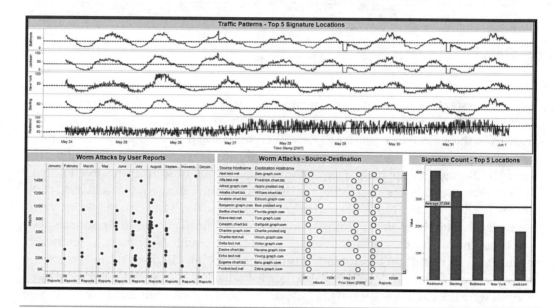

Figure 11-6   Detailed visualization of network traffic and malicious activity using Tableau software

Having confirmed their belief that there were more legitimate events being managed in their region than other regions, they presented the visualization in Figure 11-7 to their technical manager.

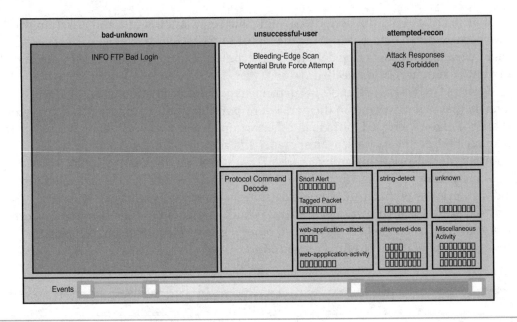

Figure 11-7   Heat map view of security alerts

The analysts chose a heat map to visualize the state of security in the Eastern region. Its main strength is in the way it visualizes specific threat signatures by proportion and priority. In this case, the consolidated view of events showed a multitude of FTP brute-force attempts, among other things. This provided sufficient evidence for the technical manager to decide to support the request for a higher share of security-related funding.

Confident that this was a perfect opportunity to enhance security, the manager set up a meeting with "holders of the purse strings." Conventional wisdom among security professionals dictates that a single group of events does not justify additional resources, unless they result in a data breach, at which point funds tend to be endless, as discussed in Chapter 12, "Return on Investment: Business Justification." Because this is the point where business and security collide—specifically budgetary discussions—key security analysts were invited to the meeting to ensure that no question went unanswered. Figure 11-8 is the first visualization that appeared in the presentation to the CFO.

Figure 11-8 is based on ranged values that generate size and color-coded alerts by geographic region. In this case, it shows a significant concentration in the East, specifically the Mid-Atlantic region. It is a good starting point and might sway the opinions of some people on its own merit, but it indicates that states on the West coast could be equally under fire thanks to Washington state and southern California. (Chapter 10 explains

12-Month Threat Analysis 2006-2007

Figure 11-8   Geographic map

how mapping intrusion detection alerts is significantly beneficial to identify pre-emptive professional attacks.)

The next slide shown is Figure 11-9. Besides visually demonstrating that a higher concentration of events exists in the East, the map shows all statistics in the context of other regions.

The first visualization, in Figure 11-8, was a good preface to the more detailed image in Figure 11-9. Because both have the continental United States as a background, a viewer's attention is fixed on the same area instead of being steered in different directions. Clarity and the simplicity of Figure 11-9 easily transferred good information to the CFO. Although Redmond, Washington had the highest number of events, four of the top five national locations were in the Eastern region, including Jackson, Mississippi, Sterling, Virginia, Baltimore, Maryland, and New York, New York.

Static reports such as these fall short of security operations center (SOC) requirements, where the most current information is critical to operational success, but they are entirely appropriate in a business setting. Security visualizations frequently show hundreds or thousands of data points, a difficult but often necessary task. There are few, if any, necessary calls for this sort of thing in presentations to senior management, although such presentations should have executive summaries based on the same production data that the SOC uses. Thus, it logically follows that graphical displays in an office presentation format are valuable when used in an appropriate situation.

Figure 11-9   Visualized state of enterprise security

The most successful data collection and reporting strategies, whether in the security space or general IT support, are those that recognize the different needs of various organizational groups. Table 11-1 lists four user audiences, along with high-level descriptions of their reporting requirements. This table does not address the unique needs of corporations and agencies; therefore, view Table 11-1 as useful guidelines.

Table 11-1   User Audiences

User Audience by Function	General Reporting Requirements
Management	Summary reports regarding an entire network or large divisions thereof, such as regions, districts, customer, or high-level network elements.
Operations	Individual circuit and device reports that include real-time prioritized alerts, short-term historical data in the smallest available increment, event correlation/filtering, and configuration and inventory management support.
Engineering	Individual and grouped circuit, device, application, protocol, and general performance reports. Include short- and long-term history, failure scenarios, trends, forecasts, and network models.
Internal and external customers	Typically include response times, network availability, application availability, and average time to repair.

Of the four user audiences, operations and engineering have similar needs that, when properly met, enable the groups to work together. Historical trouble tickets can augment baseline statistics and intelligence on current threats for solid engineering solutions. This, in turn, is fed back to operational groups who must know the network well enough to manage real-time fault conditions and threats. In a similar fashion, service-level metrics are beneficial to managers, whose responsibilities might include customer satisfaction or general business operations. A security budget is a good example of how requirements change as information is passed up to decision makers. Reports will include line items at the start, such as the number of intrusion detection system/intrusion prevention system (IDS/IPS) sensor upgrades and then become summarized by department, district, region, or other high-level increment. At points along the way, granular details become supporting information to graphical displays that justify expenses to upper management, as shown in the previous example. For technical staff members, the value of visualized data is realized at all steps and levels.

Simple aesthetics are sometimes confused with visually appealing displays of useful information in support of both management and technical functions. The most appealing graphs can sometimes harm an operation because the interesting data is masked by extraneous information. On the other hand, depending on the makeup of the intended audience, there is a definite place for aesthetics. If the environment is such that the presenter needs to attract users to reports that are being ignored, a slick presentation that is similar to marketing literature might get the audience's attention. Two key points to consider for the decision are knowing when to give weight to aesthetics and knowing how to fashion a marketing literature-style report while maintaining the report's usefulness.

STATISTICAL GRAPHING TECHNIQUES

The types of graphs shown in Figures 11-10, 11-11, and 11-12 provide information that is a staple of the daily activities of network support analysts and engineers. They preface the visualizations discussed in the remainder of this chapter, which focuses on the security aspects of data visualization. In this way, readers who are relatively new to visualization concepts can better understand which graphs are most appropriate in a given situation.

Figure 11-10 uses a time series graph that was produced by Simple Network Management Protocol (SNMP) polls in 30-second increments over 31 days. It represents 89,280 data points that demonstrate the linear relationship of circuit usage to time. It has the following main characteristics:

- Represents inbound and outbound traffic over a single network link
- Time series data application
- One independent variable (x-axis) and one dependent variable (y-axis)

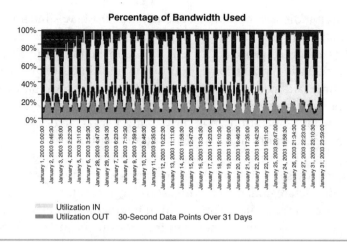

Figure 11-10 Time series graph

Figure 11-10 is an example of a circuit that is operating close to full capacity on an ongoing basis. When presented to a network-savvy audience, the transfer of that knowledge is virtually instantaneous. Graph interpretation begins with variables on the *y-axis*, which, in this example, are expressed as percentage values. The typical alternative form of display is by volume, and it would be shown in kilobits or megabits per second, depending on the circuit. Packets or bytes per second are also popular values. In this case, percentages are effective because most viewers, however savvy they might be, know by routine the theoretic capacity of every circuit in the network. The *x-axis* reflects a time progression in 30-second increments over 31 days. Moving from left to right and viewing the intersections of percentage values and time stamps, a viewer immediately knows how busy the circuit has been at specific points in time.

In keeping with an ethical presentation of statistics, the author of this graph clearly displays relevant facts. The label 30-Second Data Points Over 31 Days describes the polling interval, which is the frequency with which data was acquired from the device. SNMP systems count the number of bytes that pass through an interface between the current and last observation and calculate an average for the set, which becomes a single point on the graph. This graph shows that the percentage of available capacity in use is frequently in the upper nineties and has occasional spikes to full capacity. It is safe to assume that traffic is also reaching full capacity in the seconds between observations. In performance terms, this means that packets are being dropped and users are more than likely experiencing degraded service levels.

Some systems are configured to display data points at wider intervals than the actual polling interval. For example, a data collector might take a sample every 5 minutes and feed it to a reporting engine that uses the average of three samples to produce a single point on a graph. This is a 5-minute polling interval and a 15-minute data display rate. The graph needs to then include a second label to differentiate the values, which resemble a 5-minute polling interval and 15-minute data display rate.

From a security perspective, the extreme peaks and valleys in Figure 11-10 are significant, but there is no obvious evidence of statistical outliers that might indicate anything more than a capacity problem. The logic is that peaks and valleys of similar degrees occur at regular intervals over time, which means that it is probably just a busy circuit. In relevant material of his book, *Extrusion Detection* (Addison-Wesley, 2006), Richard Bejtlich highlights the need to consider spikes of egress traffic.

Figure 11-11 is a different look at portions of the dataset from the previous time series graph. It offers a closer look at traffic by using the same size graph to display data points in a much shorter timeframe.

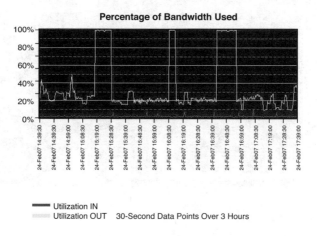

Utilization IN
Utilization OUT   30-Second Data Points Over 3 Hours

Figure 11-11   Sustained utilization peaks

The graph now shows a time period of three hours, which is reflected in a new label, and reveals three sustained traffic bursts, ranging from approximately 8 to 18 minutes. This technique, called *drilling down*, is used in conjunction with sets of graphs that show longer timeframes. An example is a monthly review of production circuits. If there were 20 circuits to analyze for the review, it would be impractical to graph them all at this level of granularity. The analyst instead views 20 graphs of 30-day timeframes, and then selects those with high peaks or other interesting data points for further analysis. The technique applies to both static and real-time reports.

Time series graphs are an excellent way to characterize information over time when a small number of variables are involved, as is the case with utilization on a single circuit. High-density datasets, those with a lot of variables, are more challenging to visualize. Security events fit this model.

The parallel coordinate plot, shown in Figure 11-12, is widely used in network security to explore relationships between a large number of variables. It represents observations as lines passing through parallel vertical axes with respect to their minimum and maximum values; observations are noted along the horizontal x-axis. This particular rendition draws each vertical y-axis as dots rather than as solid lines. The highlighted area that begins on the left side of the graph comes from a technique called brushing, which allows users to select interesting areas at will. The vertical solid line has been placed to note the beginning of the active brushing.

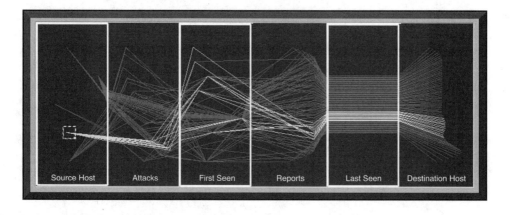

Figure 11-12   Parallel coordinate plot

This graph shows an Internet worm attack launched from multiple hosts against multiple hosts. Moving from left to right, values indicate the following:

- **Source Host**. This is how the graph happens to be labeled. Other options might be selected, such as port numbers 0–65,535 or IP octet values 1–255.

- **Attacks**. Visualizes the launch of attacks and associates them with source hosts by connected lines.

- **First Seen:** Based on log file time stamps at the start of attacks.

- **Reports:** Derived from user reports.
- **Last Seen:** Perpetrators ended this apparently coordinated effort on the same day.
- **Destination Host:** Victim machines.

There are elements of a time series graph present, but they are more of a chronology than a time progression. In its purest definition, parallel coordinate plots represent temporal and spatiotemporal data as horizontal lines that pass through vertical axes, with minimum and maximum values at the lower and upper limit of each axis, respectively. Visualizations become increasingly cluttered as the number of variables increases; in this case, that would be more source and destination hosts. Users are divided on whether this is a good or bad thing. Extremely dense displays can be desirable when the purpose is to visualize areas with the most activity, and analysis can be enhanced by a drill down or zoom option, if desired. If the zoom function is not an option, authors can mitigate the clutter problem by making real-time filters available to users, although they must avoid filtering critical events along with clutter. Another valid approach is to spread the dataset across multiple graphs in meaningful categories.

TECHNOLOGICAL CONSIDERATIONS

So far, this chapter has discussed the human perception of graphics, user audiences, graphing techniques, and fundamental terminology. For implementation purposes, whether an open source or a commercial product is under consideration, there are technological considerations that accompany using the software. This section discusses scalability, installation, support, and data-management issues.

SCALABILITY

In addition to the influence of user audiences, decisions regarding a reporting strategy are directly related to the amounts and types of data being represented. For example, if the requirement is to characterize the makeup of traffic on an intranet, aggregate data can be categorized by application and displayed in a pie chart. Because data is summarized, the use of capital resources—storage space, and server CPU time—is minimal, and report manipulation is an easy task. Characterization of that sort is more of a general network management use of graphs than a security application, but an awareness of the quantity of data involved applies to both situations.

There are obvious technical challenges involved in graphically conveying information, not the least of which is scalability. Device log files, the primary data source for visualizing security information, can translate into a sizable dataset for report generation. Large datasets that cannot be accurately represented by summarized data are a serious concern when choosing an appropriate graph. A balance between resource consumption and effective reporting often comes when report authors "forego the aesthetic in favor of the useful." Readers who choose to do further research on visualizing data will be presented with scores of wonderful reports, many of which belong in an art gallery instead of a production environment. As such, scalability is a key issue associated with report generation, and decisions must be made that differentiate critical datasets from those that are secondary, which means that they should be observed, collected, and archived for future use.

INSTALLATION AND SUPPORT

There is a good selection of tools in the industry for visualizing all types of information, including a substantial list of graphing products that focus on network security. Whether the visual toolkit is open source or commercial software, its installation and/or support must be considered before decision time. Some of the best products come with dependencies to be satisfied during installation, dependency on user expertise, and little, if any, ongoing technical support. Although this should not discourage their use, it can change implementation human resource requirements enough to make it an item for thoughtful consideration. Rather than welcome an increased mean time to repair (MTTR) in the event of a product failure, take proactive steps to ensure that support personnel have the appropriate set of knowledge, skills, and abilities.

Software dependencies, patches, fixes, and upgrades are not always easier to manage for commercial off-the-shelf (COTS) products, so the installation and support considerations shown in Table 11-2 apply to them. For example, early evaluations of *risk assessment* software that imports firewall, router, and switch configurations, along with IDS alerts, Windows Server Update Services (WSUS) logs, and Nessus scans showed that the import of Nessus reports required a specific file extension, .nbt, which required the Nessus client to be installed. If only the Nessus server application was running, Nessus results could not be incorporated. This created a gap in the risk assessment software from a lack of compatibility with various imported Nessus formats, precluding a security "seal of approval." Although it might seem that switching Nessus formats sounds easy, a modification of that magnitude in a government production environment requires deployment testing, deployment strategizing, budgetary considerations, and more importantly, a significant change in current procedures. Although the restricted ability to convert Nessus file extensions has been corrected, it was once a make or break technological consideration.

Table 11-2   Installation and Support Considerations

Consideration	Description
Compatible input	Ensure compatible support for all desired data formats, such as log files; SNMP MIBs and alerts; CSV; NetFlow records; tcpdump/pcap; txt; XML; STF; Argus; and others.
Compatible output	Research product capabilities for providing user access to reports. It must be relatively easy to produce output in standard formats, such as image files and Web pages. Also, consider management presentations in products like PowerPoint. Although PowerPoint has received harsh criticism in the past, it remains the standard for presenting material, including data visualizations.
Functionality	Develop a list of functions that must be supported. Be aware that many products have limited capabilities and might offer only a percentage of the desired functions. For example, investing time and effort in evaluating products that support only 80 percent of a required 100 percent functionality is major red flag. The *Pareto Principle* might reveal that obtaining the last 20 percent of the desired functions will consume 80 percent of the budget.
Parsers	When data compatibility becomes an issue, determine which parsers are required and whether they are readily available. This can also be a consideration regarding organizational technical skills. Some examples are Perl programming language, Python object-oriented programming language, UNIX Stream Editor (SED), and AWK.
Scaling	Consider the scalability of the application, database, and system hardware. Where possible, get specifics from the supplier regarding the number of devices and records that are supported, including long-term data storage. Some visualization requests that span terabytes of data require ample disk space, computation resources, and time to display and analyze results. Considering the size of their networks, this is a common problem for corporations and agencies that mine IDS alerts.
Structured data	If a tool requires that data be represented according to a particular specification, compare it to other systems in its intended operating environment. Uniqueness is an expensive attribute in most data centers.
Support	Support issues include technical support; training; patches and upgrades; pricing and purchasing; and feature enhancements. Try to ascertain whether a product is likely to be discontinued in the predictable future. Always inquire about the company or open source organization's *best practices* for the product, which might indicate unanticipated maintenance tasks.

DATA MANAGEMENT

The technical prerequisites for bringing data from its source to a computer monitor can vary according to several factors. For this discussion, the assumptions are 1) If more than one system is involved, the fundamental interface requirements between systems have been met, and 2) pointers to metadata that characterize color tones is not a problem. Assumption 2 is a topic of discussion for software developers to have at the print shop.

After the basic interface questions are answered, focus on whether long-term reports will be graphed. Visualizing security data involves a short-term dataset first and foremost, because potentially harmful activity must be flagged and quickly analyzed. In the absence of an operational specification for a software application, determining what is considered to be short-term data is somewhat unique to an organization. Organizational definitions usually involve the individual or group that pays the disk storage and management bills, and it is a good idea to address budgetary issues early in the project cycle. Disk space is relatively cheap these days; however, the processing power needed to index, analyze, and display the dataset can quickly drain a budget when not anticipated accurately before implementation. Financial considerations aside, data that is not aggregated is generally left intact for a period of 90 days. In some cases, this means that, on day 90, an analyst can see a complete set of available records of failed login attempts for the 90-day period. On day 91, reports are limited to a daily, weekly, monthly, or quarterly average, depending on the roll-up scheme, which is developed by and unique to each organization.

The practice of data forensics and, to a lesser degree, trending and forecasting, are the main drivers behind long-term data storage. Data forensics, where data is stored "as collected" for extended periods of time, is a fairly straightforward topic, because the only variable is whether or not it is necessary. In Department of Defense (DoD) and law enforcement environments, which are among the most common applications of data forensics, proponents of the function prevail every time. Trend and forecast reporting are more debatable because the statistical methods used depend on the nature of network traffic patterns. For example, if observations of traffic over time reveal fairly consistent patterns with low standard deviation numbers, a series of weekly or monthly averages should produce the same trend lines and forecasts as more granular data. This is the first of several debatable points, and it needs to be approached with historical evidence and some knowledge of statistics.

Most data-collection applications operate with some sort of aggregation scheme, where data are rolled-up in predefined increments. For example, data points are collected every 5 minutes, and then aggregated to 30-minute data points, and then to hourly, and so forth. Systems typically store the granular data for a limited amount of time, which makes it available for graphing. In many companies, the data retention policies are determined by regulatory compliance, law, or contract-specific agreements. Products, such as Cisco IOS Flexible NetFlow or video surveillance systems, support aggregation at the source. In general, NetFlow technology has value for managing data of many types, including security events. In business, NetFlow records are a common source to track network usage by customer or internal organization. Because it collects information regarding who is using the network and for what purpose, NetFlow is an excellent data source for executive reports, including those that characterize the state of network security. Depending on which vendor's management software is deployed, NetFlow records can track intrusion attempts using an anomaly-based detection approach.

Statistical outliers are not much of a storage concern, but they can be challenging from an analytical perspective. Outliers appear as spikes in times series patterns or as isolated points in scatterplots that are considerably farther from mean values than other data points. They are most interesting in a visualized report when its purpose is to track nonthreatening activity, especially when patterns are expected to be consistent. The visual display of exceptions in historically flat data patterns is a good way to monitor suspicious activity and is a perfect example of visualization in support of anomaly detection. The term *historically flat* is notable, because it justifies long-term storage of seemingly mundane data. There's only one caveat: There is nothing special about outliers when reports clearly show that they have been appearing daily and without incident for weeks or months. The long flat line or scatterplot followed by a series of spikes can indicate malicious activity. The caveat is that intruders might attempt to emulate normal patterns to avoid detection, and the previously mentioned analytical challenge is to design reports that flag anomalous activity. A well-designed visualization is a powerful tool to accomplish this goal.

Moving data from collection points to a reporting system is a task that can consume many labor hours, and the methods used are almost as varied as the actual reports. Commercial products tend to do a better job at this than freeware and open source products, although there is still a significant amount of ongoing maintenance. On the other hand, noncommercial solutions that require scripting and programming skills to operate are part of a technical community that likes to give things away for free. There are hundreds or thousands of available free scripts, programs, and utilities that make systems run better.

The Data Analysis and Visualization Linux, called DAVIX, is a bootable CD[5] constructed by Jan Monsch. It offers a broad range of visualization tools, most of which are freeware. It is freely available, the user community is knowledgeable and supportive, and virtually anyone who is computer literate can use it. Tools are offered to capture, process, and visualize data. These operational characteristics should exist in an organization's support plan for visually communicating data.

SECURITY EVENT VISUALIZATION

Companies that provide data collection and reporting tools for general network management purposes have been virtually iconic in the IT world, and most organizations still look to them for tools and methodologies. However, network security companies and .org Web sites, like www.secviz.org and www.vizsec.org, have quietly grown at a fast pace and might soon eclipse other sources as the place to look for good data-visualization techniques. Buyers of such products should go about their search with an understanding of a key difference between the two sources. Traditional data-collection and reporting tools focus on statistical aspects of data that support forecasting and trending, while most visualization tools do just what their name implies. When the goal is to produce displays that interact with human visual perception, traditional reports are a supplement, albeit an important one.

The practice of visualizing security events can be in a class of its own if there is a heavy requirement for event correlation. Plotting parallel coordinates for large numbers of connections can be labor intensive to produce or require the use of sophisticated algorithms. If viewed strictly from the perspective of underlying technology, data visualization operates at a higher level of complexity than traditional reporting products. Network data collection and reporting technology, like its cousin in the financial sector, can rely entirely on dependent and independent variables to produce meaningful reports, as is the case with time series utilization graphs.

For security-related event management, the issue of scalability is addressed under the umbrella of meta-alert generation, because of its power to reduce large numbers of events to a single alert. A port scan against a single computer can generate an event for each port, for a total of 131,070 unique alerts (65,535 TCP and 65,535 UDP). In most cases, even with a good visualization strategy, this is an unnecessarily large dataset for graphic presentations, where critical events might blend with others and huge amounts of system resources would be consumed. Event correlation is a valid way to address this problem, as long as the associated complexities, which can be significant, are acceptable.

Considerations for meta-alerting go beyond scalability to those that are of an architectural nature. Depending on size and scope, it is likely that sensors are distributed throughout the network, and each sensor might have to know about, and stay in sync with, all others to avoid generating redundant events, especially when tangling host- and network-based IDS. Other questions to consider when designing a meta-alert solution include the following:

- What constitutes a low-level event as opposed to one that is critical?
- Should correlation occur per session or strictly by device address?

- Are outbound events included?
- Are severity levels elevated as correlated events increase?
- Should statistical sampling be used?

As an alternative to meta-alerts, visualization is not subject to the aforementioned issues, with the possible exception of avoiding redundancies that might come from distributed data sources. But, the issue is more of an administrative burden than an operational liability, because duplicate events tend to overwrite each other on most graphs. The salient point is that visualization offers virtually all the required data and can negate the need for a sophisticated correlation engine. It is reasonable to say that, because visualized information is a single, total view of data, correlation is accomplished in the time it takes for the human brain to process a picture. Because the right strategy is usually unique to each organization, solutions that use meta-alerts to complement visualization should be considered.

EXAMPLE GRAPHS

This chapter alludes to the limitless amount of visualizations that can be drawn from network security data points, including everything from intrusion alerts, failed logon attempts, firewalls, and asset discovery to more managerial graphs that focus on departmental statistics and other information. The following example visualizations were generated with both freeware and commercial products. Each section begins with a list that includes the type of graph or chart and the name of the company that produced it, followed by its URL. As a practical matter, only a small representation of current visualization techniques are shown here. Hopefully, these graphs offer an idea of all that is available and stimulate the creative thought processes of anyone who analyzes or presents information.

Topology

GraphViz

www.graphviz.org/

The linked graph shown in Figure 11-13 is based on a sniffer trace and was generated with GraphViz, which is a popular open source package. The most common method of using the tool involves external data, although graphs can be manually created. This flexibility puts it in a class far above traditional drawing packages. It can also represent network and port traffic within a network so that security analysts can identify suspicious network communication. For example, if an e-mail server suddenly starts to communicate with the FTP server or vice versa, it is highly possible that it is malicious.

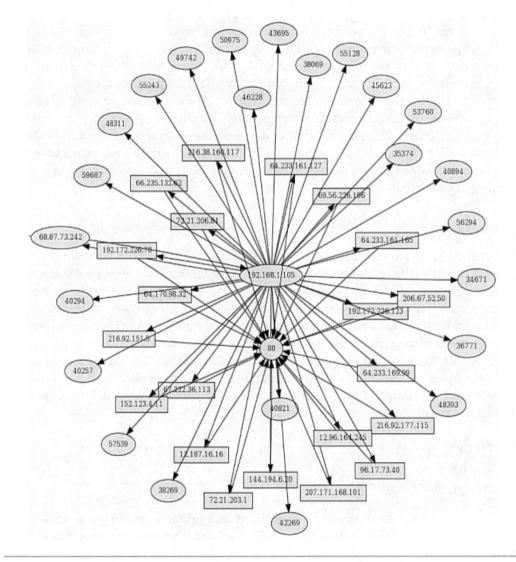

Figure 11-13   Example of a topology graph

Histogram with Normal Curve

Minitab 15, Minitab

www.minitab.com/

A frequency distribution of certain network statistics is a good way to characterize network traffic. The frequency distribution shown in Figure 11-14 shows the number of times in a reporting period that traffic consumed specific percentages of available bandwidth. In this particular graph, the bell curve has been imposed over the data as a point of comparison. A security analyst can use this information to assess the patterns and degree of dispersion of outbound traffic or to compare weekly Internet Service Provider (ISP) results. Utilization is also characterized and, if a significant change is identified, further research can determine if there is a legitimate reason, such as new customers, software release updates, or the implementation of a third party disc-to-disc backup.

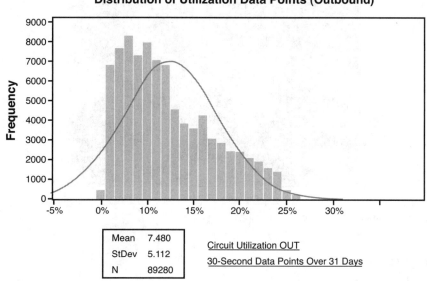

Figure 11-14 Example of a histogram

3D Traceroute

Scapy

www.secdev.org/projects/scapy/

Figure 11-15 is based on the output of a `traceroute` command, and it can display addresses and host names over a network path. The Scapy TCPTraceroute is unique, because it simultaneously sends out all the packets as opposed to sending them out one at a time. This provides a much faster result. By concatenating the results, you can identify that, at the fourth hop, the packet paths changed routes. By Control-clicking a colored ball, the program displays the ports investigated. Scapy requires ImageMagik or GraphViz to create the 3D image.

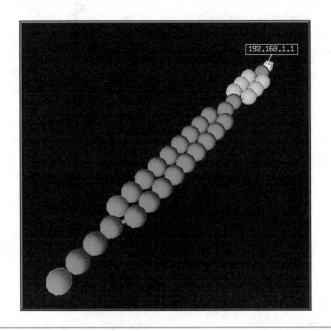

Figure 11-15 Example of 3D traceroute graph

Contour Plot

Minitab 15, Minitab

www.minitab.com/

The contour plot shown in Figure 11-16 shows, over time, the number of successful intrusions that occurred because of lag time. Lag time is the number of hours it takes the industry to produce a threat signature after the threat is first recognized. The shaded area, shown in four contours, are times when there were greater than six successful intrusions, the striped area had between four and six successful intrusions, and so forth.

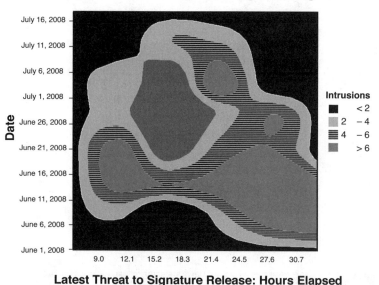

Successful Intrustions by Threat-Signature Lag Times

Figure 11-16   Successful intrusions by threat-signature lag times

2D Surface Plot

Cytoscape, Cytoscape

www.cytoscape.org

Figure 11-17 shows a global view of network elements and was produced with a freeware tool called Cytoscape. Global views are critical for identifying rogue devices, especially considering that it is now fairly common to see employees implementing unauthorized and unsecure wireless access points (APs) at the office. Employees tend to do this so that they can carry a laptop and still remain connected. As coworker laptops pick up the signal, suddenly, the company has an entire human resources department roaming around, which can potentially transfer sensitive information over an unsecure wireless network.

Figure 11-18 reflects the same network, but it is zoomed to give you a closer look at elements in an alert status.

Like Graphviz, Cytoscape is an open source software tool that offers network visualizations, which is about the full extent of similarities between the products. Cytoscape was originally designed for use in *bioinformatics*, where knowledge is extracted from biological data through computer analysis, but has been adapted for use in network visualization and analysis. The analysis feature sets it apart from GraphViz, which is not an analytical package.

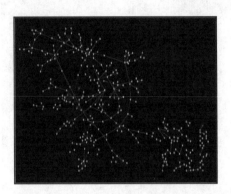

Figure 11-17   Example 2D link graph

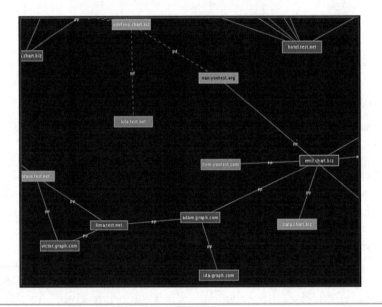

Figure 11-18   Example of zooming on part of a 2D link graph

Sparklines

Microcharts, BonaVista Systems

www.bonavistasystems.com/

A sparkline type of display shows trends over time for multiple network links. In Figure 11-19, entries in the column labeled 1 Month are the most commonly used sparklines, but various others are available.

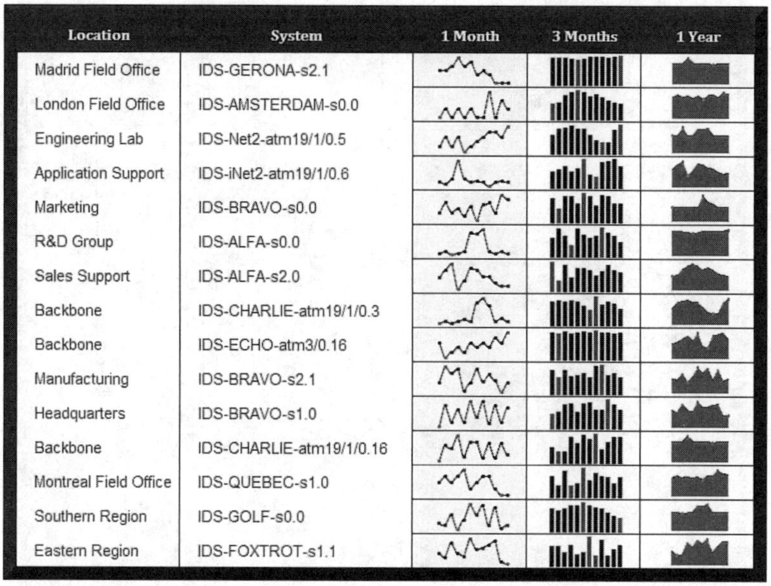

Location	System	1 Month	3 Months	1 Year
Madrid Field Office	IDS-GERONA-s2.1			
London Field Office	IDS-AMSTERDAM-s0.0			
Engineering Lab	IDS-Net2-atm19/1/0.5			
Application Support	IDS-iNet2-atm19/1/0.6			
Marketing	IDS-BRAVO-s0.0			
R&D Group	IDS-ALFA-s0.0			
Sales Support	IDS-ALFA-s2.0			
Backbone	IDS-CHARLIE-atm19/1/0.3			
Backbone	IDS-ECHO-atm3/0.16			
Manufacturing	IDS-BRAVO-s2.1			
Headquarters	IDS-BRAVO-s1.0			
Backbone	IDS-CHARLIE-atm19/1/0.16			
Montreal Field Office	IDS-QUEBEC-s1.0			
Southern Region	IDS-GOLF-s0.0			
Eastern Region	IDS-FOXTROT-s1.1			

Figure 11-19   Example sparklines graphical display

Histogram With Scatterplott

Statistical Data Visualization System, Mondrian

http://rosuda.org/Mondrian/

Mondrian is a general purpose statistical visualization system that offers a common scatterplot function, but with the addition of supporting histograms (see Figure 11-20).

The next two sections introduce powerful visualization commercial products; one that does not cater specifically to network security data, Starlight Visual Information System, and one that does, VisNet.

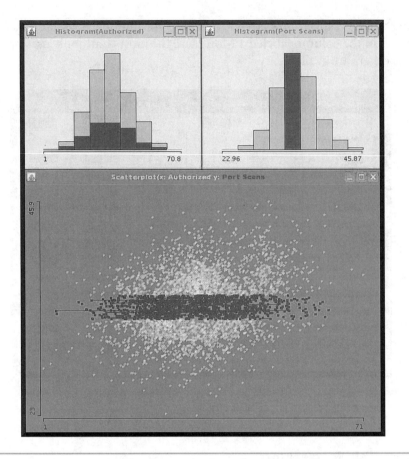

Figure 11-20   Example Mondrian scatterplot with supporting histograms

STARLIGHT VISUAL INFORMATION SYSTEM

Among the most powerful visualization products that are available today is the *Starlight Visual Information System*, which is available through Future Point Systems (www.futurepointsystems.com/). Conceived by the U.S. Department of Energy's Pacific Northwest National Laboratory (PNNL) under the name Mercury, it was originally only used by government and military agencies. Starlight Visual Information System is powerful enough to import nearly any data type (which need not be related to security), and it enables users to identify elements and visually represent the dataset using numerous formats and effects—2D, 3D, data link array, hierarchical views, categorical views, time series, and more. The application is rich in features and subsequently requires a significant amount of time to learn (for example, its powerful automated import batch process). But, once the core logs are imported and parsed, the client-server software maintains a "batch process" and has the intelligence to perform scheduled redundant automated steps. The software also has a powerful indexing scheme, so sorting millions of records literally takes seconds.

Starlight is a unique visualization tool to select for a network security book, specifically because of the product's nonagnostic capability to visualize any number of datasets from any department (not strictly network security). I analyzed and researched endless network security visualization tools and, ironically, most of the tools' drawbacks stem from their inability to import various data sources. Networks consist of a multitude of security logs, so finding a tool that can correlate as many as possible is extremely important. Starlight might not be the answer to *all* of your problems, but because it can import any delimited data source and has powerful visual options, it is worth evaluating.

Figures 11-21 through 11-24 provide an idea of Starlight's capabilities to visually display Snort datasets. Figure 11-21 groups the dataset by alert category and location. For example, the large circle at the top of the image encapsulates all the MS-SQL SA brute-force login attempts in the dataset. The smaller circles within the larger circle derived from geocoding the source IP address. The size of the circles is determined by the number of homogeneous alerts. This allows an analyst to quickly determine what the attack is, where it is coming from, and its intensity. The other circles mimic the same autonomy.

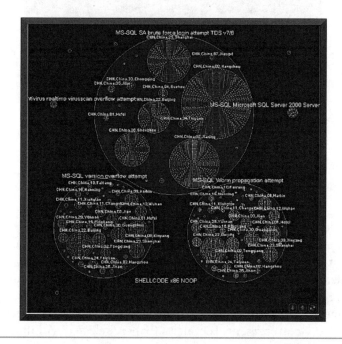

Figure 11-21   Starlight Visual Information System displaying Snort alerts identifying alert type, source IP, and attack intensity

Figure 11-22 represents the same data points, but alters the view from 2D to 3D, which is usually based on individual preference. In this example, 2D provides a better view because all the alerts are simultaneously visible. The 3D view, although fancier, actually detracts from the alert monitoring practice, because the user cannot see the alerts on the opposite side of the globe, known as occlusion, from which most 3D displays suffer. *Occlusion* is the masking of data points behind other data points, similar to the relationship between foreground and background. The same type of effect would occur; an analyst can see only a single data point at a time, therefore forcing the analyst to interact with the display.

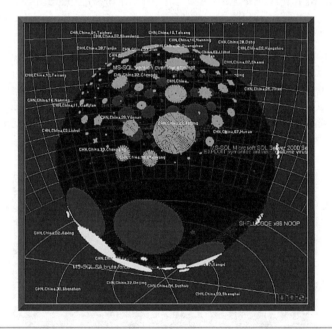

Figure 11-22   Starlight Visual Information Systems displaying the same Snort dataset in 3D

Figure 11-23 depicts the time series view with IDS alerts from December 15, 2007, to July 22, 2008. There are actually several different time series views that can be controlled. The time series at the top of the image displays the entire dataset and a quick-view histogram of the alerts. The main time series view with the black background in the center allows the user to focus on smaller intervals of time. In Figure 11-23, the main time series displays one month with the individual days identified below; weekends appear gray. Finally, the 3D view represents IDS alerts that are selected within the identified time series.

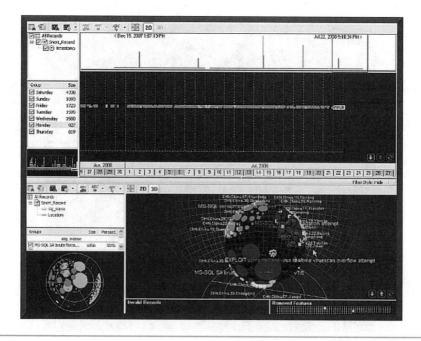

Figure 11-23 Starlight Visual Information System displaying Snort alerts based on chronological timeline

Figure 11-24 shows the source and destination IP address relationship as each line represents an alert. This view is too clustered and is fairly useless using the selected time series, showing how important it is to use the filtering capabilities. This visual design might be greatly improved by the ability to filter by alert severity or alert types to help minimize clutter. In the current view, the only true beneficial security takeaway is that more "to-from" lines to a point denotes more alerts launched either to or from that server. Although Starlight is a powerful visualization tool, not all visual designs prove useful.

ETRI: VisNet and VisMon

Throughout an interesting InfoSec career, this humble author, Ryan, has been privileged to witness some of the security industry's most technologically advanced SOCs, including government, private commercial, and managed security service provider (MSSP). From sizing-up their intrusion correlation software for monitoring network health, it becomes clear that the key for a successful SOC is to provide the security analysts monitoring the network complete situational awareness. An enterprise SOC floor plan mimics an auditorium layout where a primary screen is at the front and provides a holistic view of the network and/or security events. The individual analysts have multiple computer monitors to multitask. Of course, all SOC operations are slightly different, but a reasonable

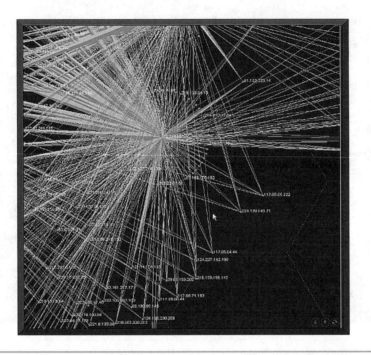

Figure 11-24   Starlight Visual Information System displaying the same Snort dataset in another graph format

SOC provides analysts with three monitors, including a copy of the primary screen, a second screen with additional security alerts, and a monitor that has Internet access for research. Most, if not all, SOCs collect too many network statistics and alerts to efficiently display them all on a single screen. Typically, the second monitor displays any data points that do not fit on the primary screen, IDS, and firewall alerts.

Electronic and Telecommunications Research Institute (ETRI) (http://amtrac.etri.re. kr/eng/main.html) is a nonprofit, government-funded research organization that was founded in Korea in 1976. ETRI is developing an ideal SOC-like product line, which is encouraging to visualization perfectionists. Two of its products, VisNet and VisMon, nicely complement each other with an intelligent discovery of anomalous traffic and filtering capabilities that group related attacks by behavior and pattern. The visualizations that these products produce are incredible and are particularly valuable for SOC operations as a real-time operational tool.

Figure 11-25 shows the VisNet screen display. It demonstrates that a useful, real-time display of relevant security information can be represented in a comprehensive manner by visualizing network traffic. Geographic source and destination IP addresses, source and destination ports, protocols, and IP and port counts are shown without cluttering the screen and completely overwhelming the viewer. The information shown in Figure 11-25 is standard for real-time network security monitoring, but it lacks intrusion alert details (most likely found on the secondary screen). As manageable as this visualization is, if you incorporated additional alerts from IDS/IPS sensors, firewalls, syslogs, antivirus software, or operating systems, the screen would greatly suffer from clutter and turn a visually effective screen into an overwhelming information security collage.

If the network encountered a DoS or DDoS attack, the screen would definitely be overwhelming and would force the analyst to use the interactive capabilities, including filtering traffic or zooming in to suspicious patterns. When viewing a potentially vast number of data points, user interaction is absolutely mandated. Figure 11-25 and Figure 11-26 would be useless in an offline presentation because the images do not convey clear useful information. However, by giving the user the ability to filter traffic and/or extract certain suspicious traffic patterns, the images are providing critical microanalytical capabilities. Screens such as this emphasize visualizing data in the hope of finding outliers/anomalies or abnormal patterns.

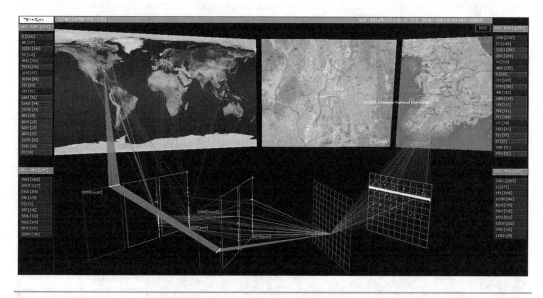

Figure 11-25 ETRI's VisNet

Figure 11-26 represents the ETRI VisMon cube view, which consists of the same data points as the VisNet screen, but it displays that information in a different format. This reinforces the point that a visualization's success directly depends on the user's individual interpretation of the data. Whether the viewer gravitates to the VisNet or VisMon visualization is a prime example of user preference. The VisNet screen (in Figure 11-25) shows parallel coordinates between the source IP, source port, destination port, and destination IP. What if an analyst preferred the cube view over the parallel coordinate graph? The cube view (in Figure 11-26) is a common network security visualization for identifying ping sweeps, port scans, and other anomalous traffic.

In Figure 11-26, notice the six minicubes at the top of the screen that display permutations of the information in the parallel coordinates. This enables simultaneous investigation of data streams from all angles without the analyst having to rely on shifting the cube to a specific angle or view to see the suspicious traffic. (This is no doubt ETRI's attempt to minimize occlusion with its 3D displays.) It provides a superior level of efficiency in a console or dashboard. If something suspicious is identified, the minicube is selected for zooming and, as the cube is enlarged in the bottom left, a level of situational awareness is maintained with the other minicube views. In Figure 11-26, the analyst is currently zoomed to the minicube on the far right; a close look reveals that it has a small frame box around it to identify it as the enlargement. A superior visual application should have features that provide as many options as possible without drastically detracting from the visual benefit. Helpful features include filtering events to extract smaller subsets of data for analysis; highlighting and tagging events; and the ability to modify colors for analysts who might be fully or partially color blind (and therefore cannot see red, which represents a warning).

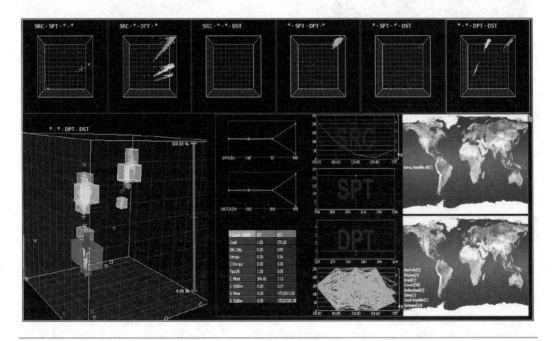

Figure 11-26 VisMon

USE-CASE: SECURITY AUDIT

In the 1965 film, *Doctor Zhivago*, there is an interesting scene where the lead character, Dr. Zhivago (played by Omar Sharif), is being questioned by the disgruntled Bolshevik, Pasha. The doctor had apparently piqued the interest of local authorities by involving himself in suspicious activities and by maintaining such a calm demeanor in spite of the current political and social turbulence. How could this be, they wondered, when half of the country is starving and the other half is overfed and drunk with power. Surely, Zhivago must be an assassin or spy. With a bloody war moving its death machine closer each day and whispers of revolution in the air, Pasha wants to talk to this arrogant, young doctor.

Against this backdrop of misery, Pasha relentlessly interrogated the doctor, probing deeper with each angry denial. Eventually, at his wit's end, Pasha's most combative diatribe was reduced to basic sarcasm. At this point, the fictitious character, Pasha, gave real-life actor, Tom Courtenay, the opportunity to deliver one of the best lines in the movie. Unhappy with the perplexed look on Zhivago's face and his answer regarding what he did with an old kitchen knife he kept with his eating utensils, Pasha replied, "You put your knife with a fork and a spoon, and it looks quite innocuous. Perhaps you travel with a wife and child for the same reason."

The point of this tangent is that the writers of this scene understood that, when presented with identical images, people can see different things. You can only assume that the writers also understood the deeper point, which is that differences in perception among people must be recognized and resolved before a common ground can be established to further the relationship.

It might not be as dramatic, but the modern business equivalent to the movie scenario might involve a security consultant who, after completing an audit of a customer's network, is ready to present his findings. Suppose that the customer directed the consultant to attend two confidential, one-on-one meetings to share and discuss the audit results. The first is with the chief information security officer (CISO), and the second is with the comptroller, whose motivation to discuss technical details comes from a personal stake in the findings. It was his discovery of irregularities in the accounting system that led to the security audit.

Based on facts that they had before hiring the consultant, both officers knew that the legal and financial ramifications might cripple the company for years to come. But, they did not know the extent of the problem, which is why they hired the consultant. At the initial meeting, all three of them agreed that the irregularities were the result of a criminal act, most likely from within the organization.

The consultant's approach was to equally weigh likely and unlikely possibilities, in spite of the smoking gun of internal mischief. Conformance with the customer's *information security model* also became part of the reporting plan, so reference materials included proprietary documents that were supplied by the customer under a nondisclosure agreement. Figure 11-27 shows an example summary section from the consultant's audit report.

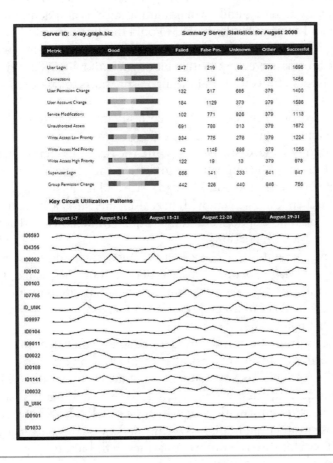

Figure 11-27 Audit report sample

The top portion of the sample page summarizes activity for the accounting server, x-ray.graph.biz, and serves as the cover sheet for several pages of tabular statistics and text. The purpose of the sparklines on the bottom part of the form is simply to show traffic patterns over what the company considers to be critical circuits. The ID field in the left column links to circuit details that include, among other things, a full complement of NetFlow reports. It also represents the last four digits of a user's unique company login ID; the entries in this list are actually a NetFlow *Top N* report on host conversations to the accounting server for the reporting period. With the exception of a few drawings, summary pages like this one show the highest level of information in the report. All other pages include granular technical details and supporting verbiage, which is what the consultant presented to each manager.

The first meeting took place according to plan, with only the consultant and the CISO in attendance. It lasted for 45 minutes, during which time, the CISO asked a series of questions and took notes, but withheld comments on all aspects of the consultant's report.

The second meeting, which was with the comptroller, was different, and the general tone was characterized by a cordial mismatch of technological and financial paradigms. At its conclusion, both participants felt assured that the most critical concepts were successfully communicated.

Readers might want to go back a page and again consider the sparklines, but with traffic anomalies in mind. That is how the CISO viewed the report, and it is the reason why the two managers, both of whom saw nothing remarkable about the server statistics, saw completely different things in the sparkline images. To the nontechnical comptroller, there are enough peaks in the rows of traffic patterns to produce an unremarkable mental image, even to the extent of being innocuous. To the technically focused CISO, the third line, which is associated with ID0002, is Zhivago's knife, spoon, and fork. The peaks are simply too close to being equal in amplitude for such a short time interval to not be considered anomalous.

SUMMARY

Such are the considerations for visualizing security events, network traffic, and other IT datasets. The key concepts discussed in this chapter, not the least of which is human visual perception, come from a well-rounded outlook on the visualization discipline. Readers who are new to visualization concepts, and those who are experienced and continuing to learn, benefit most from this chapter by keeping these ideas in mind:

- Technological concepts are inexorably tied to our strengths and weaknesses as human beings; create useful visualizations that work for the most diverse audience.
- Keep it simple when possible; make it complex when necessary. If a spreadsheet works, offer the spreadsheet, but be prepared to visualize thousands of data points for cases when none can be overlooked. Security is critical.

Remember William Playfair! He invented a visualization that, in 1801, people thought was genius. It honestly showed each person or entity's share of the entire pie and was easy to produce. The history and writings of William Playfair, creator of the much maligned pie chart, teach us to use the right tool for the right job. Nothing is wrong with a pie chart until it visualizes too much data.

TERMINOLOGY

Table 11-3 includes graphing terms and definitions that you need to know when you design visualizations.

Table 11-3 Graphing Terms and Definitions

Term	Definition	Example
Area graph	Color-shaded areas that show and compare frequency counts over time.	
Bar chart	Color-shaded bars that display frequency counts by category.	
Chart	Diagram, table, or graph that visually displays summary groupings of data.	
Choropleth map	Geographic map that displays statistics in color-coded regions.	
Contour plot	A 2D representation of a 3D surface. Contours are color shaded and graphically depict the changes in Z as a function of X and Y.	
Dependant variable	Data being observed (for example, y-axis time series data).	
Descriptive statistics	Provide facts about a dataset.	
Dotplot	Stacked dots that compare datasets.	
Factor	Things that affect variables.	

Table 11-3 Graphing Terms and Definitions

Term	Definition	Example
Graph	Pictorial representation of quantitative data.	
Heat map	Type of graph that demonstrates location-based variables.	
Histogram	Frequency counts for values of a continuous variable.	
Independent variable	Predictor values (for example, X-axis scale and time series graph).	
Inferential statistics	Branch of statistics that makes inferences about a population from an analyzed sample.	
Line plot	Lines that compare variable statistical functions to two factors.	
Maps	Geographic maps are immediately identifiable and can overlay variable datasets.	
Multivari chart	Minitab 15 chart; graphically shows the relationship between a predictor/explanatory/factor variable and a response variable.	
Multivariate	Multiple predictor variables and multiple response variables arranged in a matrix.	
Outlier	A data point that is well above or below the observed norm.	
Parallel coordinate	Variables with matching coordinate on a plane, usually vertical axes.	
Pie chart	Circular segmented display that reveals the share of the entire chart taken by each segment.	

Table 11-3 Graphing Terms and Definitions

Term	Definition	Example
Scatterplot	Uses symbols (such as dots and triangles) to represent and compare data points. Used for irregular datasets and can represent time series or static data.	
Spatial	Existing in physical space.	
Spider diagram	Shows existential relationships within an Euler or Venn diagram.	
Surface plot	Continuous surface that relates three variables in a 3D view.	
Temporal	Existing in time.	
Time series plot	Sequential data points that are plotted over time and usually represented by a line. Dot plots, scatterplot, and bar charts are also used for time series analysis.	
Tree map	Type of graph that visualizes space-constrained, hierarchical data.	
Variable	Any numeric value that is subject to change.	
X-axis	The horizontal line in a graph.	
Y-axis	The vertical line in a graph.	

ENDNOTES

[1] In this discussion, the word figure is used interchangeably with the words picture or display.

[2] www.caida.org/home/.

[3] www.itl.nist.gov/div898/.

[4] In this context, performance management regards tracking business key performance indicators (KPI) rather than network response times and availability.

[5] DAVIX is available at http://secviz.org/content/the-davix-live-cd.

REFERENCE

Tufte, Edward R. *The Visual Display of Quantitative Information.* Graphics Press, 2007.

Return on Investment: Business Justification

There is no such thing as a truly secure system. With enough time, resources, and determination on the part of a malicious attacker, not to mention human error, any system can be breached, including government and military networks. In the adversarial world of security, you are challenged by a constantly moving malicious opponent target. As you study your adversaries' strategies, they study yours. They parry and counter your every move, so a majority of malicious attackers are never more than a half-step behind you, whereas the remaining minority are even more sophisticated. They create zero-day exploits and remain slightly ahead of the white hat security community.

The primary goal of a company's Security Department is to provide security solutions that do not hinder customers or employee productivity while simultaneously maintaining regulatory compliance within budget constraints and evaluating cyber liability insurance (CLI). Because there are so many possible combinations, this is often an insurmountable challenge that might lead to a flawed defense strategy. Realistic security can only come from the ability to reduce the probability of a breach and minimize its impact. Accepting the inevitability of attacks lets you refocus your efforts on preparing for an attack rather than reacting to one.

During the first half of 2008, security breaches reached an all-time high in the United States. Between January 1 and June 27, there were 342 publicly reported data breaches, representing a 69 percent increase over the same period in 2007. Undoubtedly, the true count is even higher because of the fact that many breaches go unreported or are under-reported as a single event when numerous entities might have been affected. For example, many companies that maintain client data comingle data because, years ago, the cost of supplying each client with its own database server was too expensive and the legacy architecture is still in production today. So, say that a managed security service provider (MSSP) is compromised; although it is a single data breach, the client data that was stolen included information from 25 of their clients. Technically, in the laws of contracts, that MSSP is an "extended arm" of the organization and the data extracted still belongs to each monitored organization. However, in the data breach surveys, the breach is only considered a single compromise when, technically, it should be considered as 26 breaches (25 clients + 1 MSSP = 26).

The number of security breaches has been on the rise because formal tracking began in 2005. In 2005, there were 140 incidents involving more than 55 million people's records. In 2006, 492 breaches were reported, in 2007, documented breaches dropped to 440, and in 2008 increased to a staggering 573. In total, more than 354 million records containing sensitive personal information have been involved in security breaches since January 2005.[1]

These drastic statistics forced the security industry to seek additional standardized security measures in the form of frameworks (CoBIT, ISO, ITIL, NIST, and FISMA) and regulatory compliance efforts (HIPAA, PCI, and SOX). Frameworks are equivalent to "industry best practices" and form more of a guideline that focuses on internal company policies and procedures, whereas regulatory compliance involves legal requirements that companies must enforce when handling certain types of personal/sensitive information.

Appropriately handling private data is a legally protected right of your customers. The fallout from mishandling data resulting in a data breach extends throughout an organization, affecting virtually every function. Although there is a shared interest in protecting data, the decision-making process for investment in additional security resources is hampered by the varying perspectives held by related parties. Corporate executives are concerned with reducing breach risks to an acceptable level commensurate with the level of investment. On the other hand, security managers are dedicated to implementing the most secure design. A uniform cost-benefit analysis metric provides a uniform level of assessment so respective solutions hounding other departments can also be fairly judged across the board.

The first section of this chapter covers the reality of "not if, but when" and the security frameworks. The next section covers security breaches and their costs. The following several sections address the economics issues and how to estimate the return on investment (ROI) in security measures. Finally, this chapter closes with an overview of liability insurance.

NOT IF, BUT WHEN

The IT security industry has an undeclared security anthem: "It's not if you get hacked, but when you get hacked." This anthem might stem from a subconscious self-motivation for preservation or to remind management that everybody is mortal. Although the phrase is generally spoken sarcastically, it has an underlying hint of truth. Security breaches impact the public sector and private industry, global corporations, and local businesses. Certain sectors, such as government agencies, financial services, colleges/universities, and healthcare services, are especially attractive targets, because of the nature of the data that their systems contain. Companies with less advanced security policies leave their sensitive data especially vulnerable. But, no industry segment is spared, as Figure 12-1 and Figure 12-2 show. For virtually every organization, it is not a question of if, but of when, their customers' sensitive records are compromised. The increasing rate of data compromises has compelled companies to seek a financial failsafe in the form of cyber liability insurance (CLI). CLI is an additional insurance coverage that specifically addresses IT and electronic needs.

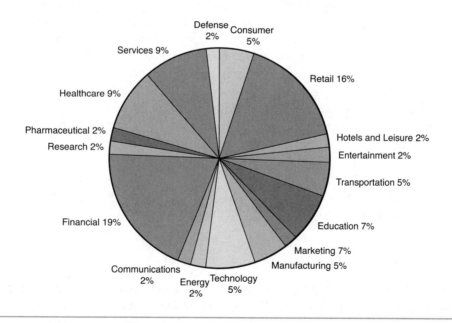

Figure 12-1   2008 data breaches by industry[2]

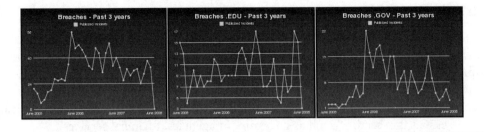

Figure 12-2   Data breaches over the past three years[3]

COMPLIANCE PLAYS A ROLE

The security industry has tried to normalize security processes/procedures to help IT departments adhere to common frameworks. Several frameworks, including ISO 27001/ISO 27002 (successors to BS 7799 and BS 17799), ITIL, and CoBIT, try and fill the gaps and cut through the confusion to provide some standard guidance. CoBIT and ISO 27002 help define "what should be done" to protect a company's network, whereas ITIL helps define "how to" best implement a coherent methodology. ISO 27001/ISO 27002, ITIL, and CoBIT are standards introduced in the UK and are widely used in the European Union (EU), India, and Japan. However, the UK developed frameworks are gaining legitimacy and, therefore, acceptance in the U.S., as any common ground provides an additional layer of uniformity. Companies in the U.S. are not held to these standards, because it has some of its own: the Health Insurance Portability and Accountability Act of 1996 (HIPAA) security regulations, the Payment Card Industry Data Security Standard (PCI-DSS), and the Federal Information Security Management Act of 2002 (FISMA). These are just a portion of the "common" frameworks and regulatory compliance that help system and business owners manage their resources, but the section is not meant to encompass every single possible regulatory guideline.

The rest of this section provides a brief take on each framework.

CoBIT FRAMEWORK

CoBIT stands for Control Objectives for Information and related Technology. It is published by the IT Governance Institute (ITGI) and provides best practices for monitoring and managing IT activities. It helps executives and technical network owners better understand and manage IT investments and align them with the business direction. The entire framework consists of five components:

- Plan and organize
- Acquire and implement
- Deliver and support
- Monitor and evaluate
- Information criteria

Several CoBIT volumes tip-toe around using intrusion detection when mentioning risk evaluation and vulnerability assessment, but refrain from specifically saying IDS. However, intrusion detection is explicitly discussed in Deliver and Support Section 5, Ensure Systems Security (DS5.10), which states the following:

> Use security techniques and related management procedures (e.g., firewalls, security appliances, network segmentation, intrusion detection) to authorize access and control information flows from and to networks.

ISO 27001/27002 FRAMEWORKS

The ISO 27001/27002 standards are published by the International Organization of Standardization (ISO) and International Electrotechnical Commission (IEC). Both standards are derived from the UK government's BS 7799/17799. ISO 27001 and ISO 27002 are different, but they are meant to work in tandem. The ISO 27001 standard deals with information security in an overarching broad sense. ISO 27001 discusses how to implement, monitor, maintain, and continually strengthen your Information Security Management System (ISMS). ISO 27002 provides more of a checklist of security recommendations, because it encompasses 133 topics divided into 12 chapters (totaling over 5,000 direct or derived security aspects). The chapters include the following:

- Risk assessment and treatment
- Information security policy
- Organizational security
- Asset management
- Human resources security
- Physical and environmental security
- Communications and operations management
- Access control
- Information systems

- Incident management
- Business continuity
- Compliance

Ultimately, ISO 27001 provides the strategy, and ISO 27002 provides the steps to maintain maximum ISMS defense. Intrusion detection fits securely into two modules of the ISO 27001/27002 frameworks, both in "A.6.2 – External Parties" and "A.10.6 – Network Security Management."

The task defined by the module, "A.6.2 – External Parties," is "to maintain the security of the organization's information and information processing facilities that are accessed, processed, communicated to, or managed by external parties." The subsection that more clearly defines Intrusion Detection is, "A.6.2.1 – Identification of Risks Related to External Parties," which defines "the risks to the organization's information and information processing facilities from business processes involving external parties shall be identified and appropriate controls implemented before granting access."

The task defined by the module, "A.10.6 – Network Security Management," is "to ensure the protection of information in networks and the protection of the supporting infrastructure." "A.10.6.2 – Security of Network Services" is the subsection that provides stability for the intrusion detection technology by stating, "Security features, service levels, and management requirements of all network services shall be identified and included in any network services agreement, whether these services are provided in-house or outsourced."

ITIL FRAMEWORK

ITIL, currently at version 3, is published by the UK Office of Government Commerce (OGC) and provides an industry set of concepts and policies for managing infrastructure, development, and operations in an attempt to improve the quality and reduce the costs of IT services that support their business objectives. Like ISO 27002, ITIL is divided into five core topics:

- Service Strategy (SS)
- Service Design (SD)
- Service Transition (ST)
- Service Operation (SO)
- Continual Service Improvement (CSI)

Each topic encapsulates a book that provides ample information for implementation. Intrusion detection is found within the SO module, more specifically under Chapter 5, "Common Service Operation Activities." "Section 5.5 – Network Management" identifies ten bullet points that revolve around ensuring the success of service and connectivity. The ninth bullet states, "Implementing, monitoring, and maintaining Intrusion Detection Systems (IDSs) on behalf of Information Security Management and is also responsible for ensuring that there is no denial of service (DoS) to legitimate users of the network."

HEALTH INSURANCE PORTABILITY AND ACCOUNTABILITY ACT OF 1996 (HIPAA)

HIPAA was enacted by the U.S. Congress in 1996. Due to the drastic changes Congress decided to extend a "grace period" of April 20, 2005 for all covered entities and April 20, 2006 for smaller covered entities that did not have the budget or technology already in place to make the transition. This allowed HIPAA Covered Entities time to implement the needed security regulations that called for more stringent processes, procedures and technologies. HIPAA provided, among other requirements, a generally accepted set of standards for the ownership, protection, and transport of Protected Health Information (PHI) within the healthcare industry. As technology advanced, more medical providers were transitioning from traditional paper records to electronic records to expedite efficiency and streamline communication. The HIPAA regulations that are most relevant here are broken into two primary components: The Privacy Rule and The Security Rule. The Privacy Rule defines how PHI can be used and disclosed by certain covered entities and provides for patient rights in and to that PHI, who might have access to PHI; while the Security Rule dictates how to protect PHI or Electronic PHI (E-PHI) from unauthorized access or disclosure. The Security Rule requires the implementation of three categories of safeguards:

- Administrative safeguards
  - Administrative actions
  - Policies and procedures
  - Security management
- Physical safeguards
  - Physical measures
  - Policies

- Procedures to protect electronic information systems and related equipment
- Technical safeguards
  - Technology assets and security protection for access

HIPAA was realistic about its implementation and, while requiring compliance with certain standards, categorized the "implementation specifications" under each required standard as either required or addressable to assist in prioritizing modifications and allowing for compliance to be scaled to an entity's resources and systems. HIPAA is infamously a "loose" regulation because specific technologies are not directly identified, which, unfortunately, leaves gaps for human interpretation. Intrusion detection, although not directly mentioned, fits into the administrative safeguards under "Section 164.308(a)(1) Security Management Process." This safeguard requires a covered entity to "implement policies and procedures to prevent, detect, contain, and correct security violations." What is required of every HIPAA covered entity, however, is a risk analysis and risk-management process that documents the risk analysis and the determination by an entity of how it meets the various requirements, with written policies and procedures that reflect implementation of the results of the analysis and risk-management process.

PAYMENT CARD INDUSTRY DATA SECURITY STANDARD (PCI-DSS)

The Payment Card Industry Data Security Standard (PCI-DSS) was conceived on September 7, 2006, in a joint effort between American Express, Discover Financial Services, JCB, MasterCard Worldwide, and Visa International. Like most regulatory mandates, it was developed to create universal data security standards. The joint effort ensured a global uniformity among organizations that process credit-card transactions by standardizing both technical and operational requirements. PCI is a security implementer's dream compared to HIPAA because the PCI regulations are extremely granular, leaving little human interpretation.

IDSs are specifically annotated within PCI in several places, but predominantly in Requirement 11, "Regularly Test Security Systems and Processes," in Section 11.4, which states, "Use intrusion detection systems, and/or intrusion prevention systems to monitor all traffic in the cardholder data environment and alert personnel to suspected compromises. Keep all intrusion detection and prevention engines up-to-date."

The interesting caveat to this requirement that other compliance efforts are lacking is the last part, regarding keeping all IDS/IPS engines up-to-date—impressive!

The second and third mention of IDS is indirect, but it still reiterates the importance of the technology. Requirement 10, "Track and Monitor All Access to Network Resources and Cardholder Data," in Section 10.6 states, "Review logs for all system components at least daily. Log reviews must include those servers that perform security functions like intrusion detection systems (IDS) and authentication, authorization, and accounting protocol servers."

Requirement 12, "Maintain a Policy that Addresses Information Security for Employees and Contractors," in Section 12.9.5 states, "Include alerts from intrusion detection, intrusion prevention, and file integrity monitoring systems."

NOTE

PCI does not distinguish between host- or network-based intrusion detection, so there is still a level of preference. However, surprisingly, the regulation addresses WIDSs in Requirement 11, Section 11.1.a, which is investigated in Chapter 8, "Wireless IDS/IPS."

FEDERAL INFORMATION SECURITY MANAGEMENT ACT OF 2002 (FISMA)/NATIONAL INSTITUTE OF STANDARDS AND TECHNOLOGY

The Federal Information Security Management Act (FISMA) was developed to strengthen network security within the federal government and government contractors. FISMA is a kind of regulatory Network Access Control (NAC), because it imposes a baseline standard that must be followed by all information systems before connecting to federal systems. The regulation actually encompasses HIPAA and Federal Information Processing Standards (FIPS), the Privacy Act of 1974, and the globally recognized National Institute of Standards and Technology Special Publications (more commonly known as the NIST 800 series).

Because, among these standards, intrusion detection is exclusively discussed by NIST, this section focuses on that. Historically, *NIST-31 IDSs*, developed by Rebecca Bace and Peter Mell, opened the door to the technology and discussed how to effectively implement the technology within a network architecture. The 51-page document covered the fundamental need-to-know concepts. Although there is no copyright date on the special publication, the latest date referenced within the document is 1999, therefore categorizing itself as being somewhat outdated. (This information might not be available on the NIST Web site.) However, natural evolution saw its replacement draft published in

February 2007 by Karen Scarfone and Peter Mell. The latest version, *NIST-94 Guide to Intrusion Detection and Prevention Systems (IDPS)*, amends the original and brings the technology into the twenty-first century.

NOTE

FISMA has been under attack by some security experts who claim it is just a paper-work fire drill because it only requires compliant organizations to report whether they have followed procedures to check for system vulnerabilities instead of whether they have implemented procedures that directly remediate the vulnerabilities. In laymen's terms, the vulnerability scanner might have identified 20 missing patches, but there is no requirement to apply the patches to the system.

SECURITY BREACHES

Businesses that experience security breaches involving credit-card information, social security numbers, or other sensitive customer data pay a high cost. These events permeate an organization, impacting relations with current and potential customers, business partnerships, employees, regulators, and the public. The high cost and pervasiveness of security breaches has led the Federal Bureau of Investigation (FBI) to rank cyber crime as its top priority, behind terrorism and espionage. In addition to the *hard* costs of a breach, including legal fees, notifications, fines, restitutions, and internal investigations, there are also *soft* costs, such as brand damage, diminished market performance, and customer attrition.

A unifying benchmark is found within cost-benefit analysis. This methodology quantifies both the hard and soft costs associated with security risks, providing metrics to assess an organization's security expenditures and their bottom-line impact. Cost-benefit analysis monetizes the balance between management's need to achieve acceptable risk levels while maintaining a minimalistic investment budget.

The stimulus law passed by the Obama administration, the American Recovery and Reinvestment Act of 2009 (ARRA), emphasizes the importance of these issues. Among many other provisions, ARRA extends the requirements of the HIPAA Security Rule directly to business associates (contractors) of HIPAA covered entities, increases penalties for noncompliance, and expands enforcement of the HIPAA regulations to the state Attorney General. Moreover, ARRA enacts two new security-breach notification laws: one applicable to HIPAA covered entities and business associates for the unauthorized acquisition, access, use, or disclosure of unsecured PHI, and the other applicable to vendors of personal health records and their contractors with respect to the personal information in their custody. These provisions require notice to the federal government of all incidents, thus removing the possibility of flying under the public radar when a breach occurs.

BREACH COSTS

While companies grapple with the challenge of frequent attempts and the inevitable security breaches, the costs associated with a failure to adequately protect data are also rising. In 2008, the average total cost of a security breach reached $6.6 million, up from $6.3 million per incident in 2007, and $4.8 million per incident in 2006.[4]

As shown in Figure 12-3, this represents a cost of $202 per impacted customer record, which is up more than 2.5 percent over the 2007 cost of $197, and up more than 10 percent over the 2006 cost of $182.

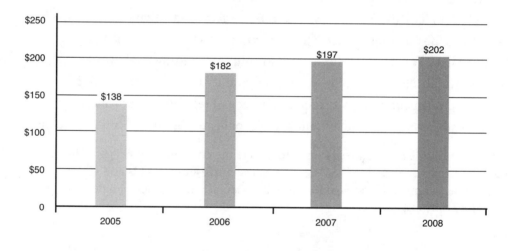

Figure 12-3   Average per record cost of a data breach (2005–2008)[5]

In most organizations, IT managers and IT security officers are responsible for developing an incident response plan that includes security breach procedures and devising the response to security breaches. Yet most costs associated with security breaches are incurred outside of the IT realm. Costs are born by marketing departments, primarily in the form of customer attrition associated with damage control and public relations. Customer support, legal departments, and audit and risk-management functions can all be staggered by the costs associated with the loss of sensitive data.

SECURITY INVESTMENT WITHIN THE ORGANIZATION

The decision-making process for devising the response to security breaches is muddied by the various interests held by the related parties. IT managers are concerned with reducing breach risks to an acceptable level commensurate with the level of investment in security technologies. Security managers are dedicated to implementing the most secure design. The executive decision makers within an organization look across a broad business spectrum as they evaluate the financial risks posed by security breaches. The investment has to make good business sense and must be justified by its impact on the organization's bottom line. The executive team typically is not overly concerned with system architecture as a defensive posture. It could be a firewall or a pit bull minding the data—executives don't really care. They look to answer core fundamental questions pertaining to an organization's bottom line:

- What is the current level of security investment?
- How does the existing security architecture affect productivity and profitability?
- What is the financial impact if the current architecture is breached?
- What is a cost-effective solution to mitigating the existing level of risk?
- How would alternative solutions impact productivity and profitability?
- Is the investment in security required by federal regulatory guidelines?
- Is the investment in security contractually obligated by customer requirements?

A major hurdle for organizations is to bridge the communication gap between IT (CIOs), security managers (CISOs), and the executive suite (CFOs and CEOs). There needs to be a common language for assessing security needs and a single benchmark for evaluating options.

DATA BREACHES AND THE LAW

Even the most secure organizations must operate under the presumption that sensitive data is eventually compromised. Although there have always been considerable costs associated with security breaches, the stakes are higher in the current environment. With a slew of well-publicized incidents, recent regulatory mandates, and sky-high fines and penalties for noncompliance, there is an assumption on the part of both the public and regulators that due diligence is taken. Failure to do so is simply unacceptable.

At least 44 states have enacted legislation requiring organizations that possess sensitive personal information to notify individuals when their security is breached. As with most technologically advanced laws, California led the way in the creation of these laws, with most states following and often expanding on the requirements of the California statute. Table 12-1 shows the trending of states adopting disclosure laws.

Table 12-1   Running Total of States Adopting Data Breach Disclosure Laws

Year	Running Total
2003	1
2004	1
2005	12
2006	29
2007	34
Pending	44

   Breach notification laws have significantly contributed to a heightened awareness of the importance of data security throughout organizations. As you might expect, breach notification costs can quickly accumulate, primarily because the targeted corporation/institution cannot reasonably determine which customer's information is compromised and, therefore, it is required by law to notify *all* customers. With the current statutory emphasis on breach detection, intrusion IDSs are not just a weapon, they're defense, too. Although specific notification requirements vary by state, most statutes adhere to the conditions found in the California Senate Bill 1386, which allows a company to forgo public notification if a breach was detected before information could be wrongfully acquired or the information was encrypted. According to the Ponemon Institute's "2007 Annual Study: U.S. Cost of a Data Breach," the increase of lost/stolen laptops, backup tapes, or USB flash drives, which accounted for a staggering 49 percent of reported breaches in its 2007 survey (36 percent in the UK), have practically forced companies to encrypt all mobile/portable devices to avoid aforementioned breach notifications laws.

   Marcy Wilder, a nationally recognized HIPAA expert at Hogan and Hartson who specializes in data breach management, says that at least 44 states have enacted data breach notification laws. She has also seen cases where there was a contractual obligation to notify the customer (on whose behalf a vendor or supplier was holding data) of a security incident, even when the information was encrypted.

Breach notification laws have also significantly contributed to heightened public awareness of the importance of information security. The media glorify data breaches and usually only publicize the deficiency of the company's security posture (method of compromise exploited). Hollywood attempts to emphasize the simplicity of cracking into systems (Hugh Jackman in *Swordfish* or Harrison Ford in *Firewall*), leaving the general public in an uninformed paranoid state, which might actually be beneficial given today's casual laziness. This increased sensitivity has profound consequences in the event of a security breach. There are substantial costs related to the notification process, and there are even more significant costs related to a tarnished image and loss of customer confidence. Although the security of private records might not be a marketable attribute for companies to sell to consumers, the perceived absence of security can be devastatingly costly. It's a key element of the cost structure that is assembled for ROI modeling.

ROI AS A UNIFYING BENCHMARK

"The day before a breach, the ROI is zero," said Dennis Hoffman, RSA vice president of enterprise solutions. "The day after, it is infinite" (www.gcn.com/online/vol1_no1/42229-1.html).

This topic is finding its way into the writings of several mainstream security bloggers (Bruce Schneier, Richard Bejtlich and Anton Chuvakin), and that quote from one of Richard's devoted readers stands out. Bruce Schneier points out that, "Any business venture needs to demonstrate a positive return on investment, and a good one at that, in order to be viable."[6] However, it is apparent that there is no universally accepted security investment approach. Some core algorithms (ROI, Return On Security Investment [ROSI], Net Present Value [NPV], and so on) aid security managers to better calculate a reasonable security budget, but all have received criticism regarding the true value that they actually provide.

But before getting into the details of ROI frameworks, here's a common misconception that even I have intentionally used to attract attention to this chapter. Richard Bejtlich explains

Security is not an investment that provides a return. It's an expense that, hopefully, pays for itself in cost savings. Security is about loss prevention, not about earnings, and while security can't produce ROI, loss prevention most certainly affects a company's bottom line.

Applying this simple metric to security investments poses some unique problems. Unlike spending in other areas, security investments do not create anything tangible that contributes to a company's bottom line; therefore, the educated estimates taken within the calculations drastically fluctuate. The "gain" from an investment in a security technology is derived from the benefits of loss prevention. Because a prevented loss is an event that never occurred, the gain must be assigned a value so that it can be understood from the various perspectives of risk, security, productivity, and profitability. (As a side note, if you are the "lucky" one responsible for the security budget in your firm, take ROIs supplied by security vendors and security Value Added Resellers [VARs] with a grain of salt because there are always alternative motives behind those extreme numbers—similar to the "sale by fear" tactic. Always replace their calculations with your own numbers for a more accurate estimate.)

Typically, organizations rely on ROI to evaluate expenditures. ROI is at the heart of all business decision making and provides that unifying understanding among management. It distills business activity down to its essence and levels the playing field for every facet of an organization. ROI is a simple and versatile performance measure that quantifies the efficiency of an investment and provides a uniform metric to enable comparisons between investment alternatives. To calculate ROI, the cost of the investment is subtracted from the gain from an investment and then is divided by the cost of the investment. The result is expressed as a ratio or percentage:

$$ROI = \frac{(\text{Gain from Investment - Cost of Investment})}{\text{Cost of Investment}}$$

To calculate the value of the benefit gained through loss prevention, values must be assigned to its various components. In basic terms, these components are the presumed costs associated with the risks that are mitigated and the presumed risk likelihood and frequency of losses. The quantification of these factors gives the approximate hard numbers needed to calculate the ROI of an organization's security investment. By expressing breach costs and exposure risks in the common language of ROI, security investments can be evaluated and funded in the same manner as all other expenditures.

COST BREAKDOWN

Breach costs have the same effect on companies as a motorcyclist getting sideswiped by a careless driver. The point of collision is swift, the damage is extensive, and, if you are lucky enough to limp away from the accident, the effects are felt for years to come. This section looks at the direct costs, indirect costs, and fines associated with historic data breaches.

Direct Costs

The direct costs of a security breach relate to specific activities stemming from the breach. These measurable hard costs pertain in large part to the discovery, escalation, customer and vendor notification of the breach, and internal IT costs to resume normal business activity. The following expenses generally make up the direct costs:

- Free or discounted products /services to offset customers' inconvenience and/or frustration
- Notification of customers and vendors
  - Mail/e-mail campaign
  - Call centers
- Public relations/public notifications
- Web and media announcements
- Legal fees
  - Defense services
  - Criminal investigations
- Financial services
  - Accounting services (such as monitoring customers' credit reports for upwards of six months)
  - Internal and external audits
  - Investor relations
- Internal investigations
  - Forensic investigations
- Lost productivity
  - Post-breach repair time spent by IT staff
  - Inaccessible systems due to downtime resulting from the breach
  - Inaccessible systems due to seizures of equipment by law enforcement
- Compromised data
  - Cost of restoring from backup data
  - Repair or replacement of missing or altered data
  - Reassessment of strategic plans that have been disclosed or compromised
- Security and audit services
  - Additional procedures mandated by an industry governing board

Indirect Costs

The indirect costs of a security breach relate to lost business opportunities as a result of a data breach. Lost opportunity costs tend to be the most significant cost component of total breach costs, and they are generally the fastest rising. The following lost business opportunities generally make up the indirect costs of a security breach:

- Lost business due to system downtime
- Customer attrition
- Increased customer acquisition costs
- Brand/credibility damage control

The Ponemon Institute and the PGP Corporation, in their National Consumer Survey on Data Security Breach Notification, questioned consumers who had received notification that their private and confidential data had been mishandled, exposed, or lost. This survey illustrates the severe opportunity cost implications of a data breach. As Figure 12-4 shows, the majority of consumers reacted extremely negatively to this notification. Almost 60 percent terminated or considered terminating their relationships with the relevant company, 27 percent of those surveyed expressed moderate concern, and the smallest group, only 14 percent of those surveyed, expressed a lack of concern about the handling of their records.

Customer Impact of Breach Notification

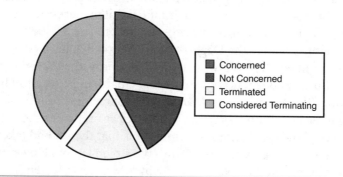

Figure 12-4   Customer impact of breach notification[7]

Fines and Restitution

The appropriate handling of private data is a guaranteed right of your customers, and failure to do so can result in criminal and civil penalties. This final category of breach costs is often the most difficult to quantify. Regulatory fines can range from $0 to $10 million, depending on the industry, number of compromised records, and the overall extent of the breach.

Fines might be imposed on an organization in both civil and criminal courts. Restitution for damages suffered by customers greatly differs across industries, but a financial-services company can expect a high level of public scrutiny and significant penalties in the event of a security incident.

Fines have become so excessive that many companies are seeking insurance to financially rescue them from possible bankruptcy if a compromise occurs. "Cyber liability insurance (CLI) addresses the first- and third-party risks associated with e-business, the Internet, networks, and informational assets. CLI coverage offers cutting-edge protection for exposures arising out of Internet communications."[8] A more in-depth look at CLI coverage is discussed in the section, "Cyber Liability Insurance (CLI)."

Silver Lining (If There Is Any)

There is a silver lining to a data breach, if only a small one. As Dennis Hoffman points out in his quote mentioned earlier, the day after a data breach, a company typically throws more money at the problem than it would have needed to successfully mitigate the compromise in the first place. Therefore, it's reasonable to assume that the company will better defend itself going forward than a company that does not have first-hand knowledge of the effect of a data breach. For example, let's use the highly publicized Department of Veteran Affair's stolen laptop fiasco in 2006. Unfortunately, it took a breach to strong-arm government agencies to standardize encrypting mobile devices. It is an expensive technology to deploy and maintain, but it's a necessary evil. Compare the cost to a recent legal agreement (albeit three years later) to pay $20,000,000 to settle several class-action lawsuits against the Department of VA on behalf of current and former military personnel. Immediately following the media frenzy, the VA tightened data security policies, procedures, and technology deploying Guardian Edge, a full hard-drive encryption solution. Two years later, in March 2008, following a residential burglary in Austin, Texas, another VA laptop was stolen. This once again proves the "not if, but when" theory, although this time, the silver lining was that the VA had taken preventive measures against the ability to extract data from the stolen laptop. However, the hypothetical question still needs to be asked: If that laptop was never stolen in 2006, would the Department of VA have been prepared for the 2008 theft?

COST-BENEFIT ANALYSIS: BUILDING AN ECONOMIC MODEL

Whether intrusion detection is maintained internally or through an MSSP, a unifying benchmark is found within the cost-benefit analysis. This methodology quantifies both the hard and soft costs associated with security breaches and provides metrics to assess an organization's security expenditures and its bottom-line impact.

The versatility of ROI and its ease of calculation have made it a popular metric, used nearly twice as often to evaluate security investments as other commonly used methods (see Figure 12-5).

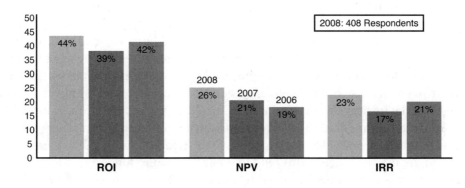

Figure 12-5 Percentage of organizations using ROI, NPV, and IRR metrics[9]

The following examples explain security investments using ROI, NPV, and internal rate of return (IRR) to determine whether a medium-size financial institution should deploy IDSs and, if so, whether it should be maintained internally or outsourced to an MSSP.

Let's begin with the *ROI* ratio:

$$\text{ROI} = \frac{(\text{Gain from Investment - Cost of Investment})}{\text{Cost of Investment}}$$

To calculate a firm's ROI in an IDS, you must define and quantify the metrics of its elements.

GAIN FROM INVESTMENT

You already know that the gain from investing in an IDS is derived from the benefits of loss prevention. Because a prevented loss is an event that never occurred, the gain must be assigned a value based on the presumed costs associated with the risks that are mitigated and the presumed risk likelihood and frequency of losses.

The total cost associated with a single security breach, or the *single breach exposure* (SBE), is multiplied by the expected *annual rate of occurrence* (ARO) to calculate the *annual loss exposure* (ALE), which represents the gain to a firm that can successfully reduce the risk of breach occurrence through its security investment:

Gain from investment = ALE = SBE × ARO.

Let's deconstruct these terms to quantify them. SBE is comprised of the direct and indirect costs. Direct costs are typically measurable hard costs that relate to specific activities stemming from the breach incident. The indirect, or soft, costs relate to productivity issues within the organization stemming from the breach incident.

For these purposes, let's examine the cost structure of a security breach impacting a financial-services firm. Customer expectations of trust and privacy tend to be higher for the financial-services industry, and public scrutiny and awareness of breaches tend to be more acute than for other industries. Liability and compliance requirements also tend to be more stringent because of the heightened need to secure the types of information and data that financial institutions maintain, such as credit-card account information, bank-account information, and other sensitive, personally identifiable information (PII). According to the 2008 Annual Study: Cost of a Data Breach, conducted by Ponemon (see Figure 12-6), financial-services firms tend to incur the second highest incident costs, illustrated by a cost of $240 per breached record for 2008 versus an overall average cost across all industries of $202 per breached record, and nearly twice the breach costs that retail vendors experience ($131).

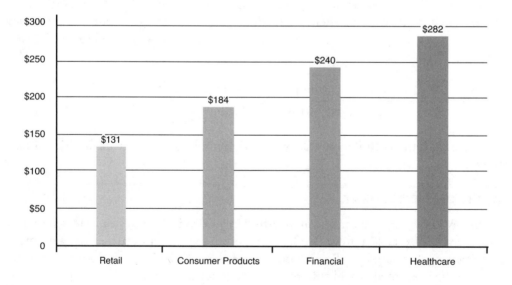

Figure 12-6   Industry average breach costs

Figure 12-7 breaks down the costs by type and year.

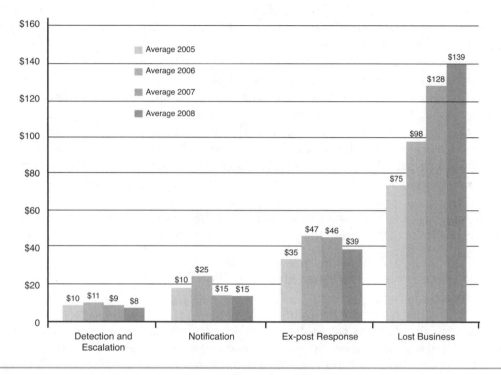

Figure 12-7   Cost of breach recovery per record by type and year

Figure 12-7 can be summarized as follows to yield a value for a single breach exposure (per record):

SBE = Indirect Costs + Direct Costs = $240

Computation of the ALE requires that you make certain assumptions about the scale, scope, and frequency of data breaches on an annualized basis. The Privacy Rights Clearinghouse, a nonprofit consumer advocacy organization, reported 330 separate data breach incidents in 2007. However, the vast majority of breach incidents go unreported. According to a survey conducted at this year's RSA conference, 89 percent of breaches went unreported.[10]

Most susceptible to breach incidents were educational institutions (29 percent), closely followed by municipal, state, and federal governmental agencies (26 percent).

Private businesses, such as retail corporations, reported 22 percent, healthcare organizations reported 16 percent of the incidents, and financial services reported the lowest occurrence of unauthorized disclosure of any industry (7 percent).[11] These figures align with the premise that industries that implement a higher standard, even though a target, are less likely to sustain a data breach.

Financial institutions, which are held to the highest standards of privacy and security, are exceedingly risk averse. In its 2007 report on global security, Deloitte Touche reports that 92 percent of financial-institution respondents are willing to tolerate risk at only the lowest of levels, from zero to "necessary and approved risks" only.[12]

At least one attempt (not including network scans) was reported by 46 percent of respondents during 2007, down from 52 percent in 2006. Of that 46 percent who responded affirmatively, 1–5 attempt incidents were reported by 41 percent, 6–10 incidents were seen by 11 percent, and 26 percent experienced more than 10 breach attempts.

To estimate the *ARO* for this fictitious firm, use these averages as a starting point. Throwing out the outliers from the survey, assume a 46 percent probability of 3.2 breach attempts:

ARO = risk probability × expected number of occurrences

ARO = $0.46 \times 3.2 = 1.5$

Of course, the mathematical probability of 1.5 occurrences does not mean this firm would necessarily expect to see between one and two breach incidents during a year. Instead, the calculation of ARO gives you a quantifiable average mitigated by risk factors.

The Computer Security Institute reported an average loss per breach incident (attempts with any degree of success) or single breach exposure of $345,005.[13]

NOTE

The average loss per breach incident research yielded extreme discrepancies. For example, the Computer Security Institute reported the average loss per breach incident for 2007 as $345,005; however, the 2007 Annual Study: U.S. Cost of a Data Breach, published by Ponemon, identifies the average cost per reporting company was more than $6.3 million per breach. The discrepancy can stem from numerous variables. However, this chapter uses the Computer Security Institute's calculation because that report consisted of nearly seven times more supporting data.

If you quantify your model with these averages, the annual loss exposure is as follows:

$ALE = SBE \times ARO$

$ALE = \$345,005 \times 1.5 = \$517,508$

We previously defined the gain from an investment in an IDS as the benefits derived from loss prevention. If a security investment can prevent or mitigate all losses, the *gain from investment* is the full *ALE*:

Gain from investment $= ALE = \$517,508$

With a near zero tolerance for risk (as reported by the financial-services participants in the Deloitte Touche survey), we assume a goal of 100 percent loss prevention.

COST OF INVESTMENT

There are unlimited variables used to calculate the total annualized cost of the deployment and management of an IDS. For this model, assume that the equipment is leased and that an MSSP manages the maintenance and monitoring of the equipment. The generalized cost structure shown in Table 12-2 is based on several estimates provided by three global MSSPs.

Table 12-2   Investment per Security Device per Year

Cost	Dollar Amount
Equipment lease	$4,000
Device management and monitoring service	$10,000
One-time installation charge	$1,000

*Prices are estimated for illustrative purposes.

A mid-sized financial institutional with typical security needs might deploy 12 NIDS/HIDS devices, which results in the following first-year *cost of investment (COI)*:

$COI = [\text{no. of devices} \times (\text{lease} + \text{management and monitoring costs})] + (\text{no. of devices} \times \text{installation})$

$COI = [12 \times (\$4,000 + \$10,000)] + \$12,000 = \$180,000$

RETURN ON INVESTMENT

With all components quantified, you can now calculate the *ROI:*

$$\text{ROI} = \frac{\text{gain from investment } - \text{ cost of investment}}{\text{cost of investment}}$$

$$\text{ROI} = \frac{\$517,508 \ - \ \$180,000}{\$180,000} = 1.875$$

The resultant positive ROI of 1.875 tells you that the net gain (gain from investment – cost of investment) exceeds the COI. Generally, an organization chooses to undertake investments with positive ROI, and the ROI speaks to the magnitude of the return. In due diligence, a security manager needs to evaluate multiple security technologies that might benefit his environment and, upon determining each technology's ROI, select to implement the technology that returns the greatest/highest ROI.

ROI values can generally be interpreted as shown in Table 12-3.

Table 12-3   What ROI Means

ROI Value Versus Investment	Interpretation
ROI > investment	The investment adds value to the firm.
ROI = investment	The investment has no impact on the firm's value.
ROI < investment	The investment subtracts value from the firm.

ROI is not without its detractors. Its versatility and flexibility can be its downfall. Its calculation is only as good as its inputs, and it is often difficult to construct plausible measures, especially with regard to risks and benefits. There is always a degree of subjectivity that can be manipulated to suit a user's purpose. There are also challenges inherent in calculating the return on a security investment that stem from the notion of "return." Rather than a true economic return that can be seen concretely in a firm's bottom line, it is the imputed gain derived from loss prevention. In the case of an IDS, this is calculated by measuring breach-detection rates based on historical measurements of breach occurrences.

NET PRESENT VALUE

An alternative means of analyzing security investments is *Net Present Value (NPV)*. NPV considers the cost of the capital required to fund an investment in an IDS. It measures the investment in the IDS against alternative uses of the same capital by comparing the rate of return imputed from the security investment against the rate that might be earned if the organization invested the same amount of capital into another project with a similar risk profile. By analyzing just the capital costs, NPV can measure rates of return throughout an organization. The narrow prism of NPV allows for an apples–to-oranges comparison, provided that the associated investment risks are similar. Security investments can, therefore, be contrasted with investments in Sales and Marketing, Human Resources, and Facilities.

NPV calculates the sum of the flow of capital both to and from the investment over time and discounts it back to the present value of those funds. The rate at which it discounts the funds is the rate of return assigned to the alternative investments:

C_t = net cash flow = (gain – investment) at a given time, t

r = the rate of return that an organization expects to earn through alternative investments

The *present value (PV)* of each cash flow over the life of the investment is calculated as follows:

PV of a single net cash flow = $C_t/(1+r)t$

Each investment and return is treated as a separate cash flow and discounted back to its present value. The NPV is the sum of each of those terms:

NPV = Σ $C_t/(1+r)t$

Table 12-4 provides interpretations of NPV values.

Table 12-4   What NPV Means

NPV Value	Interpretation
NPV > 0	The investment adds value to the firm.
NPV = 0	The investment has no impact on the firm's value.
NPV < 0	The investment subtracts value from the firm.

NPV can be especially useful when the costs of an investment are immediate, but the benefits are long term. In theory, it should allow an organization to find the most worthwhile project in which to channel its capital. But, security investments are not merely one of many investment options. If the NPV of an IDS is less than that of alternative investments, or even negative, the decision *not* to invest in security improvements can result in value destruction that exceeds the positive capital flow achieved through alternative investments. For example, say that a company decided to spend the investment budget on hiring five more HelpDesk personnel instead of the IDS, which resulted in a data breach three months later. As you can see, the absence of adequate security has implications for a firm's value, such as the erosion of trust and negative publicity that can affect value but might not be factored into the NPV equation.

INTERNAL RATE OF RETURN

Internal rate of return (IRR) is another metric used to analyze security-investment decisions. IRR uses essentially the same principles and metrics as NPV. But, where NPV lends itself to comparisons between competing investment opportunities by assigning value or magnitude to various options by valuing a stream of cash flows, IRR computes the break-even point of an investment as an indicator of that investment's efficiency. IRR is the discount rate at which the present value of the cash flows of a series of investments is equal to the present value of the returns on those investments.

Think of the IRR as the rate of growth that an investment is expected to generate. This growth rate can then be compared with the IRR of alternate projects or measured against the prevailing rate of return in the securities market.

The IRR is defined as the rate, *r*, at which the NPV of an investment's net cash flows equal zero:

Ct = Investment's stream of cash flows over time

r = Rate at which the present value of a single cash flow equals zero

N = Number of payments under consideration over a period of time, t

Each investment and return is treated as a separate cash flow and discounted back to its PV:

PV of a single net cash flow = $Ct/(1+i)t$

The NPV is the sum of each of those terms:

NPV = Σ $Ct/(1+i)t$

To calculate the IRR, solve for *r*:

$$NPV = \sum_{t=0}^{N} \frac{C_t}{(1 + r)^t} = 0$$

Like NPV, IRR addresses the notion of timeliness by looking at future adjusted cash flows related to the investment. IRR calculations identify the annual rate of return of the security investment that result in a NPV of zero. Because an NPV of zero represents no gain or loss to an organization, the IRR is essentially the break-even rate of the security investment, essentially a cut-off rate. A project with a negative IRR has an unfavorable impact on a firm's bottom line. It suggests that the benefits of the investment are not justified in terms of either the cost of the capital required to fund it or in terms of the rate of return, as compared with other possible investments.

ROI VERSUS NPV VERSUS IRR

The question with both NPV and IRR is what to do with the results. NPV demonstrates the value added to (or subtracted from) an organization's bottom line from an investment in an IDS, while IRR can offer the simplicity of yea or nay. But as shown, security is not just another investment for an organization. The loss associated with a security breach can be monetized, but its impact is not just economic. A firm might be willing to tolerate the monetary losses from direct costs but not the loss of faith and trust from customers and vendors associated with indirect costs. When the tolerance for risk approaches zero, as is the case with financial services organizations, the decision making offered by NPV and IRR become meaningless.

ROI is best suited to compare similar types of investment returns within the IT world. It integrates the hard, directly economic costs and the soft costs and risk factors associated with security breaches. If consistency is used in assigning values to its components, the comparisons are accurate. Where ROI is often seen as falling short is when the ROI of security investments are measured against the ROI among different classes of capital investments within an organization.

To illustrate this, return to the example of an IDS investment with an ROI of 1.875. An alternative investment within the firm (for example, sales automation software) might require the same level of investment and generate the same ROI. The investment in sales automation software derives its returns from the improved efficiencies of its sales organization. It directly affects the bottom line through hard cost savings by decreasing costs through sales staffing reductions. The investment in IT security can generate a comparable gain from the same investment, but that gain is a value based on the presumed costs associated with the risks that will be mitigated and the presumed risk likelihood and frequency of losses. Additionally, you have seen that, within the realm of security, there is little (if any) tolerance for the probability associated with security breaches. Therefore, security investment decisions are not generally framed by the question of "if" the investment will be made but rather "how much" will be invested. The next section addresses the "how much" costs associated with the management and monitoring of an IDS and whether it makes financial sense to outsource it to an MSSP or keep it in house.

SECURITY INVESTMENT: SHOULD SECURITY OPERATIONS BE OUTSOURCED?

Managing an IDS is a challenge for even the most talented and well-staffed IT organizations. Companies can no longer defend their networks by using a single firewall at the perimeter. Now, companies need to use a defense-in-depth (also known as depth-in-defense) methodology, which requires multiple layers of devices throughout the network. The extensive implementation is followed by the constant and grueling task of monitoring, maintaining, and upgrading the system. Outsourcing some or all of the functions related to a company's defensive posture might be efficient, but this needs to be decided on a company-by-company basis, because MSSPs come with positive and negative realities. As mentioned previously, security investments do not produce a tangible ROI, and often, when profits significantly decline and staffing levels deteriorate, a company's decision makers are forced to route their investments into projects that generate revenue, not security.

BENEFITS OF MSSPs

Let's start by diving into the beneficial reasons to outsource to an MSSP. A security specialist offers certain advantages that come from specialization. An MSSP's narrow focus and specially trained, experienced staff should allow it to reap and pass along economies of scale and operating efficiencies that cannot be achieved by an in-house Security Department. Companies typically have a small handful of employees that concentrate on specific IT security tasks in the same sense that companies do not have more than one CFO or CIO because too many high-level executives in the same position is not efficient and cost prohibitive, whereas the only function of an MSSP is to staff multiple security experts of all kinds—security engineers, security analysts, regulatory/compliance experts, security architects, incident response experts, vulnerability assessment (VA) specialists, and penetration-testing professionals. It's apparent, from that list of specialties, that MSSPs offer a wide range of services but, more importantly, provide an extensive foundation of expertise.

NOTE

Never ever use your own MSSP for your penetration-testing firm because of the obvious conflict of interest; instead, let it handle application assessments.

There can also be great benefit when an MSSP has multiple clients within a single industry. Professional security intruders frequently focus on a specific industry because they have to fully understand the logistics of that industry/company to properly assess and design a breach. If I'm a professional attacker with a buyer for credit-card numbers, and I'm familiar with the banking system's data flow, there is an extremely high probability that I will attack only financial institutions and their customers; it wouldn't make sense for me to attack a healthcare company. State-of-the-art MSSPs have identified this logic and are analyzing their data not only independently for internal anomalies but also segregating customer's alerts by industrial sectors looking for nefarious commonalities within similar industries (banking, healthcare, retail, education, and so on). The pooled information and the external activities learned by other monitored clients in the same industry can improve the speed and accuracy of breach prediction; you just have to keep your fingers crossed that your company wasn't the attacker's proof of concept.

A final benefit from outsourcing to an MSSP (excluding the cost aspect, which is tackled soon) is having a failover redundant site in the unfortunate event that certain network segments are knocked offline, usually by environmental causes, including hurricanes, tornadoes, flooding or the "backhoe" factor. Also, keep in mind that, even if the MSSP's systems remain online, the chances its employees continue their same hours is unrealistic because an employee's primary concern is to ensure that his personal responsibilities are protected (such as family). For example, if your company's MSSP was hit by Hurricane Katrina, which devastated the U.S. southern coastline in August 2005, there is a chance that your MSSP was not affected by the hurricane and systems remained online. However, the MSSP's employees who lost their houses most likely did not report to work for days, if not weeks, in the effort to resume some level of personal normalcy. So, confirm their hot/warm site is a sufficient geographic distance from the production environment. I concede that most companies that handle Security Operations Center (SOC) functions internally have the funding and support for hot/warm site failover strategies as well, but it's never a guarantee because, when push comes to shove, getting failover mission-critical operational infrastructure online takes precedence over maintaining security infrastructure without a second thought (meaning an in-house hot/warm site might not be equipped with NIDS).

DOWNFALLS OF MSSPs

As much as letting someone else worry about your network's health sounds good, there are a few disadvantages. There is no guarantee that each MSSP firm has the extensive and dedicated staff that the last section mentioned. Small to medium-size MSSPs face the same monetary issues that nag all companies and, for the sake of maximizing their profit margins, an MSSP might often hire entry-level positions at the lower end of salary ranges. This results in security analysts without the appropriate experience to adequately monitor a company's alarms. However, MSSPs try to mitigate this issue by using a tiered approach. A majority of the analysts on the floor can appropriately be labeled as security analysts I, the entry-level people focusing on monitoring the automated alerting system, letting the sensors do the heavy lifting, and letting the analyst perform the brunt of the research and legwork. If they find something suspicious and their inexperience surfaces, they can escalate the issue to a security analyst II/security analyst III. A security analyst II is more experienced and has 2–3 years of security analysis under his belt and can identify attack vectors and corresponding vulnerabilities more quickly than analyst I. I am digressing, but in the interest of full disclosure, the final level of escalation is security analyst III. The final tier is equivalent to senior security consultants. The people at this level are considered experts in the field. They are the final line of defense and typically have attained higher levels of education (a master's degree or doctorate degree) or have earned a laundry list of IT certifications, such as GCIA, GSEC (or another "G" level equivalent), CEH, CCNA, CCIE, Security+, MCSE, or CISSP.

NOTE

Certifications are another industry battle: Are they worth it? In my opinion, certain certifications are absolutely more established and respected than others. I have had colleagues literally just memorize questions and answers and get their Microsoft certifications (primarily for a small bump in pay). Recently, I attended a one-day course on virtualized security; after the training, there was a certification exam that required a 70 percent passing grade to receive yet another three-letter acronym amended to your resume. I opted out of the exam/certification for the sheer fact that any certification that can be achieved in a single day of lecture is not worth having! In the past several years, "makeshift" certifications are popping up all over the place, to the detriment of the concept of certification.

Another disadvantage that plagues MSSP (and internal security departments) is the volume of security analyst turnover. It takes a rare breed of individual to truly enjoy being a security analyst; the long hours, potential shift work, and the endless supply of security alerts that mostly can be categorized as a false positive and are ultimately viewed as wasted time (silver lining: chock it up to experience) make the vocation not attractive to everyone. A friend of mine (who asked to remain anonymous) runs a SOC in the U.S. and states that his firm experiences 20 percent employee turnover each year. High turnover can greatly affect internal team dynamics and the managing approach.

A third disadvantage is the rocky transition from the "courting" process dealing with sales and moving into operations. After your company's security alerts are transplanted into the MSSP's current clientele database, there is no longer any personalization. The stereotype that separates IT and Sales is spot on in the sense that the sales team is more personable, whereas the security analyst is happier doing packet analysis than discussing it on the phone with you. The sales engineer that you dealt with during the courting process, who promised two hour e-mail responses or he could seamlessly implement your Incident response policy/procedures into his process is no longer returning e-mails or phone calls because he has other potential clients to handhold. The takeaway from this example is to be sure to check references and verify that you are satisfied with an MSSP's long-term process and procedures, and not just the service you received during your initial service pilot.

The final and most significant disadvantage for outsourcing to an MSSP is the lack of knowledge its security analysts have of your internal network. Industry reports generally state that internal breaches account for approximately 85 percent of the total compromises. Is it possible that an outsourced entity can monitor your network against internal attacks better than if you had an internal security team? Absolutely not. Most MSSPs request a network diagram and require a conference call with your IT department so that they can have a general understanding of your topology and data traffic patterns, but given the number of clients they monitor, the high employee turnover, and the dynamic nature of your enterprise, it's just not realistic that an MSSP can effectively protect you from an internal attacker who is familiar with the network. However, that being said, it can be nearly impossible for an internal security team to pinpoint an internal attacker using ultra-ninja-like tactics.

As revenues have stagnated or (more likely) declined, the use of MSSPs has increased. As a result of economic hardships, outsourcing has increased, but unfortunately, a rise in the number of breach incidents where a third-party provider is accountable for the event is also significantly increasing. In 2008, 44 percent of all breaches were directly linked to outsourced security functions, nearly doubling the rate since 2005 (see Figure 12-8). In the same period, the cost per compromised record related to outsourced security functions rose at a faster rate than the per-record costs associated with breaches that were handled in house, according the Ponemon 2008 study.

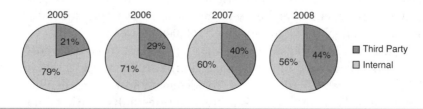

Figure 12-8   First- and third-party data breaches[14]

THE FINANCIAL ASPECT OF AN MSSP

Finally, let's dive into the financial views of outsourcing your network security alerts to an MSSP. Contracting your security alerts to an MSSP is cost effective for small and medium-size companies because the cost of hiring several specialized full-time employees outweighs the cost of hiring a MSSP. Small companies, and some medium-size companies, don't have the profit margins or demand for 24x7 monitoring that justify hiring a dedicated second- or third-shift person to continue to monitor network security alerts during off-peak business hours. Even if the small or medium-size company only needs to maintain the security monitoring over a single shift, it likely needs to hire a security analyst III that has an abundant amount of security experience and can juggle the system's monitoring, analysis, and daily maintenance. This sort of person is likely to command a low six-figure salary, depending on your geographic location and cost of living. Larger companies that require 24x7 monitoring can allocate the funding to create a SOC by centralizing all the company's network security alerts to a central location; especially when that company is intelligent enough to locate the operation in a cost-effective geographic location. Large companies handling security internally, and MSSPs, apply the same principles to minimize overhead costs and maximize their revenue by locating their facilities in the suburbs of larger metropolitan areas so that they can take advantage of the IT skillset that such areas attract without paying the higher real-estate costs that are inevitably seen inside metropolitan borders.

Let's peel off another layer of the "financial onion" and look at the monetary effects. Let's compare the costs associated with hiring an MSSP and an equivalent in-house staff. Previously, this chapter evaluated the ROI of implementing an IDS system for a medium-size company. Let's briefly review that calculation.

A mid-sized financial institutional deploys 12 devices, resulting in the following COI:

COI = [no. of devices × (lease + management and monitoring costs)] + (no. of devices × installation)

COI = [12 × ($4,000 + $10,000)] + $12,000 = $180,000

This calculation included a one-time installation cost, which does not play into the on-going costs of management and monitoring; therefore, subtract the last $12,000 from the total to make the final MSSP monitoring $168,000 per year.

Preserving the same scenario, determine the employment costs to support an internal security department for a medium-size financial firm deploying 12 security devices (NIDS/FW) that require 24x7 monitoring. To adequately sustain this deployment with constant ownership, the company needs to support three shifts. The breakdown looks like this:

- First shift (8 AM–5 PM)
  - One security manager
  - Three security analyst Is
  - One security analyst III
- Second shift (4 PM–1 AM)
  - Two security analyst Is
  - One security analyst II
- Third shift (12 AM–9 AM)
  - Two security analyst Is
  - One security analyst II

The first shift requires two additional bodies for several reasons:

- The security managers themselves do not monitor or analyze alerts because they are stuck in management meetings for the majority of the day.
- Because the first shift works during normal business hours, there is a likely need that other departments within the organization need assistance from the security department, whether to run a virus scan on an external drive, evaluate a new security product line, or evaluate a new security technology.

NOTE

It's a bit off topic, but a crucial point is that all shifts have a one-hour overlap so that the analyst team can appropriately hand off the events that occurred during that shift.

You can make the argument that second and third shifts need only two analysts, not three. However, you could also argue that each shift requires a minimum of three employees, to take into consideration vacations, high turnover that usually stems from the graveyard shifts, and the fact that finding analysts for graveyard shifts is extremely difficult. So, having an additional analyst doesn't cripple the shift's routines. Ideally, it makes sense to have a security analyst III on staff for the second and third shifts; however, to reduce cost, a security analyst II suffices. The strategy for the second and third shift is to have the security analyst II handle all escalating alerts, or if he is unsure of a situation, prepare a summarized report for the first-shift security analyst III.

You might think, "How is he going to try to normalize the salary for these careers to avoid contaminating your real-world scenario?" The salary calculations I use are derived from two variables: identify a city that is deemed to be among the average for IT salaries and use the salaries for the positions within that geographic location. Figure 12-9 displays the results of the DICE 2007 Tech Salary Survey that identifies 16 metropolitan cities salaries throughout the country. Dallas/Ft. Worth appears exactly in the middle and is the geographic location in this case study.

METRO AREA SALARIES, 2005 - 2007				
	2005	2006	2007	2006 - 2007 % Change
Silicon Valley	$85,430	$90,430	$93,876	3.95%
Boston	$79,211	$80,308	$83,465	3.93%
Baltimore/Washington D.C.	$75,593	$79,911	$81,750	2.30%
Los Angeles	$73,911	$79,583	$81,039	1.83%
New York	$76,382	$80,006	$80,039	0.95%
Seattle	$73,105	$79,787	$79,770	-0.19%
Denver	$74,823	$77,317	$77,846	0.68%
Dallas/Ft. Worth	$71,494	$74,656	$76,560	2.55%
Chicago	$71,496	$75,154	$76,407	1.67%
San Diego	$72,163	$79,416	$75,994	-4.31%
Atlanta	$73,684	$72,323	$74,822	3.46%
Philadelphia	$71,881	$72,786	$74,442	2.28%
Hartford	$72,265	$71,796	$73,372	220%
Houston	$68,358	$71,526	$72,733	1.69%
Phoenix	$70,023	$74,976	$71,246	-4.97%
Detroit	$64,154	$67,080	$67,271	0.28%

Figure 12-9   Metro area salaries from the DICE 2007 Tech Salary Survey[15]

A friend of mine works in a SOC located in close proximity to Dallas, Texas, and he agreed to share the salary breakdown that his firm uses when hiring security analysts (under the condition that his firm remain anonymous). According to this research, here are the following salaries corresponding to job titles:

- Security analyst I = $47,000–$52,000; average = $49,500
- Security analyst II = $52,000–$80,000; average = $66,000
- Security analyst III = $80,000–$95,000; average = $87,500
- Security manager = $95,000–$115,000; average = $105,000

I use the average for each pay scale, although my friend mentioned that his MSSP company lean toward the lower end because they typically invest a considerable amount in individual security training and compensate the technicians for certifications and advanced academic degrees.

Now, just plug in the numbers:

Total = (1 Security Manager) + (1 Security Analyst III) + (2 Security Analyst II) + (7 Security Analyst I)

= (1 × $105,000) + (1 × $87,500) + (2 × $66,000) + (7 × $49,500)

= $671,000/year

Obviously, the costs associated with the round-the-clock monitoring and management required to support a security department is significantly higher than outsourcing that function to an MSSP firm that can pool the needs of multiple clients and achieve economies of scale.

The cost of keeping the security function in-house is $671,000/year (not including equipment costs) versus the cost of outsourcing it to an MSSP ($168,000/year) is so dramatically different that it should not come as a surprise that MSSPs gain in popularity every year. Currently, 27.8 percent of companies outsource part or all of their IT security monitoring functions.[16] Even with the best of circumstances, outsourcing is not a seamless solution. Regardless of whether you outsource your network alerts, security-related tasks are still performed internally, and the relationship with the outside MSSP is inherently risky and might fail to prevent a data breach. A short-sighted view of outsourcing contracts is cited as a leading cause of security outsourcing failure and the most likely reason a firm brings these functions in house.[17] Few MSSPs offer a complete one-stop shop for all of your security needs. Some offer IDS and firewall monitoring and management, but do not include log collecting or NetFlow analysis. Others specialize in NetFlow analysis, but do not provide vulnerability assessment reporting. Unfortunately, it is extremely difficult to find an MSSP that provides service offerings for every security requirement that your company needs, and this forces companies to outsource security to several different vendors. Unlike other procurement arrangements, outsourcing security contracts creates a hybrid entity that needs to be treated as an extension of a firm's

IT department sharing outcomes and liabilities. To be efficient, your company must work coherently together to successfully minimize breach risks.

This does not imply that every firm requires a 24x7x365 monitoring of security alerts. Some organizations might require security events to only be looked at on a daily basis (or even weekly, depending on the industry) and only need one security analyst. If that's the case, it's recommended that you have either a security analyst II or security analyst III and, from a financial viewpoint, it makes sense to keep security in house as opposed to outsourcing to an MSSP. Ultimately, every company has different requirements and, as such, needs to reflect on its industry requirements, financial budgets, and how confident its risk mitigation strategy is to determine its own data breach recourse.

CYBER LIABILITY INSURANCE (CLI)

Data breaches have, unfortunately, become a daily occurrence. They no longer carry the same jaw-dropping stigma they did five years ago. This is not so different than when you hear a car alarm in a parking lot. Whereas people used to immediately react, now people don't flinch. Over the past decade, as the frequency of data breaches increases, it's now commonplace for people to get notification letters over the course of a year informing them that their sensitive information was somehow disclosed. Unfortunately, it has even gotten to the point where contracts and proposals are awarded with contingent requirements that the contractor holding the sensitive information is required to add third-party cyber liability insurance (CLI) endorsements onto its existing policy, sometimes in excess of $50,000,000, therefore protecting the clientele of the awarding contract from identity theft, fraudulent credit-card transactions, and so on.

The Open Security Foundation (OSF) maintains a Web site at http://datalossdb.org/ with the sole purpose of collecting breach information and informing the general public of the latest breach news. The Web site is an eye-opening experience, because it extends to breach articles, statistics, and a downloadable database of breach incidents. According to the OSF Web site, the graph in Figure 12-10 breaks down each breach type that has been reported and made public knowledge. Changing the category to reflect only incidents in 2008 displays differences of only +/-1 percent.

NOTE

The graph in Figure 12-10 estimates that approximately 50 percent of the identified breaches could not have been avoided by implementing an IDS/IPS. Does that undermine the ROI case study? Absolutely not, because deploying an IDS/IPS solution into the corporate environment could have mitigated approximately 37

---

percent of those breaches. This supports the fact that ROI scenarios need to be calculated for various security investments to determine the best solution for your investment. The hypothetical financial firm had hypothetically already deployed hard-drive encryption, which accounts for nearly 30 percent of the identified 50 percent!

Because data breach costs can significantly increase as the numbers of compromised records accumulate and regulatory penalties are incurred, some companies are forced to explore every possible avenue to re-coup costs to avoid filing for bankruptcy. As most companies have discovered, traditional policies, including errors and omissions, general liability, property, crime, kidnap, and ransom (cyber extortion could feasibly be considered a ransom, but it is out of scope in most policies) and others either exclude or do not affirmatively address coverage for the following:

- Damage to third-party data
- Nonbodily injury or property damage/economic loss to a third party
- Unauthorized access of information or network systems
- Intentional acts of the insured
- Federal, state, or local statute violations
- Personal injury coverage limitations

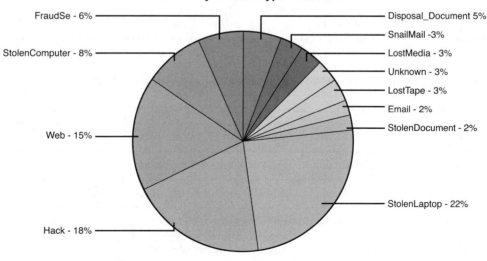

Figure 12-10   Incident breakdown by breach type

This ultimately leaves the victim company to financially fend for itself.

The need for insurance policies to evolve into the twenty-first century is becoming abundantly apparent, given the daily unauthorized disclosure of sensitive information. In its simplest form, CLI includes coverage for perils that can cause a loss by or through your computer system, applications, or the Internet that are caused by a breach of security or programming error. In its broadest form, it includes third-party network security liability, privacy liability, first-party data assets, computer network business interruption, and extra expenses and extortion. An important initial consideration to address is whether your company is looking for first-party coverage, third-party coverage, or both. First-party coverage is defined as the company itself, whereas the third party is defined as clients, customers, applicants, and students (in the situation where an educational institution is the victim). Additionally, coverage can include direct expenses to a client that are related to a security or privacy event, such as customer notification expenses, public relations expenses, credit-monitoring service expenses, and regulatory action defense expenses.

CLI COVERAGE TYPES

Insurance providers have developed additional coverage policies deemed as CLI that covers IT breach incidents (see Table 12-5). Because policies can get granular in nature, even these broad coverages can be broken down into smaller policies.

Table 12-5   Coverages and Definitions

Coverage	Definition
Privacy liability	Harm suffered by others because of the disclosure of confidential information
Network security liability	Harm suffered by others from a failure of your network security
Property loss	The value of data stolen, destroyed, or corrupted by a computer attack
Loss of revenue	Business income that is interrupted by a computer attack
Cyber extortion	The cost of investigation and the extortion demand
Notification costs	The cost of complying with the various breach notification laws and regulations
Regulatory defense	Legal defense for regulatory actions
Media liability	Infringement of copyright or intellectual property

PRIVACY LIABILITY INSURANCE

Privacy liability insurance covers damages and defense costs suffered by others because of a failure to protect confidential information or the wrongful disclosure of confidential information. This coverage is not tied to a negligent act or a security failure, but the coverage can include failure to disclose or warn third parties of potential identity theft, along with coverage for legal expenses related to regulatory violation actions.

NETWORK SECURITY LIABILITY INSURANCE

Network security liability insurance covers damages and defense costs suffered by others because of a failure of security that involves your computer network, including liability caused by a transmission of a computer virus, unauthorized access, DoS, disclosure of confidential information, and identity theft.

PROPERTY LOSS INSURANCE

Property loss insurance covers direct first-party losses involving the value of data that is stolen, destroyed, or corrupted because of a failure of security involving your computer network and the inability to prevent a computer attack. Coverage is necessary because traditional property forms require that there be a "direct physical peril" that causes the loss, and a cyber-related incident does not necessarily involve "direct physical peril." Also, traditional property forms cover damages to "tangible property," and courts have upheld the decision that "data" is intangible property; therefore, it is not considered to be property within the coverage grant.

LOSS OF REVENUE INSURANCE

Loss of revenue insurance covers direct first-party business income that is interrupted because of a failure of security involving your computer network and the inability to prevent a computer attack. Coverage is necessary because traditional property forms require that there be a "direct physical peril" that causes the loss, and a cyber-related incident does not necessarily involve "direct physical peril." Additionally, there is no contingent business interruption coverage in the traditional form for third-party hacking incidents. This is especially true when you consider that many computer networks rely on third parties for their uptime, and standard extra expenses property forms do not provide coverage for electronic forensic expenses.

CYBER EXTORTION INSURANCE

Cyber extortion insurance is coverage only offered as a first-party policy and is used when a malicious attacker blackmails your company by threatening to launch a DoS, Distributed DoS (DDoS), or Reflective DDoS (RDDoS) attack (a resource-starvation attack that blocks legitimate users from accessing services). This technique gained exposure in the past five years as organized crime syndicates extorted mainstream e-commerce Web sites in return for some staggering amounts of money. Another cyber extortion technique is having an attacker hold sensitive information hostage, threatening to release the information to the general public unless he is given a disclosed amount of money (similar to holding a hostage for ransom).

NOTIFICATION COSTS INSURANCE

Notification costs insurance covers related expenses that are paid directly to the customer because of incidents that are caused either by a failure of network security that involves your computer network or the wrongful disclosure of confidential information. Coverage includes the cost to notify affected individuals and the fees and expenses associated with rectifying the repercussions of the compromising event (such as credit-monitoring services and the charges and fees associated with the services of a public-relations firm that restores the company's image). Coverage is necessary because traditional property and casualty forms do not affirmatively address coverage for the expenses related to federal or state notification requirements or the providing of services to a third party as "goodwill." They also do not normally assist a company with its need to re-establish its public image.

REGULATORY DEFENSE INSURANCE

Regulatory defense insurance coverage is only offered as first-party coverage to help financially assist companies paying regulatory compliance penalties.

MEDIA LIABILITY INSURANCE

Media liability insurance covers damages incurred by infringement of intellectual property, copyright laws, or trademark infractions; it ultimately protects a company against defamation and/or invasion of privacy claims.

As with most traditional insurance policies, CLI policies are generally offered in an a la carte format, which gives the firm any number of possible combinations and pricing schemes to custom fit its business needs. When my company was engaging in our CLI policy bids, we received proposals from different insurers, where each insurer included up to eight different options, just for the third-party component of the policy.

CLI UNDERWRITING PROCESS

The CLI underwriting process works like any other insurance policy:

1. Identify all the cyber-related risks and exposures, including privacy, network security, business interruption, extra expense, cyber extortion, or media.

2. Complete a Technical Risk Assessment and/or obtain a third-party vendor security assessment questionnaire.

3. Complete the Insurance Carrier Cyber Insurance application.

4. If necessary, participate in a technical conference call with the insurance carrier to clarify any ambiguous points as a result of the questionnaire. For example, the questionnaire has a Yes or No checkbox for encrypting data at rest. Is it referring to data at rest within a database? Or possibly encrypting backup tapes (because those are stolen/lost more often than a compromise)? Or is it generalizing the question to reflect any mobile storage unit with potential sensitive information? Obviously, the intricacies of the question cannot accurately be conveyed in a Yes/No answer.

5. After the underwriter's technical team is familiar with your inner workings, it can provide the appropriate CLI options.

6. Take all the submitted CLI proposals and internally decide which best fits the company.

The CLI policy, as expected, reads like a legal contract (see the following note) and, although every insurer includes slightly different formats to its proposal, there are some core components, including the endorsements and the exclusions that are imperative to focus on. The endorsements are written for modifications that either amend or retract provisions from the general policy. The endorsements are critical, because that is where all the coverages and exclusions are identified. The context of the term "coverages" is obvious, but let's visit the term "exclusions." No insurance company likes to pay out when the insured company itself is grossly at fault (grossly being deemed as beyond the point of reasonable doubt). For example, if a company submits the Technical Risk Assessment and indicates that it constantly applies released Microsoft patches using its Patch Management Policy, after a data breach occurs, the insurer might ensure that all or a majority of the workstations/servers are up-to-date with its Windows patches. If the insurer discovers that patches haven't been applied to workstations or servers for eight months, it opens the possibility of gross negligence on the part of the company and, therefore, voids the CLI contract. It is the responsibility of the company seeking CLI insurance to bring to light any feasible exceptions that the insurance company needs to be aware of. For example, say that the insured company has legacy applications that are not compatible with Microsoft Office or Internet Explorer updates. Therefore, the company has decided not to apply patches to the legacy application and deems it an "acceptable risk." This must be brought to the attention of the insurance company up front.

Another example is if a company specifies that its network engineers only use Secure Shell (SSH) to remotely administer the network gear, but after a data breach, the insurer discovered (through logs) that most of the network hardware is actually managed using Telnet. As a cleartext protocol, the insured network administrators are therefore sending administrator credentials unencrypted and in a form easily recovered using a packet sniffer, no matter how long or difficult the password is. That said, it's meaningful to point out that insurance vendors are aware that network topologies are highly dynamic and typically requests the insured to submit some variation of a Technical Risk Assessment Questionnaire on an annual basis to ensure the policy coverage and costs adequately represent the needed CLI requirements.

NOTE

Disclaimer: The goal of this section is to introduce you to some industry-offered insurance coverages and policies. It is *not* meant to reflect *all* the possible intricacies of *all* CLI insurance providers. If your company decides to explore CLI, it is in your best interest to research all possible policy plans. Given my experience with CLI, I highly recommend consulting with legal counsel or an insurance broker to help guide you through the tedious process and ensure the policy covers all of your needs.

SUMMARY

Reported data breaches are reaching monumental numbers, and companies are forced to absorb staggering financial retribution both in the form of hard and soft costs. Figure 12-11 shows a global map representing approximately 33 percent of the locations where a data breach has been publicly acknowledged in 2008. Companies are forced to re-evaluate their own security investments to determine if current funding is sufficient or if it's financially beneficial to outsource that functionality to an MSSP. Calculating the appropriate security investment is a tricky and exceptionally subjective undertaking, and this chapter elaborated on three credible techniques: NPV, IRR, and ROI. Unfortunately, the lack of profitable margins as a result of security investments entices a company's decision makers to minimize the security spending and redirect those funds to projects that generate capital gains. Security managers need to fight to preserve funding in hopes of minimizing negative effects on their data loss prevention strategy. However, the ROI model provides a unifying benchmark throughout the company and, therefore, gives management the capability to equally assess investments across the board. The final question to be answered is, "Do we outsource our security functionality or do we implement an in-house solution?" MSSPs frequently publicize the amount of savings that comes from reduced staffing and minimized security equipment costs; however, all service offerings don't make sense for all companies, and security managers must fully evaluate their investment options and weigh the risks associated with implementing either an internal or external solution.

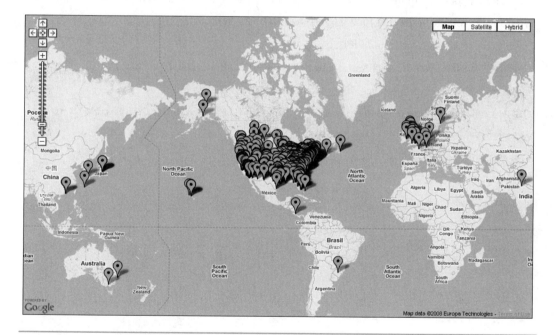

Figure 12-11   Map of approximately 33 percent data breaches in 2008[18]

ENDNOTES

[1]Breach statistics courtesy of www.datalossdb.org.

[2]Courtesy of PGP's Annual Study: Cost of a Data Breach (2008)

[3]http://etiolated.org/

[4]Courtesy of Ponemon Institute, Annual Study: Cost of a Data Breach (2006, 2007, 2008)

[5]Courtesy of Ponemon Institute Annual Study: Cost of a Data Breach (2006, 2007, 2008)

[6]www.schneier.com/blog/archives/2008/09/security_roi_1.html

[7]Courtesy of Ponemon Institute Annual Study: Cost of a Data Breach (2006, 2007, 2008)

[8]www.insurenewmedia.com/pages/cyberliability.asp

[9]Source: Computer Security Institute, CSI 2008 Computer Crime and Security Survey

[10]www.informationweek.com/news/security/attacks/showArticle.jhtml?articleID=209901208

[11]www.informationweek.com/news/security/attacks/showArticle.jhtml?articleID=209901208

[12]www.deloitte.com/dtt/research/0,1002,sid=1013&cid=170582,00.html

[13]http://i.cmpnet.com/v2.gocsi.com/pdf/CSISurvey2007.pdf

[14]Courtesy Ponemon Institute 2008 Annual Study: Cost of a Data Breach(2006, 2007, 2008)

[15]http://marketing.dice.com/pdf/Dice_2007_TechSalarySurvey_1-31-08.pdf

[16]Gallaher et al., *Economic Analysis of Cyber Security and Private Sector Investment Decisions*, 2006

[17]CSI 2007 Computer Crime and Security Survey

[18]http://etiolated.org/map

Bro Installation Guide

Bro was originally funded by a Department of Energy grant at Lawrence Berkeley National Labs (LBNL). This Intrusion Detection System (IDS) was built as a network application framework to enable the group at the LBNL to analyze network protocols and how they function. The Bro team has been releasing major versions every 6 to 12 months with minor bug fix versions distributed in between. Bro is designed to run on FreeBSD, Linux, and Mac OS. However, the user following has since ported it to NetBSD, OpenBSD, and Solaris (*not* Windows!). There are always two versions of the current release of the Bro code: a stable version and development adaptation. The stable version is used in production environments and is available via the Bro Web site (www.bro-ids. org/download.html). The development version of the code is only available through an online Subversion code repository. It requires you to "check out" the latest version of the code and then set up the directories for compiling (see Figure A-1).

The last notable caveat about Bro versions is that most major developers keep their own branches of the code so they can choose to either share the code (Robin Sommer's case) or keep the code private (Vern Paxson's case). These branches commonly contain beta code that a specific developer is working on for a dedicated project, and he posts the code along with comments to the Bro Wiki or the mail distribution list. The distributed-development support of the Bro user community means that documentation of bug fixes and small modifications is a challenge. The CHANGES file was included to help mitigate this documentation obstacle and accompanies each distribution of the Subversion development version. It includes all the changes and a brief description of each change. This process results in the CHANGES file being automatically generated for each submission of changes to the Bro Subversion repository.

```
Host:bro_xx user$ svn checkout http://svn.icir.org/bro/trunk/bro Bro_1_4
A    Bro_1_4/linux-include
A    Bro_1_4/linux-include/net
A    Bro_1_4/linux-include/net/slcompress.h
...... cut for brevity ..........
A    Bro_1_4/testing/istate/base/persistence-read/stderr.log
A    Bro_1_4/testing/istate/base/persistence-read/vars.log
A    Bro_1_4/testing/istate/rndseed.dat
A    Bro_1_4/testing/README
A    Bro_1_4/install-sh
A    Bro_1_4/libpcap.bufsize.patch
Checked out revision 6653.
Host:bro_xx user$ ./autogen.sh

              BRO Build Tools Setup
===================================================
...... cut for brevity ..........
Host:bro_xx user$ ./configure --options-you-choose; make; make install
|
```

Figure A-1   Commands to run Bro

A Bro developer named Christian Kreibich developed the Bro Communications Library (BROCCOLI) to help centralize communication streams between multiple Bro instances and other devices. BROCCOLI became a staple need and, by default, now accompanies all Bro distributions. The library has several uses that definitely appeal to users running multiple Bro instances:

- Sharing event feeds from multiple Bro devices. For example, all events that relate to a specific type of traffic forward their information to a central Bro instance.
- Synchronizing information between multiple Bro instances. This helps asynchronous routing environments reassemble the data streams.
- Utilization by the LBNL group to feed IP address and port information about a hostile connection to an access control list (ACL) and have the connection dropped via a router/firewall block.
- Processing and acting as a NetFlow collector. It is useful for large networks where capturing LIBPCAP streams on infrastructure devices (routers, switches, taps, and so on) cannot be performed. This functionality is brand new to Bro 1.4, so check the wiki, blog, and mailing list for any recent changes and additions.

COMPILING AND BUILDING OPTIONS

The Bro tool can seem large, complex, and overwhelming, but here are several key pieces of helpful information. After you choose the version (stable or development) you want to install, you need to be aware of several options and settings, including the default location where it will be installed on the system. If you choose to perform a full install of the Bro distribution on a system, it installs to the default location /usr/local/bro and includes all the supporting directories under that path. However, you can change that by using the configure time option of `—prefix=/new/path/for/bro`. This example just introduces the flexibility that the application provides to the installer. (The path location is at the installer's discretion.) Table A-1 describes other major options that you can enable or disable by using the configuration parameter during runtime.

Table A-1   Bro Options

Bro Configure Option	Description
`—enable-brov6`	**IPv6 support.** Enables Bro to capture and read IPv6 packets but can only interpret basic connection information because of a limitation in LIBPCAP. This is memory intensive and causes the Bro daemon to take almost double the memory than with any other option included.
`—enable-broccoli`	**BROCCOLI support.** The default option is to enable this support. However, if you won't use any BROCCOLI components, disable it. This saves some Bro memory and keeps the Bro daemon smaller.
`—enable-shippedpcap`	**LIBPCAP support.** Bro ships with an older version of LIBPCAP, so leave this option disabled. If this parameter is left disabled, the compiler uses the system version that you install (which is likely a newer version).
`—enable-debug`	**Debugging support.** Enabling this parameter causes the Bro daemon to have a larger footprint than normal; however, for newbies, if you encounter problems, keeping a debug build compiled is beneficial.
`—enable-perftools`	**Google performance-debugging tool support.** Requires a working copy of Google's tools to be already installed on the system. This works well only on Linux OSs, not on *BSD or Mac OSs.
`—enable-activemapping`	**Host TCP/IP stack tracking.** Works on the same principle as the Snort Frag3 preprocessor. With this enabled, a Bro daemon stores information related to each machine in the local network and how each machine structures its TCP/IP stack. This helps defeat or detect some fragmentation attacks.

Table A-1   Bro Options

Bro Configure Option	Description
—with-openssl	**SSL support.** Tells the compiler that a newer version of OpenSSL is installed on the system.
	WARNING: If you don't provide the path to the version you want to use, the compiler won't correctly pick up SSL support.
	Here is an example:
	`./configure —other-options —with-openssl=/path/to/openssl`

OPERATIONS USE

After Bro is configured with your options and installed to the default path, several options and variables can assist the operator/analyst in running it properly for his specific environment. The first option deals with what form of data Bro will handle. Like all command-line interface (CLI) daemons, arguments can be passed to Bro that tell it how to run. To enable Bro to sniff packets off the wire as an IDS tool, pass it the `-i <interface_name>` option. Another option is to replay a set of already recorded/sniffed traffic to Bro by using `-r <pcap_file>`. Finally, to record LIBPCAP traffic into a file to allow a security analyst to analyze the data stream another time, use the `-w <pcap_file_name>` option. The CLI also can tell the Bro daemon what analyzers/policy files to use on the type of traffic. For example, the following code tells the Bro daemon to play back the LIBPCAP file web.pcap by using the TCP connections, scan detection, weird, and alarm analyzers. (See the section, "Bro: An Anomaly-Based IDS," in Chapter 3, "Intrusion Detection Systems," for information on alarm analyzers.)

```
Bro -r web.pcap tcp scan weird alarm
```

The following example shows Bro listening to a FreeBSD network interface named em0 and loading all analyzers in the mt file. The mt.bro file, located in the default site policy directory, acts as a loader and order of operations for multiple analyzers. Use this if you want to have Bro run a series of analyzers across data streams but do not want to include all the parameters in the CLI:

```
Bro -I em0 mt
```

Bro has three major environmental variables that can customize your Bro instance based on specific needs. Table A-2 demonstrates these variables and their appropriate options.

Table A-2 Environmental Variables and Options

Bro Environmental Variable	Options/Descriptions
BROPATH	Specifies the directories or path that Bro uses to search for policy scripts. `export BROPATH=/usr/local/bro/site:/path/two`
BRO_LOG_SUFFIX	Sets the log suffix for Bro log files; the default is *.log. The following example uses the date and time for all files to keep track of them: `export BRO_LOG_SUFFIX=`date +y-%m-%d_%H.%M.%S`
BRO_DNS_FAKE	Sets or unsets DNS resolution for Bro. It has only two options: "1" to enable and "0" to disable. `export BRO_DNS_FAKE="1"`

After generating some Bro logs, several support scripts installed with Bro can help a security analyst. These scripts are in the aux directory under the main path for the default Bro installation. Table A-3 presents a small subset of the scripts that are generally the most useful.

Table A-3 Selected Support Scripts

Tool Name	Tool Description
Cf	Converts Bro time stamps into human-readable format and is usually run like this: `Cat my_bro_log ¦ cf > new_log_file`
Hf	Replaces IP addresses in Bro log files with the currently resolved host name.
Rst	Issues forged TCP Reset flag packets to both sides of a TCP connection. You can use this over the sniffing interface of a Bro sensor or a management interface. Note that this tool has two caveats: • The interface has to be a read *and* write interface, which is not usually the case for sniffing interfaces. • The traffic *must* pass the interface from which you are issuing the packets.

Table A-3   Selected Support Scripts

Tool Name	Tool Description
Nftools	Ftwire2bro. Converts NetFlow version 5 wire-formatted data into Bro format.
	Nfcollector. Collects NetFlow data and writes it into an output file. The default port is 1234/tcp (not the standard 2055/tcp).

RESOURCES

This introduction exposed you to Bro's options and power. If you still have questions, aside from rummaging through the documentation that comes with the distribution, here are more resources to use:

- **Main page.** www.bro-ids.org
- **Wiki.** www.bro-ids.org/wiki
- **Mailing list.** http://mailman.icsi.berkeley.edu/mailman/listinfo/bro
- **Blog.** http://blog.icir.org
- **Bug Tracker.** http://tracker.icir.org/bro

Index

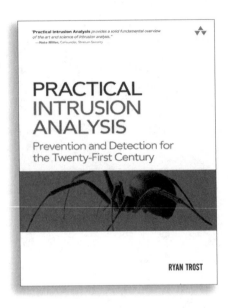